The Economic and Political Aspects of the Tobacco Industry

An Annotated Bibliography and Statistical Review, 1990–2004

Tom Diamond

The Scarecrow Press, Inc.
Lanham, Maryland • Toronto • Oxford
2005

SCARECROW PRESS, INC.

Published in the United States of America
by Scarecrow Press, Inc.
A wholly owned subsidiary of
The Rowman & Littlefield Publishing Group, Inc.
4501 Forbes Boulevard, Suite 200, Lanham, Maryland 20706
www.scarecrowpress.com

PO Box 317
Oxford
OX2 9RU, UK

Copyright © 2005 by Tom Diamond

All rights reserved. No part of this publication may be reproduced, stored in a retrieval system, or transmitted in any form or by any means, electronic, mechanical, photocopying, recording, or otherwise, without the prior permission of the publisher.

British Library Cataloguing in Publication Information Available

Library of Congress Cataloging-in-Publication Data

Diamond, Tom.
  The economic and political aspects of the tobacco industry : an annotated bibliography and statistical review, 1990–2004 / Tom Diamond.
    p. cm.
  Includes bibliographical references and index.
  ISBN 0 8108 5161 X (hardcover : alk. paper)
  1. Tobacco industry—Economic aspects—Bibliography. 2. Tobacco industry—Political aspects—Bibliography. I. Title.

Z7882 .D53
[HD9130.5]
016.3381'7371—dc22

2005011483

∞™ The paper used in this publication meets the minimum requirements of American National Statndard for Information Sciences—Permanence of Paper for Printed Library Materials, ANSI/NISO Z39.48-1992.
Manufactured in the United States of America.

Contents

Acknowledgments		v
Introduction		vii
1	Economic Aspects: Advertising and Marketing	1
	Packaging	1
	Products	8
	Promotions	20
	Sponsorships: Arts	50
	Sponsorships: Philanthropy	54
	Sponsorships: Research	56
	Sponsorships: Sporting Events	59
2	Economic Aspects: Distribution Channels	69
	Duty-Free	69
	Illegal Trade	73
	Military	92
	New and Emerging Global Markets	94
	Prisons and Jails	100
	Retail and Wholesale	102
3	Political Aspects	113
	California and the Tobacco Industry	113
	International	117
	Politics, Politicians, and Lobbyists	121

Tobacco Litigation	145
Tobacco Settlement Agreements, 1997–1998	150
Post–Tobacco Settlement Agreements, 1999–2004	168
Appendixes	
Appendix A Statistical Tables	181
Appendix B Tobacco Company Profiles	199
Appendix C Tobacco Litigation: Selected Court Cases	209
Appendix D Tobacco Websites	213
Index	217
About the Author	241

Acknowledgments

The creation of this work involved contributions from others in the library, government, nonprofit, and commercials worlds. I would like to recognize all these individuals and thank them for their assistance: Jennifer Cargill, dean of libraries, Louisiana State University (LSU); Edward Kurdyla, editorial director, Scarecrow Press (Lanham, Maryland); Ian Galloway, editorial assistant, Scarecrow Press (Lanham, Maryland); Martin Dillon, acquisitions editor, Scarecrow Press (Lanham, Maryland); Nicole McCullough, assistant editor, The Rowman & Littlefield Publishing Group (Blue Ridge Summit, Pennsylvania); Melissa Ray, formerly assistant managing editor, Scarecrow Press (Lanham, Maryland); Theresa Gardella and Ann Loftus of the Advocacy Institute (Washington, D.C.) for allowing me access to the institute's tobacco files; Darryl Jason, vice president, Tobacco Merchants Association (Princeton, New Jersey) and Judith Mathus, formerly of the Tobacco Merchants Association, for graciously allowing me to visit its library and providing information through e-mail requests; Gary White, head, Schreyer Business Library, Paterno Library, Pennsylvania State University Libraries, for his usual excellent assistance; the U.S. Department of Agriculture, for providing various statistical data; Desiree Sundelin and Malin Eriksson, Generation AB (Örnsköldsvik, Sweden), for allowing me access to its online database and for answering all my e-mails; Garfield Mahood, executive director, Non-Smokers' Rights Association (Ottawa and Toronto, Ontario, Canada); Trevor Haché, outreach and information coordinator, Non-Smokers' Rights Association (Ottawa and Toronto, Ontario, Canada); the Office of the Hon. Senator John Breaux (Democrat-La); Alice Daugherty and Sigrid Kelsey, LSU Libraries; Donna Simpson, freedom of information coordinator, Navy Exchange Service Command (Virginia Beach, Virginia); Carole W. Marsh, freedom of information officer, Defense Commissary Agency (Fort Lee, Virginia); and Cindy Reiber, freedom of information officer, Army and Air Force Exchange Service (Dallas, Texas).

Introduction

The *Oxford English Dictionary* defines "big" in a number of ways, when the word is used as an adjective. One meaning conveys a sense of great size or bulk, as in the phrase "Big Dipper" or "big band." Another definition refers to the word's use in "phrases or numerals to designate a combination of three or more important things, persons, or nations." "Big Business" is a good example. Alternatively, the word can be used in a pejorative sense to portray a sense of evilness and wickedness—to warn of roguish behavior or ominous tidings. A company or entire industry can be plastered and marked forever with the word "big." In this negative context, "big" assumes the role of the "Scarlet Letter."

Industries and their members become unwilling and convenient targets for the word "big." During the 1970s, the oil industry found itself unceremoniously transformed into "Big Oil," thanks to the "windfall profits" earned during the 1973–1974 Arab oil embargo. More recently, the fast-food and pharmaceutical industries morphed into "Big Fat" and "Big Pharmacy," respectively, to reflect negative perceptions of their operations. Likewise, the tobacco industry became known as "Big Tobacco." The phrase crept into the literature surrounding the industry. A search through the newspaper database in LexisNexis Academic as of November 6, 2004, revealed over 2,700 occurrences of the phrase "Big Tobacco" since January 1, 1980. Nearly two thousand of these had occurred after 1995. Undoubtedly, the tobacco settlement discussions played a huge role in its deployment. "Big Tobacco" is now a permanent fixture of the lexicon.

The world of Big Tobacco and its broad-leafed plant *Nicotiana tobacum* take root in many facets of the global economy. Farmers plant, harvest, and cure the tobacco leaves. Tobacco is graded for quality, stored, cured, and prepared for final processing into cigarettes and other tobacco products. Sales generate tax revenues for government at different levels and revenues for the tobacco manufacturers. Tobacco monies are used for advertising and marketing the product, making philanthropic contributions, burnishing a company's image, making political contributions, and tobacco litigation. The leaf's economic and political tentacles spread wide and deep.

The tobacco industry burst into the 1990s with hope and promise of building bridges to new and emerging global markets while maintaining and nurturing opportunities on the home front. The U.S. industry pried open markets in Japan, Taiwan, and South Korea during the 1980s (with the assistance of the U.S. government) and then set its sights on the burgeoning markets in Eastern Europe and the former Soviet empire. Soon thereafter, the industry's footing began to show signs of cracks and fatigue. Haunted by the burgeoning antitobacco movement, growing new brands became more difficult. For example, R. J. Reynolds failed in its attempt to launch its Uptown and Dakota cigarette products. The company had developed the products to target African-Americans (Uptown) and women (Dakota). In April 1994, the chief executive officers of the major tobacco companies appeared before a congressional hearing and testified that nicotine is not an addictive product. This lit the fuse that eventually led to the historic 1998 Master Settlement Agreement. The industry agreed in that instrument to unprecedented restrictions on its advertising and marketing capabilities and to the use of characters to promote its products (the Marlboro Man met his demise in April 1999). Currently, the industry is fighting a tidal wave of individual and class-action lawsuits. The industry is locking horns with the U.S. Department of Justice in a $289 billion lawsuit. The tobacco industry's roller-coaster ride throughout the 1990s and into the new millennium has been dramatic.

This book is an attempt to document the economic and political aspects of the tobacco industry, using for that purpose the form of an annotated bibliography. It is intended to serve as a research tool for academic researchers and scholars, public libraries, librarians working in such special libraries as those of nonprofit organizations, and the general public. Its goals are to document quality published materials and to serve as a standard and comprehensive historical reference source for locating documents that examine a critical side of the tobacco industry. Though not originally so conceived, the book follows in the footsteps of Louise O. Bercaw's *The Tobacco Industry: A Selected List of References on the Economic Aspects of the Industry, 1932–June 1938,* published by the Department of Agriculture's Bureau of Agricultural Economics in 1938.

The book's primary focus is on the tobacco industry's global cigarette manufacturers, with special emphasis on the major players: Philip Morris (now a subsidiary of Altria Group); British American Tobacco; R. J. Reynolds Tobacco and Brown & Williamson (now known as Reynolds American); Lorillard Tobacco (a subsidiary of Loews Corp.); and Liggett Group (a subsidiary of Vector Group Ltd.). Other companies include Altadis SA (Madrid and Paris), the Gallaher Group (United Kingdom), the Imperial Tobacco Company (United Kingdom), Japan Tobacco, and Rothmans, Benson & Hedges (Canada).

The book covers materials published from January 1, 1990, through November 3, 2004. The principal research materials reviewed include journal and periodical literature, U.S. and European government documents, books, and Internet documents. Materials not reviewed include theses and dissertations, book reviews, and legal articles. The author accessed numerous library research collections and catalogs and also aggregate databases to collect the materials included in this work. Library research collections and catalogs include those of the Advocacy Institute; the Federal Trade Commission; the Legacy Tobacco Documents Library (legacy.library.ucsf.edu); the Library of Congress; Louisiana State University Libraries; *Melvyl,* the catalog of the University of California Libraries (melvyl.cdlib.org); the New York Public Library (main library); the Science, Business, and Industry Library, New York Public Library; the Statistical Reference Index Microfiche Library; the Tobacco Merchants Association; University of California at Berkeley Libraries; the University of Kentucky's William T. Young Library; and numerous websites. Aggregate databases researched include Business & Company Profile ASAP, General Reference Center Gold, Health Reference Center Academic, and OneFile from the

Gale Group; Ebsco's Academic Search Premier and Business Source Premier databases; Elsevier's LexisNexis Academic database; and ProQuest Information and Learning's ABI/Inform database.

The book's content is structured in three chapters. Chapter 1, "Economic Aspects: Advertising and Marketing," covers packaging, products, promotion, and sponsorship. The sponsorship section is subdivided into the arts, philosophy, research, and sporting events. This is followed by chapter 2, "Economic Aspects: Distribution Channels." Distribution channels covers duty-free sales, illegal trade (for example, counterfeit and smuggled cigarettes), the military, new and emerging global markets, prisons and jails, and retail and wholesale outlets.

Chapter 3, "Political Aspects," covers six different areas. California and the tobacco industry document some of the important events in this major battleground, where two formidable opponents struggled. The international section covers the industry's political machinations in foreign lands. Politics, politicians, and lobbyists covers a wide variety of areas, including political contributions and organizations, political influence, and taxes. Tobacco litigation covers selected court cases. The final two sections cover events unfolding during the discussions surrounding and leading to the various tobacco settlement agreements (1997–1998) and the subsequent period of enforcement (1999–2004).

Four appendixes follow. Appendix A contains an extensive list of statistical tables. The tables paint a portrait of the industry's global monetary impact. These include tobacco farm cash receipts at the state level, advertising and promotional expenses, military and commissary exchange sales, duty-free and tax-free worldwide sales, state government tobacco sales tax collections, and federal cigarette excise tax collections. Appendix B provides profiles for thirteen national and international tobacco companies. Appendix C provides a snapshot of major tobacco litigation as of November 3, 2004. These summaries supplement the abstracts documented in the tobacco litigation section of chapter 3. Appendix D is a list of tobacco websites for further research. An extensive author and subject index completes the work.

1
Economic Aspects: Advertising and Marketing

PACKAGING

1. Bateh, Freddie. "Playing the Market-Share Pack Card." *World Tobacco*, no. 116 (May 1990): 26, 28.

    The tobacco industry places increased emphasis on the cigarette package in three areas: marketing the brand, projecting a brand image, and protecting the product. Sales and profits are tied to the graphics displayed on a package. In Japan, Brown & Williamson sells its Kent cigarette in a hinge-lid pack. The hinge-lid packaging is used as "miniature billboards" to convey an image, attract customers to the product, and provide maximum protection.

2. "Reynolds Introduces FlavorSeal to Rejuvenate Winston." *Tobacco Journal International*, no. 5 (September/October 1991): 51–52.

    R. J. Reynolds is fighting decreased sales of its Winston brand by packing the cigarette tobacco and cigarette package tighter, upgrading visual cues in such ways as using whiter paper and brighter printing, and introducing a new packaging outer wrap called FavorSeal. The outer wrap offers superior protection by retaining cigarette moisture and blocking air penetration. A projected $22 million advertising campaign includes media such as outdoor, print, and direct mail. Also, the company employs items such as danglers and new pack displays in retail settings. Advertising slogans include "The Wrap-Fresh Taste Breakthrough" and "The Wrap—Only Winston Has It."

3. "Concealed Treasures." *Tobacco Journal International*, no. 4 (July/August 1992): 10.

    British American Tobacco's German subsidiary created a unique package for its HB cigarette brand. The package does not carry the brand name, the word "undercover" appears on both sides, and the front side displays a self-adhesive label. Removing the label reveals an "obscure object," such as a plaster. The tear tape to open the package, instead of being placed on the black hinge-lid, appears at the bottom. This facilitates easy removal of the foil.

4. Horne, Barbara. "More Sophistication Less Weight for Cigarette Packaging." *Tobacco Journal International*, no. 5 (September/October 1995): 52, 55–58, 60, 62, 64–65.

   In relation to tobacco products, European environmental concerns over consumer goods spawned "eco-profiling," or "eco-balancing." This covers the "cradle to grave" process of manufacturing and disposing of tobacco packaging materials. Cigarette packaging must meet environmental regulations, serve its purpose in protecting the product, continue to be affordable to the consumer, and maintain high quality standards. Government restrictions or bans on advertising and the placement of health warnings heighten the package's role as a "silent communicator." Manufacturers enhance the packaging with tear tapes and innovative packaging designs to communicate messages and convey environmental concerns.

5. Mehegan, Sean. "The Aesthetic Smoke." *Brandweek* 37, no. 24 (June 10, 1996): 17, 20.

   With its line of nine "microsmokes," R. J. Reynolds's Moonlight Tobacco Company conveys a hip/contemporary and retro image with each package. The unique and eye-catching designs draw from the present and also hark back to olden times. For example, the company used gas station signs and refrigerators from the 1940s to design the packaging for its Icebox brand. The other new Moonlight brand introduced is Planet. Its package design reflects a few simple elements and the "look of handmade Japanese paper."

6. Crescenti, Marcelo G. "What's in a Pack?" *Tobacco Journal International*, no. 4 (July/August 1996): 40–42.

   Tobacco Journal International interviewed Italian design consultant Maurizio di Robilant about packaging designs for tobacco products. According to Mr. Robilant, the cigarette pack assists in selling the product and reflects the consumer's attitudes and character. The consumer carries the package, which becomes a reflection of the individual. The package's personality is reflected in its color and logo, and it helps to position the brand with a specific target group. It is very important to understand a country's cultural differences when designing a package and positioning a brand.

7. Crescenti, Marcelo G. "Overwrapping Moving with the Times." *Tobacco Journal International*, no. 5 (September/October 1996): 54, 56.

   Tobacco manufacturers are awakening to the usage of overwrapping, once an unsung marketing tool. Opaque films attract consumers' attention to new product launches or special sale offers printed on cartons. Overwrapping assists in selling special packages in duty-free outlets. Philip Morris sells ten Marlboro cigarettes packs in one oversized flip-top box in U.S. duty-free markets. In Europe, tobacco manufacturers create a "facsimile" pack, or one large cigarette pack, by using paper or film wrapping to collate four twenty-five cigarette packs. European supermarkets are beginning to market these packages.

8. Crescenti, Marcelo G. "Life Getting Harder for the Soft Pack." *Tobacco Journal International*, no. 6 (November/December 1996): 52, 54.

   Smokers are beginning to favor hinge-lid cigarette packs versus soft packs. Smokers attach images of solidness and protectiveness to the hinge-lid pack; multinational producers use the lid as an imaging tool to attract smokers' attention. The soft pack requires less material, is more environmental friendly, and costs less to produce. Soft packs still dominate in Latin America and Asia, but European and North American markets are moving more toward hinge-lid packs. Soft pack material suppliers are developing lighter materials to give them a cost competitive advantage.

9. "The Pack Is the Message." *Tobacco Journal International*, no. 2 (March/April 1997): 54.

    The German tobacco manufacturer Reemstma used different packaging designs to promote its flagship West cigarette brand. From 1991 through 1996, the company marketed West Lemon Fresh, West in Space, West in Space II, and West Cola, all with specially designed packages aimed at attracting the consumers' attention. The West in Space promotion began with the brand's emblem splashed across a Russian rocket launched in Kazakhstan. West in Space II followed, with each package displaying a quotation from a Russian cosmonaut. In 1994, consumers purchasing the brand through a vending machine could have received a package with the brand name printed in Arabic, Chinese, Russian, Hebrew, German, or Thai.

10. "The Trick with the Click." *Tobacco Journal International*, no. 3 (May/June 1997): 64.

    A market research report by ICON Research and Consulting served as the basis for an experimental cigarette package developed by German printer Carl Edelmann GmbH. ICON's research concluded that the cigarette package will serve as a critical marketing tool and identified three trends likely to impact the future of the cigarette: individuality and aestheticism, enjoyment and ritual, and living legend and transcendence. Using this research, Carl Edelmann GmbH created a fantasy niche brand called Spirit. When opened, the Spirit package created a "click effect" and provided "added value" sought by the consumer. In an independent project, Edelmann created another fantasy brand package, Blues. When removed, the package's horizontal flap could be used as an ashtray, to carry matches, or to carry a lighter.

11. "Creative Approach with Interactive Packaging." *Tobacco Journal International*, no. 4 (July/August 1997): 74.

    Rothmans is using cigarette packaging overwrap as a tool to build brand loyalty and brand reinforcement. Produced by Lawson Mardon Packaging Flexibles, the polypropylene wrap features the directive "Get the Message, Win £50,000." Inside the package, the smoker will find a card printed with a hidden message. Placing a red square, printed on the reverse side of the package, over the card reveals a message. By completing a winning sentence, such as "Get/the/message" or "You/are a/winner," a smoker can win a prize ranging from five to fifty thousand pounds.

12. Link, Emily. "The Hinge-Lid Success Story." *Tobacco Journal International*, no. 1 (January/February 1998): 48, 50–51.

    Smokers regard hinge-lid cigarette packs as conveying quality, safety, value, and status; these packs are increasing in popularity. In 1993, Philip Morris marketed an oval hinge-lid carton in France. The packaging never achieved permanence with the French, and Philip Morris withdrew the product. Since 1993, however, the cigarette brand Davidoff Classic has come in an octagonal flip-top pack. In New York City, R. J. Reynolds is test-marketing a "side-slide" pack of its Salem brand cigarette. The pack opens sideways by pressing the inner pack. The company markets the product with the slogan "It's Not What You Expect."

13. Sosnowski, Tom. "Print and Pack Bind." *Tobacco International* 200, no. 2 (February 1998): 40, 42, 44.

    Pending advertising restrictions are forcing the tobacco industry to look more closely at using the printing and packaging aspects of cigarettes as a means to advertise and attract new customers. Netherlands-based TSO Packaging is looking at the "upgrading of product presentation" and using more colors in printing and packaging tobacco products. Saueressig GmbH & Co. points toward printing cigarette packages filled with advertising and also issuing collectors' items. Other possible trends include promoting other brands on the packages, building brand identity and image through quality packaging materials, switching to hinged-lid cartons from softcup labels, and using lower-weight board to help protect the environment and add to the companies' bottom line.

14. Mehegan, Sean. "B&W Set to Roll Out New Kool Packs." *Brandweek* 39, no. 9 (March 2, 1998): 44.

    In April 1998, Brown & Williamson's (B&W) Kool cigarettes were marketed with a new packaging design. The packaging sported the motif of a waterfall that the company uses in its print advertising. Inserts in the current packaging and direct mail were used to notify smokers about the design change. Also, smokers learned that the design changes did not mean a change in the formula used to manufacturer the cigarettes.

15. Escher, Sandra. "The Visiting Card of a Brand." *Tobacco Journal International*, no. 3 (May/June 1998): 54, 56.

    Swiss packaging designer Irene Hitpold discusses her creations for Philip Morris's Swiss brand called Star. Hitpold designed five completely different versions, and these became fodder for collectors. The packaging changed every six months. Advertising restrictions now mean more infrequent changes in the design. Hitpold describes the cigarette package as a smoker's "visiting card"—one that displays status.

16. Neubauer, Bernd. "Films for the Future." *Tobacco Journal International* (1999 Suppl): 16, 18–19.

    Companies manufacturing cigarette package films must meet demands to reduce costs, address environmental concerns, protect the contents from damage, and retard the penetration of moisture. The transparency, glossiness, and tightness-of-fit attributes of films also enhance the product's selling qualities. The cigarette Peter Stuyvesant features a new twist in films with its recloseable "innerpack."

17. Rommel, Christian. "Cigarette Packaging: A Window on the Chinese Soul." *Tobacco Journal International* (1999 Suppl): 42, 44–46.

    Art designs appearing on Chinese cigarette packages are a reflection of the country's art and culture. These representations include tourist attractions (for instance, architectural monuments), the animal kingdom, mythical creatures, and political propaganda. Brand names such as The Great Wall and Powerful Lion and illustrations serve to touch the smoker's emotions. Colors are also used as a tool to create brand identity and loyalty.

18. Beltrame, Julian, and Gordon Fairclough. "Strong Smoking Warnings Are Proposed for Canada." *Wall Street Journal*, January 20, 2000: B16.

    Cigarette packages sold in Canada display one out of a possible sixteen warning messages. Themes including diseased lungs and rotting teeth cover the top portion of both the front and back side of each package. *See also* entry 21.

19. Rossel, Stefanie. "Special Editions: The Art of Smoking." *Tobacco Journal International*, no. 3 (May/June 2000): 48–50.

    Cigarette package special editions are very popular in Germany. Reemstma uses such images as a tiger, leopard, and grizzly bear to grace the package of its West cigarette brand. Camel cigarette packages depict a cuddly, cute camel and "cheeky commentaries" (for example, news, events) designed for the German market. The special edition images are used throughout Europe, but the slogans are market specific. The images are used to enhance and support the brand's image.

20. Glogan, Tim. "The Art of Perfect Packaging." *Tobacco Journal International*, no. 6 (November/December 2000): 50, 54, 56, 58.

    Limited-edition picture packs are used to promote a brand at the point of sale and communicate a message to the consumer. In August 2000, Philip Morris launched its first-ever German special edition package campaign, Marlboro Country Specials Limited Edition. Five red/yellow picture designs represent full-flavored cigarettes, and ten blue picture designs represent "light" cigarettes. Different names used include Chili, Neon Cowboy, Wolf, and Snow Burners. Text or illustrations printed on wrappers are used to promote brands. Other factors considered in packaging are the use of economical and environmentally acceptable paperboard and the ability to combat counterfeiters.

21. Barrington, Stephen. "Canada Battles Smoking." *Advertising Age* 71, no. 50 (December 4, 2000): 3, 56.

    Effective December 23, Health Canada's new antismoking measures require that fifty percent of each tobacco package be covered with health warnings. The sixteen new warnings comprise headlines, brief messages, and shocking color photographs of cancer-laden body areas affected by smoke. Each package contains health-related information (for example, how to stop smoking). Health Canada refers to these as the most stringent rules in effect worldwide.

22. Lewis, Jay. "Fighting Back." *Tobacco Reporter* 127, no. 12 (December 2000): 58, 60–61.

    The packaging industry is working with tobacco manufacturers to combat the surge of counterfeit cigarettes. Five new and updated tools are being used in the battle. Tear tapes convey information such as health warnings and also promote the brand. Films are used for brand promotion, enhancement, and protection. Sophisticated tax stamps can defer counterfeiters. The printing process can incorporate such items as microtext and security inks. Holograms, or optical variable devices, are very difficult for counterfeiters to copy.

23. Fox, Barry. "Quit or Die, Says Talking Cigarette Packet." *New Scientist* 169 (March 10, 2001): 25.

    The cigarette machinery–manufacturing firm Molins has patented (GB 2351061) a talking cigarette packet. When the packet is opened, a health warning is uttered. The health warning could appear in different languages. A Molins representative asserted that this innovative package could appeal to the tobacco industry.

24. Wakefield, M., C. Morley, J. K. Horan, and K. M. Cummings. "The Cigarette Pack as Image: New Evidence from Tobacco Industry Documents." *Tobacco Control* 11, Suppl 1 (March 2002): i73–i80.

    The authors researched tobacco industry documents to learn the interrelationship between cigarette package design and marketing strategies created by the tobacco industry. The researchers studied three areas: the interrelationship between the packaging and advertising in grounding the brand's imagery; the interrelationship between the packaging colors/design and smokers' perceptions about the strength and taste of the cigarettes; and the importance of packaging when appealing to youth and women. They concluded that governments should consider regulating cigarette packaging.

25. Dipasquale, Cara B. "New Look for B&W's Kool." *Advertising Age* 73, no. 18 (May 6, 2002): 3, 62.

    Brown & Williamson is repackaging its Kool cigarettes with an eye toward appealing to the twenty-one-to-thirty age group. The new package will sport either a bright green or blue monochrome look. Advertisements promoting the new look will feature the tagline "Look at Kool now. Time to step into the house." This dovetails with the overall marketing theme "We built the house of menthol."

26. Wakefield, M., and T. Letcher. "My Pack Is Cuter Than Your Pack." *Tobacco Control* 11, no. 2 (June 2002): 154–56.

    In Australia, British American Tobacco Australasia (BATA) introduced package changes for two of its major brands. With the Benson & Hedges brand, the company introduced five "clubber's edition" packs under the theme of "Festive 2." The changes served to attract attention and interest to the brand and altered the standard trademark. For the Winfield Super Mild 25s brand, the company resuscitated an old tagline, "anyhow . . . ," set against an eye-catching colorful image. The authors speculate that BATA made the changes to attract new smokers and to encourage brand switching.

27. Rutkowski, Liane. "Cigarette Manufacturers to Face EU Directive." *Tobacco Journal International*, no. 5 (September/October 2002): 24.

    The European Union's new directive for tobacco products took effect on September 30, 2002. The directive requires larger health warnings to cover the front (30 percent) and back (40 percent) of each cigarette package. The warnings must be placed within a black frame set against a plain white background, and the words must appear in bold, black letters. Also, the directive prohibits the use of product descriptors like "light" and "mild." Cigarette manufacturers were required to implement the new rules by September 30, 2003.

28. Link, Emily. "Brand New Gowns." *Tobacco Journal International*, no. 1 (January/February 2003): 54–56.

    The tobacco industry is embracing innovative changes in cigarette packaging design. In April 2002, R. J. Reynolds (RJR) unveiled new packaging for its Winston brand. The Evo Flask packaging, manufactured with crushproof recyclable plastic, provides sturdier protection and resistance to water. A 2002 joint venture between RJR and Gallaher Group produced the Reynolds cigarette brand in a slide-box package. In 2002, British American Tobacco manufactured its Lucky Strike brand in a "push the button" box package. Smokers press on the brand logo to slide out the box containing the cigarettes. In 2000, Imperial Tobacco Group tweaked hinge-lid box packaging with an angular lid and rounded corners to introduce its new Fusion brand.

29. Rommel, Christian. "The World in Your Hand." *Tobacco Journal International*, no. 5 (September/October 2003): 148–52.

    Global cigarette brand packaging for special or limited editions feature special themes designed to attract new smokers and enhance brand identity and loyalty. Tourism, trade fairs (for instance, 1990 Milan Fair), and cultural history (for example, Buddhist and Taoist deities) themes are used on packages. Western cigarette special-edition packages tend to promote the themes of sport, leisure, lifestyle, and pleasure. East Asian packages tend to be more experimental, using themes of education and dissemination of knowledge (such as classical painting, poems, and chess games). The Amigo brand in Brazil is used to educate the public about the disappearance of children.

30. Bhatti, Jabeen. "European Smokers Snuff Out Cigarette-Package Warnings." *Wall Street Journal*, February 12, 2004: D4.

    European cigarette smokers are using creative methods to cover warning labels on cigarette packages. Pro-smoking stickers such as "Live hard, die young" are sold on the Internet and at stores. Smokewear, a Frankfurt-based company, has sold two hundred thousand stickers. Slipcases are also used to cover the unsightly warnings. One slipcase from Spain reads, "Let's have a cigarette and a drink." Flowers and a picture of Che Guevara grace some of the slipcases used in France.

31. Paersch, Emily. "Chaos Creates Chances." *Tobacco Journal International*, no. 1 (February/March 2004): 58, 61.

    Several global regulatory constraints are challenging the tobacco industry to build and enhance brand equity via the cigarette package. Health warnings could be placed either on the top or turned upside down on the package. Like the health warning, the brand can be placed within a thick black border. Pictures, such as of traffic jams, can be used to offset the negative warnings. "Wrapsy," a cosmetic shell, is available to hold and conceal the health warnings. Cigarettes can be individually wrapped in promotion-enhanced paper, connected, and stored in a simple cardboard package.

32. Brinson, Brandy. "True Colors." *Tobacco Reporter* 131, no. 4 (April 2004): 22–24.

    A recent European Union directive, effective September 30, 2003, forbids cigarette manufacturers from using the terms "full flavor," "light," or "mild" to describe their cigarettes. Companies are devising new strategies to inform smokers about their products. Some manufacturers are including the box color in the product name. Product names incorporate a color (for instance, 555 White), but the color name is not printed elsewhere on the package. Three possibilities exist by which manufacturers can use colors to help distinguish brand styles: change the design elements, use lighter colors, and change the brand name. Color selection becomes critical, because it elicits different meanings and interpretations among different people and cultures.

33. Rommel, Christian. Global Trendsetters: China. "Traditional Chinese Forms Mix Easily with Modern Fantasies to Establish a Bond between Consumer and Package." *Package Design Magazine,* September/October 2004. www.packagedesignmag.com/issues/2004.09/trendsetters.shtml (accessed October 11, 2004).

Through the lens of cigarette packaging, Chinese brands reflect the country's art and culture, changing technologies in the industry, and the penetrating influence of Western ideas. Throughout the 1990s and into the twenty-first century, Chinese cigarette packages rapidly changed with an eye toward connecting with Western themes, creating an aura of modernity and progressiveness, and breaking away from traditional forms of cigarette packaging. A plethora of cigarette packages display the technological advances achieved through such devices as innovative designs and holograms.

34. "Most Effective Use of Product Design and Packaging." *Media* (October 8, 2004): A11.

Gold and silver awards are given to companies reflecting use of product design and packaging. The gold award went to Heineken (Hong Kong), and British American Tobacco (BAT) Japan received the silver award. BAT Japan issued its Lucky Strike brand with vintage cigarette packaging. The company used the 1916 Original box style (September 2003) and the 1942 Classic style (December 2003) for relaunching the Lucky Strike brand in Japan. The campaign theme emphasized heritage and authenticity in the complex world faced by Japanese consumers.

PRODUCTS

35. Schiffman, James R. "After Uptown, Are Some Niches Out?" *Wall Street Journal,* January 22, 1990: B1, B8.

R. J. Reynolds (RJR) made public its decision to halt test-marketing of its new menthol cigarette Uptown. In 1988, RJR created Uptown to counter market share losses to Lorillard Tobacco's Newport menthol cigarette. RJR targeted Philadelphia as the initial test site and explicitly target-marketed blacks. It is estimated that RJR spent $2–$10 million to develop the cigarette. RJR capitulated to pressure applied by antismoking groups and by Louis W. Sullivan, head of the U.S. Department of Health and Human Services.

36. "Launched with a Sporting Chance." *World Tobacco*, no. 114 (January 1990): 31.

The Italian Monopoly issued MS Mundial, a line extension of its flagship brand MS. This is to take advantage of the World Cup soccer championships played throughout Italy. The cigarette package is decorated with a "multi-coloured soccer ball motif."

37. Specter, Michael. "Marketers Target 'Virile Female.'" *Washington Post*, February 17, 1990: A1, A8.

   Just weeks after shelving plans to market Uptown, a menthol cigarette targeted to blacks, R. J. Reynolds planned to market a new cigarette named Dakota. According to a marketing report prepared by Promotional Marketing, Inc., the cigarette would target "young adult female smokers" aged eighteen to twenty-four. These "virile females" are characterized as high school-educated women who love to cruise, party, and attend sport events like tractor pulls and hot rod shows. Promotions could include using the slogan "Where smooth comes easy," creating a "Dakota" rock group, and soliciting media preferences (for example, movies and rock groups) through "on-pack" promotions.

38. Bird, Laura. "Tobacco Manufacturers Face a Marketing End-Game." *Adweek's Marketing Week* 31, no. 9 (February 26, 1990): 2, 4.

   A leaked marketing report obtained by the Advocacy Institute and subsequently the *Washington Post* about R. J. Reynolds's (RJR) plan to market a new cigarette named Dakota to "virile females" sparked a storm of protest and generated another bad dose of publicity for RJR. In a memo, RJR chairman James W. Johnston vowed to catch the pilferers for confiscating RJR property. Investigators hypothesized that an internal source or an external spy planted within RJR leaked the report.

39. Ramirez, Anthony. "Times Change: The Man Rides On." *New York Times*, March 8, 1990: D1, D8.

   Philip Morris's Marlboro brand reigns as the global king of cigarettes, even in the face of increasing pressure against the tobacco industry. The heart and soul of Marlboro lie in the theme "Come to where the flavor is. Come to Marlboro country" and in its cowboy icon. Both the slogan and the rugged individualist allowed Marlboro to segue from television to print and outdoor advertising. Thirteen product-line extensions, packaging differentiations playing off the Marlboro Red mother brand, and a "no-discount policy" all play roles in keeping Marlboro the industry leader.

40. Koeppel, Dan. "Japan's Mild 7 Cigarette Targets Asians in the U.S." *Adweek's Marketing Week* 31, no. 33 (August 13, 1990): 4–5.

   Considered the "Philip Morris of the Pacific Rim," Japan Tobacco, through its JATICO U.S. subsidiary, imports and markets Mild 7, the best-selling cigarette in Japan. Pitched with the slogan "An Encounter with Tenderness," Mild 7 is establishing a solid foothold among the Asian-American community. Los Angeles's Koreatown and Little Tokyo are blanketed with billboards trumpeting Mild 7.

41. Siragusa, Gail. "De-Nicotine Cigarets Are Struggling in Test." *Supermarket News* 40, no. 44 (October 29, 1990): 20.

   Next DeNic, Merit DeNic, and Benson & Hedges DeNic cigarettes contain less than 0.1 mg of nicotine. Philip Morris uses a proprietary process to extract the nicotine in the tobacco leaf. Philip Morris is test-marketing these products in Hartford, Omaha, Tampa Bay, and Toledo (Next); Spokane (Merit); and Phoenix (Benson & Hedges). Brand loyalty and the de-nicotine taste pose major hurdles for the new cigarettes.

42. Dagnoli, Judann. "Quirky Cigarettes Join the Pack." *Advertising Age* 63, no. 5 (February 3, 1992): 17.

    The leading tobacco manufactures have marketed line extensions to grab market share and public attention. Line extensions save companies from $170 million to $270 million in start-up costs. R. J. Reynolds (RJR) will roll out "Camel Wides," a cigarette 80 mm long and 29 mm wide. In 1991, in the western United States, RJR launched a cigarette 99 mm long, the Camel 99s. Philip Morris marketed its five-pack-set as the "Collectors Choice" cigarette series. The set includes the Skyline and Americana series. The five cigarette brands in the Skyline series are New Yorker, Park Avenue, Plaza, Broadway, and Fairmont. The five cigarette brands in the Americana series are Arizona, California, Freeport, Long Beach, and Monterey.

43. "Iran to Market a U.S. Cigarette," *New York Times*, January 26, 1993: A10.

    According to the Iranian newspaper *Salam*, the Iranian government's Iranian Tobacco Organization (ITO) has begun marketing R. J. Reynolds's (RJR) Winston cigarette under the name Bistoon. Bistoon is a mountain name and similar to Winston. This financial arrangement is the product of negotiations between the two parties to settle a complaint filed by the ITO with the Iran-U.S. Claims Tribunal stemming from the 1979 Iranian revolution.

44. "Using the Health Message as Marketing Tool." *Tobacco Journal International*, no. 1 (January/February 1993): 35–36.

    Death Cigarettes, Ltd., United Kingdom, began marketing "Death" cigarettes in the United Kingdom in October 1991. The package is draped in black and features a skull and crossbones. The package contains an admonishment from the manufacturer: "Cigarettes are addictive and debilitating. If you don't smoke, don't start! If you smoke, quit!" The cigarette's target markets include smokers enjoying the brand image and taste, smokers purchasing the brand in a self-attempt to quit smoking, and nonsmokers purchasing the product and giving it to their smoker friends. The company is marketing the product in such retail outlets as restaurants and record shops.

45. Myerson, Allen R. "Philip Morris Cuts Cigarette Prices, Stunning Market." *New York Times*, April 3, 1993: 1, 52.

    Philip Morris slashed the price of its flagship brand Marlboro approximately 18 percent. Wall Street responded by lopping $14.75 off the company's share price. The company responded to the dramatic price impact of discount and generic brands and smokers' preference to pay less money for cigarettes. This "special promotion" action was followed up with discount coupons, mail promotions, and price cuts at the wholesale level.

46. "Making the Most of the 25's Cigarette Pack Niche in France." *Tobacco Journal International*, no. 3 (May/June 1993): 26–27.

    During 1992, cigarette companies began tapping a niche market for twenty-five-pack cigarettes. Rothmans reached the market first with its twenty-five-pack Golden American brand. The company stated that the product's success could be traced to the "generosity concept," as opposed to the price and quality advantages. Silk Cut, the distributor for the brand Bastos NY 25s, sensed an economic advantage in tapping a perceived drop in consumers' disposable income. Reynolds France's entrant, Gold Coast, is perceived to be successful due to the price rather than because of the twenty-five-pack concept. The success of Philip Morris Trade Marketing's twenty-five-pack L&M brand is attributed to the brand's international image.

47. Barford, Michael F. "What Marlboro Price-Cutting Means." *Tobacco Journal International*, no. 4 (July/August 1993): 26–28.

Even in the face of strong branding measures to identify, win, and keep loyal consumers, Philip Morris's decision to slash prices on its Marlboro brand reflected a need to guard market share, protect profits, and repel gains made by discount cigarettes. By the end of 1992, consumer preference for discount cigarettes enabled the category to command a 33 percent market share. However, when compared to the top line premium brands such as Marlboro, deep discount cigarettes generate far less profits, possibly as much as 90 percent per pack. Philip Morris and other premium cigarette manufacturers may be exhausting the cachet attached to the word "premium." The word "debasement" tends to undermine customer confidence and loyalty and to breed cynicism.

48. Warner, Fara. "Marlboro Medium Goes on I.D. Hunt." *Brandweek* 34, no. 42 (October 18, 1993): 1, 6.

In 1991, Philip Morris launched Marlboro Medium, a line extension of Marlboro, with the same ad campaign used for its flagship brand: cowboy symbols and images like the Marlboro Man and cowboy boots. The latest ad campaign features "Cowboy's Place," a bar slapped with the slogan "Well, come on in" and devoid of the typical cowboy trappings. In addition, Philip Morris assigned the brand its own unique motto: "There are no strangers here, only friends we haven't met."

49. "New West Pack a Challenging Idea." *Tobacco Journal International*, no. 6 (November/December 1993): 48–49.

Reemstma has announced a new German cigarette called New West. The entire package sought to bring together the elements of quality, enjoyment, and environment friendly. Competitors filed for an injunction and are successfully preventing Reemstma from shipping the cigarette. Competitors objected to the advertising slogan "Does a cigarette really need perfume in its tobacco?" and the words "unscented tobaccos" on the cigarette box.

50. Margulis, Ronald A. "The War of '93." *Tobacco Reporter* 121, no. 4 (April 1994): 22, 24.

Philip Morris's April 1993 decision to cut the price of its Marlboro brand signaled a market share—and not a price—war. The seeds for this move began with R. J. Reynolds's 1989 decision to end trade loading. The need for higher profit margins led distributors to carry discount brands. A recession, coupled with booming sales in discount and private label brands, led to decreases in market share for premium brands, especially for Marlboro. Based on this data, Philip Morris announced on April 2, 1993 that it would decrease the price of its premium brands and increase the price of its discount brands. Geoffrey C. Bible, Philip Morris's group chief of worldwide tobacco, proclaimed the move served to protect Philip Morris's premium brand's long-term value and to win back discount-brand smokers.

51. "Taking Stock." *Tobacco Reporter* 121, no. 4 (April 1994): 26, 28, 30.

Tobacco Reporter presents an edited transcript of a speech given by Geoffrey C. Bible, Philip Morris's executive vice president for worldwide tobacco operations. He spoke before the Consumer Analyst Group of New York in Scottsdale, Arizona. His talk focused on brand strategies, the discount market, tax increases, and international business. Bible also commented on Philip Morris's April 2, 1993, decision to cut the price of Marlboro and its other leading premium brands. Philip Morris sought to recover lost market share by narrowing the price differential between the premium and discount brands; this helped protect the long-term value of the premium brands. Also, the company sought to reinforce quality, imagery, preference, not just price, as the main attributes driving customers' purchasing decisions.

52. Kimelman, John. "Defensive Maneuver." *Financial World* 163, no. 13 (June 21, 1994): 32, 34.

British American Tobacco's (BAT) decision to purchase American Tobacco, the U.S. subsidiary of American Brands, is seen as protecting the brand equity of Lucky Strike and Pall Mall. These brands are produced and marketed in the United States by American Brands but globally by BAT, which feared American Tobacco would reposition the cigarettes as discount brands and cheapen their global image. In non-U.S. markets, Lucky Strike is marketed as an "American Original."

53. Margulis, Ronald A. "A Conversation with Bill Campbell." *Candy Wholesaler* 48 (September 1994): 38–40.

Philip Morris USA president and CEO Bill Campbell commented that "Marlboro Friday" marked the company's commitment to emphasize and defend its trademark/premium brands, such as the flagship Marlboro brand. Getting involved in price-only strategies would transform products into commodities and degrade the clout inherent in the trademark/premium. The redesigned Wholesale Masters program, involving partnerships with distributors, emphasizes marketing and merchandising at the point of sale and places greater demands on investment in technology to share information with Philip Morris. The company does not favor the use of coupons as a strategy.

54. Moore, Pamela. "Russia's Rip-Off Smokes." *Fortune* 130, no. 8 (October 17, 1994): 19–20.

Bogus tobacco manufacturers based in Southeast Asia (especially China and Indonesia) are producing and marketing "American blend" cigarettes throughout Russia. Smokes include Clinton (named after President Bill Clinton), Kennedy and Johnson (also American presidents), and the R. J. Reynolds brand Dakota. The cigarette packs are labeled "U.S. Tax Exempt for Use Outside U.S.," which American tobacco companies print on packs exported to foreign countries.

55. Kaplan, Andrew. "Wholesaler Unveils Line of Discount Cigarettes." *U.S. Distribution Journal* 222, no. 1 (January 15, 1995): 5.

New York wholesaler King Maker Marketing has launched a new low-priced brand named Checkers. King is a private label distribution and merchandising firm. Indian Tobacco Company (ITC) (India) Ltd.'s U.S. subsidiary, Fortune Tobacco Co., manufactures the product.

56. Rubel, Chad. "Dave's: A Smoke with Attitude." *Marketing News* 29, no. 3 (January 30, 1995): 1, 11.

Philip Morris began selling its new discount cigarette brand, Dave's, in Denver, Colorado, in November 1994. Marketed, using a fictitious character, to cigarette advocates, the brand promotes an antiestablishment message in various outlets, such as direct mail and point-of-purchase.

57. "X Cigarettes Pulled Off Market." *Boston Globe*, March 17, 1995: 35.

Manufacturer Star Tobacco and distributor Stowecraft Brook Distributors withdrew their Boston-based X menthol cigarette following storms of protest by African-American individuals and groups. The populace complained that the "X" evoked Malcolm X.

58. Sullivan, Barbara. "Smoke Signals Courtroom Battles." *Chicago Tribune*, April 3, 1995: sec. 4: 2.

In the face of mounting tobacco lawsuits and legal entanglements, Harley-Davidson, the motorcycle maker, is attempting to abrogate a 1986 licensing agreement with Lorillard Tobacco. Lorillard sought to develop and market a cigarette built around the brand name Harley-Davidson. In 1993, the companies disagreed over a proposed advertising rollout of a motorcycle rider resembling Darth Vader. Lorillard never nationalized the cigarette, opting only to sell the product in test markets.

59. Crescenti, Marcelo, and Barbara Horne. "Downpricing: A Last Resort or Ingenious Marketing Strategy?" *Tobacco Journal International*, no. 3 (May/June 1995): 26–29.

Philip Morris's decision to cut the price of Marlboro eventually led to similar actions by companies in other countries. In Turkey, R. J. Reynolds International introduced a new brand, Monte Carlo, and Philip Morris introduced L&M as low-priced alternatives for smokers hurt by the country's recession and ensuing drop in purchasing power. In Brazil as well, Philip Morris's marketing propelled L&M to the top of its best-selling list. Souza Cruz, the country's leading cigarette manufacturer, reacted by introducing the cheap cigarette brand Derby. The brand flew past L&M to become Brazil's best-selling cigarette brand.

60. Horne, Barbara. "Will Consumers Ever Accept a Smokeless Cigarette?" *Tobacco Journal International*, no. 3 (May/June 1995): 72, 74.

R. J. Reynolds Tobacco is developing a new smokeless cigarette called Eclipse. This is the company's follow-up to its failed Premier smokeless cigarette, introduced in the late 1980s. Eclipse contains a charcoal tip and a standard filter. The center piece contains tobacco and glycerine. When puffed by the smoker, the cigarette does not emit smoke, does not produce ash, and does not burn down like conventional cigarettes.

61. Hundley, Lars. "Micro Smokes." *Tobacco Reporter* 122, no. 10 (October 1995): 60.

R. J. Reynolds executives Dirk Herman and Diane Robert will lead a new independent division called Moonlight Tobacco Co. The company's new, offbeat cigarettes will be offered in dynamic, eye-catching packaging and in flavors, like honey-toasted tobacco. Seven new brands will be marketed under the parent name in Seattle, Chicago, and New York. Herman states that the cigarettes are targeted to the general public and especially smokers with "attitude."

62. Margulis, Ronald A. "Lolita Seduces Russian Smokers." *Tobacco Reporter* 122, no. 12 (December 1995): 46, 48, 50.

In 1993, New York–based Celadon Corporation introduced its new cigarette brand Lolita in Russia. The brand is manufactured in Sweden. Its packaging is upscale, with the cover featuring a sexually provocative woman. In Moscow and St. Petersburg, armed guards distribute the product in secured vans. The company will market the Lolita cigarette next in Israel—without the provocative packaging.

63. "HB907 Launched in Bid to Revive Numbers." *World Tobacco*, no. 152 (May 1996): 65–66.

January marked the unveiling of British American Tobacco (BAT) Germany's line-extension brand HB907. The brand aims to meet two goals: to pump life in the brand's parent, HB, and to attract young adult smokers. BAT has marketed the brand with the theme "HB, that's me."

64. Penteado, Claudia. "Cultivating Cigarette Brand in Fertile Territory." *Advertising Age* 67, no. 29 Suppl (July/August 1996): 12.

British America Tobacco's Brazilian subsidiary, Souza Cruz, produces the cigarette Hollywood. Hollywood is a sixty-year-old brand with brand equity rivaling that of Coca-Cola. The cigarette is backed with a $50 million budget that supports such advertising campaigns as print ads, sporting event sponsorships, and rock concerts. The company's universal advertising slogan is "The Hollywood Way." Advertising and marketing strategies implemented in Eastern Europe have made the cigarette the company's best-selling brand. U.S. and European markets would be future targets.

65. "Tobacco Fashions: Veni, Bidi, Vici." *Time* 148, no. 20 (October 28, 1996): 28.

"Beedies," the imported Indian "poor man's cigarette," has risen to cachet status on college campuses. Looking like a "joint," the Bidi resembles a miniature cigar but is a hand-rolled cigarette, less than 50 percent of the diameter of a regular cigarette. Bidis are manufactured in flavors of clove, menthol, and strawberry; they come in brands names like Mangalore Ganesh and Kailas.

66. Baker, Donald P. "A Small Cigarette Maker Tries to Blend In." *Washington Post*, March 24, 1997: 5.

In 1996, a new cigarette named Bailey's appeared on the market. The retail price is about half that of a pack of Marlboro or Camel cigarettes. During the initial rollout, the Bailey's logo appeared on a race car entered in a Winston Cup event. Before the race began, Winston Cup sponsor R. J. Reynolds (RJR) enforced its contractual right to dictate sponsorship and required Bailey's to tape over its logo. A federal judge, citing a contractual agreement, dropped a lawsuit filed against RJR by Bailey's.

67. Koerner, Brendan I. "A New Breed of Smokes." *U.S. News & World Report* 122, no. 15 (April 21, 1997): 8.

"Microsmokes" are the latest cigarette entries being pitched to high school and college students. These cigarettes have special characteristics, such as eye-catching packages, bold advertising, and off-the-wall flavors. The new crop includes Death cigarettes, with its "I like 'em and I'm going to smoke 'em" motto. R. J. Reynolds's Moonlight Tobacco subsidiary markets brands like Planet, Icebox, and Red Kamels. Red Kamels are marketed with the slogan "Back for no good reason, except they taste good."

68. Mandel-Campbell, Andrea. "Smoking-Savvy Argentina Gets New Cigarette." *Marketing Magazine* 102, no. 19 (May 19, 1997): 6.

    The Western Hemisphere inaugural launch of Philip Morris's cigarette Chesterfield Browns occurred in Argentina. The company backed up the launch with a $1 million campaign featuring billboard, newspaper, television, and radio advertising. This includes the *Chesterfield Music Box* radio program, two television commercials, and distribution of free samples and other free products in Buenos Aires nightclubs.

69. Weiss, Edward. "Competition Hots Up as RJR Challenges BAT's Kenyan Bastion." *Tobacco Journal International,* no. 3 (May/June 1997): 78–79.

    British American Tobacco (BAT) Kenya Limited dominates the Kenyan market with its Sportsman and Embassy brands. The annual value equals 8.5 million shillings; market share is 85 percent. R. J. Reynolds (RJR) International is challenging this dominance with its Aspen brand. The company began marketing the brand in December 1996 with a goal to achieve a 10 percent market share. RJR is spending at least 16.8 million shillings to promote the brand. This is spurring heated competition between the companies. Reports indicate that merchandisers who carry the Aspen brand are being threatened and that Aspen billboards and posters are being stolen.

70. Coleman, Tim. "Lettuce Light Up." *Tobacco International* 199, no. 6 (June 1997): 76–78.

    Dr. Puzant C. Torigan's company Safer Smokes Corporation worked to market a cigarette made of lettuce leaves manufactured at a plant in College Park, Georgia. Like tobacco leaves, lettuce leaves are cured, blended, naturally flavored, and manufactured into cigarettes. In July 1997, the company unveiled the new products, Bravo and Fumarillo, in the United States.

71. Shirouzu, Norihiko. "Low-Smoke Cigarette Catches Fire in Japan." *Wall Street Journal*, September 8, 1997: B1.

    R. J. Reynolds Tobacco Company (RJR) introduced its new Japanese cigarette, Salem Pianissimo, in August 1995. The cigarette, once marketed in the United States in 1991 as Salem Preferred, is designed for women, commands a current market share of 1.2 percent, and generates approximately $3.3 million in sales. Promotional ads use the slogan "Little smoke and odor, so it's No. 1." The cigarette's introduction caused RJR's competitors to issue its own "low-smoke" and "better-smelling" brands. Philip Morris International introduced Virginia Slims One, and Japan Tobacco introduced Bevel Flair and Frontier Pure.

72. Pritchard, Chris. "Critics Attack Rothmans for Its 'Kiddie Packs.'" *Marketing Magazine* 102, no. 34 (September 15, 1997): 6.

    In Sydney, Australia, Rothmans has introduced a new twenty-pack version of its Holiday cigarettes. The slimmer cigarettes and package costs $2.95 (Australian dollars) versus a regular pack costing about $6 (Australian dollars). Antismoking groups described the new offering as a "kiddie pack" designed to target teen smokers.

73. Murray, Barbra. "Smoke a Head of Lettuce?" *U.S. News & World Report* 123, no. 16 (October 27, 1997): 66.

    Nicotine-free cigarettes are increasing in popularity while the major tobacco companies remain mired in public contempt. One such brand, Bravo, returns after a twenty-eight-year absence. Manufactured by Safer Smokes Corp., the cigarette uses enzyme-treated lettuce in lieu of tobacco. Company president P. C. Torigian says the cigarette "tastes good like no cigarette could."

74. "Imperial Gets Serious about U.S. Brand." *Marketing Management* 102, no. 45 (December 1, 1997): 1.

    Mercer was a new cigarette being test-marketed in Portland, Oregon. The cigarette contains no additives and is purely natural. The promotion was backed with outdoor ads, in-store displays, and other promotions. The test-marketing continued for nine months; a national rollout followed. Imperial Tobacco, Ltd. (Canada) manufactures the cigarette.

75. Filipov, David. "Russia-Made Starts Making a Comeback." *Boston Globe*, December 15, 1997: A2.

    Moscow billboards are hawking the Russian-made Yava Gold cigarette. The ads use the slogan "Retaliatory Strike" and show the Statue of America about to be attacked by a huge pack of Yava Golds. The message is that Western-made cigarettes are controlling Russia's tobacco market. Interestingly, British American Tobacco manufactures the cigarette.

76. Belluck, Pam. "Omaha Tribe Turns to Cigarettes for a Better Life." *New York Times*, March 17, 1998: A12.

    At its own tobacco plant in Macy, Nebraska, the Omaha Indian tribe is manufacturing its Full-Flavor cigarette, with North Carolina tobacco. The cigarettes first went on sale in September 1997 and are going to be distributed to twenty-six tribes, off-reservation outlets, and overseas. Interestingly, the manufacturing plant once housed the tribe's health club and wellness center. The Seattle-based Washington Confederate Tribes of the Chehalis Reservation will finance two additional assembly lines at the plant. The Omaha tribe is lobbying to be exempt from the advertising restrictions of the pending tobacco settlement being debated in Congress.

77. Schwartz, John. "Liggett to Sell 3 Brands of Cigarettes to Philip Morris." *Washington Post*, November 21, 1998: A6.

    Philip Morris has purchased three brands from the Brooke Group's Liggett Group tobacco subsidiary. Philip Morris paid $300 million to purchase L&M, Lark, and Chesterfield. This is $100 million more than Brooke Group's total market capitalization.

78. Baker, Donald P. "High-Tech Device Makes Smoking Less Smoky." *Washington Post*, December 8, 1998: D1, D4.

    Accord is Philip Morris's new cigarette for which a smoker uses a "Puff Activated Lighter" box and puffs from the protruding filter tip. The lighter emits only 10 percent of the smoke produced by a regular cigarette. After an investment of $200 million over the last ten years, Philip Morris began to market the cigarette last August in the Richmond, Virginia, area. A smoker purchases a starter kit costing from forty-five to fifty dollars; it includes the lighter, a "how to use it" videotape, and a carton of cigarettes.

79. "Philip Morris Alters Labels on Some Brands." *Richmond Times-Dispatch*, June 24, 1999: B8. LexisNexis Academic (accessed March 8, 2004).

   Philip Morris's recent purchase from Brooke Group's Liggett tobacco subsidiary of its Lark, Chesterfield, and L&M brands has brought another change. Philip Morris removed the "Smoking is addictive" label from each brand and will insert one of a number of federally mandated warning labels. Liggett agreed to the harsher label as part of its 1997 agreement to settle lawsuits filed by the states.

80. Hwang, Suein L. "Philip Morris Tests New Menthol Type of Marlboro Brand." *Wall Street Journal*, July 26, 1999: B5.

   Pittsburgh and Atlanta will be the test markets for Philip Morris's Marlboro Mild, its new menthol cigarette. The company is attempting to penetrate a market that has so far eluded it. The menthol cigarette market is growing despite price increases implemented to pay for the national tobacco settlement.

81. Meier, Barry. "Philip Morris Says It Has a Safer Paper." *New York Times*, January 11, 2000: A20.

   A cigarette paper designed to prevent fires is set to be test-marketed by Philip Morris. During the manufacturing process, paper is added to specific parts of a cigarette. The objective is to retard oxygen, reduce the burn rate, and decrease the heat generated by the burning cigarette. Initially, Philip Morris is slated to add the new paper to its Merit cigarettes. Should the test be successful, the company could apply the new technology to its other brands.

82. Link, Emily. "Striving for a 'Healthier' Cigarette." *Tobacco Journal International*, no. 6 (November/December 2000): 66–67.

   Discount cigarette manufacturer Star Scientific, Inc., is introducing its Advance cigarette brand. The company produces the cigarette's tobacco in a manner that reduces cancer-causing nitrosamines. The packaging includes information about the product's benefits and the negative health aspects of tobacco consumption.

83. Fairclough, Gordon. "RJR Fires Up New Winstons and Camels." *Wall Street Journal*, April 11, 2001: B8.

   Winston S2 is a new brand-related product introduced in May 2001 by R. J. Reynolds, backed by the slogan "Quantum Smooth." The package color is metallic silver, and black outlining highlights the Winston name. The company also unveiled Camel Turkish Jade, a new menthol cigarette designed to capitalize on the successful launch of Camel Turkish Gold in 2000.

84. Fairclough, Gordon. "Will Smokers Swallow a Different Kind of Nicotine?" *Wall Street Journal*, April 27, 2001: B1, B3.

   Star Scientific, Inc., has been marketing a new nicotine lozenge called Ariva. Nicknamed "cigaletts" and resembling Tic Tacs, the product is a mixture of powdered tobacco, eucalyptus, and mint flavorings. In late 2001, Dallas and Richmond, Virginia, were the initial test markets. In the United States, Brown & Williamson obtained the rights to market the product. Ariva's marketing as a smoking-cessation product is not subject to regulation by the Food and Drug Administration. *Note*: As of November 3, 2004, Star Scientific and Reynolds American continue to jointly test market Ariva.

85. "Simple but Sophisticated." *Tobacco Reporter* 128, no. 5 (May 2001): 34.

    Reemstma's new Polo cigarette brand is meant for the "less expensive but classy cigarette" market. Trendy, young German adult smokers fit this profile. The packaging and name are designed to be modern and contemporary. The slogan used to market the cigarette is "Life can be so simple."

86. Finora, Joseph. "RJR Moves on Strength." *Tobacco International* 01, no. 9 (November 2001): 31–32, 34.

    R. J. Reynolds's "core four" lineup of cigarettes—Camel, Winston, Doral, and Salem—will be the focus of new product offerings and packaging improvements. Camel line extensions include seven "exotic blends" and the Turkish Jade brand family of menthol cigarettes. The Winston line-extension brand S2 comes in silver packaging with the name "Winston" wrapped around the package. The packaging is eye catching and is marketed to tie in with the company's "No Bull" campaign. Doral cigarettes are packed with more tobacco to create a slower-burning smoke. Doral smokers receive the publication *Doral & Co.*, filled with color photographs and discount coupons.

87. Fairclough, Gordon. "Decking the Halls with a Brand New Cigarette." *Wall Street Journal*, December 4, 2001: B1, B4.

    For the Christmas 2001 season only, Philip Morris promoted a new cigarette called M, with the slogan "A Special Blend for a Special Season." Store signs and mailings to adult smokers were used to promote the seasonal cigarette. The packaging design featured a classy black-coated container splashed with the Marlboro chevron and topped with the letter "M." Tobacco analysts speculate that Philip Morris used the holiday season to conduct market tests with the possibility of offering the cigarette throughout the year.

88. Dipasquale, Cara B. "B&W Leads Lower-Toxin Pitch." *Advertising Age* 73, no. 25 (June 24, 2002): S-22.

    In November 2001, Brown & Williamson (B&W) and Vector Tobacco introduced new premium-priced low-toxin cigarette brands. B&W launched Advance Lights (only in Indianapolis) and Vector introduced Omni nationally. Both brands sport warnings that the low-toxin smokes do not reduce harms caused by cigarette smoking. Both cigarettes are regarded as niche brands.

89. Dipasquale, Cara B. "RJR Rolls Out Camel Turkish Royal." *Advertising Age* 73, no. 25 (June 24, 2002): 16.

    R. J. Reynolds has been distributing a new cigarette in the Camel Turkish family, Camel Turkish Royal. The new cigarette, along with Turkish Gold and Turkish Jade, is promoted under the "Pleasure to Burn" theme.

90. Link, Emily. "The Cigarette as Cessation Tool." *Tobacco Journal International*, no. 5 (September/October 2002): 91.

    Vector Tobacco's new premium nicotine-free Quest cigarette is manufactured with three different amounts of nicotine and tar: "low nicotine" (Quest 1), "extra-low nicotine" (Quest 2), and "nicotine-free" (Quest 3). Initial marketing efforts targeted seven states, including Indiana, Michigan, and New York.

91. Fairclough, Gordon. "Cheap Smokes Are Squeezing Big Tobacco." *Wall Street Journal*, November 14, 2002: C1, C3.

    Cigarettes priced at bargain levels and manufactured by smaller companies are taking market share and taking advantage of hefty price increases by the major tobacco companies. Steep price increases to cover the cost of the national tobacco settlement, combined with big state excise tax increases, are weakening the major companies' hold on the market and jeopardizing their strategy to increase profits. Cheap-smoke manufacturers are enjoying a 10 percent market share, up 7 percentage points in just the last four years. Brands such as Rave, Hi-Val, and Double Diamond are undermining established brands' foothold on the market.

92. Fairclough, Gordon. "R. J. Reynolds Rings in New Smokes." *Wall Street Journal*, December 16, 2002: B6.

    R. J. Reynolds's Salem cigarettes have been revamped and issued under two new names: Salem Black Label and Salem Green Label. New packaging has been created for each brand and a "stir the senses" advertising campaign entices smokers. The Black Label sports a "richer tobacco flavor" hook; the Green Label emphasizes its new menthol taste. The ad theme is "One World. Two Sensations." Both new brands became available in 2003. *Note*: Both cigarettes continue to be marketed by Reynolds American, the parent company of R. J. Reynolds.

93. Beirne, Mike. "Camel Smoke Is RJR's New Year's Resolution." *Brandweek* 44, no. 40 (November 3, 2003): 9.

    In 2003, R. J. Reynolds issued an end-of-the-year limited-edition cigarette called Midnight Madness. Part of the Camel Exotic Blends family, the brand was available only during December and was backed by the advertising theme "Uncork the Excitement." Other limited edition brands issued during the year under the Camel banner included Bayou Blast (only during Mardi Gras), Beach Breezes, and Margarita Mixer.

94. Fuyuno, Ichiko. "Japan Tobacco Plans New Cigarettes." *Wall Street Journal*, February 3, 2004: D5.

    As of April 2005, Japan Tobacco is no longer manufacturing Marlboro cigarettes for Philip Morris International. The company introduced thirteen new cigarette brands in an attempt to overcome the impending loss. Lucia, one new cigarette, is targeted toward women. Another new brand is the rum-smelling "hi-lite" Rum Menthol. In November 2003, the company launched Mild Seven Prime Super Lights. The slogans "New Smoking Way" and "We won't let anyone say we stink of tobacco anymore" support the new strategy.

95. Beirne, Mike. "Philip Morris Thinks Big with Smaller Marlboro 72." *Brandweek* 45, no. 7 (February 16, 2004): 6.

Philip Morris's new Marlboro 72 (72 mm) menthol cigarette is designed for smokers who must quench their smoking thirst outdoors because of indoor smoking bans. The smaller cigarette will be packaged in green, with appeal to the smoker forty-five and older, and blue for the younger smoker. The national rollout took place on March 1, 2004.

96. Paersch, Emily. "Risqué, Irreverent, Quirky Brands." *Tobacco Journal International*, no. 1 (February/March 2004): 65–66.

In 2003, United Kingdom tobacco manufacturer Shag Tobacco Company launched its Shag cigarette brand. It is targeted to the student market, with the tagline "Have you had one lately?" Because of the advertising ban in the country, the company is using point-of-sale techniques such as the Shag fashion line (not available in the United Kingdom due to trademark restrictions) and Shag-branded condoms.

97. Ives, Nat. "Kool Cigarettes in New Flavors Draw Criticism." *New York Times*, March 9, 2004: C1, C11.

Brown & Williamson's (B&W) new line of "Smooth Fusions" Kool cigarettes came in four different exotic flavors: Caribbean Chill, Midnight Berry, Mocha Taboo, and Mintrigue. The packaging was visually appealing and unique, with rounded corners and eye-catching colors, and it unfolded like a book. The company marketed the limited-edition line in adult magazines such as *Vanity Fair*, bars and clubs catering to adults, and through direct mail to adult smokers. B&W pulled the new line of cigarettes from the market in October 2004. *See also* entry 785.

98. Areddy, James T. "Leader of the Pack Is Black and White and Sought All Over." *Wall Street Journal*, May 26, 2004: A1, A13.

Once manufactured solely for the Communist Party, Panda cigarettes are slowly being marketed to the Chinese smoker. The citizenry prizes the cigarette because the late Chinese leader Deng Xiaoping smoked only this brand. Few smoke the cigarettes, however; instead, they give them away as gifts to thank or influence people. Shanghai Tobacco, the cigarette's manufacturer, is currently producing them in limited quantities. This is creating a black market, where purchasers pay huge premiums for a single package.

99. "Philip Morris to Launch New Brand in UK." *Marketing Week* 27, no. 27 (July 1, 2004): 5.

In August 2004, Philip Morris launched the cigarette brand Basic. It was the company's first entry in the British market in over two decades. Northern England was the initial rollout market. An advertising campaign, including point-of-purchase, promoted the brand.

PROMOTIONS

100. Corn, David. "Smoke Gets in Your Eyes." *Nation* 250, no. 6 (February 12, 1990): 192.

Along with the National Archives, Philip Morris has begun an advertising campaign to promote the Bill of Rights. Philip Morris is spending $60 million to launch the campaign over a two-year period.

101. Kiley, David. "As Nelson Mandela Walks Free, the Marlboro Man Walks In." *Adweek's Marketing Week* 31, no. 8 (February 19, 1990): 2.

   Nelson Mandela walked out of his jail cell on February 11, 1990. During news coverage of this historic event, Philip Morris resumed its ads hailing the Bill of Rights' centennial celebration. Philip Morris's advertising agency, Ogilvy & Mather, attempted to have networks air the spots directly after their coverage of Mandela.

102. Dagnoli, Judann, and Steven W. Colford. "American Tobacco Draws Criticism over New Book." *Advertising Age* 61, no. 11 (March 12, 1990): 6.

   The American Achievers is the title of a new book published by the American Tobacco Company. American Tobacco and the Smithsonian Institution profile one hundred famous Americans. Profiled Americans include Dr. Michael DeBakey (heart surgeon) and Will Rogers (philosopher and humorist). Antitobacco groups claim that American Tobacco's goal is to link itself with "historically positive images." Critics see parallels between American Tobacco's book and Philip Morris's sponsorship of the Bill of Rights national campaign.

103. Chadha, K. K. "Tobacco Ads Disappear from Airwaves." *Tobacco Reporter* 117, no. 3 (March 1990): 24.

   As of December 31 1990, Hong Kong's television and radio stations were barred from airing tobacco advertisements. Tobacco companies shifted their advertising dollars toward the sponsorship of sports, culture, or pop music. The English channel Television Broadcast (TVB) aired the program *A Video a Day*, sponsored by Salem; TVB's Chinese channel aired the program *Solid Gold Music Video Corner* sponsored by Japan Tobacco's Mild Seven. Video jukeboxes sponsored by the industry were accessible through such outlets as fast-food restaurants and bowling alleys. Part of the proceeds from a Luciano Pavarotti concert sponsored by Philip Morris went to the Sports Foundation for the Physically Disabled. Gifted disabled athletes were provided with money to help them train year round.

104. McCarthy, Michael J. "Tobacco Critics See a Subtle Sell to Kids." *Wall Street Journal*, May 3, 1990: B1, B6.

   Tobacco companies deny they engage in youth-oriented promotions, but critics point to incidents clearly implicating the companies. Charlotte (N.C.)-based Sunbelt Video's Winston Cup newsletter includes a "Kid's Korner" section. The child selected as writing the best caption for a Winston Cup photograph would be rewarded with a Winston Cup sweatshirt. Teenagers dialing an 800 number listed in *Sports Illustrated* receive a free Camel T-shirt and discount coupons for Camels. In a video arcade game, Sega Enterprises displayed the Marlboro logo on race cars speeding past Marlboro signs. Software maker Electronic Arts' home video game includes multiple references to the Marlboro name and logo. Kool candy cigarettes, cigarette pack, and lighter toys appear on the market. The tobacco companies counter that they monitor these trademark infringements and attempt to eliminate them.

105. Seaman, Debbie. "French Tobacco Ad Ban Threatens Sports, Events." *Adweek* (Eastern Edition) 31, no. 19 (May 7, 1990): 49.

   A proposed cigarette and alcohol advertising ban by the French government would be the death knell for nontobacco brands built by the tobacco industry. Philip

Morris created the men's clothing store Marlboro Classics. American West tours are available through Marlboro Country Travel, a creation of Air France and Philip Morris. R. J. Reynolds and its advertising agency, J. Walter Thompson, provide information about New York and France.

106. Goldstein, Carl. "Losing a Packet." *Far Eastern Economic Review* 150, no. 51 (December 20, 1990): 54.

The tobacco ban that was implemented in Hong Kong on January 1, 1991, cost the leading television stations a major source of advertising revenue. In 1990, Television Broadcasts and Asia Television earned nearly $23 million in tobacco advertising revenues. The tobacco players increased expenditures in other media, such as magazines and newspapers; yearly expenditures amount to nearly $9 million. Sports sponsorships such as the Salem Open Tennis (R. J. Reynolds), the Viceroy Cup soccer tournament (British American Tobacco), and the heavily sponsored Macau Grand Prix received increased attention. Philip Morris opened two Marlboro Classics stores selling specialty menswear.

107. Dagnoli, Judann. "Gas Fuels Magna Offer." *Advertising Age* 62, no. 2 (January 14, 1991): 42.

R. J. Reynolds and Emro, Inc., will sponsor a joint promotion across fifteen states. Smokers sending in twenty-five Magna cigarette proof-of-purchase seals will receive a certificate for a ten-dollar gas purchase at any of Emro's service station/convenience stores. Emro operates stores under trade names such as Speedway, Checker, and Starvin' Marvin.

108. Rosenfield, James R. "A Breathless Promotion." *Direct Marketing* 53, no. 11 (March 1991): 22–23.

Database marketing is a tool mastered by R. J. Reynolds and now implemented by Philip Morris. The author's cat received a mailing from Philip Morris tempting her to jump to Marlboro Country. The mailing included the "Marlboro Brand 1991 Calendar" along with discount coupons. If the cat completes and submits the attached questionnaire, Philip Morris will brand a Marlboro Brass Lighter with the cat's initials. The package expounds upon the brand name, prods the smoker to switch brands, and helps build a marketing database.

109. Bird, Laura. "Joe Smooth for President." *Adweek's Marketing Week* 32, no. 21 (May 20, 1991): 20–22.

In 1974, R. J. Reynolds (RJR) resurrected the Joe "Smooth Character" Camel cartoon spokesman during a French prohibition of advertisements featuring people. RJR hatched the idea of using a cartoon spokesman to sidestep the rules. In 1988, during the brand's seventy-fifth anniversary, RJR imported Ol' Joe stateside to lead the final advertising procession with the tagline "75 years and still smoking." During 1990, the brand ranked as the third most recognizable print ad campaign, dropping from number two in 1989. For 1990, the *Special Events Report* newsletter reported that RJR spent $7.5 million on sporting-event sponsorships for Camel.

110. Horovitz, Bruce. "Cigarette Ad Ploys Spark More Protests." *Los Angeles Times*, June 15, 1991: D1, D6.

Philip Morris employs "consecutive-page" advertising to market Marlboro Medium. In a recent newspaper ad for the product, the first segment appears on the right hand of the page. A cowboy boot is all that appears on the page, except for the slogan "Introducing a special place in Marlboro Country." Two pages later appears the rest of the ad, a package of Marlboro Medium and the health warning. No health warning appears on the first page; this invoked protests from antismoking groups. In 1990, Philip Morris published a Marlboro car-racing team ad in *Sports Illustrated*; the ad contained a warning label on only one page of an eight-page foldout.

111. Dagnoli, Judann. "Three Faces of Kool." *Advertising Age* 62, no. 44 (October 14, 1991): 54.

Brown & Williamson (B&W) unveiled two new promotional campaigns for its flagship Kool menthol brand. The "What Kool Is Today" and "Kool Penguin" themes targeted young people and portrayed the brand as being hip. The campaign included the renaming of Kool Filter Kings to Kool Classic. Both themes ran concurrently with the "Kool and Milds Today" campaign for the Kool Milds brand. B&W supported the promotions with free Kool Penguin T-shirts and caps.

112. Konrad, Walecia, and Christopher Power. "Smoking Out the Elusive Smoker." *Business Week* (March 16, 1992): 62–63.

Traditional tobacco media advertising expenditures are declining, but the industry is creating other channels for spreading its messages and marketing its products. Database marketing allows for the collection of names and addresses of smokers using one's own brands and another company's brands. For its new Marlboro Medium cigarette, Philip Morris targeted smokers of Winston and Camel cigarettes with a colorful ad, three-dollar discount coupons for carton purchases, and a box containing five free packs. Apparel catalogs and posters provide another avenue to connect smokers with specific brands. R. J. Reynolds inserts Camel Cash coupons into Camel packs; the coupons are exchangeable for Joe Camel merchandise. Also, the industry surveys smokers about brands both old and new.

113. Freedman, Alix M. "Marlboro Country: Land of Come-Ons." *Wall Street Journal*, June 23, 1992: B1, B14.

Philip Morris changed its "push-through" advertising strategy for Marlboro cigarettes. Promotions abounded, such as "Buy one carton, get a half free" and "freebies," such as barbecue lighters and watches. It was rumored that Philip Morris, to protect the brand's market share, considered the distribution of five-pack cartons instead of the industry-standard ten-pack carton. Also, the Retail Masters Program provided incentives for retailers to prominently display and sell more packages of cigarettes.

114. "Tobacco Firms Go Sample Crazy." *Marketing* (July 23, 1992): 3.

British brands Rothmans Light and Dunhill Light were marketed aggressively in pubs and bars. "Sampling girls" targeted smokers and offered to exchange brands. Dunhill targeted pubs and bars with a "bar team." The team included two boys, two girls, and a manager. Over one weekend, the team's goal was to visit one hundred bars and pubs in London.

115. Elliott, Stuart. "Adoring or Abhoring the Camel." *New York Times*, July 29, 1992: D17.

    R. J. Reynold's Camel cigarette's popularity and market share has leaped dramatically thanks to a two-pronged advertising campaign. "Camel Cash" coupons entitle the user to redeem them for merchandise such as hats, T-shirts, playing cards, watches, and lighters. "C-Notes" are included in every pack of Camel. The second part is a merchandise catalog aimed at enticing the reader into a Camel wonderland. The smoker is beckoned to enter Club Camel or Camel After Hours, or to travel Camel Road. Merchandise offered includes "Camel Tracks" slippers, the walking surfaces of which are burnished with the word "Camel."

116. Lipman, Joanne. "Philip Morris to Push Brand in Gay Media." *Wall Street Journal*, August 13, 1992: B1, B6.

    Philip Morris placed an ad in *Genre*, a magazine geared toward gay men. In the October/November 1992 issue, Philip Morris advertised its brand-extension 85 mm Benson & Hedges Special Kings. According to the consulting firm Overlooked Opinions of Chicago, Benson & Hedges ranks second in cigarette brands smoked by members of the gay and lesbian market. According to the magazine's publisher, Don Tuthill, the gay market consists of brand loyal buyers and shoppers with discretionary dollars to spend. Those dollars would be spent with an advertiser willing to market to gays.

117. Warner, Fara. "Cool Camel Shells P-M Adventurers." *Brandweek* 34, no. 3 (January 18, 1993): 7.

    R. J. Reynolds unveiled its Camel Cash III marketing program to compete against Philip Morris's Marlboro Adventure Team. Called "Tell 'Em Joe Sent You," the program included point-of-sale advertising, print advertisements, and a new Camel catalog of goods featuring Joe Cool and the Hard Pack hanging out in places such as Joe's Diner and Joe's Lounge.

118. Warner, Fara. "Winston Comes Out Smoking, Spending." *Adweek* (Eastern Edition) 34, no. 4 (January 25, 1993): 9.

    R. J. Reynolds plans to increase significantly its advertising expenditures, with the goals of countering discount brands' invasion of its turf and going head to head with Philip Morris's Marlboro brand. The new point-of-sale promotional campaign "That's Worth a Winston" will support both the Winston Select and Winston brands. The signage is positioned to entice the buyer to try either brand and so enjoy a special moment. Magazine ads will pit Winston Select against Marlboro, with the byline "You select. The Choice is yours. Make the Select move."

119. "Marlboro Country: Still Untamed." *Tobacco Reporter* 120, no. 1 (January 1993): 16, 18.

    In an interview with the periodical, Philip Morris CEO William I. Campbell discussed the new Marlboro Adventure Team promotion and the Retail Masters Program. The Marlboro Adventure Team promotion began in early 1993. Ten winners engaged in an eleven-day, six-hundred-mile trip across Colorado and Utah filled with white-water rafting, motorcycling, four-wheel driving, and horseback riding. The Retail Masters Program seeks to maximize profits for both Philip Morris and the retailer. The program seeks to incorporate such merchandising principles as prominently displaying the leading brands and using cigarette promotions to build store traffic.

120. Doolittle, David E. "Adventure." *Tobacco Reporter* 120, no. 4 (April 1993): 42–44, 46.

    Adventure, sport, freedom, and the development of trust and bonding form the heart and soul of the Marlboro Adventure Team, as sponsored by Philip Morris GmbH of Munich. The German subsidiary beckons German males aged eighteen and over to apply and ideally experience a trip through the rugged parts of as many as five American states. Promotional teams visit "action points," such as discos, and distribute merchandise like cards, games, and three-pack samples. All this is supplemented with posters, billboards, and ninety-second cinema commercials. The program's success inspired the U.S.-parent to roll out an American version in 1993. Reemstma's "Come Together" promotion seeks to "promote understanding of even the most widely differing races and cultures." For two weeks, the company pays for five Germans to live with a family not based in Germany. Each person selected must be fluent in English and must have passed two days of a grueling barrage of questions exploring their state of mind.

121. Ecenbarger, William. "America's New Merchants of Death." *Reader's Digest* 142 (April 1993): 50–57.

    An investigation into the marketing and advertising practices of the tobacco companies revealed that across twenty countries, attempts to prop up a flagging U.S. tobacco market are primarily targeting children. In Buenos Aires, fifteen- and sixteen-year-old high school students are tempted with free Camels distributed from a Camel-coated Jeep. In Taipei, video arcade games are decorated with free American cigarettes. In Manila, a local Boy Scouts snack bar has sold cigarettes. In Malaysia, a Lucky Strike ad has appeared in a comic book geared toward elementary-school students. In Budapest, rock concert or disco attendees receive free Marlboro sunglasses just for testing a Marlboro. In addition, "brand stretching" is used to market nontobacco products, such as the Salem Power Station (Malaysia), the *Marlboro Hit Parade* radio broadcast (Budapest), and the Kent International Sailing Regatta.

122. Elliott, Stuart. "Another Tobacco Company Is Trying to Entice Smokers with Offerings of Merchandise." *New York Times*, May 28, 1993: D15.

    R. J. Reynolds is rolling out a new national ad campaign titled "Winston Weekends." Smokers age twenty-one and over will be enticed to clip "Worth a Winston" proof-of-purchase coupons from Winston and Winston Select brands and then select items from a twenty-four-page catalog. Stores, not magazine inserts, will be the primary distribution vehicle. Interestingly, a smoker would need to smoke 19,600 cigarettes to collect the required 980 Winston seals needed to purchase a leather jacket.

123. Zinn, Laura. "The Smoke Clears at Marlboro." *Business Week* (January 31, 1994): 76–77.

   Philip Morris is thought to be pursuing a three-pronged marketing strategy to rebuild and strengthen the Marlboro brand. On April 2, 1993, dubbed "Marlboro Friday," the company lowered the price of its premium cigarettes in order to fend off discount smokes. The strategy worked, and the company is expected to begin raising the price by perhaps as much as four cents per pack. "Continuity programs," such as Country Store and the Marlboro Adventure Team, are designed to reward smokers with branded merchandise and, in return, provide the company with valuable demographic data to build databases and create customer loyalty. The company is considering the introduction of Marlboro Express, a 70 mm cigarette designed to provide hurried workers with quick smokes.

124. Myerson, Allen R. "Selling Cigarettes: Who Needs Ads?" *New York Times*, March 3, 1994: D1, D6.

   Sandwiched between the salvos launched by the U.S. surgeon general and the Food and Drug Administration, tobacco companies are applying new marketing tools to pinpoint only smokers and not the mass market. Philip Morris uses the "Marlboro Adventure Team" promotion to reach millions of smokers. Puffers earn "Marlboro Miles" by submitting cigarette package symbols and bar codes. The miles give them an option to purchase items like jackets, sleeping bags, and watches. R. J. Reynolds tweaked its demographic database and targeted Camel smokers and individuals who prefer a competitor's brand, or base their purchasing decisions on price, taste, or image.

125. Elliott, Stuart. "Cigarette Giants Switch from Fantasy to Empathy." *New York Times*, March 30, 1994: D1, D18.

   Tobacco companies are employing "empathy advertising campaigns" to bond with smokers who feel cast aside by new social antismoking norms. Philip Morris's newest cigarette, the 100 mm Benson & Hedges, will be unveiled with the campaign slogan "The Length You Go for Pleasure." Advertisements will show smokers glued to airplane wings and fixated on outdoor platforms attached to office windows. This is in stark contrast to the "disadvantages" ad campaign launched in 1966. Those ads poked fun at the brand by showing a newspaper-reading smoker burning a hole in the paper, and having elevator doors smother an extra-length Benson & Hedges cigarette in the mouth of a smoker.

126. Kevin Berg and Associates. *Camel Trend Influence Marketing Program*. April 14, 1994. Bates 516067044/7077. legacy.library.ucsf.edu/tid/hgz82d00 (accessed June 14, 2004).

   Trendsetters, or "hipsters," are people who frequent "hip" establishments like nightclubs/bars and restaurants, retail stores, coffee houses, cafes, concerts, and events. The goal of the Camel Trend Influence Marketing Program was to convert "hip" individuals to Camel smokers in the hope that they in turn would influence their friends, convert them to Camel smokers, and enhance Camel's brand equity as "hip." Trend Influence Marketing takes place underground, associates Camel with trendsetters and "hip" people, and causes the brand to be perceived as "cool." The "Camel Club Program" was used to penetrate these trendy markets. Alternative local media (free periodicals) and national outlets such as *Spin* and *Details* were used to align with hipsters and lend credibility to the Camel brand.

127. Spethmann, Betsy. "RJR D-Base Plans Snag." *Brandweek* 35, no. 27 (July 4, 1994): 1, 6.

    R. J. Reynolds (RJR) is pursuing one direct marketing plan with retailers while shelving another marketing plan. RJR worked with Smith's Food & Drug Centers to issue a retailer magazine, *Shopper's Advantage*. Smith's dropped out of the project due to financial and marketing concerns. RJR continued to work on the project, seeking partnerships with other retailers. Another program, Leisure USA, had targeted nearly eight million households with mass mailings tailored to the customer's demographics. RJR scrapped the program due to its high cost.

128. Warner, Fara. "Philip Morris Defends Its Turf as Anti-Smoking Forces Grow." *Brandweek* 35, no. 29 (July 18, 1994): 20–21, 24–25.

    Philip Morris has mastered the marketing concept of "family branding." Family branding attempts to identify the core concepts of a company's major brand families, to develop techniques to consistently keep the family in vogue, and to guard against any deterioration in the family's heritage while building brand loyalty. Philip Morris's family of brands includes Marlboro, Benson & Hedges, Merit, and Basic. Line extensions and "value-added programs" support the family brand. Value-added programs, which are used to keep the family stable "consistent and contemporary," include the Marlboro Adventure Team and Marlboro Country Store. "Team" transformed Philip Morris into a direct-mail powerhouse, and "Store" is projected to achieve similar results.

129. Warner, Fara. "Cowpokin' Joe." *Brandweek* 35, no. 31 (August 1, 1994): 1, 6.

    Joe Camel takes on the Marlboro Man in a new ad campaign for the R. J. Reynolds brand. Transit media or billboard advertisements show Joe Camel rushing out toward the viewer and saying, "Genuine Taste. Never Boring." A western sunset ("Marlboro Country"), a horse, and its rider ("Marlboro Man") sitting on the ground provide a backdrop for Joe. The campaign is estimated to cost approximately $50 million.

130. Philip Morris. "Marlboro Music 1994 Marketing Plan." 1994. Bates 2041953076/3095. legacy.library.ucsf.edu/tid/hzj52e00 (accessed March 8, 2004).

    This document outlines the program objectives for the 1994 Marlboro Music tour. The overall goal is to embellish the image of Philip Morris's leading cigarette brand. Country music artists, both established and new stars, will be featured. Venues include arenas, theaters, and military bases. Merchandising the Marlboro brand will also be a key feature. The program is targeted to the young adult male and female music lovers.

131. Elliott, Stuart. "Whoa Horse! The Marlboro Man Adds Cranked-Up Electric Guitar to 'Home on the Range.'" *New York Times*, March 21, 1995: D5.

    The Marlboro Man makes way for the Marlboro-less man. The new ads for Philip Morris's flagship cigarette will feature all-text ads and more contemporary cowboy imagery. Ellen Merlo, senior vice president for Philip Morris USA, states that "Marlboro

Country is open to many different interpretations. It's traditional, but it's also new and today. It's not a place as much as a state of mind." The new imagery features items such as electric guitars and parking one's car at a red-hot roadhouse.

132. Sandomir, Richard. "New Formations for Stadium Signs." *New York Times*, June 7, 1995: D3.

    Philip Morris has signed a consent decree with the U.S. Justice Department to settle a lawsuit charging the company with violating the public law banning television advertising. Signs promoting Marlboro had been prominently displayed in clear view of television cameras. The consent decree affected advertising at such venues as Giants Stadium, Shea Stadium, and Madison Square Garden.

133. Martin, Michele. "Are Style Magazines the New Face of Tobacco Advertising?" *Campaign* (June 23, 1995): 30.

    In the United Kingdom, tobacco companies are beginning to publish quarterly magazines to cement brand loyalty. Gallaher's Silk Cut is to issue its own magazine. But the leader is Rothmans Marlboro's *Icon* magazine. This lifestyle magazine is targeted to the eighteen-to-thirty-four-year-old bracket. It uses strong brand imagery to drive home the points that smoking is stylish, trendy, and sophisticated. It is estimated that such a magazine would cost £3.4 million annually to produce.

134. Weisz, Pam. "Doral Continues Premium Promo Strategy with 'Taste' Giveaway." *Brandweek* 36, no. 32 (August 21, 1995): 13.

    The low-price image of Doral cigarettes will be boosted by a premium-brand advertising campaign aimed at defending its category against Philip Morris's Basic and Brown & Williamson's GPC cigarettes. R. J. Reynolds will begin a "Taste of America" sweepstakes to help achieve these objectives. A crossword puzzle will appear in such magazines as *Country America* and *Woman's Day*. Contestants complete the puzzle, send it to the company, and become eligible to win prizes like steaks and Pacific salmon. Each entrant receives a Doral discount coupon.

135. Weisz, Pam. "Away from the Pack." *Brandweek* 36, no. 33 (September 4, 1995): 21–22.

    In addition to its new "Taste of America" sweepstakes, in the summer of 1995, R. J. Reynolds implemented the "Discover America" sweepstakes for its Doral cigarettes. One hundred winners selected from among four national parks (Niagara Falls, Yellowstone, Great Smokey Mountains, and the Grand Canyon) and won a free trip. Advertising for "Discover America" appeared in magazines like *Field & Stream* and *Road & Track*. The ad included the slogan "Discover the Doral difference."

136. Taylor, Cathy. "Why Joe Camel Shies Away from the Net Surfing Crowd." *Adweek* (Eastern Edition) 36, no. 37 (September 11, 1995): 14.

    In the wake of rising antitobacco sentiment, the Internet would seem to be the perfect vehicle for tobacco companies to reach out to the smoking public and expand their database marketing. However, both R. J. Reynolds Tobacco Company and Philip Morris disdain the Web. The 1971 law banning television and radio advertising muddies the waters, specifying that tobacco advertising cannot be done on "any medium of electronic communication subject to the jurisdiction of the Federal Communications Commission." The Federal Communications Commission (FCC) states that its regulatory authority over the Internet is murky; however, the tobacco companies are taking no chances.

137. Williamson, Debra Aho. "Marlboro Offers Up CD-ROM 'Challenge.'" *Advertising Age* 66, no. 43 (October 23, 1995): 54.

Philip Morris's "Marlboro Unlimited" promotion went interactive with the distribution of a CD-ROM game designed to heighten awareness of the Philip Morris catalog. Philip Morris targeted big-city bars. Bars broadcasted the games on big-screen televisions while contestants attempted to "point-and-click-and-match" images from the campaign: a "Marlboro Unlimited" train, the Marlboro Gear catalog, and trips to Marlboro Country. Top point scorers were rewarded with promotional materials like T-shirts and caps.

138. Sumner, Walton, II and D. Gene Dillman II. "A Fist Full of Coupons: Cigarette Continuity Programmes." *Tobacco Control* 4, no. 3 (Autumn 1995): 245–52.

The authors focus on tobacco "frequent smoker programs" (continuity programs), their economic importance to the industry, and potential future incentive programs. Cigarette packages, mass media cigarette advertisements, point-of-sale advertisements, and information received via mailing lists provided all data between 1993 and 1995. Details are provided for continuity programs offered by Philip Morris, R. J. Reynolds, American Brands, and Brown & Williamson. Specific programs include the Marlboro Adventure Team, Camel Cash, and Winston Weekend.

139. Richards, J. W., Jr., J. R. DiFranza, C. Fletcher, and P. M. Fischer. "RJ Reynolds' 'Camel Cash': Another Way to Reach Kids." *Tobacco Control* 4, no. 3 (Autumn 1995): 258–60.

In this study, the authors' objective was to survey students at two high schools to measure their awareness of R. J. Reynolds's (RJR) "Camel Cash" campaign. Camel Cash, or "C-Notes," burst onto the scene in 1991. C-Notes are included in packs of Camel and can be redeemed for Camel merchandise. On the heels of this successful program, RJR launched similar promotion campaigns. These included "The Catalog II," which promoted Club Camel and Camel After Hours, "Tell 'Em Joe Sent You," "Joe's Place," and "Camel Cash Lotto." In early 1995, the company premiered "Camel Classifieds" and promoted "The Camel Company." In addition, RJR introduced "Winston Weekends" and offered smokers merchandise and seven sweepstakes. For its Virginia Slims brand, Philip Morris offered the "V-Wear" collection of fashions and accessories. The authors found that adolescents were purchasing Camels and collecting C-Notes.

140. Marsh, Ann. "Red Thunder." *Forbes* 157, no. 1 (January 1, 1996): 238.

"Marlboro Unlimited" is the latest and most lavish promotion offered by Philip Morris. Philip Morris awarded two thousand sweepstakes winners, who were required to be smokers, with a thousand dollars each and an all-expense-paid five-day train excursion throughout four mountain states, including Colorado and Idaho. Media promotion costs were estimated to reach nearly $500 million, nearly $20 million to construct the train. The "red thunder" rolling cigarette express was expected to attract media attention and provide public exposure despite the federal ban on television advertising.

141. Elliott, Stuart. "At Home on the Frontier, Marlboro Will Cross One, as the First Cigarette in the Marketing Hall of Fame." *New York Times*, April 10, 1996: D6.

   On June 5, at the American Marketing Association Effies Awards, the Marketing Hall of Fame inducted Marlboro as the first-ever tobacco product. The induction recognized the product's "enduring success in the marketplace." Also, the Virginia Slims theme "You've come a long way, baby" was replaced with "It's a woman thing." Player's Navy Cut was a "retro-chic brand" test-marketed by Philip Morris. "Hero" donned the cap worn by the brand's cowboy-evoking sailor.

142. Warner, Fara. "Tobacco Brands Outmaneuver Asian Ad Bans." *Wall Street Journal*, August 6, 1996: B1, B3.

   In the Pacific Rim, tobacco companies build brand equity and loyalty by "trademark diversification"—using their brand names on businesses that are in the public eye. Rothmans of Pall Mall's (Malaysia) travel agencies are renamed with the company's Peter Stuyvesant brand; the agencies then promote the televised "smoke-free Olympics." Philip Morris attached the Marlboro name to Classics stores that sell clothing all across Europe and Asia. Malaysia hosts the Benson & Hedges Bistro, the first of its kind anywhere in the world. The Bistro's gold interior nearly matches the color used in the package. Throughout Asia, R. J. Reynold's Camel brand is licensed to businesses by its World Brands International unit. These businesses use the brand name to market "adventure gear" clothing.

143. Efron, Sonni. "Lighting Up World of Smokers." *Los Angeles Times*, September 8, 1996: A1, A6.

   Foreign tobacco advertising continues even in countries that have implemented ad bans. Images of sexy women and beautiful scenery drape Russian billboards, bus stops, and subway walls. The L&M cigarette slogan "Date with America" accompanies a picture of the Golden Gate Bridge. In Buenos Aires, a billboard shows movie star Antonio Banderas promoting Parliament cigarettes. In 1994, the Polish government's smoke-out day competed with a Camel sweepstakes. R. J. Reynolds selected the names of winners on the same day; their prize offerings vastly outweighed the government's lone prize. In China, Philip Morris sponsors the Marlboro Soccer League, the 555 Hong Kong–Beijing car race, and a bridge championship.

144. Friedland, Jonathan. "Under Siege in the U.S., Joe Camel Pops Up Alive, Well in Argentina." *Wall Street Journal*, September 10, 1996: B1.

   Nobleza Picardo SA, British American Tobacco's Argentine subsidiary and Camel licensee, launched a Smokin' Joe campaign aimed at increasing market share and brand awareness. Select Camel cigarette packs are fitted with playing cards bestowed with the imprint of Joe Camel and his Hard Pack buddies. Smokers can return the cards and compete for prizes like posters, shot glasses, boxer shorts, and Harley-Davidson motorcycles. The promotion is a spin-off of an earlier toll-free telephone promotion giving away Joe Camel stickers and posters to smokers of legal age.

145. Parker-Pope, Tara. "Tough Tobacco-Ad Rules Light Creative Fires." *Wall Street Journal*, October 9, 1996: B1–B2.

Strict United Kingdom tobacco advertising rules require the Advertising Standards Authority to approve all tobacco advertising. Ads cannot show "beautiful people," promote laughter, highlight scenes of serenity such as rivers and mountains, or be appealing in any way. This has not stopped the creative juices flowing from the tobacco companies and their ad agencies. American Brands' Gallaher Tobacco promotes its Benson & Hedges and Silk Cut brands with unusual advertising. In advertising Benson & Hedges, the brand's gold box acts like a mouse trap set in front of a mouse hole; in another ad, ants haul off the booty as if snatched from a picnic table; another ad shows a swinging gold watch transfixing an onlooker. Silk Cut advertising includes cancan-dancing, scissors wearing silk dresses, a purple silk cap penetrated by a rhinoceros horn, and an unattended and unadorned purple silk curtain waiting to be slashed à la *Psycho*. Marlboro Country is advertised through a folding map of the United States, under a tobacco health warning.

146. Kelly, Keith J., and Judann Pollack. "Marlboro Mag Looks at Going Mainstream." *Advertising Age* 68, no. 4 (January 27, 1997): 1, 44.

    Hachette Filipacchi Magazines and Philip Morris are drawing closer to inking a deal to market nationally Philip Morris's *Unlimited* magazine. *Unlimited* has a circulation of 1.5 million, consisting of subscribers paying either $6.95 per year or remitting one hundred "Marlboro Miles" proof-of-purchase coupons.

147. Mehegan, Sean. "Smokes and Mirrors." *Brandweek* 38, no. 8 (February 24, 1997): 28–31.

    In spite of new and pending government regulations, the tobacco companies are forging ahead with brand-equity programs. Retailer-specific programs like Philip Morris's Retailer Masters Program aim to tie product sales to monetary incentives. Continuity programs seek to enhance the value of trademarks, develop customer loyalty, and enhance brand awareness, especially when advertising budgets are reduced. Examples include Philip Morris's *Unlimited Gear Built for Adventure* catalog, the *Benson & Hedges Home Collections* catalog, and Marlboro's *Success*. Sport sponsorship is an important tool for R. J. Reynolds. The company continues to sponsor the Winston Cup NASCAR race, Smokin' Joe's Racing Team, and the American Pool Player Association.

148. Ross, Chuck, and Ira Teinowitz. "Luckies Strike Web with Stealth Tobacco Site." *Advertising Age* 68, no. 8 (February 24, 1997): 1, 86.

    In the San Francisco area, Brown & Williamson is sponsoring four-page newspaper inserts touting its Lucky Strikes brand and the "Circuit Breaker" Web page. The website is promoted as a "lifestyle site" providing information about Bay Area social clubs and various social activities. Believed to be the very first brand-enhancing Web page, the site never mentions Lucky Strikes or Brown & Williamson. The site does prompt smokers aged twenty-one and over to complete a questionnaire and provide such information as name and address.

149. Pollack, Judann. "Old Joe Is No-Show in New Camel Ads." *Advertising Age* 68, no. 10 (March 10, 1997): 1, 44.

    R. J. Reynolds is temporarily shelving Joe Camel advertisements. Instead, Camel ads show a woman, head back, allowing smoke in the form of a camel to drift from her mouth. The new slogan, "What You're Looking For," is one of four new advertisements used in the Camel campaign. The others depict the bottom of a bar glass lifted to display the camel image on the table, a man's jeans showing the camel in a frayed area, and a camel smoke image emanating from a cigarette inserted into a guitar neck.

150. Wentz, Laurel. "Tobacco Marketers Eye Global Models for U.S." *Advertising Age* 68, no. 19 (May 12, 1997): 22.

    In overseas markets, tobacco companies and their advertising agencies deploy creative ways to market cigarettes despite restrictions mandated by host countries. In Germany, Philip Morris International solicits advertising ideas from event attendees for its Chesterfield brand. In Argentina, the company spent $1 million on a media campaign for its Chesterfield Brown brand. The campaign includes sponsoring the *Chesterfield Music Box*, a radio program playing alternative music. In the United Kingdom, Gallaher is seeking to create a strong brand image for its Benson & Hedges cigarette before the imposition of stronger regulations. One ad shows a large, eye-catching, gold box in an out-of-the ordinary setting. Likewise, for its Silk Cut brand, the company deploys silk rendered by cat's claws and a purple curtain fronted by synchronized high-kicking scissors.

151. Dwek, Robert. "Rising from the Ashes." *Marketing* (May 29, 1997): 21–22, 25.

    The British government is planning to impose a ban on tobacco advertising. Tobacco companies are preparing to meet this challenge by engaging in "below the line" advertising. Imperial Tobacco is using data-driven marketing to reach new customers. Gallaher has teamed with Forward Publishing to target the tobacco company's Silk Cut smokers with a tailor-made magazine. The magazine lacks a title, contains lifestyle-oriented articles filled with references to the cigarette, and is marketed in a manner to make the smokers feel part of an "exclusive club." Specialist Publications is producing Rothman's *Rendezvous* magazine. The magazine's circulation is limited to one hundred thousand, contains lifestyle articles, and is published with a "club feel."

152. Leo, John. "Boyz to (Marlboro) Men." *U.S. News & World Report* 122, no. 21 (June 2, 1997): 18.

    Tobacco companies use "depth psychology" to convey certain messages and images to specific age groups. Ads for Newport cigarettes depict scenes of "outdoorsy horseplay." The underlying themes impart the message of females doing battle against domineering males. Military images permeate advertising for Marlboro and Pall Mall. The red chevron used on Marlboro packs is a military insignia. Packaging for both brands includes Roman military mottoes conveying the message of conquest and victory. Overall, cigarette brands sell the themes of rule-breaking, self-control, combating adult control, and a sense of belonging.

153. Teinowitz, Ira. "FTC's Camel Case Hinges on Ads' Power over Kids." *Advertising Age* 68, no. 22 (June 2, 1997): 4, 45.

    The Federal Trade Commission (FTC) voted three to two in favor to issue a complaint against R. J. Reynolds and its use of Joe Camel. The FTC alleged that the dromedary icon entices underage children to smoke. An administrative law judge will review the FTC's actions and the merits of the case. To counter the FTC's accusation, the tobacco company cited a study by Audits & Surveys Worldwide, underwritten by the company, holding that only 3.1 percent of smokers under the age of eighteen smoked Camels.

154. Pollack, Judann, and Ira Teinowitz. "With Joe Camel Out, Government Wants the Marlboro Man 'Down.'" *Advertising Age* 68, no. 28 (July 14, 1997): 3, 34.

    Recently, R. J. Reynolds decided to withdraw permanently its Joe Camel advertising campaign. During the tobacco settlement negotiations, government representatives asked Philip Morris to withdraw the Marlboro Man from public view. The company is considering the request; also, it may look at modifying the campaign.

155. Hwang, Suein L. "Health Groups Challenge Winston Ad Claims." *Wall Street Journal*, August 25, 1997: B1, B3.

    In early August 1997, as part of its "No Bull" campaign, R. J. Reynolds (RJR) unveiled a new advertising campaign for its flagship Winston brand. The ads greet the reader with "Yours have additives . . . New Winstons don't" and "What the heck have you been smoking?" The company claims that the newly reformulated Winston is safer and additive-free, as opposed to competitors' brands. On August 22, the American Cancer Society, the American Heart Association, and the American Lung Association challenged this claim in a jointly signed letter to the Federal Trade Commission. The groups are requesting an investigation into the new campaign; they see the advertising as stating a "health claim" and request proof of that claim from RJR.

156. Elliott, Stuart. "Kool Cigarettes' New Campaign." *New York Times*, October 14, 1997: D8.

    In November 1997, Brown & Williamson began a new marketing program for its Kool menthol cigarettes. The theme, "B Kool," featured men, not visible to the viewer, smoking Kools, carrying packs, and being eyed by beautiful women. The women were either straddling motorcycles or hanging out in pool halls. These ads replaced marketing themes set against scenes of waterfalls, ski slopes, and beaches.

157. Murphy, David. "Tobacco's Last Stand." *Marketing* (February 19, 1998): 33–34.

    A pending European Union directive banning most forms of tobacco advertising over the next eight years is focusing the industry on eye point-of-purchase (POP) advertising as a "safe haven." In the United Kingdom, POP techniques include gantries (back-wall displays), illuminated strips, and beeping and flashing electronic devices. For its Benson & Hedges brand, British American Tobacco is investing in a huge wall display in Folkestone's Eurotunnel Duty Free shop. Also, the company has started the Benson & Hedges Coffee line in Malaysia. Tobacco companies are using "brand coloring" as a means to correlate colors with specific brands.

158. Glass, Chris. "Splat Packs." *Tobacco Reporter* 125, no. 3 (March 1998): 56–58.

    Crotia bars the usage of traditional tobacco advertising tools: billboards, brand images, "parallel" products such as lighters and hats, and displays of the company's name in an advertisement. Rothmans International nevertheless wanted to launch, advertise, and connect potential consumers to its new products, Pall Mall Export and Pall Mall Lights. The company began using a "globe" on its packages. The globes appeared on the outer wrapping, gave the illusion of being three-dimensional, and appeared to be splattered all over the package—hence the name "splat packs." Rothmans used billboard, television (for a very brief time), and the cinema to advertise the "globe" concept. Rothmans employed image-building to connect the consumer with the globe concept, the product, and the company with the consumer. The company has stated that the products achieved a 6 percent market share immediately.

159. Pollack, Judann. "RJR Takes Brazen Tone in New Camel Campaign." *Advertising Age* 69, no. 19 (May 11, 1998): 2.

A new $50 million Camel cigarette series of advertisements will feature the slogan "Mighty Tasty" and prompt the reader to locate hidden Camel images. The new tagline replaces the "What you're looking for" campaign. The four new ads spoof the U.S. surgeon general's admonitions and the antitobacco campaign's position that minors should not view cigarette ads. R. J. Reynolds's strategy is to build the brand as offbeat and entertaining. For example, the Camel images are placed in a maid's hairpiece and the window shade in a shotgun ad.

160. Baird, Roger. "BAT Bids to Catch Up in Tobacco Wars." *Marketing Week* 21, no. 17 (June 25, 1998): 19–20.

British American Tobacco (BAT) moves forward in its trade market diversification (TMD) strategy with its Lucky Strike Originals mail-order catalog. Customers can purchase premium goods manufactured just for Lucky Strike. BAT is supplying the catalog in Germany and will begin test-marketing it in the United Kingdom, Holland, and Spain. Other BAT TMD projects include a Benson & Hedges coffee bar in Malaysia and an Asian travel agency named for its Kent cigarette brand name. Philip Morris's worldwide Marlboro Classics stores sell clothes, such as jeans, and R. J. Reynolds operates a Camel line of clothes.

161. Beirne, Mike. "Doral's Direct Line." *Brandweek* 39, no. 31 (August 10, 1998): 24–25.

R. J. Reynolds its strengthening the brand equity of its Doral cigarette by promoting it as being manufactured by heartland people with heartland values. At retail outlets, advertisements for the "The Big American Adventure" beckon customers to "Discover the Difference" and enter the Doral sweepstakes. Sweepstakes winners would receive an all expense paid nine day trip filled with such activities as touring Doral's manufacturing plant in Winston-Salem, North Carolina ("Tobaccoville, USA"), participating in a VIP tour of Graceland in Tennessee, and riding in a hot-air balloon in Albuquerque, New Mexico. Brand equity is cemented further by the Doral newsletter and annual get-togethers à la Saturn automobile owners.

162. Headden, Susan. "The Marlboro Man Lives!" *U.S. News & World Report* 125, no. 11 (September 21, 1998): 58–59.

Facing advertising and promotion restrictions at home and abroad, tobacco companies are employing "brand stretching," using nontobacco products to promote cigarette brands. For example, in Finland and Vietnam, Philip Morris promotes Marlboro not with words but by splashing the red and white chevron across various advertisements. Marlboro athletic bags are sold in Beijing. Marlboro child-sized T-shirts are sold in Kenya. Other advertising promotions include Philip Morris's "Hip Hop BBQ" in Berlin, R. J. Reynold's (RJR) Camel Rock musical program in Kiev (Ukraine), and RJR International's Salem Attitude clothing line.

163. Hwang, Suein L. "Cigarette Makers in Discount War to Lock in Share." *Wall Street Journal*, September 23, 1998: B1, B4.

In anticipation of a possible settlement of all state Medicare lawsuits, the tobacco companies are flooding the market with discounts and promotional specials. Their goal is to lock in market share and freeze out their small competitors. Philip Morris will discount Marlboro cigarettes significantly with a "buy three, get two free" promotion. Other promotions will be left to retailers and will vary across the country. Also, the companies are rushing to market new products like Philip Morris's Marlboro Ultra Lights.

164. Glass, Chris. "No Bull." *Tobacco Reporter* 125, no. 9 (September 1998): 46–47.

Backed by positive test results in Florida, R. J. Reynolds (RJR) has begun a nationwide marketing campaign for its new additive-free, "No Bull" Winston cigarette. Red and white billboards and national magazines advertise the repositioned brand with catchy phrases like "Thank you for not smoking additives," "At least you can still smoke in your car," and "There's enough bull out there, you shouldn't have to smoke it." Also, RJR is using the campaign to sponsor the "No Bull Five" NASCAR race team. At five various NASCAR events, RJR will offer the "No Bull Five" race drivers up to $1 million in prize money. RJR will offer the same purse to five Winston smokers.

165. "Marlboro Sparks Marketing Campaign in Triangle Bars." *Tobacco International* 200, no. 9 (September 1998): 6.

In upscale bars and beer havens across over forty U.S. cities, Marlboro representatives, decked out in Marlboro colors, promote the country's best-selling cigarette brand. Young men and women distribute such free promotional items as banners, T-shirts, and fishing rods; cigarettes are not distributed, and the reps are forbidden to smoke. This is a part of Philip Morris's new "event-marketing" approach to promote products with more innovative, aggressive, but less publicly offensive marketing techniques.

166. Doroba, Steve. "The New Frontier." *Tobacco Reporter* 125, no. 10 (October 1998): 198, 200.

On-Premise Marketing is offering the tobacco industry a new tool for advertising to the public—electronic entertainment promotion. One product, the TouchTunes digital jukebox, allows consumers to engage in interactive games and view video images; the tobacco companies in return enhance their database marketing efforts. TouchMaster countertop video games allow the tobacco companies to enhance brand awareness with customers. A third product, the Ticker News Network, is a satellite-based system that does not require a satellite dish or phone lines. It is a mobile piece of equipment that can fit anywhere in a retail outlet or bar. From it, consumers can get the latest news, sports, and entertainment; the tobacco companies can exclusively sponsor advertising and gain the customers' confidence.

167. Marsh, Harriet. "Big Brands Hit the Club Scene." *Marketing* (November 26, 1998): 18–19.

British American Tobacco (BAT) and nightclub operator Ministry of Sound are rumored to be readying a new marketing deal. The deal will allow the Sound's nightclubs in China, Russia, and Eastern Europe to promote BAT brands such as State Express 555, Benson & Hedges, and Lucky Strike. BAT is targeting the eighteen-to-twenty-four-year-olds who frequent the clubs. BAT and the Ministry of Sound already have a separate marketing contract promoting club nights in Asia and the United Kingdom.

168. Coleman, Tim. "On the Offensive or Just Plain Offensive?" *Tobacco International* 200, no. 11 (November 1998): 16–20.

Before advertising restrictions become effective, Philip Morris and R. J. Reynolds are boldly promoting their products with aggressive advertising campaigns. Philip Morris is seeking to preserve Marlboro's Great American West brand imagery with its new "Party at the Marlboro Ranch." Adult smokers complete an official entry form in hopes of winning a five-day, four-night stay at a first-class Marlboro ranch in either Montana or Arizona. In contrast, R. J. Reynolds is issuing ads satirizing the current antismoking environment. The ads portray the antismoking cadre as people seeking to spoil the smoking pleasure of those wishing to smoke. Ads include the tagline "Viewer Discretion Advised." One ad for Winston's "No Bull" campaign proclaims, "Judge me all you want, just keep the verdict to yourself."

169. Rosenfield, James R. "Cigarettes Are Good for You! and—They're Not Addictive." *Direct Marketing* 61, no. 7 (November 1998): 36–38.

The author critiques mailings received from Brown & Williamson (B&W) for their Capri and Carlton cigarettes. One Capri mailing beckons the recipient to "soothe away stress" and "relax, refresh, retreat" with a Capri. Aromatherapy tips are suggested to rid one of everyday cares. The author believes B&W implies thereby that cigarettes are good for you and that aromatherapy can be an alternative to conventional medical treatment. The Carlton mailing shows two successful and attractive businesswomen declaring, "The decision to smoke is mine," "It's my decision to smoke," and "Carlton is my choice." The mailing includes discount coupons. The author comments that the advertisement is reminiscent of the Virginia Slims campaign and its attempt to meld with the women's liberation movement.

170. Pollack, Judann. "B&W's Carlton Relaunch First since New Ad Rules." *Advertising Age* 70, no. 9 (March 1, 1999): 12.

Brown & Williamson's campaign for the relaunching of its Carlton brand will emphasize package, in-store, and custom magazine advertising. The product packaging will feature raised lettering and a switch to a creamy color from the standard red. The package will promote "product attributes" such as 1 mg of tar. The company views in-store advertising as "a targeted communication channel." Custom magazines, a direct-mail campaign, and the new tagline "Isn't it time you started thinking about

Number One?" will promote the brand. This is the first marketing push by any major tobacco company since the industry agreed to sign last year's settlement agreement with forty-six states.

171. "TV Ad Shows Souza Cruz Going Hollywood." *Tobacco International* 201, no. 6 (June 1999): 42.

    In Brazil, British American Tobacco's Souza Cruz subsidiary has produced a television commercial to promote the company's Hollywood cigarette brand. Sao Paulo's Duailibi Petit Zaragoza Propaganda created the "Flying Lap" commercial, featuring a globetrotting Indianapolis 500 racing car. An outdoor campaign will be created around the "Flying Lap" theme.

172. Pollack, Judann. "Loyalty Program Takes RJR's Doral to No. 3." *Advertising Age* 70, no. 36 (August 30, 1999): 4.

    Doral Celebration is R. J. Reynolds's major annual loyalty promotion program. This year's celebration will be held in Winston-Salem Tobaccoville, North Carolina, and will also mark the stopping point of the company's "Rally across the Heartland" motor tour. The success of the Celebration program, which started in 1994, has rocketed Doral to the number-three best-selling brand in America. The program is backed by a $30 million war chest, fierce brand loyalty, merchandise, magazines, price breaks, and advertising conveying an image of consistency.

173. Pollack, Judann. "Tobacco Brands' Main Events Are Now by Invitation Only." *Advertising Age* 70, no. 36 (August 30, 1999): 4.

    Tobacco companies use "invitational" advertising strategies designed to target market smokers. For example, R. J. Reynolds employs "alternative media" strategies for advertising their products. In clubs, the company uses napkins, coasters, matches, and samples to promote the Camel brand. Bar napkins appear in alternative weekly publications to promote the Winston brand with taglines such as "Your phone number here" and "Your real number here." Bathroom stall doors and urinals are offbeat vehicles used to promote the Salem brand.

174. Pollack, Judann. "Virginia Slims Translates Theme for Many Cultures." *Advertising Age* 70, no. 38 (September 13, 1999): 3, 73.

    African, Asian, and Hispanic women are target markets for Philip Morris's $40 million marketing blitz for its Virginia Slims brand. The "Find your own voice" theme commenced in December 1999 and has appeared in magazines such as *Essence*, *Latina*, and *Glamour*. "Never let the goody two shoes get you down" is the tagline aimed at African-American women. "Dance around naked with a rose between your teeth if you want. But do it like you mean it" is the tagline aimed at Hispanic-American women. The company is using the tagline "In silence I see. With wisdom I speak" for Asian-American women. Ellen Merlo, senior vice president of corporate affairs for the company, stated the ads represent today's women in terms of multiculturalism, diversity, and empowerment.

175. Torry, Saundra. "The Butt of a Marketing Joke?" *Washington Post*, September 18, 1999: E1.

Brown & Williamson customers have noticed an 800 number printed on cigarette packs. Callers are greeted by a male voice stating, "We're a giant corporation and you make us feel like a little kitten. Thank you . . . lover." The male voice leaves the caller with this line: "By the way, the other tobacco companies hate you and think you're ugly. They told us so."

176. Elliott, Stuart. "Camel Goes from an Audacious Campaign to a 'Classic' One." *New York Times*, September 22, 1999: C7.

R. J. Reynolds's advertising agency is changing the advertising slogan for Camel cigarettes. It will replace the "Might Tasty!" slogan with "Pleasure to Burn." The new slogan allows the tobacco company to "telegraph their message" to customers in print, direct mail, bars, clubs, and signs in stores. These are the advertising tools still available to the industry by the national tobacco settlement agreement. The "Mighty Tasty!" slogan, used only since May 1998, paints smokers as rebels and lampoons the antitobacco movement.

177. Darby, Ian. "Silk Cut Campaign to Mock Ads Ban." *Marketing* (October 28, 1999): 5.

With the United Kingdom ban on cigarette ads to begin on December 10, 1999, Gallaher will roll out a major campaign to advertise its Silk Cut cigarette. The tongue-in-cheek tagline will be "It's not over until the fat lady sings." The campaign goals are to poke fun at the upcoming ban and to give the brand maximum exposure.

178. Hays, Constance L. "With Joe Camel Put Out to Pasture, Tobacco Makers Like R. J. R. Try a More Direct Approach." *New York Times,* November 24, 1999: C5.

R. J. Reynolds (RJR) is starting a new quarterly magazine called *CML*, which the company refers to as a "magalog," or a combination of a magazine and catalog. The magazine's focus will be on fashion, food, travel, and shopping articles. The magazine will serve as the sole promotion and marketing tool for selling exotic new blends of the Camel brand. In addition to RJR, Brown & Williamson is publishing *Real Edge* and *Flair*. The magazines target men and women, respectively. In 1996, Philip Morris began publishing *Unlimited: Action, Adventure and Good Times*, which concentrates on outdoor adventure and contains no smoking-related articles and photographs.

179. Kuczynski, Alex. "Big Tobacco's Newest Billboards Are on the Pages of Its Magazines." *New York Times*, December 12, 1999: sec. 1: 1, 40.

Faced with limited avenues by which to advertise their products, tobacco companies are entering the "custom publishing" business. They work with commercial publishers to produce magazines targeted to their customers and distributed for no charge or a small fee. Hearst Publishing produces *Flair* and *Simple Living*, and EMAP Petersen produces *Real Edge* for Brown & Williamson. Hachette Filipacchi publishes *Unlimited* for Philip Morris. Time, Inc.'s *Wallpaper* magazine staff produces R. J. Reynolds's magazine *CML: The Camel Quarterly.*

180. Pollack, Judann. "RJR Tries Out Direct Sales of Three Cigarette Brands." *Advertising Age* 71, no. 1 (January 3, 2000): 8.

R. J. Reynolds (RJR) is attempting to jump-start sales of three slow-moving brands with a direct-mail campaign in seven states. A six-page catalog is sent to adult smokers only, promoting the More, Now, and Vantage brands. Smokers can find retailers who stock the brands by dialing a toll-free number given in the catalog. The initial test markets are California, Georgia, Kentucky, Michigan, Pennsylvania, Tennessee, and Texas.

181. Pritchard, Chris. "Aussie Cig Girls Make a Comeback." *Marketing Magazine* 105, no. 7 (February 21, 2000): 3.

    "Cigarette girls" have staged a comeback in Sydney clubs and pubs. These "scantily clad young women" wear tobacco-brand colors, carry cigarette trays, and seek to persuade young adult smokers to try half-priced cigarettes. Antismoking advocates refer to the girls as "angels of death." Cigarette boys saunter through gay venues promoting cigarette brands.

182. Teinowitz, Ira. "Philip Morris USA Rolls Marlboro Milds to National Audience." *Advertising Age* 71, no. 10 (March 6, 2000): 3, 63.

    In April 2000, Philip Morris USA entered the national market with its menthol cigarette entry Marlboro Milds. The tagline "A New Menthol" was used, with laid-back cowboy imagery. Also, the company continued its "Cowboy's Place" contest, a national $3 million sweepstakes tied to the Marlboro brand stable. Contestants had a chance to win such prizes as steaks or a visit to the Marlboro ranch. Started in February 2000, the sweepstakes continued for two more months.

183. Meier, Barry. "R. J. Reynolds to Promote Cigarette Brand as Posing Lower Cancer Risk than Others." *New York Times*, April 20, 2000: A23.

    For its Eclipse cigarette brand, R. J. Reynolds began advertising a claim that the cigarette could potentially reduce the risks of cancer and chronic bronchitis. R. J. Reynolds became the first cigarette manufacturer to claim these attributes; the company cited new scientific data as the basis for them. Philip Morris said it would not make similar claims until the government reviewed the issues.

184. Beardi, Cara. "Lucky Strike Takes an Original Ad Turn." *Advertising Age* 71, no. 22 (May 22, 2000): 13.

    Brown & Williamson's "free-thinking" marketing campaign for its Lucky Strike brand includes two themes. The "Lucky Strike Band to Band" events take place at bars and clubs. Local bands perform, and attendees select the best. A compact disc with songs performed by the contest bands will be distributed at no charge to adult smokers completing cards and sharing personal information. A second theme is a national sweepstakes, allowing contestants to alter the brand's longtime slogan "Lucky Strike means fine tobacco." Contestants think of their ultimate dream prize and insert the name in lieu of "fine tobacco."

185. Beardi, Cara. "Eclipse Tries Again via Web, Direct Sales." *Advertising Age* 71, no. 23 (May 29, 2000): 48.

    In April 2000, R. J. Reynolds relaunched a campaign for its Eclipse cigarette, which heats tobacco instead of burning it. The company is unveiling a two-pronged approach: print advertising only in Dallas–Fort Worth magazines like *Newsweek* and

Sports Illustrated, and targeting thirty-eight states for direct-mail and Internet-only sales. The magazines carry the two-page taglines "The best choice for smokers who worry about their health is to quit," followed by, "Here's the next best choice." Buyers will be able to dial a toll-free number or log on to the brand's website and must verify their age before purchasing the cigarettes.

186. Beardi, Cara. "Winston Revamps, Puts New Ad Spin on 'No Bull' Theme." *Advertising Age* 71, no. 24 (June 5, 2000): 1, 66.

    R. J. Reynolds upgrades its Winston cigarette blend to "100% first cut" and no reprocessed sheet tobacco. This is in addition to being 100 percent additive-free. The new advertising strategy for the brand piggybacks on the "No Bull" campaign, with such taglines as "No additives. No sheet. No bull," and "Leave the bull behind."

187. Beardi, Cara. "Radio Promotion Aims to Give Kool Younger Profile." *Advertising Age* 71, no. 28 (July 3, 2000): 33.

    Brown & Williamson retailed four million Kool cigarette packs each containing a miniradio. The company hoped to make the brand attractive to the twenty-one-to-thirty-year-old smoker group. The tagline "We Built the House of Menthol" buttressed the strategy. The promotion fit in with the company's "guerilla warfare" one-to-one marketing campaign. The campaign included the Lucky Strike "Strike Force." The Strike Force performed such activities as greeting smokers outside buildings and providing free coffee or extending invitations to view fireworks displays, like the "Project Independence Day" promotion. A boat stationed in New York Harbor was used for viewing the fireworks display.

188. Beirne, Mike. "B&W's Capri Blows 'Less Smoke' Message." *Brandweek* 41, no. 27 (July 3, 2000): 6.

    Brown & Williamson unveiled a marketing campaign for its Capri and Capri Superslims cigarettes. The Capri campaign was aimed at females aged twenty-four to thirty-five and used the tagline "Distinctly Slimmer, Surprisingly Tasteful, Remarkably Stylish." Targeted magazines included *Glamour* and *Cosmopolitan*. For the Superslims, the tagline "Superslim Capri means less smoke for those around you" addressed older women smokers.

189. Beardi, Cara. "PM Pushes Paper with New $20 Mil Merit Effort." *Advertising Age* 71, no. 30 (July 17, 2000): 4, 64.

    Philip Morris began manufacturing its entire line of Merit cigarettes with the new PaperSelect paper, designed to rapidly extinguish the cigarette if it lies idle in an ashtray. In contact with certain fabrics, it has a smaller chance of starting a fire. The $20 million campaign appeared in selected newspapers and magazines carrying the tagline "You still get the same rewarding taste, only now with our patented cigarette paper." Information explaining the new paper and the tagline "Looks the same, tastes the same . . . Not the same" was printed on an informational insert included in every pack of Merit cigarettes.

190. Kucharsky, Danny. "Tobacco Co. Creates Own Magazine." *Marketing Magazine* 105, no. 48 (December 4, 2000): 3.

About ten thousand Canadian smokers will begin receiving copies of Imperial Tobacco Canada's magazine *Real Edge*. Started by Brown & Williamson, the magazine targets the male smoker aged nineteen to thirty-four years. The company says the magazine is legitimate and is in compliance with the country's rules and regulations on tobacco advertising.

191. Sargent, James D., Jennifer J. Tickle, Michael L. Breach, Madeline A. Dalton, M. Bridget Ahrens, and Todd F. Heatherton. "Brand Appearances in Contemporary Cinema Films and Contribution to Global Marketing of Cigarettes." *Lancet* 357 (January 6, 2001): 29–32.

    The authors analyze tobacco-brand appearance (for instance, brand name, logo, billboards, actor endorsement) in 250 U.S. box-office films of the years 1988 to 1997. The data is segregated into a prevoluntary paid-product-placement ban period (1989–1990) and a post-ban period (1990–1997). Most noteworthy was that actor endorsement (i.e., the actor handles or uses the brand) rose 10 percent (in absolute terms) during the transitional period. Brand appearances by Marlboro (42 percent), Winston (17 percent), Lucky Strike (12 percent), and Camel (11 percent) dominated the silver screen.

192. Beardi, Cara. "B&W's Biggest Mail Blitz to Light Up New Pall Mall." *Advertising Age* 72, no. 10 (March 5, 2001): 14.

    Brown & Williamson's (B&W) new filtered Pall Mall will received a major marketing blitz when the company sent nine million adult smokers information about the cigarette. The matchbook look-alike documents had the tagline "Smoother, slower, longer" splashed across the cover. Inside, a follow-up theme read "The New Filtered Pall Mall. It's everything you've been looking for in a cigarette." B&W repositioned Pall Mall as a premium-quality cigarette and declared that the cigarette provided more puffs than Marlboro or Doral.

193. Stamler, Bernard. "Circumscribed by the Law, Tobacco Companies Look for New Ways to Get Their Message Across." *New York Times*, May 2, 2001: C7.

    Despite the marketing restrictions of the national tobacco settlement, Brown & Williamson flexed its creative muscle to market a new filtered Pall Mall cigarette. The company targeted magazines of adults where they constituted at least 85 percent of the readership. This included publications such as *Playboy* and *Ladies' Home Journal*. Point-of-sale promotions, a critical and strategic piece of the puzzle, included event promotions in such venues as bars and in point-of-sale displays. Another major resource was a direct-marketing database comprising adult smokers opting to receive sample products and other giveaways.

194. "Imperial Opens Smokers' Lounges." *Marketing Magazine* 106, no. 18 (May 7, 2001): 1A.

    The Toronto-Dominion Centre hosted a new courtyard lounge being offered to smokers by Imperial Tobacco Canada. Open from April 30 to May 25, 2001 (weekdays only), the lounge accommodated up to a hundred people, to whom the company provided free coffee or tea and market its new Matinee Ultra Mild cigarette. Also, Imperial collected names and addresses for its direct-marketing database. In exchange for personal information, Imperial offered cash and luxurious spa appointments to smokers who registered for a chance to win these prizes.

195. Beardi, Cara. "Trying to Keep Kool with Under-30s." *Advertising Age* 72, no. 21 (May 21, 2001): 14.

Brown & Williamson (B&W) is attempting to upgrade the image of its Kool brand and increase market share by targeting music lovers and smokers in the under-thirty age bracket. The company is sponsoring the ten-city Kool All Access Hip-Hop Tour. The tour features such stars as Da Brat and Memphis Bleek. The philanthropic organization 100 Black Men of America and urban communities will receive proceeds from the tour. Last year, in another B&W marketing foray for the brand, disc jockeys competed in the Kool MIXX program.

196. Rosenfield, James R. "U.S. Cigarette Marketing, 2001: The Lowest Ring of the Inferno." *Direct Marketing* 64, no. 1 (May 2001): 52–55.

The author takes a cynical look at recent mailings from Brown & Williamson. One mailing, a sweepstakes for the Lucky Strike brand, declares that "L.S./M.F.T." is defined as "Lucky Strike/Means Fabulous Tan." The recipient needs to "think of a dream prize beginning with the letters F and T." The advertisement ends with "Lucky you. You get a free pack of Luckies." A second mailing is for the magazine *One World*, produced with the African-American community in mind. Another mailing, for Carlton, shows an attractive young woman pictured in a 1960s-drenched nostalgic setting and thinking about "Number One." This is tied to the mailing's theme— "Isn't it time you started thinking about Number One?"

197. Beirne, Mike. "B&W Draws Jokers for 20s Smokers." *Brandweek* 42, no. 37 (October 8, 2001): 14.

Brown & Williamson's (B&W) "Smokers Appreciation Night" took place from October 16 to November 21, 2001. This tour of comedians took place in selected clubs in Columbus (Ohio), Kansas City (Missouri), Louisville (Kentucky), and Minneapolis (Minnesota). The company collected information for its database marketing efforts and also provided free samples to attendees. B&W sponsored the tour to promote the new Pall Mall brand.

198. Fairclough, Gordon. "R. J. Reynolds Retools Doral Brand to Be 'a Little Less Down-Home.'" *Wall Street Journal*, November 20, 2001: B15.

Doral cigarettes account for 25 percent of R. J. Reynolds's cigarette production; they outshine even the marquee brands Camel and Winston. However, slumping sales are prodding the company to make a number of changes. The cigarette's recipe and blend of tobaccos will be upgraded. The slogan "New splendidly blended. You gotta taste this" will be used to promote the "new" cigarette. "Blending" will be the theme used to advertise in magazines and newspapers. A previous advertising campaign to trumpet the company's putting more tobacco in each Doral used the slogan "Imagine getting more." The new advertising campaign will be buttressed by a Web version of the cigarette's quarterly magazine *Doral & Co*.

199. Poetschke-Langer, Martina, and Susanne Schunk. "Germany: Tobacco Industry Paradise." *Tobacco Control* 10, no. 4 (December 2001): 300–303.

In Germany, smoking is socially permissible, and voluntary agreements to restrict advertising are not enforced. Over eight hundred thousand vending machines provide unrestricted access to minors. During the 1990s, the tobacco advertising expenditures totaled approximately $2.5 billion. A Marlboro billboard campaign targets the "Marlboro Woman." Camel is promoted through events such as "Camel Snow Crew" and the "Camel Speed Vision."

British American Tobacco promotes Lucky Strike cigarettes through promotions such as the "Lucky Strike Trend Scout." During the summer of 2001, the winner traveled to New York City. Philip Morris's philanthropic efforts continue with, for example, the Philip Morris Science Award. The company presents $200,000 to scientists for their work in modern technology. Reemstma sponsors the "Ladies Lunch in Berlin," with its Davidoff cigarette slogan, "The More You Know," serving as the luncheon's title. The German parliament's restaurant serves as the meeting site.

200. Sepe, Edward, Pamela M. Ling, and Stanton A. Glantz. "Smooth Moves: Bar and Nightclub Tobacco Promotions That Target Young Adults." *American Journal of Public Health* 92, no. 3 (March 2002): 414–19.

The authors review tobacco industry documents to determine the historical development and impact of targeting teenagers—or "young adults" in industry parlance—through bar and nightclub promotions. Generally, these promotions began in the mid-1980s with strategies targeting parties, concerts, spring breaks, and nightclubs for one-to-one interactions and winning over "entry-level" smokers. Promotions have included live music, games, and distributing free cigarettes. Tobacco companies have sought partnerships with business owners by providing free supplies (for example, napkins, ash trays) and financial incentives (such as displaying advertisements). Promotions have allowed the companies to conduct research and build marketing databases, stay in compliance with clean-indoor-air laws, and implement "under the radar" or "below the line" marketing programs so as not to be accused of targeting children. The industry has deemed alternative presses, such as newspapers and magazines, attractive places to advertise their bar and nightclub events. Peer influence, or "trend influence marketing," has become a major factor influencing smoking among young adults. "Social leaders" or "trendsetters" surfaced in three categories: bar owners/club promoters, bar employees, and trend-setting patrons.

201. Mekemson, Curt, and Stanton A. Glantz. "How the Tobacco Industry Built Its Relationship with Hollywood." *Tobacco Control* 11, Suppl 1 (March 2002): i81–i91.

The authors searched various tobacco Web archives for materials related to the integral and favorable business relationships developed between the tobacco and entertainment industries. The documents reveal that both parties viewed movies as excellent tools for brand placement, exposure, and depiction; emphasized celebrity usage, endorsement, and association with the product; and stressed the development of advertising campaigns through industry-related magazines and events. Philip Morris and its Marlboro brand dominated the cinematic screen during the 1990s.

202. Ling, Pamela M., and Stanton A. Glantz. "Using Tobacco-Industry Marketing Research to Design More Effective Tobacco-Control Campaigns." *JAMA: The Journal of the American Medical Association* 287, no. 22 (June 12, 2002): 2983–89.

The authors searched tobacco Web archives for materials related to the industry's marketing research. They report industry patterns of analyzing smoker personalities and motivations, social behavior, concerns, interests, and attitudes toward smoking, and also examining brand positioning and identifying new areas of opportunity. A table outlines the market segmentation strategies of Philip Morris and R. J. Reynolds from the 1960s through the 1990s. This data can be used to strengthen tobacco-control efforts in such ways as encouraging activism against the industry and decreasing the social acceptance of smoking.

203. Lawton, Christopher. "Cigarette Ads Butt in at World Cup, Despite a Tobacco Ban." *Wall Street Journal*, June 18, 2002: B1, B6.

   The Federation Internationale de Football Association, the governing body of soccer, has declared the 2002 World Cup tobacco-free. The stadiums are to be tobacco-free with respect to both ads and products. World Cup logos are not to be used by tobacco manufacturers. However, broadcasters are still free to air tobacco ads. In Pakistan, for example, Lakson Tobacco (Pakistan) is marketing its Diplomat cigarette and launching a sweepstakes on television, all tied to the World Cup. British American Tobacco is the national sponsor in Malaysia. Korea Tobacco & Ginseng Corporation terminated its sponsorship and pulled its "Time 2002" cigarettes from the market.

204. Kleinman, Mark. "BAT Launches Kent Mag and Retail Zone." *Marketing* (June 20, 2002): 2.

   In anticipation of legislation banning tobacco ads, British American Tobacco is seeking new ways to promote its Kent cigarettes. The company created a new marketing "zone" at London's Heathrow Airport and created the magazine *Discover*. The zone is used to share information with travelers about the cigarette. The magazine covers areas such as lifestyle, travel, and using tobacco technology to improve the taste of cigarettes.

205. Ling, Pamela M., and Stanton A. Glantz. "Why and How the Tobacco Industry Sells Cigarettes to Young Adults: Evidence from Industry Documents." *American Journal of Public Health* 92, no. 6 (June 2002): 908–16.

   The authors have searched various tobacco Web archives for materials related to the industry's efforts to target market eighteen-to-twenty-four-year-old young adults or their lifestyle activities (for instance, attending bars and performing military service). The research revealed three conclusions. First, smoking entails a series of stages, from the first puff to the pack-a-day habit. Marketing strategies are designed to match each stage. Second, the industry emphasizes leisure and social activities and the environments where new behaviors are adopted (for example, new workplace or school). Third, the industry analyzes attitudes, concerns, and various social settings and devises appropriate strategies to penetrate these areas. Tobacco-control strategies can be created to counterattack the tobacco industry.

206. Dipasquale, Cara B. "Philip Morris Plans $350M in Price Promos." *Advertising Age* 73, no. 32 (August 12, 2002): 3, 22.

   Since July 2002, Philip Morris has been spending (and will continue through December) $350 million to promote its premium brands through sweepstakes, events, and price promotions. Starting in August, the "Boot Up" sweepstakes was launched.

Purchasers of Marlboro two-packs had the opportunity to win a custom-made pair of boots, to be awarded in January 2003. Also, the company has expanded the Marlboro Miles program. Each pack of Marlboros contains "currency" that can be exchanged for items listed in the *Marlboro Cowboy Chronicles* catalog. Marlboro's Live Auction program, held in bars, gives smokers the chance to use their miles by bidding on various goods. In May 2002, Philip Morris expanded this program to include the Trading Post program. Bars house trading-post stores where miles may be redeemed for goods. This fall, the Trading Post program will be rolled out nationally. All these events are tied to point-of-sale advertising and provide maximum visibility and exposure for the brands.

207. Shamasunder, Bhavna, and Lisa Bero. "Financial Ties and Conflicts of Interest between Pharmaceutical and Tobacco Companies." *JAMA: The Journal of the American Medical Association* 288, no. 6 (August 14, 2002): 738–44.

Using documents obtained from tobacco Web archives, the authors have created three case studies to document the integral relationships developed between the tobacco and pharmaceutical industries in the development and marketing of nicotine replacement therapies (NRTs). Philip Morris pressured Dow Chemical to drop its physician-related *Smoking Cessation Newsletter* and its support of a public-health organization, the National Interagency Council on Smoking and Health. Dow began marketing its Nicorette NRT with the tagline "If you want to quit smoking for good, see your doctor." Also, Philip Morris financially pressured Ciba-Geigy to end its "Smokebusters" diploma program and later its Habitrol transdermal nicotine patch advertisements. Instead of targeting all smokers, the advertisements target smokers wanting or needing to quit. In addition, subsidiary companies of Philip Morris and Procordia AB collaborated in the development of NRTs.

208. Dipasquale, Cara B. "Kool Tries Card-Playing Promo." *Advertising Age* 73, no. 35 (September 2, 2002): 8.

In October 2002, Brown & Williamson (B&W) sponsored a sixteen-city tour of a "Play on the House Spades Slam" card tournament. B&W research identified playing cards as a key lifestyle activity for its consumer base. Caesar's Palace hosted the finale, where the winning two-member team won the fifty-thousand-dollar top prize. Each of the sixteen team entrants received five thousand dollars and stayed at Caesar's for two nights. B&W promoted the tournament through direct mailings, magazines like *Urban Latino* and *GQ*, and decks of playing cards included with Kool packs.

209. Dipasquale, Cara B. "Call It 'Marlboro Thursday.'" *Advertising Age* 73, no. 39 (September 30, 2002): 1, 60.

During the fourth quarter of 2002, Philip Morris spent $600–$650 million in an effort to regain market share, increase sales volumes, and promote all its brands. The price promotion effectively discounted a cigarette pack as much as eighty cents. Philip Morris chairman/CEO Louis Camilleri also cited other reasons, such as combatting the popularity of deeply discounted cigarettes and the proliferation of cigarettes illegally imported into the country, for the bold move. Deep-discount cigarettes and "fourth-tier" manufacturers are cutting premium-cigarette sales and margins.

The penalty provisions contained in the Master Settlement Agreement do not apply to these manufacturers.

210. Kleinman, Mark. "Rothmans Finds on-Pack Route to Dodge Ads Rules." *Marketing* (November 21, 2002): 1.

    The Tobacco Advertising and Promotion Bill disallows direct marketing of tobacco products. Only if customers request information may a communication take place. To work around this rule, Rothmans' Royal cigarettes include a "pub quiz" and an invitation to share answers by contacting the company. Once contacted by a consumer, Rothmans are able to promote other brands and products.

211. Curtis, James. "Tobacco after the Ban." *Marketing* (January 16, 2003): 24–25.

    In the United Kingdom, the Tobacco Advertising and Promotion Bill took effect on February 14, 2003, banning Internet, magazine, and newspaper advertising. "Exceptional global events," such as Formula One car races, are allowed until September 2006, but domestic sponsorship is banned as of July 2003. The authors review strategies for tobacco company advertising in the areas of product (for instance, colors); Internet and viral (i.e., creating a phony cult following by "spoofing" a major brand's advertising) marketing, sampling and face-to-face marketing; promotions and direct marketing (magazines, limited-edition packs); packaging; public relations; merchandising and brand sharing; and point-of-sale (for instance, British American Tobacco's Lucky Strike 451° F store).

212. Bates, James. "Warner Douses Smoking Promo." *Los Angeles Times*, March 5, 2003: C2.

    For twelve weeks, the "Rothmans Experience It Cinema Tour" visited cities in Nigeria. The cinema showings included *Ocean's Eleven* and *The Matrix*. Rothmans' parent, British American Tobacco (BAT), purchased the film screening rights from Warner's South African distributor, Warner Nu Metro. During the screenings, limited to people aged eighteen and over, viewers received free promotional cigarettes. When informed of the promotion, Warner Brothers issued BAT cease-and-desist letters. According to the parent company, the South African distributor had not received permission to engage in these business practices.

213. Butalla, Laura. "Winston Promotes Itself with Holography." *Converting Magazine* 21, no. 4 (April 2003): 72. ABI/Inform (accessed December 18, 2003).

    R. J. Reynolds will be using HoloPRISM® holographic paper to help differentiate its new Winston Evo Flask brand at the retail level. PROMA Technologies created the new paper. The company feels the new point-of-sale papers will let customers know that the new brand is "the most modern, exciting brand" in its class.

214. O'Connell, Vanessa. "Last Call for Camel, Marlboro Ads in Bars." *Wall Street Journal*, May 9, 2003: B1, B4.

    Even in bars where smoking is still acceptable, R. J. Reynolds (RJR) and Philip Morris will be ending efforts to market and promote their cigarette brands. RJR cites "business pressures" for its decision to withdraw from the market; Philip Morris is emphasizing instead theme events, such as the Marlboro Ranch in Montana, to market its products. Also, both companies are providing more funds for wholesalers and retailers. Initiatives such as two-for-one offers and financial incentives are offered to these distributors. In New York and Miami bars, Freedom Tobacco employs "leaners" to get male patrons to step outside the bar and try the company's Legal cigarette. These "good looking young women" work for Freedom Tobacco.

215. Balbach, Edith D., Rebecca J. Gasior, and Elizabeth M. Barbeau. "R. J. Reynolds' Targeting of African Americans: 1988–2000." *American Journal of Public Health* 93, no. 5 (May 2003): 822–27.

The authors have examined tobacco industry Web archives to document R. J. Reynolds's (RJR) marketing approach to the African-American community. The authors compared 1989–1990 advertisements with 1999–2000 advertisements appearing in the publications *Jet*, *Ebony*, *Essence* (JEE), and *People Weekly*. They examined and compared both periods for the occurrence of four themes appearing in JEE versus *People Weekly*: escape/fantasy, expensive objects, nightlife, and mentholated products. Also, the authors document RJR's development and potential marketing strategies crafted for the new, and subsequently withdrawn, cigarette product Uptown.

216. Smith, Elizabeth A., and Ruth E. Malone. "The Outing of Philip Morris: Advertising Tobacco to Gay Men." *American Journal of Public Health* 93, no. 6 (June 2003): 988–93.

The authors have examined company documents available through Philip Morris's Web page, major national newspapers, and lesbian and gay periodicals to track the company's marketing approach to the gay community. Philip Morris sought to promote a brand extension of Benson & Hedges. At the behest of its advertising agency, Leo Burnett, and the gay magazine *Genre,* the company placed an advertisement in the periodical's October/November 1992 and December/January 1993 issues. Philip Morris sought to contain the negative publicity surrounding an article appearing in the *Wall Street Journal* (see entry 116), particularly the fallout in the gay and African-American communities.

217. O'Connell, Vanessa. "Smokes Return to Runway." *Wall Street Journal*, September 15, 2003: B1, B3.

New York–based Freedom Tobacco's Legal cigarettes stole the spotlight during a recent fashion show sponsored by the company. The fashion team of As Four smoked and promoted the brand during the gala event, conducted television interviews with the cigarette logo in the background, and had their clothing covered with Legal cigarette packs. Each person attending the show received two cigarette packs stuffed in a gift bag. R. J. Reynolds, another sponsor, distributed free cigarettes during a post–fashion show party. R. J. Reynolds has also been involved with funding the work of young musical artists and their work with the Sean John and Phat Farm recording labels, owned by Sean "P. Diddy" Combs and Russell Simmons, respectively.

218. Häusel, Hans-Georg, Dr. "Branding with Brains." *Tobacco Journal International*, no. 5 (September/October 2003): 174–75.

"Limbic branding" uses neuroscience to influence buying decisions and the placement of brands in the minds of consumers. The three underpinnings of all human behavior—dominance, stimulation, and balance—combined with the three "composed motives" of adventure/thrill, discipline/control, and fantasy/pleasure form the basis of limbic branding. With Marlboro, the brand is positioned between the axis of stimulation and dominance, covering the composed motive of adventure/thrill. This gives the brand characteristics such as rebellion, autonomy, impulsiveness, and creativity.

219. "'Cigarette Girls' Target of Complaint." *Marketing Magazine* 108, no. 38 (November 10, 2003): 2.

    A report in the *(Montreal) La Presse* noted that Imperial Tobacco's two divisions, Canal 2 and Evenement Rumbling Walls, has employed "cigarette girls" to promote the company's brands in clubs. These "very sexy" women dispense du Maurier cigarettes from assigned posts. Quebec's Health Department is to investigate whether this "lifestyle advertising" violates the country's rules and regulations on tobacco advertising.

220. Carter, S. M. "Going below the Line: Creating Transportable Brands for Australia's Dark Market." *Tobacco Control* 12, Suppl III (December 2003): iii87–iii94.

    Federal Australian law and the 1992 Tobacco Advertising Prohibition Act outlaw, with some exceptions, most forms of tobacco advertising, including television, radio, cinema, and print. The tobacco industry refers to this restrictive environment as the "dark market." The authors have reviewed the industry's "above the line" and "below the line" non-point-of-sale marketing activities within these constraints. These include advertising in imported international magazines, brand stretching, and event promotions. Imperial Tobacco's Peter Stuyvesant brand is analyzed in a case study.

221. "RJR Faces State Probes on Eclipse Marketing." *Los Angeles Times*, March 6, 2004: C3.

    Vermont's attorney general has served R. J. Reynolds with a civil subpoena over the company's advertising for its Eclipse cigarette. Reynolds claims that extensive scientific testing demonstrates that Eclipse is less harmful than regular cigarettes. Attorneys general from Maine and Connecticut are also seeking information about the cigarette.

222. Beirne, Mike. "B&W Blends Music, Art, Extensions to Play It Kool." *Brandweek* 45, no. 10 (March 8, 2004): 9.

    Brown & Williamson (B&W) enters the sixth year of its Kool hip-hop promotion. The company continues its fourteen-city disc jockey competition, ending with the Kool Mixx Master award. The competition, along with the compact disc *Soundtrack to the Streets* featuring hip-hop music from emerging stars, will be included in selected issues of magazines like *Rolling Stone* and *Spin*. The hip-hop themes of DJ, MC, dance, and art will appear on limited-edition packages of Kool MIXX cigarettes. Purchasers of special two-pack Kool packages will receive a Stick Radio and, after submitting a survey, will be eligible for a free subscription to one of five "urban lifestyle magazines," such as *Details* and *OneWorld*. Also, B&W will introduce its new "Kool Smooth Fusions" flavored cigarettes.

223. Thomas, Daniel. "Ashes to Ashes for Tobacco Branding?" *Marketing Week* 27, no. 11 (March 11, 2004): 22–23.

   The United Kingdom's ban on tobacco advertising has basically stopped the introduction of new brands, frozen market shares, and blocked new competitors from entering the field. Even point-of-purchase advertising will be restricted in the coming months. Tobacco advertising expenditures will be channeled toward packaging, in-store furniture, and use of brand names to launch product extensions.

224. Beirne, Mike. "RJR Lights Plans for 'Summer.'" *Brandweek* 45, no. 12 (March 22, 2004): 5.

   R. J. Reynolds ran its Winston "Endless Summer Sweepstakes" from late March through July 31, 2004. Twenty cartons of Winston, twenty thousand dollars, and plane tickets were awarded to the winner. The "Board Meeting" theme appeared in point-of-purchase ads. The promotion followed up on the January launch of the "Winston Escapes," designed to allow smokers to redeem UPC codes for merchandise.

225. Smith, E. A., and R. E. Malone. "'Creative Solutions': Selling Cigarettes in a Smoke-Free World." *Tobacco Control* 13, no. 1 (March 2004): 57–63.

   The authors examine Philip Morris's 1994–1996 "Creative Solutions" U.S. advertising campaign for its Benson & Hedges brand. The campaign combined the themes of empathy and risk management to provide comfort and solutions to smokers facing restrictive smoking environments (for example, clean-indoor-air laws and regulations). Ads used by Philip Morris also promoted the company's "Accommodation Program." The program sought to drive a wedge through regulatory efforts meant to restrict smoking, instead promoting its social acceptance. The authors conclude that the campaign has failed to counter the efforts undertaken to control tobacco smoking.

226. "Kool Alters Tack after Maine Says Ads Targeted Teens." *Wall Street Journal*, April 26, 2004: B5. (Associated Press).

   Brown & Williamson has informed the Maine attorney general, Steven Rowe, that the company will no longer print images of hip-hop personalities on its Kool cigarette packages, advertise the Kool promotion in magazines, or distribute a CD-ROM containing hip-hop music. Mr. Rowe commented that the campaign appeared to be especially targeting African-American youth and to be in violation of the 1998 national tobacco settlement.

227. Brinson, Brandy. "Colored Tips." *Tobacco Reporter* 131, no. 5 (May 2004): 32–33.

   Tipping papers used to manufacture cigarette filters are another potential way to differentiate cigarette brands, especially in light of the European Union's directive restricting the use of product descriptors. Colored tipping papers are yet to be embraced, however, by cigarette manufacturers and consumers. However, preprinted logos on customized tipping paper are being used in the European Union. Increased demand for such papers is foreseeable in areas like North Africa and the Far East.

228. "Imperial Tobacco Giveaway Ruled as Breaching Ad Ban." *Marketing Week* (August 12, 2004): 7.

The Bristol (U.K.) City Council Trading Standards, with support from the Department of Health, has charged Imperial Tobacco with violating the Tobacco Advertising and Promotions Act of 2002. Both bodies have concluded that the inclusion of "Supertrivia" cards in Superkings cigarette packages violated the 2002 law in two ways: the cards advertised the company's tobacco products, and they constituted a "free product." Imperial Tobacco received a slap on the wrist for its actions, avoided the payment of a fine, and promised not to promote its products.

229. "Tobacco Brands Plan to Sell In-Store Ad Space." *Marketing Week* (October 21, 2004): 6.

    The British government has proposed point-of-purchase restrictions on tobacco advertising at retail outlets. The industry owns over sixty-six thousand retail units and may sell the space to other companies. For example, Gallaher Group owns 27,000 gantries, and British American Tobacco owns 3,200.

230. "JTI Extends Lounge Concept." *Travel Retailer International* (October/November 2004): 94.

    Japan Tobacco International's "smoking lounge" concept will be implemented at the Zurich airport. The company will open a Camel lounge and a Winston lounge. The lounges are located near departure gates, for quick access. The new airport lounges are in addition to those already open at Madrid (Barajas airport) and Athens International. In addition, the Madrid and Athens airports will feature the new "Winston Smoking Station," a portable station for the airport smoker.

SPONSORSHIPS: ARTS

231. Waddell, Ray. "Marlboro Music Festivals Team Newcomers with Established Acts." *Amusement Business* 103, no. 17 (April 29, 1991): 7. Infotrac OneFile (accessed October 29, 2004).

    In 1991, Philip Morris sponsored four Marlboro Music Festivals. The festivals featured country music artists, matching veteran performers with upcoming stars. For the fifth consecutive year, Second Harvest National Food Bank Network was the main beneficiary. Over the years, the food bank has received over $825,000. During the festivals, upcoming country music talent competed for thirty thousand dollars and forty hours' studio work in the national Marlboro Music Talent Roundups. Also, for the third consecutive year, Marlboro Music visited twelve military bases throughout the United States, Puerto Rico, and Canada. The Morale, Welfare, and Recreation Fund of each military base received all admission charges and concession sales.

232. Robinson, Robert G., Michele Berry, Michele Bloch, Stanton Glantz, Jerie Jordan, Keith B. Murray, Edward Popper, Charyn Sutton, Keith Tarr-Whelan, Makani Themba, and Sue Younger. "Report of the Tobacco Policy Research Group on Marketing and Promotions Targeted at African Americans, Latinos, and Women." *Tobacco Control* 1, Suppl (Autumn 1992): S24–S30.

    This report focuses on the interlocking relationship between the tobacco industry and the African American, Latino, and female populations. The industry influences these populations through advertising, marketing, and promotional activities; these take place through, civic, social, and political outlets affecting each community. In the African American community, tobacco contributions support cultural activities such as the Parliament World Beat Concert Series and the Black Art: Ancestral Legacy Tour. In the Latin American community, tobacco support funds a national tour of The Latin American Spirit: Art and Artists in the United States, 1920–1970 and supports newspapers and magazines. Women's groups receive tobacco support for the Joffrey Ballet and the American Ballet Tour. In addition, tobacco contributions support various political and fraternal organizations in each group.

233. Johnson, Danny R. "Tobacco Stains." *Progressive* 56, no. 12 (December 1992): 26–28.

The tobacco companies target African Americans with event marketing, lifestyle advertising, and image advertising. Event marketing includes Marlboro's support of arts groups such as the Alvin Ailey Dance Theater and music tours like the Parliament World Beat Concert Series. Lifestyle advertising has included R. J. Reynolds's More cigarettes long-running support of the Ebony Fashion Fair, though the company has discontinued this support due to public pressure. Image advertising includes support of history, culture, institutions, and leaders. Examples include Philip Morris's support of Black History Month and R. J. Reynolds's "Salute to Black Scientists and Inventors" ad in the magazine *Essence*.

234. Johnson, Robert. "Philip Morris: The Arts Are Good for Business." *Dance Magazine* 68, no. 5 (May 1994): 18. Infotrac Expanded Academic ASAP (accessed November 26, 1997).

Since its initial sponsorships in 1959, Philip Morris has substantially increased its financial and moral support of the arts. Philip Morris has funded such organizations as the American Ballet Theatre and the Paris Opera Ballet. Support for the Arts Forward Fund made Philip Morris the initial leader and soon the leading corporate contributor in seeking long-term financial solutions for the dance world. Recently, with a special emphasis on dance, Philip Morris announced that it would contribute $405,000 to the arts.

235. Solomon, Alisa. "The Other Nicotine Addiction." *Theater* 25, no. 2 (Fall 1994): 5–8.

In October 1994, the New York City Council considered an ordinance enacting strict smoking restrictions. Philip Morris threatened to relocate its corporate headquarters and enlisted the aid of arts organizations that receive funding from the company. The company's largesse has been spread across state organizations such as the Brooklyn Academy of Music and the INTAR Hispanic American Arts Center. Many of these organizations have Philip Morris employees as board members.

236. Chidley, Joe. "Tobacco's Soft Sell." *Maclean's* 108, no. 52 (December 25, 1995/January 1, 1996): 53

The Canadian tobacco industry faces proposed government sponsorship restrictions as a result of a Supreme Court of Canada ruling that the Tobacco Products Control Act is unconstitutional. The proposed regulations are unsettling organizations dependent on tobacco's overflowing coffers. For example, the annual du Maurier Ltd. New Music Festival, a nine-day event promoting Canadian and international composers, is partly dependent on Imperial Tobacco, Ltd.'s financial contribution. Supporters fear a ban on tobacco sponsorship will spell the end of the festival.

237. Levin, Myron, and Tony Perry. "Museum Ditches Philip Morris as Sponsor." *Los Angeles Times,* May 1, 1996: D2, D5.

The San Diego Museum of Art canceled an upcoming exhibit of Montana artist Deborah Butterfield's wild horse sculptures. The exhibit was scheduled to take place during the Republican National Convention, with Philip Morris as the exhibit's sponsor. Previously at the museum, Philip Morris, through its Kraft Foods subsidiary, sponsored shows tied to the America's Cup yacht race, Pat Oliphant's political cartoons, and Australian photographs. Philip Morris encountered additional public backlash; the Del Mar Fair Board canceled the company's participation in the upcoming summer fair and also at the Fiesta Latino Day.

238. Hollós, Mihály. "Slovakia: Not Alone with a Monopoly." *World Tobacco*, no. 154 (September 1996): 55–56.

Tobacco sponsorship of the arts is flourishing in the Slovak Republic. In the capital, Bratislava, Reemstma's Slovak International Tabak AS sponsors such arts events as stage performances and the cabaret West Theatre. Slovak International also sponsors the national ice hockey team, the annual snowboard race, and the West Beach Volley Cup competition. Philip Morris's (PM) Slovakia Tabak sponsors the PM Ballet Flower Award. The award recognizes the top ballet dancer in the Slovakia Republic, the Czech Republic, and Hungary.

239. Farley, Christopher John. "C'mon, Baby, Light My Fire." *Time* 149, no. 4 (January 27, 1997): 66.

Woman Thing Music is the latest music label entrant to target the youth market. In this case, the sponsor is Philip Morris. The company named its new label after the "It's a Woman Thing" slogan used for its Virginia Slims cigarettes. Female performers will receive support from the company for their albums and performance tours. Martha Byrne, star on the soap *As The World Turns*, is the first performer; her album will be available for five dollars. The CD-ROM is available only with the purchase of two packs of Virginia Slims.

240. "Canadian Designs on the Catwalk." *Maclean's* 110, no. 14 (April 7, 1997): 14.

Imperial Tobacco, Ltd., the Canadian manufacturer of brands such as du Maurier and Players, agreed to sponsor two annual fashion shows. Funding from other sources to sponsor the fall and spring shows appeared to be in jeopardy until Imperial Tobacco came to the rescue. The spring show became the "Matinee Fashion Ready to Wear" show, named after the company's Matinee cigarette.

241. Hanson, Gayle M. B. "Will a Settlement Hurt the Arts?" *Insight on the News* 15, no. 10 (March 16, 1998): 11.

The proposed tobacco settlement being debated by Congress threatens to depress financial support of the arts and cultural events. Over the past thirty-five years, Philip Morris's monetary contributions include sponsorship of the Museum of Modern Art's Pop & Op show, the Martha Graham Dance Company, and choreographer Twyla Tharp. Over the past twenty years, Philip Morris contributed at least $27 million to dance companies and, in 1997, funded new works with over a million dollars.

242. "Cancer Group Is Upset over Gift Because of Link to Philip Morris." *New York Times*, June 10, 1998: A17.

Philip Morris has contributed twenty-five thousand dollars to sponsor and reserve a table at a gala banquet for an upcoming traveling exhibit called "Dresses for Humanity," featuring dresses worn by the late Diana, Princess of Wales. The Boys and Girls Club of America will receive funds raised at the banquet. Philip Morris's involvement surprised and angered the Cancer Research Foundation, especially after it received a donation from the charity exhibition's sponsor, the People's Princess Charitable Foundation. Also, the foundation Inova H.I.V. Services declined a twenty-five-thousand-dollar donation from Philip Morris.

243. Myerson, Allen R. "Can Joe Camel Grow Up?" *New York Times*, July 4, 1999: sec. 3: 7.

R. J. Reynolds has sponsored an artistic event at the Brooklyn Bridge Anchorage Building in Brooklyn. The Camel brand name appeared on brochures, cocktail napkins, and projected onto the floor. Attendees identified as smokers received free T-shirts or note pads and information about other events. Also, the Camel representative inquired about their smoking habits and registered their names for free direct mail and e-mail news.

244. Barbieri, Kelly. "Tobacco Legislation Takes Bite Out of Sponsorship at Toronto Jazz Fest." *Amusement Business* 112, no. 17 (April 24, 2000): 2, 6.

Restrictive rules effecting advertising at Canadian sporting and cultural events may force tobacco companies to completely withdraw their support from sponsorship roles. The new rules became effective in October 2000. One of these rules limits tobacco advertising in publications to events where attendees age twenty-one or older constitute at least 85 percent of the audience. The percentage must be "proven." Ninety percent of the advertisement must be dedicated to the event and only 10 percent to the tobacco product. The impending rules nearly forced Imperial Tobacco, Ltd.'s du Maurier cigarette brand to cancel its sponsorship of the 2000 Toronto Jazz Festival. At the behest of Toronto's mayor, the company donated $750,000 (Canadian). The company originally intended to donate only $250,000 (Canadian), versus the $1 million (Canadian) donated last year.

245. "Rothmans Pulls Out of Fireworks." *Marketing Magazine* 105, no. 49 (December 11, 2000): 1.

Toronto, Montreal, and Vancouver's annual Symphony of Fire fireworks displays has lost Rothmans, Benson & Hedges (B&H) as its sole sponsor. RBH has sponsored the event for the past fourteen years. The company is withdrawing support ahead of the October 1, 2003, ban on tobacco event sponsorship. Also, the company withdrew from sponsoring the Toronto International Film Festival.

246. Altria Group, "Altria Group Awards More than $3 Million to Visual Arts and Cultural Organizations across the Country." Press release, September 9, 2004, www.altria.com (accessed September 14, 2004).

Altria Group has announced the granting of over $1 million to twenty visual arts institutions and a million for specific exhibitions such as the Bronx Museum of the Arts' *A Parallel Modernity in Brazil*. Sixty-one arts and cultural organizations will receive

$990,000 in unrestricted general operating funds. The company assembled an elite committee of curators to assist in the grant selection process. The press release includes all the names of the grantees and the dollar amounts awarded.

SPONSORSHIPS: PHILANTHROPY

247. Ramirez, Anthony. "Philip Morris to Increase AIDS Donations." *New York Times*, May 30, 1991: D4.

    Philip Morris will contribute a substantial sum, perhaps nearing $3 million, to study the AIDS epidemic. The company is reacting to last year's national boycott of its Marlboro cigarettes and Miller beer by the gay rights organization AIDS Coalition to Unleash Power. It is also a response to Philip Morris's political support of antigay North Carolina senator Jesse Helms. Company spokesperson Alice T. McGillion notes that the company has contributed over $1.3 million to gay rights causes since 1987.

248. "R. J. Reynolds Company: Supports NAACP with Public Service Billboard Campaign." *Crisis* 99, no. 4 (April–May 1992): 37.

    In 1990, R. J. Reynolds (RJR) enlisted the services of outdoor billboard companies in providing free billboard advertisements to national organizations linked to the tobacco giant. RJR's efforts paid off with more than nine hundred billboards spread across forty-two cities. In 1990 and 1991, the service's beneficiaries included the National Urban League, the National Association for the Advancement of Colored People (NAACP), and the National Council of La Raza. Over the last two years, the program's value totaled over $2.5 million.

249. Nicklin, Julie L. "Philip Morris Boosts Aid to Colleges, but Critics Question Tobacco Company's Motives." *Chronicle of Higher Education* 40, no. 8 (October 13, 1993): A36–A37, A39.

    Philip Morris has become one of the leading corporate contributors to education, especially in the field of teaching. In 1993, the company is expected to donate approximately $22 million to education-related causes. John I. Goodlad of the University of Washington created the Philip Morris Leadership Program with a $500,000 grant. In 1992, Teach for America received a $3 million challenge grant for recruiting and training college graduates. In 1992, the Foundation for Independent Higher Education received $1 million to create a scholarship program for minorities. Philip Morris's Miller subsidiary has funded the Thurgood Marshall Scholarship Fund with $150,000 annually.

250. Burritt, Chris. "A Troubled Conscience." *Atlanta Journal and Constitution*, July 28, 1996: A10.

    Tobacco and tobacco money are integral to the economic vitality of North Carolina. For example, R. J. Reynolds Tobacco (RJR) funded Duke University's nicotine research center with twenty thousand dollars to sponsor a conference about Eclipse, RJR's new heated-tobacco cigarette. The United Way fund of Cabarrus County received $408,000 from Philip Morris's local tobacco plant. Greensboro captured Lorillard Tobacco's new corporate headquarters, valued at $15 million and an estimated $15 million in annual payroll.

251. Lerner, Sharon. "Tobacco Stains." *Ms. Magazine* 7, no. 3 (November/December 1996): 46–55.

    Women's organizations face moral and ethical questions when deciding to accept or reject philanthropic contributions from tobacco companies. Many are cash starved and could use the money to fund valuable programs. However, accepting any monies will make them susceptible to charges they are "in the pocket" of Big Tobacco and serve the industry's desire to sweeten its image. In 1995, Philip Morris contributed funds to more than one hundred women's organizations, as well as approximately $3 million from 1990 through 1995.

252. Glass, Chris. "Making a Difference." *Tobacco Reporter* 124, no. 11 (November 1997): 50–52, 54.

    Since 1956, Philip Morris's corporate philosophy has been to give back to the community, promote itself as socially responsible, and communicate to the outside world the values of the company. The company contributes funds to various philanthropic efforts, including hunger relief and AIDS research. Since 1990, Philip Morris has contributed over $34 million and its Kraft subsidiary over $81 million for hunger relief and nutrition programs. This includes a $125,000 grant to D.C. Central Kitchen to expand its program of teaching basic kitchen skills to men and women in twelve cities. Kraft Foods donates funds to help feed AIDS-stricken people unable to leave their homes. During 1996, over one hundred environmental organizations received in excess of $1.6 million from Philip Morris.

253. "BAT: Working within the Community." *World Tobacco*, no. 166 (September 1998): 45, 48.

    British American Tobacco Hungary strives to be a corporate model of good citizenship. In the town of Pecs, the company contributes approximately seven thousand dollars annually to support the Diagnostic Centre. Also, it donates money to the National Theatre to recognize the best actor or actress, as selected by audiences. The company contributes funds for homeless shelters, medical conferences, a women's soccer team, and the National Gathering of University and College Students.

254. "The War on Hunger." *Tobacco International* 201, no. 4 (April 1999): 42, 44.

    Philip Morris and its Kraft Foods subsidiary works to battle hunger across America. The company supports programs and services through its Philip Morris Fight against Hunger. The fund has provided money for such initiatives as Senior Helping, assisting homebound elderly through the National Meals-on-Wheels Foundation; Positive Helpings, by which people inflicted with HIV/AIDS receive meals, through the National AIDS Fund and the AIDS Nutrition Services Alliance; and the Native American Hunger Program, assisting Native American reservations to address hunger, through the First Nations Development Institute. Kraft Foods, Second Harvest, and Foodchain Network of Food Rescue work together for the Kraft Fresh Produce Initiative, a program designed to supply fresh produce to needy people.

255. Elliott, Stuart. "Tired of Being a Villain, Philip Morris Works on Its Image." *New York Times*, November 11, 1999: C12.

With advertising firm Leo Burnett handling the ads, Philip Morris is launching a national campaign called Working to Make a Difference. The People of Philip Morris. The campaign's objectives are to repair and build the company's image as a corporation that cares and to draw attention to its positive contributions to national charitable, philanthropic, and social activities. The multimedia campaign also features Kraft Foods and Miller Brewing, divisions of Philip Morris, and touches on topics like hunger and domestic violence.

256. Branch, Shelly. "Philip Morris's Ad on Macaroni and Peace." *Wall Street Journal*, July 24, 2001: B11A.

In an ongoing effort to bolster its public image, Philip Morris has sponsored a sixty-second ad called "Molly's Story." Shot in Prague, the ad depicts a fictional Philip Morris employee reporting on the cargo delivery of Kraft foods to hundreds of Kosovar refugees. It is based on company public-affairs executive Molly Walsh's journey to Albania in connection with the delivery of Kraft foods. The ad is both a mixture of corporate philanthropy and marketing.

SPONSORSHIPS: RESEARCH

257. Fitzgerald, Mike, and Brent Shearer. "How Far Down the Tobacco Road?" *Columbia Journalism Review* 30, no. 2 (July/August 1991): 51–52.

The University of Missouri–Columbia's Rob Logan, director of the school's Science Journalism Center, has spent two years negotiating with Philip Morris for a $150,000 grant. The grant, much needed in the wake of budget reductions, would support research into the relationship between statistics and risk assessment, and invitations to leading science writers to speak on environmental and health topics, for videotape. After much discussion and input from university faculty and colleagues from other schools, Logan rejected the grant in March 1991. Faculty did not have the opportiunity to meet, discuss, and vote on the grant.

258. Golden, Daniel. "Boston-Area Researchers Benefit from Tobacco Funds." *Boston Globe*, December 17, 1993: 1, 20–21.

In June 1993, the American Medical Association released a statement recommending that schools and universities reject tobacco research grants. Scientists contend, however, that cutbacks in state and federal funds force them to seek alternative sources, including tobacco industry grants. In Boston and surrounding metropolitan areas, hospitals and medical schools, including Harvard Medical School and Boston Medical University, have accepted tobacco money awarded by the Council for Tobacco Research. Many of these institutions are reexamining their policies.

259. Walsh, Raoul A., and Rob W. Sanson-Fisher. "What Universities Do about Tobacco Industry Research Funding." *Tobacco Control* 3, no. 4 (Winter 1994): 308–15.

The authors have surveyed Australian higher institutions of learning about their current policies and practices with respect to accepting tobacco funds from three major organizations. The Australian Tobacco Research Foundation and the Rothmans Foundation Education Division provide funds for postgraduate scholarships and fellowships for postdoctoral research, respectively. The Tobacco Research and Development Council was created by the Primary Industries and Energy Research and Development Act of 1989. The tobacco-growing sector is the main recipient of its funding. The authors conclude that close ties remain between these groups even though Australian institutions are increasingly rejecting funds tied to tobacco.

260. Rutter, Terri. "US Journals Veto Tobacco Funded Research." *British Medical Journal* 312 (January 6, 1996): 11.

The American Thoracic Society's two scientific journals, *American Journal of Respiratory and Critical Care* and the *American Journal of Respiratory Cell and Molecular Biology*, will ban research funded by the tobacco industry. The research is regarded as biased and unable to pass the test of peer review. The society's parent body is the American Lung Association. The American Cancer Society's three journals, however, do not have a similar policy. The editorial board of the *New England Journal of Medicine* accepts tobacco-funded research but requires the authors to disclose the names of the financial contributors.

261. Cohen, Jon. "Philip Morris Gives Institute a Head Start." *Science* 272 (April 26, 1996): 489.

To the research institutes in La Jolla, California, will soon be added the Molecular Sciences Institute (MSI). MSI will focus on cell signal transduction. Dr. Sydney Brenner, a highly respected molecular biologist, will head the institute. At the heart of the institute is its benefactor, Philip Morris. The tobacco company is committing $15 million per year for fifteen years. The initial grant sum is $225 million, adjusted for inflation. Philip Morris will have no involvement in the day-to-day operations but will have licensing rights to a limited number of non-tobacco-related inventions. Former Philip Morris chair R. William Murray is slated to serve on the board of trustees.

262. Cohen, Jon. "Institutes Find It Hard to Kick the Tobacco Funding Habit." *Science* 272 (April 26, 1996): 490.

Some research institutions are still accepting funds from the tobacco industry and its Council for Tobacco Research. However, institutions in the United States and Australia are banning their researchers from accepting tobacco funds. These institutions include Brigham and Women's Hospital, the M. D. Anderson Cancer Center, and the University of Sydney.

263. Hearn, Wayne. "Journals Urged to Decline Tobacco-Funded Research." *American Medical News* 39, no. 27 (July 22, 1996): 3. Infotrac Health Reference Center (December 8, 1997).

A vote taken by the American Medical Association's (AMA) House of Delegates recommended that tobacco-funded research be rejected by scientific journals. Opponents, such as the Section on Medical Schools, complained that the action interfered with editors' rights to judge the scientific value of the work. Safeguards are already in place to prevent publishing biased research, such as disclosing the names of third-party contributors and the relationships of the authors to any third parties. The American Lung Association already enforces the AMA's position.

264. Motluk, Alison. "The Dirtiest Dilemma of All." *New Scientist* 151 (August 31, 1996): 12–13.

   Tobacco sponsorship of scientific research is increasingly being put under the microscope. The British-funded Cancer Research Campaign may no longer fund Cambridge University, because of its acceptance of funds from British American Tobacco (BAT). BAT's money would fund an international studies chair named after former BAT chairman Patrick Sheehy. BAT has sponsored Cambridge's postgraduate studentships and the Royal Commonwealth Society Library. Tobacco money has funded such institutions as the University of Bristol, Duke University, and the Russell Group (upper echelon universities including Cambridge and Oxford).

265. Williams, Nigel. "Tobacco Funding Debate Smolders." *Science* 274 (October 4, 1996): 28.

   Cambridge University's acceptance of a $2.5 million gift from the United Kingdom–based British American Tobacco (BAT) has elicited cries of outrage from the British research community. Cambridge intends to fund an international relations professorship to be named after Sir Patrick Sheehy, the former chair of BAT. In response, the Cancer Research Campaign has issued a stern warning that acceptance of the donation would cause it to cease allocating research funds to Cambridge. Cambridge has suspended its public relations head, Mary Rice, for stating that the money would smear Cambridge's image "as an impartial source of scientific knowledge." BAT has also donated $220,000 to the Medical Research Council, an organization funded by the government, to study the health effects of nicotine usage by at-risk Alzheimer's patients.

266. Buckby, Simon, and Clive Cookson. "Universities Warned on 'Tobacco-Tainted' Funds." *Financial Times*, October 15, 1997: 18.

   Universities receiving tobacco industry research funds could possibly be barred from accepting research funds from grant-giving government bodies. The United Kingdom's Cancer Research Campaign's draft code of practice has so recommended. It is estimated that the tobacco industry's annual contribution to medical research totals several million pounds. The draft code came to light after last year's announcement that Cambridge University had received £1.5 million from British American Tobacco to endow a chair in international relations.

267. Hirschhorn, Norbert, Stella Aguinaga Bialous, and Stan Shatenstein. "Philip Morris New Scientific Initiative: an Analysis." *Tobacco Control* 10, no. 3 (September 2001): 247–52.

   Philip Morris's Worldwide Scientific Affairs has created a new research-granting entity titled the Philip Morris External Research Program. The program has a number of purposes: to fund research proposals, reduce the health risks through cigarette design, repair the company's scientific credibility, and build elements of peer review and scientific integrity.

268. Blumenstyk, Goldie. "Taking Cash from Tobacco Will Cost Researchers." *Chronicle of Higher Education* 50, no. 24 (February 20, 2004): A1, A25–A26.

   Since July 2005, the American Cancer Society no longer provides research grants to scientists receiving research funds from the tobacco industry. Proponents in favor of the new policy state that the tobacco industry uses research grants to distort the dangers of smoking and to push its own agenda. Opponents reply that the new policy infringes upon academic freedom and endangers science.

SPONSORSHIPS: SPORTING EVENTS

269. Spolar, Christine. "Park Service Bans Tobacco Sponsors." *Washington Post*National Association of Stock Car Auto Racing's (NASCAR) August 16, 1991: C6.

The National Park Service's settlement of a lawsuit filed by the nonprofit Action on Smoking and Health will spell the end of tobacco-sponsored Virginia Slims tennis tournaments. For the final tournament, tobacco sponsors must comply with strict advertising limits and cease providing attendees with free tobacco products. In addition, signs posted throughout the tournament site must state that the Park Service "does not imply endorsement of any product."

270. "Vons Rides Camel GT Stop; Move Matches RJR Tobacco's New Strategy." *IEG Sponsorship Report* 11, no. 15 (August 10, 1992): 1–2.

R. J. Reynolds Tobacco's (RJR) sports marketing arm, Sports Marketing Enterprises, is giving first strategic priority to retail sales and bucking competitors such as Philip Morris. To implement its strategy, the company has signed agreements with Vons Companies, Fay's, Inc., and Food City to sponsor motor sports events. Tie-ins to RJR occur via retail tools, such as exclusive sales of tickets, television exposure (for example, ESPN), signage, appearances by drivers, and event-themed displays. RJR is heightening exposure of its motor sports sponsorships (for instance, Winston Racing Series, Winston West, and the National Hot Rod Association) and golf sponsorships (such as the Vantage Championship).

271. Whalen, Jeanne. "Cigarette Interest Flags in Racing." *Advertising Age* 64, no. 51 (December 6, 1993): 28.

Tobacco companies are reconsidering their event marketing strategies in the face of tough government advertising regulations. R. J. Reynolds Tobacco (RJR) is dropping its Camel GT Series and Camel Mud Monster Truck Racing Series. For National Association of Stock Car Auto Racing (NASCAR) and National Hot Rod Association (NHRA) competition, the company created the Smokin' Joe's Racing Team sponsorships. RJR will retain its NASCAR Winston Cup, Winston West Series, Winston Racing Series, and the NHRA Winston Drag Racing Series. In the Indy Racing League, Philip Morris will pay an estimated $8 million to sponsor an additional car.

272. McCollister, Tom. "RJR Defends NASCAR Visibility." *Atlanta Journal and Constitution*, June 21, 1995: C3.

R. J. Reynolds Tobacco (RJR) is defending its right to place signs at such motor vehicle events as National Association of Stock Car Auto Racing's (NASCAR) Winston Cup, the National Hot Rod Association (NHRA), and IndyCar racing teams. It is responding to Philip Morris's decision to redeploy signs at sporting events away from the camera's eye, under pressure from the U.S. Justice Department. RJR says their signs do not promote a brand name, in that at NASCAR events "Winston" is almost exclusively associated with the Cup. During 1995, the NASCAR point fund will receive $3.5 million from RJR, and the NHRA point fund $2.3 million.

273. Dohrmann, George. "Tobacco Might Have to Butt Out of Racing." *Los Angeles Times*, August 24, 1995: C1, C4.

Tobacco sponsorship of motor racing and sporting events faces near-fatal advertising regulations proposed by President Clinton and the Food and Drug Administration. Television coverage of National Association of Stock Car Auto Racing (NASCAR), Indy Race League (IRL), and National Hot Rod Association (NHRA) events has been a lucrative way to build brand equity and enhance brand loyalty. This advertising occurs in spite of the 1971 public law banning tobacco television advertising. The tobacco industry's financial contributions are significant. During 1995, the industry provided $15 million, $50 million, and $10 million to NASCAR, IRL, and NHRA, respectively.

274. Keenan, Faith. "Staying in the Game." *Far Eastern Economic Review* 158, no. 43 (October 26, 1995): 67.

Chinese authorities have implemented a new "one banner" rule allowing tobacco companies to display only one corporate-named banner each at sporting events. Previously, companies had been allowed to display multiple banners. In addition, tobacco companies are prohibited from advertising corporate logos and product facsimiles at sporting events. Because the Chinese market offers tremendous profit opportunities, any association with sporting events, such as the 555 China Open Badminton Championships (British American Tobacco) or the Chinese Basketball League and Marlboro Soccer League (Philip Morris), continues to be attractive.

275. Rashid, Ahmed, and Jonathan Karp. "Bowling for Dollars." *Far Eastern Economic Review* 158, no. 43 (October 26, 1995): 68.

Pakistan, India, and Sri Lanka have jointly won the bid to host the 1996 World Cup, a twelve-nation competition of the world's cricket powers. The troika is set to collect sponsorship fees totaling $60 million. The fees will be boosted significantly by revenue sharing (except for Sri Lanka, which did not participate in financing the winning bid). Additional fees will come from the tobacco giant Indian Tobacco Company (ITC), which placed the winning bid to name the games. They will be the "Willis World Cup"; Willis is the company's popular cigarette brand. ITC is estimated to have paid $12 million for the winning bid and will spend $6 million for advertising.

276. Glass, Chris. "The Winston Circuit." *Tobacco Reporter* 123, no. 4 (April 1996): 32–34, 36.

In 1971, the National Association of Stock Car Auto Racing (NASCAR) embraced its first nonautomotive sponsor, R. J. Reynolds Tobacco (RJR). RJR created the Winston Cup and a bonus fund awarded to the driver achieving the highest season point total. For the twenty-five year period, RJR has funded bonuses totaling $30 million; in 1996, the Winston Cup winner received $1.5 million. Winston Cup events are great opportunities to attract customers at the retail level and to use luxury booths to entertain corporate clients.

277. Perrone, Vinnie, and Josh Barr. "Racing Feels a Pinch." *Washington Post*, August 24, 1996: F1, F3.

Proposed regulations aimed at curbing teenage smoking and severely limiting Big Tobacco's ability to advertise at sporting events could have a major impact on the National Association of Stock Car Auto Racing (NASCAR) stock car racing circuit. R. J. Reynolds's twenty-six years of corporate sponsorship dominates NASCAR, which holds a thirty-one race series at eighteen racetracks. This investment has included expenditures of more than $30 million annually, including $4 million for the Winston Cup Series, advertising contracts, and bankrolling two races and one team.

278. Harverson, Patrick, and John Griffiths. "Survival of Fittest after Sport Loses Tobacco Sponsorship." *Financial Times*, May 20, 1997: 14.

Yesterday, the British government announced its intention to ban sports sponsorships by the tobacco industry. The tobacco industry makes contributions to such events as cricket, motor racing, snooker, darts, and ice hockey. The Williams-Renault Formula One motor racing team receives £15 million annually from Rothmans. Benson & Hedges provides £4 million to cricket over five years, £250,000 per year to ice hockey, and £4 million per year to the snooker Masters events. The lesser-known events, such as snooker and darts, will feel the financial pinch.

279. Brierley, David, and Robert Alexander. "Formula 1 Flotation May Spin Off Course." *European,* May 22, 1997: 3.

During the summer, the London stock market will begin trading shares in the Formula One motor racing company. The $3.2 billion stock float may be put on hold due to the government's proposed ban of tobacco advertising and sponsorship of sporting events. Formula One is heavily supported by the tobacco industry, which spends millions to sponsor teams and drivers. Brand names Marlboro, Benson & Hedges, Mild Seven, West, Rothmans, and Gauloises have major stakes in the industry. The name "Formula One" means glamor and prestige, and the racing circuit provides an excellent channel for brand advertising. During 1996, forty-one billion people in two hundred countries viewed these events.

280. Mrlilli, Denise. "No Butts about It." *Crain's Cleveland Business* 18, no. 27 (July 7, 1997): G6

Philip Morris and Brown & Williamson are major sponsors of Championship Auto Racing Team (CART) events. Philip Morris sponsors the Marlboro Grand Prix of Miami, the Marlboro 500, the Penske Racing Team, and the serieswide pole award. Brown & Williamson sponsors the Team Kool Green banner, the Kool/Toyota Atlantic Championship Series, and hot air balloon events. In addition, Kool offers monetary incentives to its drivers and teams, promotes young drivers at its "Stars of Tomorrow" breakfast gatherings, and sponsors Team Green Academy. The academy trains drivers in the areas of fitness, coaching, and the media. Overall, tobacco financial sponsorship ranges from 10 to 15 percent of the total sponsorship dollars provided to CART.

281. Vega, Michael. "Up in Smoke." *Boston Globe*, July 13, 1997: D1, D15.

In 1971, R. J. Reynolds (RJR) became a sponsor of the fledgling National Association of Stock Car Auto Racing. Over twenty-seven years, the company funded bonuses and prize money for its Winston Cup Series, to the tune of nearly $35 million. The cup now covers thirty-two races and is a guaranteed moneymaker for track owners lucky enough to snatch race dates. At a December 1997 awards banquet at New York City's Waldorf-Astoria, RJR was set to award $4 million in prize money. The proposed tobacco settlement, approved by Congress, quashed all this; the agreement commited the tobacco industry to end its involvement with sporting events and series.

282. Alexander, Robert. "End of the Tobacco Road for F1?" *European*, July 17–23, 1997: 48–49.

Pan-European proposals to ban all tobacco advertising and sports sponsorship have impacted the Formula One (F1) motor racing events. Still, F1 marketers remained bullish on the sport and anticipated that any outright bans would not take effect before the year 2000. Hedging its bets, F1 signed contracts with Malaysia and South Korea to host future races and is eyeing future markets in countries such as China, India, and Morocco. Up until the ban, tobacco companies remained committed to F1 racing teams, such as Williams Renault (Rothmans) and Arrows Yamaha (Philip Morris).

283. Rogers, Danny. "BAT Axes Suzuki to Seek F1 Deal." *Marketing* (September 18, 1997): 5.

British American Tobacco's director of global sponsorships, Tom Moser, has announced that the company will end its twelve-year sponsorship of the Suzuki's Lucky Strike Motorcycle World Championship. In the past, the company provided £20 million each year. The company is thought now to be pursuing the sponsorship of the Minardi Formula One motor racing team. The sponsorship carries an annual price tag of £100 million.

284. Griffiths, John. "BAT Buys Formula 1 Team for Cigarette Promotion." *Financial Times*, November 13, 1997: 1.

For a price of £300 million paid over a five-year period, British American Tobacco (BAT) is going to purchase the Tyrell Formula motor racing team. Tyrell builds and designs racing cars. The purchase will create three benefits for BAT. First, BAT will use the team to promote its Lucky Strike and State Express 555 brands. Secondly, BAT will become a member of the Formula One Constructors Association and thereby gain easier access to television revenues and the like. Third, in this way the company can sidestep a proposed ban on tobacco sponsorship of sport by the European Union.

285. Meier, Barry. "A Controversy on Tobacco Road." *New York Times*, December 4, 1997: D1, D11.

Formula One racing takes the spotlight in the wake of the British Labour Party's disclosure that Formula One head Bernie Eccelstone has contributed $1.7 million to the party. Also, Prime Minister Tony Blair announced Formula One would be exempt from a proposed ban on tobacco advertising. Formula One depends mightily on the tobacco industry's largesse. Brand names and logos grace the racing cars. In countries where brand names are prohibited, brand-name word plays appear on the cars. For example, "Bitten & Hisses" appears in place of "Benson & Hedges." In 1997, the tobacco companies contributed approximately $200 million to the racing circuit.

For 1998, Philip Morris spent approximately $77 million in sponsorships and prize money.

286. "Imperial to Pull Plug on Sponsorships." *Marketing Magazine* 102, no. 46 (December 15, 1997): 1.

    October 1998 marked the end of Imperial Tobacco, Ltd.'s sponsorships of three major Quebec events: the du Maurier Open tennis tournament, Player's Grand Prix of Canada, and the Montreal International Jazz Festival. The Alliance for Sponsorship Freedom estimates that these events will be able to cover only $31 million in new sponsorships. Overall, Imperial Tobacco's sport and cultural sponsorship contributions total $50 million.

287. Shuit, Douglas P. "Anti-Smoking Forces Ready to Invade Tobacco Road." *Los Angeles Times*, April 3, 1998: B1, B5.

    In Long Beach's Toyota Grand Prix, antitobacco logos graced a number of race entries. L.A. Link sponsored an entry, the American Cancer Society's logo was splashed on two entries, and SmithKline Beecham's Nicorette gum and Nicoderm nicotine-patch logos were attached to an entry. Counselors and pharmacists for SmithKline distributed information from the company's thirty-four-foot motor home, dubbed the "NicoVan."

288. Daniels, Chris. "Dunhill May Rethink Targeted Sponsorship." *Marketing Magazine* 103, no. 18 (May 11, 1998): 3.

    Since about 1996, Rothmans, Benson & Hedges, Inc.'s Dunhill cigarette brand sponsored the annual courier bike competition, the Alley-Cats Scramble. The 1998 Toronto-based two-day competition attracted over four thousand attendees and 180 competitors. The company felt the competition was the best ever and gave the brand "a chance to be part of the community." Future sponsorships will be weighted against impending sponsorship restrictions contained in the Tobacco Act.

289. Clarke, Liz. "To Attract Kids, Stock Car Racing Shifts Gears." *Washington Post*, May 22, 1998: A1, A14.

    The National Association of Stock Car Auto Racing (NASCAR) is looking to expand its market and garner new fans by focusing on the youth audience. The NASCAR name will be licensed to create theme parks, cafes, retail stores, toys (for example, NASCAR Barbie), games, and a cartoon show. NASCAR will in that way compete with other organizations, such as the National Basketball Association. This is being done while carefully racing around Winston Cup Series sponsor R. J. Reynolds (RJR). Since the company began sponsoring NASCAR in 1971, the company has provided substantial support to build the motor circuit into a marketing behemoth. RJR spends approximately $30 million annually on the series, kicking in another $5 million for prize money. NASCAR nevertheless emphasizes its own brand name, minimizing or excluding Winston.

290. Rogers, Danny. "BAT's Quest for a Winning Strategy." *Marketing* (September 17, 1998): 20–21.

    British American Tobacco has changed its sports sponsorship strategy from rallying, powerboats, and motorcycle racing to Formula One racing. The company owns a 50 percent equity interest in and an exclusive five-year sponsorship contract for its newly created British American Racing team. Of the firm's global stable of 250 brands, it is speculated that Lucky Strike, State Express 555, John Player Gold Leaf, or Kool may grace the car. Formula One offers the company access to a major global sporting event. Marketing benefits may include track signage, corporate hospitality, and stadium naming.

291. "Did RJR's Pool Haul Snooker Ex-Partner?" *Business North Carolina* 18, no. 9 (September 1998): 14–15.

In 1997, R. J. Reynolds Tobacco Company (RJR) canceled its sponsorship of the Pro Billiards Tour Association (PBTA). The company had sponsored the tour in 1996. PBTA then canceled the year's events, while RJR launched its own tour and hired away the PBTA tournament director. The PBTA has sued RJR on the grounds that the company had sponsored the tour only to shop for top talent and then put the association out of business. The suit alleges that in 1996 the association renamed the tournament the Camel Pro Billiards Series, rented space in expensive venues, such as convention centers, but RJR failed to follow through to promote the series.

292. "Philip Morris Decides to Cease Sponsoring Chinese Soccer League." *Wall Street Journal*, November 30, 1998: B13D.

For five straight years, until October 1998, Philip Morris Asia sponsored China's professional soccer league, which it referred to as the "Marlboro League." The company reportedly paid a yearly fee of $7 million. Philip Morris has discontinued sponsorship of this league. Interestingly, the Chinese themselves call the league "A-division soccer."

293. "Cigarette Brands Snooker Tie-Ups to Be Hit by Ban." *Marketing* (July 1, 1999): 3.

Starting in 2003, the Benson & Hedges and Regal brands lost their rights to sponsor snooker tournaments. This includes the United Kingdom and Irish Masters (Benson & Hedges) and the Scottish Open (Regal). The Department of Health in the United Kingdom has determined that these tournaments do not fit the criteria of a "world event" and must relinquish their sponsorships. Imperial Tobacco will still be able to sponsor the Embassy tournament for another three years, since this is deemed a "world event" and thus not subject to the European ban of tobacco sponsorships.

294. Darby, Ian. "Tobacco Loses Grip on F1 Sponsorship to Cars." *Marketing* (January 27, 2000): 3.

The start of 2000 Formula One racing season marked a shift in sponsorships to car brands, such as Jaguar, BMW, and Mercedes, from tobacco brands. Still, British American Tobacco's British American Racing team is working with Honda to have the Lucky Strike brand splashed across Honda's racing cars.

295. Siegel, Michael. "Counteracting Tobacco Motor Sports Sponsorship as a Promotional Tool: Is the Tobacco Settlement Enough?" *American Journal of Public Health* 91, no. 7 (July 2001): 1100–06.

Using reports obtained from the sports analysis service *Sponsors Report*, the author analyzes tobacco and brand-name television exposure received from 1997 to

1999 and considers on the Master Settlement Agreement's (MSA) potential impact on this exposure. The documents from *Sponsors Report* helped the author establish the approximate dollar value of nonpaid television exposure received. Race events like the Indy Lights Championship and Winston Cup garnered $156.8 million worth of advertising. For the three years, it is estimated that the television exposure generated $410.5 million in coverage. Top brands included Winston ($305.8 million) and Marlboro ($22.1 million). Under the MSA's terms, motor sports television exposure will generate $99.1 million annually. The study concludes therefore that the MSA will have little effect in this area.

296. Rosenberg, N. Jennifer, and Michael Siegel. "Use of Corporate Sponsorship as a Tobacco Marketing Tool: A Review of Tobacco Industry Sponsorship in the USA, 1995–99." *Tobacco Control* 10, no. 3 (September 2001): 239–46.

    The authors combine the results of keyword Internet searches and a customized, paid report from Chicago-based IEG, Inc., to identify tobacco sport sponsorships for the years 1995–1999. The results cover the major tobacco companies: Philip Morris, R. J. Reynolds, Brown & Williamson, and Lorillard. The authors also included snuff tobacco producer U.S. Tobacco. The authors identified three hundred sponsorships in such categories as the performing arts, minorities, motor sports, and education. Funding for these sponsorships totaled at a minimum $363.5 million. Of this total, motor sport sponsorship is identified as the top event/program/organization, with an estimated financial investment of $208.5 million. Michael Siegel's report is available at dcc2.bumc.bu.edu/tobacco (accessed March 8, 2004).

297. Kleinman, Mark. "B&H Ends Cricket Cup Sponsorship." *Marketing* (March 14, 2002): 2.

    In June 2002, Gallaher Tobacco's Benson & Hedges brand ended its thirty-one-year sponsorship of top-class cricket in the United Kingdom. Tickets for the final match of the Benson & Hedges Cup were offered at 1972 prices. The brand's sponsorship of snooker and golf tournaments expired in 2003.

298. Rossel, Stefanie. "The Oval Formula." *Tobacco Journal International*, no. 2 (March/April 2002): 61.

    Reemstma's West cigarette is being manufactured in an oval package emblazoned with a Formula One racing image. The theme is tied to the company's sponsorship of the West McLaren Mercedes Formula One racing team. The product will be marketed in Asian markets and at racing events.

299. Kleinman, Mark. "WHO Warns F1 Body on Russian Grand Prix Ads." *Marketing* (April 4, 2002): 3.

    In 2004, the first Russian Grand Prix took place in Moscow. The race's governing body, Federation Internationale de l'Automobile (FIA), received a stern warning from the World Health Organization (WHO) against allowing cars to be plastered with tobacco brands. WHO may review the FIA's membership in the Tobacco Free Sport, an initiative designed to end tobacco sponsorship of various sporting events by the year 2006. Tobacco Free Sport is tied to the WHO's Framework Convention on Tobacco Control.

300. "FIFA Admits Flaw in Tobacco-Free World Cup Claim." *Marketing* (May 30, 2002): 3.

   The 2002 World Cup will not be a tobacco-free event. The Federation Internationale de Football Association (FIFA), soccer's world governing body, has admitted that British American Tobacco (BAT) will sponsor Malaysian television coverage of the event. FIFA states that BAT's Dunhill brand's sponsorship role was finalized before the FIFA signed the Tobacco Free Sport initiative.

301. Dewhirst, Timothy, and A. Hunter. "Tobacco Sponsorship of Formula One and CART Auto Racing: Tobacco Brand Exposure and Enhanced Symbolic Imagery through Co-Sponsors' Third Party Advertising." *Tobacco Control* 11, no. 2 (June 2002): 146–50.

   Tobacco companies often cosponsor sports motor race teams or events like Formula One and Championship Auto Racing teams. Cosponsorships allow the tobacco companies to piggyback on third-party advertising and achieve promotional visibility and exposure for their products. For example, TAG Heuer of Taiwan is a Formula One sponsor and has partnered with McLaren and West cigarettes to cosponsor the West McLaren Mercedes racing team. Cobranding is another avenue by which tobacco brand names can appear jointly on products, packages, and other types of media. Cobranding is strengthened if the product association is strong and complimentary (for instance, suggesting that one product may be used with the other), is promoted thoroughly, results in a long-term relationship, and the cosponsors' products lend credibility to the tobacco brands. In addition, sponsorship contracts entered into by racing teams and individual sponsors provide room for the tobacco industry to engage in third-party advertising.

302. Bernstein, Viv. "A Cup without Winston." *New York Times*, February 8, 2003: D3.

   R. J. Reynolds's thirty-two-year sponsorship of the Winston Cup Series, one of the premier events on the National Association of Stock Car Auto Racing (NASCAR) racing circuit, will be coming to an end. Though the company recently agreed to sponsor the event through 2007, a dramatic change in the company's "business dynamics" is forcing it to end the sponsorship and thus save annual expenses ranging from $30 to $60 million. Just last month, the company withdrew its sponsorship of the Winston No Bull 5. The No Bull 5 covered five races, with million-dollar bonus prizes, also sponsored by R. J. Reynolds.

303. Kleinman, Mark. "NiQuitin CQ to Sponsor BMW Williams F1 Team." *Marketing* (April 17, 2003): 3.

   Formula One racing team BMW Williams was sponsored by NiQuitin, a nicotine-replacement therapy product produced by GlaxoSmithKline. The brand name made its debut at the San Marino Grand Prix. NiQuitin took over sponsorship from Rothmans cigarettes. Tobacco brands provide an estimated £160 million a year in financial support. In ongoing sponsorships, West backs the McLaren team, Benson & Hedges backs the Jordan team, Marlboro sponsors Ferrari, and Lucky Strike supports BAR (British American Racing).

304. Lavack, Anne M. "An Inside View of Tobacco Sports Sponsorship: An Historical Perspective." *International Journal of Sports Marketing & Sponsorship* 5, no. 2 (June/July 2003): 105–28.

   The author traces the tobacco industry's objectives and key decision areas in regard to sports sponsorship. The analysis is based primarily on British American Tobacco Company's documents stored in the Guildford Depository (Guildford, England). Key tobacco objectives cover goodwill, community relations, political support, media exposure, exploiting regulations, and brand image, recognition, and recall. Key decision areas include choosing which events to sponsor (matching event image with brand image), using sponsorship communications (such as prepromotion and postpromotion), measuring sponsorship effectiveness (for instance, television viewing audience), and fighting for the right to continue sponsoring events (for example, using third parties to support the industry).

305. "F1 Attacked over Tobacco Ads U-Turn." *Marketing Week,* 26, no. 28 (July 10, 2003): 5.

Rather than banning tobacco sponsorships of Formula One race cars by the year 2005, the Federation Internationale de l'Automobile (FIA) will only "recommend" their elimination. This is a reversal of an earlier decision to honor the ban imposed by the European Union. Racing's governing body eliminated races in Belgium and Austria; tobacco-friendly venues include Bahrain, China, Malaysia, Monte Carlo, and Japan. Antismoking forces anticipate future compliance due to the Framework Convention on Tobacco Control.

306. Kleinman, Mark. "ASH Attacks B&H-Backed F1 Feature." *Marketing* (July 24, 2003): 1.

The August 2003 issue of *Maxim* published an article entitled "F1 Special in Association with Benson & Hedges Jordan Grand Prix." In connection with the British Grand Prix, the article includes references to the brand and over forty Benson & Hedges (B&H)/Jordan logos. The Action on Smoking and Heath (United Kingdom) group claims that this article constitutes advertising through the "back door" by B&H, in violation of recently enacted prohibitions of tobacco advertising and promotion. The article also appeared in the magazine *FHM*.

307. Fowler, Geoffrey A. "Treaty May Stub Out Cigarette Ads in China." *Wall Street Journal*, December 2, 2003: B1, B6.

China has signed, and may ratify, a global treaty to restrict various forms of tobacco media advertising, raise taxes on cigarettes, and cover half of each pack with stern health warnings. This could change the face of the tobacco industry in China, especially tobacco sport sponsorship. For example, the Yunnan Hongta Group sponsors the Hongta Soccer Club and supported a visit by soccer team Real Madrid. A new Formula One race track is being built in Shanghai with tobacco advertising revenues. British American Tobacco has not commented on its possible sponsorship of the track, but the company has declared that by the year 2006 it would end all global Formula One sponsorships.

308. "Anti-Tobacco Laws Smoke F1 Teams Out." *Marketing News* 38, no. 4 (March 1, 2004): 7. (Associated Press).

The European Union's starting date of its directive banning Formula One is now set for July 2005. Originally the ban was to take place in October 2006. Britain has accepted the change, but it is wreaking havoc with formerly tobacco-sponsored teams. The teams are heavily dependent upon tobacco financing and could be forced to move their operations out of Britain.

309. Carlyle, Joshua, Jeff Collin, Monique E. Muggli, and Richard D. Hurt. "British American Tobacco and Formula One Motor Racing." *British Medical Journal* 329 (July 10, 2004): 104–6.

British American Racing has been British American Tobacco's (BAT) way to race around public health laws. Formed in 1999, the racing team has served as a tool to promote and build the company's name and image, use the broadcast media and merchandising (for example, video games, toy model cars) opportunities to promote its brands worldwide, and market the cigarette brands through events sponsored in the emerging Asian markets. BAT implemented the "Lucky Tribe Campaign" to promote its Lucky Strike brand and to trumpet the company's arrival, through team ownership, in Formula One racing.

310. "F1 Defies Ban on Tobacco Sponsorship." *Marketing Week* 27, no. 31 (July 29, 2004): 7.

Signs point to continued relationship by Formula One (F1) with the tobacco industry. This is in direct contrast to the July 2005 ban imposed by the European Union. More F1 races are occurring in tobacco-friendly countries. Tobacco companies are rumored to be looking to sponsor F1 teams.

2
Economic Aspects: Distribution Channels

DUTY-FREE

311. Ryan, Kerwin. "Government Programme Helps Lift Duty-Free Cigarette Performance." *World Tobacco*, no. 114 (January 1990): 37, 39.

    The Canadian government sponsors and controls twenty-six duty-free shops along the U.S. border. Tobacco and alcoholic products account for 60 percent of sales. Because of their success, the government will build up to nine additional shops. Imperial Tobacco sells a large volume of cigarettes through the shops. Currently, Imperial's sales total 4 percent and may reach 7 percent in 1992.

312. Philip Morris. *PM Duty Free Inc. Three Year Plan 1991–1993*. 1991. Bates 2041798054/8098. legacy.library.ucsf.edu/tid/iej62e00 (accessed June 11, 2004).

    This three-year business plan details major objectives of the company's duty-free businesses. The report provides details of various duty-free segments: ships, airports, the Mexican border, the Canadian border, and Canadian ships and airlines. Financial statements, market shares, and pricing analyses are also included.

313. "Duty-Free Success." *Tobacco Journal International*, no. 4 (July/August 1993): 6.

    Philip Morris's Fine Australian Cigarettes collection is a big hit in the Australian duty-free outlets. It is composed of eight twenty-five-pack cigarettes. The packaging features such Australian icons as the Sydney Opera House and kookaburras. The package is available only in the duty-free markets.

314. Mesquita, Lúcio. "Channel Hopping Becomes British Sport." *Tobacco Journal International*, no. 5 (September/October 1995): 37–40.

    British "cross-Channel" shoppers board ferries and travel to the French harbor town of Calais. British shoppers are allowed to purchase upward of four hundred duty-free cigarettes (two hundred each way). Shoppers purchase cigarettes in France because they cost only slightly more than duty-free goods and are cheaper than the heavily taxed product in Britain. Such traffic cost the British tobacco industry £75 million in lost sales in 1994.

315. R. J. Reynolds Tobacco Company. *1995 U.S. Duty Free Sales and Marketing Plan.* 1995. Bates 514256100/6187. legacy.library.ucsf.edu/tid/jsp41d00 (accessed October 11, 2004).

   This document reviews the sales and marketing plan for four duty-free markets: border stores (Canada and Mexico), airports, commercial ships (cargo, cruise, and fishing), and navy ships. Each section gives a brief explanation of the target market, key issues effecting the market, assumptions needing to be made for current and future business transactions, and strategy/plans for conducting business.

316. Joy, Robin. "Tobacco Showcase Threatened as E.U. Moves on Duty-Free." *World Tobacco*, no. 156 (January 1997): 39–40.

   The European Union (EU) ended sales of duty-free goods, including tobacco products, as of July 1, 1999. Overall sales were estimated to be $6.9 billion, with EU sales accounting for nearly $4.9 billion. The ban has impacted suppliers, airport shops, ferries, and airlines but has impacted only minimally the total volume sales of cigarettes. Duty-free shops are havens for the advertising and marketing of cigarettes, launching international brands, building brand loyalty, and promoting luxury brands like Dunhill, Cartier, and Davidoff.

317. "Designs for Duty-Free." *Tobacco Reporter* 124, no. 5 (May 1997): 58.

   Increasing sales of cigarettes at duty-free outlets is spawning new and attractive packaging ideas to catch the consumer's attention. British American Tobacco introduced a new brand called 555 Equinox. The packaging for both packs and cartons is a royal-blue, hard plastic, clamshell container. The brand-name lettering is gold. The packaging bespeaks luxury and is targeted toward free-spending Asian businessmen. It is marketed with the phrase "The Ultimate Expression of Smoothness." Other packaging designs created especially for the duty-free market include a "face-to-back" or "stick-pack," an octagonal cross-section pack, a clamshell or shell and slide pack, and also multipacks consisting of four hundred cigarettes (twenty packs of twenty cigarettes).

318. "Religion in Russia Is Big Business." *Humanist* 57, no. 5 (September–October 1997): 47. Infotrac General Reference Center (October 29, 1997).

   The Russian Orthodox Church is quietly engaged in certain unusual business activities designed to generate income. The church is involved in establishing banks, exporting $2 billion worth of oil through a partnership, and importing duty-free cigarettes. The duty-free cigarette business deprives the Russian government of over $40 billion in revenues. The church's financial statements do not reflect these operations.

319. Lipsith, Gavin. "Strike It Lucky: Living It Up in the City." *Duty-Free News International* 16, no. 9 (May 15, 2002): 101.

   British American Tobacco launched a new "City Life" campaign aimed to change the image of its Lucky Strike brand. The campaign took place in eight cities, including Amsterdam, Tokyo, and Rio de Janeiro, as well as fifteen airports. Passengers encountering the City Life campaign zone were able to view videotape of each of the eight cities twenty-four hours a day. The campaign targeted domestic traffic and also potential German, Spanish, and French customers.

320. Labous, Jane. "Next Year, New Strategy for JTI." *Duty-Free News International* 17, no. 3, Special Report (February 2003): 21–22.

   Japan Tobacco International is pursuing numerous strategies to increase brand exposure and gain market share. One strategy is 2002's launching of a campaign to rebrand its Camel cigarette. This included an investment in global marketing and manufacturing, a new package, and a new advertising campaign. The main targets for the launch included the duty-free and European markets. Also, the company began to deemphasize military and diplomatic business and focus on airport shops and the duty-free market. This has been backed with aggressive promotions and upgrades to the airport shops. In 2002, the "Win a Trip with Winston" rewarded winners with free trips to European cities, including Barcelona and Paris.

321. "West Promotion to Drive Growth." *Duty-Free News International* 17, no. 10 (June 1, 2003): 14.

   Imperial Tobacco is promoting its West brand and its West McLaren Mercedes Formula One racing team with the "West Racing Challenge," aimed at both duty-free retailers and consumers. To promote the brand within the shop, retailers may set up a racetrack driving simulator, a virtual racetrack tour where consumers count the number of West cigarette packages flashing on the screen, or just ask consumers basic questions leading to an opportunity to enter into a big prize contest. The grand prize is a professional driver's training course in England, nights paid at a four-star hotel, and paid airfare.

322. "Improving the Shelf-Life of Duty-Free Tobacco." *Duty-Free News International* 17, no. 11 (June 15, 2003): 23–24, 26.

   Duty-free marketing managers for Imperial Tobacco and Altadis discuss the importance of the travel-retail/duty-free markets. For Imperial Tobacco and its main brands—Davidoff, West, Lambert & Butler, Regal, and Superkings—creating the right in-store environment impacts brand image, brand awareness, and customers' purchase decisions. The merchandising units reflect shelf layout, branding, space management, and personalized furniture. All these factors create the "brand domain" or "brand world" experience. Altadis takes the same approach toward merchandising its main brands—Gauloises, Gitanes Blondes, and Fortuna. Also, the company feels that merchandising, promotion, and packaging rank ahead of advertising. Saving customers' time and making the shopping experience easier with maximum exposure to the brands is another of the company's goals.

323. Brown, Jonathan. "Luxury Brands Reign Supreme as Travel Downturn Persists." *Duty-Free News International* 17, no. 11 (June 15, 2003): 31–32, 35.

   Premium or luxury cigarettes are tailor made for the travel-retail/duty-free markets. The cigarettes generate high sales volumes, profits, and global exposure. They are manufactured with premium-quality tobaccos and are packaged to appeal to the status-conscious consumer. Smoking a luxury cigarette conveys a sense of success, reward, and upwardly mobile lifestyle. Though travel has declined, the Danish company House of Prince has unveiled a new duty-free cigarette, Christian of Demark. Other company's luxury duty-free brands include Sampoerna Santoso Effendi's S. T. Dupont Paris and Chancellor Tobacco Company's Treasurer.

324. "Bhutan Becomes First to Outlaw Duty-Free Tobacco." *Duty-Free News International* 17, no. 13 (July 15, 2003): 17.

The tiny country of Bhutan has become the first signer of the Framework Convention on Tobacco Control to ban duty-free tobacco sales. The Ministry of Finance operates the country's sole duty-free shop for diplomats.

325. Brown, Jonathan. "Imperial Revamps Furniture and Packaging for Duty-Free." *Duty-Free News International* 17, no. 17 (October 1, 2003): 19.

Imperial Tobacco aims to increase duty-free sales of its Lambert & Butler by installing new merchandising furniture. Wall systems and stand-alone towers perched at an angle mimic the brand's stripe. Lighting complements and highlights the new designs. The new designs reflect a desire to maximize shelf space and meet customers' demand for multipack (e.g., 400s, 600s, 800s, and 1000s) products.

326. "Altadis Plans Big Expansion into Worldwide Duty-Free." *Duty-Free News International* 17, no. 20 (November 15, 2003): 10.

In 2004, Altadis entered the worldwide duty-free channel and promote its Fortuna brand, the company's number-one brand in Spain. Duty-free stores also hosted a game promotion for the Gauloises Blondes brand and reward winners on the spot. Altadis employed visually attractive imagery (e.g., hostess promotions) for the campaign.

327. Brinson, Brandy. "The Beginning of the End?" *Tobacco Reporter* 130, no. 14 (December 2003): 28–30, 32, 34.

The Framework Convention on Tobacco Control recommends that countries ban duty-free tobacco sales but does not require it. The travel-retail and tobacco industries fret that bans will be forthcoming and that this wording will not make any difference. The framework would also require travel-retail shops to hide tobacco products from the public. This is already the rule in Australia and Iceland.

328. Lipsith, Gavin. "The Marlboro Man." *Duty-Free News International* 18, no. 18 (October 15, 2004): 179–81, 183.

George Farah, managing director for Philip Morris International's worldwide duty-free operations, discusses the company's role and the importance of its flagship brand Marlboro in serving the global duty-free market. Worldwide, over four thousand shops conducting business in over 150 countries are stocking more than 150 of the company's cigarette brands. Important sales channels include airport shops, border shops, and ship chandleries. In many airport shops, Marlboro serves as a "magnet brand" and commands a market share as high as 50 percent. The power and appeal of Marlboro gives Philip Morris the ability to maximize creativity in packaging, shelving, and promotion. One example is the linkup with Ferrari Formula One in Bahrain. China holds special promise for the future, especially with its thirty-three international airports. The Chinese/Hong Kong–border shop business is already big and is likely to get bigger.

329. "Tobacco Malaise Takes a Turn for the Worse." *Duty-Free News International* 18, no. 18 (October 15, 2004): 185.

Rumors are circulating that duty-free tobacco may be rescinded by the Malaysian health ministry. A media leak tipped the industry about this potential action. In

Malaysia, duty-free cigarettes have a price advantage vis-à-vis commercially sold cigarettes of up to 40 percent. In 2003, the industry faced the possibility of a ban on duty-free products in South Africa, but the industry worked together to defeat this threat.

ILLEGAL TRADE

330. KPMG Peat Marwick Thorne. *The Smuggling of U.S. Manufactured and Canadian Duty-Free Cigarettes into Canada and Inter-Provincial Smuggling.* March 5, 1990. Bates 2040237963/7973. legacy.library.ucsf.edu/tid/vaq91a00 (accessed March 8, 2004).

    This report analyzes the extent of smuggling in Canada. The focus is on smuggling points (such as the Kahnawake and Akwesasne Indian Reservations) and entry points into Canada (customs points of entry), products smuggled into Canada from the United States, Canadian products exported to the United States and then smuggled back into Canada, and the impact on tax revenues.

331. Koerner, Manfred. "Contraband Cigarettes Flooding East Germany." *Tobacco International* 193, no. 8 (May 1, 1991): 5–6.

    East Germany is being inundated with contraband cigarettes through three avenues. Semifinished cigarettes are exported to Poland, because of low Polish tax rates, and are reimported back to East Germany. Cigarettes purchased at duty-free venues by Soviet military personnel and diplomats stationed in West Berlin find their way to the black market. Shipments supposedly destined for Poland are diverted to drop-off points within East Germany and are then funneled into the black market. Annual tobacco tax losses from contraband sales are estimated to be about $300 million.

332. Ali, Syed Rashid. "Proposals and Woes of the Cigarette Industry." *Tobacco International* 193, no. 15 (August 15, 1991): 18, 20.

    Cigarette smuggling and nonpayment of duties result in estimated annual revenue losses of about 1.83 billion rupees to the Pakistan government. Losses attributed to the evasion of the central excise duty and sales taxes amount annually to 1.15 billion rupees. These activities account for about 20 percent of the total cigarette market. Losses are traced to nonpayment of duty tax on product removed from the factories (with the tacit permission of government officials), lower than normal prices on cigarette packages, and cigarettes smuggled from Afghanistan. The Afghan traffic is due, in part, to a government ban on exports to Afghanistan.

333. John, Glenn A. "Black Market Sees the Light of Day." *Tobacco International* 193, no. 18 (October 1, 1991): 26, 28, 30, 32.

    Contraband cigarette activity, mainly via the coastline, is fast becoming an epidemic in Taiwan. Products manufactured by Japan Tobacco and American and European brands account for 85 percent and 15 percent, respectively, of contraband cigarettes. Smugglers enjoy profits as high as 50 percent, retailers earn only an 8 percent profit, and the government incurs tax and revenue losses as high as $4 billion (Taiwan dollars).

334. Graham, Robert. "Italy Bans Philip Morris Sales for Month in Contraband Row." *Financial Times*, December 16, 1991: 4.

   The Italian foreign ministry can ban the sale of legal cigarettes if seized cigarette contraband exceeds five tons per year. The ministry used this power to ban sales of Marlboro cigarettes after confiscating a shipment at Ravenna. Philip Morris protested that this action would erode customer loyalty and cost it as much as £310 billion in sales.

335. Graham, Robert. "Marlboro Country, Italian Style." *Financial Times*, December 28, 1991: 6.

   Naples, Italy, is a hotbed for contraband sales of cigarettes. It is estimated the traffic generates yearly sales up to £200 billion and costs the Italian government tax revenues of £25 billion. The brands that Philip Morris manufactures in Europe account for most of the contraband cigarettes. The cigarettes are distributed through such means as trucks, cars, minors, and grocers.

336. Newton, Jon. "Where There's Smoke." *Canadian Business* 65, no. 10 (October 1992): 86–95.

   Canadian cigarettes exported to the United States are smuggled back into the country at an alarming rate. Unlike their Canadian counterparts, these cigarettes are tax exempt when exported to the United States; priced from twenty-five to thirty dollars on the black market, they reap substantial profits for smugglers. High federal and provincial taxes help create this environment. Canadian cigarette manufacturers, wholesalers, and retailers must combat a rise in crime and a lower demand for legitimately manufactured cigarettes. Steep expenses are incurred to guard cigarette warehouses and prevent break-ins. The St. Regis Akwesasne Mohawk and Kahnawake reservations serve as major distribution points for the cigarettes.

337. Harman, Alan. "Drop the Taxes!" *Tobacco Reporter* 119, no. 10 (October 1992): 32, 36.

   A group of Canadian tobacco growers, unions, retailers, and distributors estimate that U.S. cigarette and black market purchases resulted in a 1992 revenue loss of $2.2 billion (Canadian). Critics point to price disparities between American and Canadian cigarette cartons. In Quebec, a carton costs fifty-two dollars, or twenty-five on the black market; the same carton costs fifteen dollars in New Hampshire. For 1991, the Royal Canadian Mounted Police estimate that cigarette smuggling from the United States equaled fifteen million cartons. Smugglers' tools include cars, suitcases, mailed packages, and false customs declarations.

338. Ryan, Kerwin. "Smuggling Creates Crisis in Canada." *World Tobacco*, no. 132 (January 1993): 29–30, 32–33.

   Canadian cigarette smuggling is costing the Canadian government (in the aggregate) about $788 million (U.S. dollars) per year, according to the report *Contraband Tobacco Estimate: June 30, 1992*. This is attributable mainly to excessive federal and provincial taxation and duty-free sales. Upon returning from the United States, every Canadian is entitled to one carton of duty-free cigarettes, if the stay lasts more than forty-eight hours. Other avenues for smuggled cigarettes include the Canada/U.S.-based Akwesasne Reserve, fishermen, and through the French islands of St. Pierre and Miquelon, off Newfoundland.

339. Sudetic, Chuck. "Cigarettes a Thriving Industry in Bleak Sarajevo." *New York Times*, September 5, 1993: sec. 1: 3.

In war-torn Sarajevo, cigarettes help people cope with the war, serve as commodities for barter, and make money for smugglers. The sale of one black-market pack of cigarettes could feed a person for one week. Before the war, the Sarajevo Tobacco Factory manufactured Marlboro cigarettes for Philip Morris; currently, it reverses the packaging for a brand called Bosna. Even with its current limited production of four million cigarettes, the factory is suspected of feeding cigarettes to the black market.

340. Fennell, Tom. "Up in Smoke." *Maclean's* 106, no. 49 (December 6, 1993): 14–16.

Cigarette smuggling robs all Canadian governments of nearly $2 billion per year in revenues. In 1992, the provincial government of Quebec, where one-third of all cigarette consumption is related to smuggling, lost $200 million. To counteract this threat, the provincial government considered droping taxes by seventy-five cents per pack. Non-Canadian demand for cigarettes has resulted in increased exports, with approximately 90 percent of those cigarettes redirected back to the motherland. Montreal and Toronto are flooded with contraband from Cornwall, the major drop-off for cigarettes transported from the Akwasasne Mohawk reserve located on U.S. soil. The goods are transported across the St. Lawrence River and sold at huge discounts in comparison to legally sold cigarettes.

341. L'Aimable, Guy. "Government Losing War against Black Market Cigarettes." *World Tobacco*, no. 138 (January 1994): 45–48.

For 1993, the Federation of Italian Tobacconists estimates that cigarette contraband sales amounted to 26,455,440 pounds, or 13 percent of total cigarette sales. Legal sales of cigarettes are impacted dramatically, especially in cities like Naples, where legal sales totaled only 4,339,507 pounds. Naples, Rome, and Milan are strongholds for contraband sales. Favorite black-market brands are the state-owned brand and Marlboro. Contraband cigarettes are funneled into the market through duty-free shops and from Eastern Europe.

342. Kondro, Wayne. "Cuts in Canadian Tobacco Taxes." *Lancet* 343 (February 19, 1994): 470.

Canadian prime minister Jean Chretien's ruling Liberal Party lowered federal cigarette taxes in a move to reduce smuggling and battle a "breakdown in respect for the law." This is expected to decrease federal tobacco revenues by approximately $450 million. Across Canada, governments are losing about $500 million a year to smugglers. Quebec is experiencing losses from 60 to 70 percent of sales. New Brunswick lowered taxes by seven dollars a carton in an effort to reduce the $50 million lost per year to smugglers. The Ottawa government is also imposing an export tax of eight dollars per carton and an increase from 21 percent to 30 percent in the income-tax rate on tobacco manufacturing profits. This is expected to raise an additional $200 million.

343. Came, Barry. "Inside 'the Trade.'" *Maclean's* 107, no. 8 (February 21, 1994): 18–20.

Straddling Quebec, Ontario, and New York State, the Akwasasne Mohawk reserve accounts for about 70 percent of all smuggled cigarettes into Canada. The smuggled product originates in Canada, with the bulk of it manufactured in Montreal. Distributors in Buffalo and surrounding cities receive the product and sell it to Mohawk distributors on the American side of the reserve. Most of these distributors sell only to Akwasasne natives or Kanesatake (Oka, Quebec) and Kahnawake (Montreal) Mohawk natives. About 1,400 Kahnawake residents are connected directly or indirectly to the smuggling. The reserve is also well known for its "Tobacco Alley," a phalanx of stands selling discounted cigarettes. Overall, in 1993 smuggling generated $5 billion in revenues and approximately $300 million in profits.

344. Wilson-Smith, Anthony. "Pack of Trouble." *Maclean's* 107, no. 8 (February 21, 1994): 10–13.

Prime Minister Jean Chretien's administration has lowered taxes by five dollars a carton with a pledge to match up to ten-dollar-per-carton reductions imposed by each province. Carton prices in Quebec tumbled from forty-seven to twenty-three dollars; New Brunswick prices dropped from forty-nine dollars a carton to thirty. The federal government's prime motive in lowering taxes is to contain cigarette smuggling. Some officials fear that smuggling between the borders of the United States and Canada will escalate across borders between provinces that lower their taxes and those that choose not to do so. The Royal Canadian Mounted Police has announced an increase to nearly eight hundred the number of people working on tobacco smuggling. Customs Canada will add $45 million and an additional 350 officials to increase surveillance of the U.S.-Canadian border.

345. "Kreteks Threaten." *Tobacco Reporter* 121, no. 6 (June 1994): 22, 24.

In Malaysia, clove-laced contraband kretek cigarettes are eroding the market share of locally produced cigarettes. The contraband is accounting for almost the entire 17 percent share devoured by black-market cigarettes. Excise tax hikes in 1993 helped catapult sales of contraband kreteks.

346. Lindquist, Avey, Macdonald, Baskerville, Inc. *Cigarette Smuggling in the United States*. Philadelphia: The Firm, August 15, 1994. Bates 2072007294/7348. legacy.library.ucsf.edu/tid/kvb08d00 (accessed March 8, 2004).

This report analyzes global cigarette smuggling. The Firm, which provides economic damage analysis and forensic accounting services, concludes that cigarette smuggling activities face few obstacles, provide opportunities for abundant profits, and offer an easy entry for organized crime. Increases in taxes will lead to increasing smuggling activities and tremendous losses in federal, state, and local tax revenues. It is estimated that in 1994, 6 percent of total U.S. cigarette consumption escaped taxation and resulted in lost revenues of up to $345 million in federal taxes and $645 million in state taxes for California, Illinois, New Jersey, New York, and Washington.

347. Philip Morris. "How Smugglers Operate: California." August 1994. Bates 2072006921. legacy.library.ucsf.edu/tid/rdc08d00 (accessed March 8, 1994).

In California, state revenue losses from smuggling are estimated to range from $40 million to as much as, or more than, $100 million a year. One example is duty-free cigarettes off-loaded from ships or freighters and sold. "Mules," or couriers, are used in the state to transport cigarettes. In San Diego, drivers drop off smuggled cigarettes at "stash" houses (storage facilities). The cigarettes make their way back to Los Angeles and are sold for major profits. Buses are also used to carry smuggled cigarettes via luggage or cardboard boxes.

348. Barford, Michael F. "Targeting the Cigarette Smugglers." *Tobacco Journal International*, no. 5 (September/October 1994): 54–56.

It is estimated that cigarette smuggling cost governments $3.5 billion in revenues in 1992. The Italian government is attempting to choke off smuggling by implementing stringent new regulations and asking foreign manufacturers to monitor their distribution lines. Authorities can correlate the coded case markings with the manufacturers' sales records. Unfortunately, this trail is weak and stops with the wholesaler. Efforts to counteract smuggling are seen as "antisocial" in Naples, where trafficking in contraband cigarettes is a way of life.

349. Nicholson, Marjorie. *Smuggler's Charter: A Study of How High Tobacco Taxation around the World Increases Crime*. November 1994. forest-on-smoking.org.uk/publics/smuggpt1.htm (accessed April 26, 2000; site discontinued but available through www.archive.org).

The author analyzes the global effects of high tobacco taxes, with an emphasis on unintended consequences. The report is divided into five parts. Part 1 looks at the politics and economics of taxation. This includes a look at the Single European Act and the justification for tobacco taxes. Part 2 analyzes the Canadian government's efforts to increase tobacco taxes and to ban tobacco advertising. Part 3 highlights the effects of smuggling on the United Kingdom. Part 4 examines the global effects of smuggling and its future prospects, analyzing Europe, the United States, the Middle East, Southeast Asia, and the Indian subcontinent. The final part analyses the consequences of smuggling. The emphasis is on antismuggling measures in Britain, the effects of penalizing tobacco companies, and implications for civil liberties.

350. Sweanor, David, and Luc R. Martial. *The Smuggling of Tobacco Products: Lessons from Canada*. Ottawa: Non-Smokers' Rights Association, 1994.

Canadian cigarette taxes enacted between 1982 and 1992 created a hefty governmental revenue stream and reduced teenage smoking. Starting in 1993, cigarettes priced approximately $2.50 lower in the United States stoked a major increase in cigarette smuggling across the Canadian border, mainly through Quebec and Ontario. Tobacco industry activities (e.g., changes in exporting routes and cigarette packaging designed to match domestic brands) and the inability of law enforcement to thwart smuggling combined to make smuggling a major problem. In 1994, the Canadian government recognized the problem, lowered federal cigarette taxes, and agreed to match (up to a Canadian dollar per pack) the lowering of taxes by each province.

351. Stamler, R. *Plain Packaging: Its Impact on the Contraband Tobacco Market*. Lindquist, Avey, Macdonald, Baskerville. February 1995. Bates 2064807230/7250. legacy.library.ucsf.edu/tid/nxl93c00 (accessed March 8, 2004).

The introduction of plain cigarette packaging in Canada could lead to an increased presence by organized crime. Copycat brands would proliferate and become a profitable business. Plain packaging would significantly reduce packaging costs for counterfeits, erase trademark protection, create opportunities for counterfeiters to manufacture their own cigarettes, and jeopardize the integrity of brand names.

352. Joossens, Luk, and Martin Raw. "Smuggling and Cross Border Shopping of Tobacco in Europe." *British Medical Journal* 310 (May 27, 1995): 1393–97.

    The tobacco industry argues that the European Union's lifting of border patrols will lead to an increase in cigarettes smuggled from low-tax to high-tax countries. This will accompany a rise in personal consumption of tobacco products due to cross-border shopping. Thus, the industry opposes any increases in tobacco taxes. The authors counter this argument by stating that increases in cigarette taxes should be continued to combat smoking and that southern Europe is greatly affected by the sale of smuggled "international" cigarettes flowing into the region from northern Europe.

353. Shuqi, Wei, and Zou Jing. "The Current Situation of Cigarette Smuggling, Its Harm and China's Policy Responses." *Sino-World Tobacco* 30, no. 4 (December 31, 1995): 19, 22, 24–26.

    Rampant nationwide cigarette smuggling is forcing national and local government officials to implement stricter controls and enforcement of antismuggling laws. Smuggling is a major problem in coastal areas, such as Guandong, Fujian, Weihai, Dalian, and Tanggu. Each box of smuggled foreign cigarettes can yield a profit of 1,000 yuan. State coffers are deprived of approximately 1 billion yuan in customs tariffs each year.

354. Flint, Anthony. "Cigarette Firms Condemn Smuggling, Gain from It." *Boston Globe*, June 10, 1996: 1, 10.

    Cigarette smuggling has blossomed into a worldwide epidemic. Smuggled cigarettes enable tobacco companies to establish markets in countries where import tariffs are exorbitant, distribution is controlled, and state-run monopolies control the market. The World Health Organization estimates that approximately three hundred billion cigarettes exported around the globe cannot be traced to their final destinations. Eventually, the contraband market is the final destination for these cigarettes. Tobacco companies claim to have no control over cigarettes' final destination but that they take every measure to combat smuggling.

355. Wenbo, Liu. "The Chinese Government Steps Up Efforts to Crack Down on Producing and Selling Fake Cigarettes." *Sino-World Tobacco* 32, no. 2 (June 30, 1996): 30, 32.

    During spring 1996, local and national Chinese authorities initiated a campaign to combat the producing and selling of fake cigarettes. In March and April, authorities from the cities of Beijing, Tianjin, Hebei, Zhejiang, Hunan, Fujian, Guangxi, and Shanxi reported confiscating and destroying 1.60919 billion illegal cigarettes. Efforts are being concentrated on the epicenter for illegal trade, Hexian County, Guangxi, and on eliminating such activity.

356. Smith, Craig. "Smugglers Stoke B.A.T.'s Cigarette Sales in China." *Wall Street Journal*, December 18, 1996: A14.

Smuggling of cigarettes throughout Southeast Asia, and especially in China, is providing profits for the tobacco companies. Though the China National Tobacco Corporation (CNTC) is the country's only authorized importer and import duties equal about 244 percent, smuggling costs the Chinese government nearly a billion dollars yearly in lost revenues. British American Tobacco is a major beneficiary of both legal and illegal cigarette transactions. In 1995, the company is reported to have total sales of 407 billion cigarettes to the CNTC, duty-free shops, and special economic zones; $38 billion in additional sales relate to smuggling activities. In Southeast Asia, the company ships product "in bond" (duty-free) to warehouses in Singapore, Hong Kong, and the Philippines from plants located in Asia and the West. It is sold to various distributors, who allegedly smuggle the product into China. Cigarettes are also smuggled into China through truck-sized metal containers and hollow aluminum doors. The cost differential between what dealers pay for a case of cigarettes and what would be paid (cost plus duty) for importing the product is quite substantial.

357. Fleenor, Patrick. *The Effect of Excise Tax Differentials on the Interstate Smuggling and Cross-Border Sales of Cigarettes in the United States.* Washington, D.C.: Tax Foundation, 1996.

This report examines the growing national problem of cigarette smuggling and the impact upon state revenue flows. State and local governments increase cigarette excise taxes to raise additional revenues and to regulate social behavior. Consumers generally react by changing their consumption patterns. Price disparities among the states have led to increases in illegal cigarette activities. In cross-border shopping, including across the U.S.-Canadian border, consumers buy in states with lower cigarette excise taxes. Also, consumers purchase cigarettes in low-tax states (e.g., Kentucky, North Carolina, and Virginia) and sell them illegally in high-tax states. Cigarettes not subject to federal, state, and local taxes are sold on Native American reservations and military bases. The report concludes that legislators need to be more aware of the intended and unintended effects of raising cigarette excise taxes.

358. European Community. Committee of Inquiry into the Community Transit System. *Report on the Community Transit System.* February 20, 1997. www.europarl.eu.int/hearings/kelletta/default_en.htm (accessed September 28, 2004).

Chapter 6, "The Illicit Trade in Cigarettes," reviews the impact of cigarette smuggling. Smugglers benefit handsomely from exploiting price and tax differentials between various European countries. Contraband "market share" consumes hefty shares of illegal sales in such countries as Austria, Germany, and Italy. Smugglers transform in-place transit systems into tools for distributing cigarettes elsewhere in the world. Ports like Antwerp and Rotterdam are conduits for smuggled cigarettes. Suspected perpetrators include criminal organizations and established local distribution networks. Though cigarette manufacturers have not been linked to cigarette smuggling, the companies could take a more active and cooperative role when working with law-enforcement agencies.

359. Knight, Patrick. "Smuggled Cigarettes Take a Quarter Share." *World Tobacco*, no. 157 (March 1997): 38, 40.

Cigarette sales and consumption in Brazil are moving in opposite directions, due in part to cigarette smuggling. It is estimated that 25 percent of cigarette consumption is of smuggled cigarettes. Another factor is the state-imposed 70 percent total tax incident on cigarettes. In absolute terms, this is 50 percent higher than in Paraguay. Surinam and surrounding countries are launching pads from which the Amazon region is flooded with illegal cigarettes. Many cigarettes legally imported into the country are smuggled back into Brazil.

360. Williams, Bob. "Bootleg Cigarettes Heading North." *News & Observer*, June 1, 1997. LexisNexis Academic (accessed June 21, 2004).

Michigan's very high cigarette excise tax rate and the fact that it does not require tax stamps on cigarette packages make it a favorite target for smuggling, or "buttlegging," of cigarettes from other states not requiring cigarette tax stamps (e.g., North and South Carolina). North Carolina is a favorite launching pad for smuggled cigarettes. Michigan estimates that smuggled cigarettes cost it $300 million in annual sales and $140 million in uncollected taxes.

361. Bonner, Raymond, and Christopher Drew. "Cigarette Makers Are Seen as Aiding Rise in Smuggling." *New York Times*, August 25, 1997: A1, C12.

According to the research firm Market Tracking International, Ltd., the worldwide traffic in smuggled cigarettes rose from 100 billion (1989) to an estimated 280 billion, accounting for approximately 28 percent of the global cigarette production. Law enforcement officials and insiders claim the tobacco industry knowingly conducts business with dealers and traders who are mere conduits into the black market. In one major case, Spanish authorities seized the cargo ship *Wendy I.*, which carried sixteen thousand cases (160,000 cigarettes) of Winston cigarettes manufactured in the United States by R. J. Reynolds. The cargo ship had originally sailed from Antwerp, Belgium, which is described as a major hub for the distribution, both legal and illegal, of American-made cigarettes. Also, ships visiting the Spanish coastline stop beyond the twelve-mile territorial limit to off-load cigarette cargo to other transportation vessels; the cigarettes find their way into Spain.

362. Bonner, Raymond. "2 Cases Shed Light on Cigarette Smuggling in Italy." *New York Times*, September 2, 1997: C13.

Two cigarette smuggling cases highlight the impact of contraband cigarettes in Italy, which accounts for nearly 25 percent of all cigarettes sold. In one case, a "Mafia-like association" is charged with buying extremely large amounts from tobacco companies and then exerting pressure on the companies not to conduct business with any other criminal organizations. In the second case, in Belgium, Augusto Arcellaschi is charged with smuggling Marlboros into Italy through Switzerland. The product was allegedly received from Antwerp, Belgium. European law authorities regard Arcellaschi as a major figure in smuggling cigarettes within Europe.

363. Bonner, Raymond. "Rival Asserts Philip Morris Smuggles in South Africa." *New York Times*, November 22, 1997: D2.

In a suit filed against Philip Morris, South Africa's Rembrandt Group, Ltd. alleges that the American cigarette giant is actively involved in helping smugglers move product into the country from neighboring countries. Rembrandt alleges that Philip Morris is violating a 1981 agreement assigning Rembrandt the exclusive right to manufacture and distribute Marlboros. Philip Morris claims that the parties never came to a final agreement on the terms and that therefore the contract is void.

364. Rigby, Leslie. "Tobacco's Growing Gray Market." *Distribution Channels* 52, no. 1 (January/February 1998): 128, 131.

Gray market cigarettes are "export only" products, taxed and priced at lower rates, that do not produce the same paper audit trail as domestically produced cigarettes. Many cigarettes never even leave port for export but are redirected for distribution in the United States. Diverted shipments can also enter the United States through ports, customs-bonded warehouses, and foreign trade zones. Though tobacco manufacturers prohibit their distributors from marketing these cigarettes, international brokers offer their services to sell them at prices lower than domestic cigarettes. Law enforcement of these cigarettes is a major hurdle facing California and Florida.

365. Coleman, Tim. "Stuck in the Middle." *Tobacco International* 200, no. 3 (March 1998): 26–28.

The combination of rising tobacco taxes and smuggling is creating havoc for the United Kingdom. In 1996, tobacco products generated £8,063 million of revenue for the government. However, cigarettes alone accounted for £135 million in lost excise tax revenues due to smuggling activities. The London-based Tobacco Manufacturers' Association identifies the lifting of border controls tied to the European Single Market as one of the causes in increased smuggling. Sources identify smuggled cigarettes as coming from Andorra, Eastern Europe, Africa, the Canary Islands, and Belgium. Belgium is considered a major source of "bootlegged" product (tax-paid cigarettes sold elsewhere at a profit).

366. Ahmad, S. M. "Pakistan: A Heaven for Counterfeiters." *Tobacco Journal International*, no. 2 (March/April 1998): 75.

Smuggling of counterfeit national and international brands is rampant throughout Pakistan. Illegal smokes are manufactured in the northern and northwestern regions of the country. These operations are quite mobile and are able to evade the customs authorities. During the Soviet occupation of Afghanistan, counterfeit operations appeared in areas close to the Pakistani border. Estimates are that over four hundred million cigarettes evade taxation every year. This equates to a loss of governmental revenue of 420 million rupees and a loss in sales to manufacturers of 730 million rupees.

367. McIvor, Greg. "Sweden Cuts Taxes on Tobacco to Curb Growth of Smuggling." *Financial Times*, April 15, 1998: 24.

In an effort to curb smuggling from Eastern Europe, the Swedish government reduced cigarette excise taxes by 27 percent and abolished indexing tobacco prices to inflation. The tax cut was effective August 1, 1998. This made the price of Swedish cigarettes nearly equal to those of cigarettes sold in Denmark but still much higher than in Germany and other European Union countries.

368. U.S. General Accounting Office. *Cigarette Smuggling: Information on Interstate and U.S.-Canadian Activity*. GAO/T-RCED-98-182. May 4, 1998. Washington, D.C.: GAO, 1998. www.gao.gov/archive/1998/rc98182t.pdf (accessed June 21, 2004).

The General Accounting Office reviews the interrelationship between global cigarette smuggling activities and the proposed national tobacco settlement. The report addresses the reemergence of interstate smuggling from high-excise-tax states (e.g., Massachusetts and Washington) to lower-excise-tax states (like Kentucky and Virginia). Increases in international smuggling have attracted the attention of organized crime. Smuggling between Canada and the United States has increased dramatically due to the sharp increases in Canadian federal and provincial cigarette taxes. A study conducted by the Washington State Department of Health, published in January 1997, estimated that interstate smuggling costs the states of Massachusetts and Washington $52 million and $61 million annually, respectively.

369. White, David. "Kicking the Smuggling Habit Proves Costly for Andorra." *Financial Times*, May 5, 1998: 5.

Under pressure from the European Union (EU), the country of Andorra has begun monitoring the movement of cigarettes imported for wholesale and also manufactured within the country. Cigarettes transported throughout the country and into the EU black market are estimated at hundreds of millions of dollars' worth annually. Most of this product is smuggled through neighboring Spain. Smuggled product from Andorra is estimated to cost the Spanish government $180 million each year.

370. Bonner, Raymond. "Europe Turning to U.S. to Fight Illicit Cigarettes." *New York Times*, May 8, 1998: A1, A8.

In an effort to combat rising cigarette smuggling, the European Union (EU) will request help from the U.S. government. In current cases being investigated by the United States, the EU will request the names of international customers of the tobacco companies, especially the customers of the R. J. Reynolds Tobacco Company (RJR). This comes in the face of two recently celebrated seizures of tobacco cargo intended for the European black market. One case involved eighty million Winstons seized by Spanish customs authorities in Barcelona. The ship's cargo included seven long-haul trucks filled with Winston cigarettes. The second case involved the seizure by Spanish authorities of the *Sea Princess* and its cargo of 120 million Winston cigarettes. The ship's captain was longtime RJR customer Michael Hanggi, a major European trader involved in supplying smugglers with contraband RJR cigarettes. For 1997, European governments estimate that cigarettes smuggling cost them $1.5 billion in revenues.

371. Bartlett, Bruce. "Tobacco Smuggling: A Tax-Driven Problem." *Tax Notes* 79, no. 11 (June 15, 1998): 1501–10.

Governments around the world have increased cigarette taxes to raise revenues and persuade citizens not to smoke. This has led to wide tax disparities among countries and to increased trade in smuggling. Individuals and organized crime are involved in the operations that cost governments millions in revenues. In 1995, Great Britain experienced an estimated loss of $600 million in revenues from the sale of illegal cigarettes. In 1996, it is estimated that European governments lost $4.2 billion due to cigarette smuggling. Canada suffered huge losses due, in part, to large exports of cigarettes to the United States, which smugglers hauled back into the country. Other documented cases involve Malaysia, Paraguay, and South Africa.

372. "Hong Kong's Cigarette Trade Crashes." *World Tobacco*, no. 165 (July 1998): 15–16.

Hong Kong government officials are using computers, foreign government contacts, and paid informants to track the flow of cigarettes into the country and to combat smuggling. The government pays a bounty for information leading to the capture of smugglers or the sale of smuggled cigarettes. Bounty hunters are paid ten thousand dollars (HK) when between 500,000 and 1 million smuggled cigarettes are captured. For 2 million or more captured smuggled cigarettes, the bounty hunter is paid $50,000 (HK). In 1997, the authorities recovered smuggled cigarettes worth $12 million (HK) in customs revenues.

373. Brown, Richard. "Europe Seeks US Help to Combat Smuggling." *World Tobacco*, no. 165 (July 1998): 17–18.

The European Union (EU) is a major global target for smuggled U.S. cigarettes. To combat this trend, the European Commission's antifraud unit, Unité de Coordination de la Lutte Anti Fraude (UCLAF), is invoking a U.S.-EU treaty. Under the treaty, the U.S. would provide the names of initial tobacco buyers; the EU officials would use this information to combat contraband sales. One tool used for contraband sales is the "transit system," where imported goods, intending to be shipped to non-EU countries, are allowed to enter the EU duty-free. When leaving the EU, the transit form is to be stamped. Instead, cigarettes never make it to the crossing but are diverted and sold, duty-free, within the EU. It is estimated that smuggled cigarettes cost retailers 900 million (European Currency Unit) a year in legitimately earned profits.

374. Joossens, Luk, and Martin Raw. "Cigarette Smuggling in Europe: Who Really Benefits?" *Tobacco Control* 7, no. 1 (Spring 1998): 66–71.

In 1996, even after accounting for cigarettes sold in duty-free venues, the difference between global exports and imports equaled 36 percent of worldwide production. The thinking is that the difference is smuggled around the world and sold below market prices. In 1996, Philip Morris, R. J. Reynolds, and British American Tobacco products manufactured in the United States and Brazil accounted for 100,000 million cigarettes, valued at $14,000 million, shipped to the Antwerp, Belgium, warehousing facilities. In Europe, Antwerp serves as a major hub for the flow of smuggled ("in transit") cigarettes into third world countries.

375. Farah, Douglas. "In Colombia, Marlboro Country Is Smugglers' Haven." *Washington Post*, August 30, 1998: A23.

The Colombian government's Ministry of Foreign Trade issued a report about the country's contraband cigarette trade. The report noted that contraband Marlboros entered the country through the free trade zones of Aruba and Panama. Only about 20 percent of Marlboro sales are directly traced back to Philip Morris's Colombian manufacturing plant. Each year, thirty billion cigarettes are sold in the country. Over nineteen billion are contraband, eight billion are produced in the country, and three billion are imports. Contraband accounted for $700 million of the $1.02 billion cigarette sales market.

376. Schwartz, John, and Saundra Torry. "Tobacco Affiliate Pleads Guilty to Role in Smuggling Scheme." *Washington Post*, December 23, 1998: A2.

    In a case filed in the Northern District of New York, Northern Brands pleaded guilty to participating in a smuggling scheme designed to evade both American and Canadian cigarette excise taxes. U.S. authorities charged that two American import companies, Baltic Imports and LBL Importing, Inc., received twenty-six loads of Export A cigarettes from Northern Brands. Both companies declared that the shipments would be exported out of the United States. This allowed the imported product to sidestep U.S. excise taxes. Rather than being exporting, the cigarettes were channeled back into Canada via the St. Regis Mohawk Indian Reservation and eventually onto the black market.

377. Hwang, Suein L. "As Cigarette Prices Soar, a Gray Market Booms." *Wall Street Journal*, January 28, 1999: B1, B14.

    "Diverted," or gray market, cigarettes are intended for export to other nations. The cigarettes carry label warnings, packaging, and have formulations different from products sold in the United States. With prices increasing over 50 percent due to the national tobacco settlement, gray-market cigarettes are becoming an increasing presence in U.S. retail stores and through Internet shops. California-based discount store chain Cigarettes Cheaper! discounts gray-market cartons of Winstons by 20 percent. Cigarette distributors are voicing concerns that the industry is not doing enough to combat the problem. The industry counters that the practice occurs without its consent and that gray-market cigarette sales damage their major brands and customer loyalty.

378. FIA International Research, Ltd. *The Gray Market in Cigarettes in the United States: A Primer*. August 1999. Bates 158215823/5850. legacy.library.ucsf.edu/tid/kzv11c00 (accessed August 2, 2004).

    This document describes the burgeoning "gray market" of cigarette distribution and its financial consequences. The gray market consists of "America-made cigarettes intended for export but which are re-imported into the U.S." Distribution channels do not face the same regulatory controls and lack the same paper trails of the domestic cigarette distribution channels. This opens the door for infiltration by organized crime. Also, this market is influenced by state tax increases and a substantial price differential per carton in favor of international wholesalers. Florida and California are prime markets for "gray cigarettes." Other states affected include Texas, New York, Kentucky, and Michigan.

379. FIA International Research, Ltd. *Organized Crime and the Smuggling of Cigarettes in the United States: The 1999 Update*. August 1999. Bates 207006797/6883. legacy.library.ucsf.edu/tid/ucc08d00 (accessed August 2, 2004).

    This document provides a detailed review of cigarette smuggling activities in the United States. This includes a look at current activities, its consequences, the international cigarette market, the gray market in cigarettes, and details of smuggling activities in states such as California, New York, and Michigan. In 1998, 84.5 million packages represented internationally smuggled cigarettes consumed in the United States. Also, 45.5 million packages represented interstate smuggled cigarettes consumed in the United States. International cigarette smuggling is an enticing and profitable target for organized crime in such countries as Italy and China.

380. Segal, David. "Canada Sues Tobacco Giant." *Washington Post*, December 22, 1999: A7.

The government of Canada filed a billion-dollar lawsuit in federal court in Syracuse, New York, against R. J. Reynolds. The company is accused of using shell companies, trucks, boats, and snowmobiles to smuggle cigarettes into the country and avoid paying excise taxes. The Canadian government accuses the company of ferrying cigarettes across the U.S.-Canadian St. Regis Akwesasne Indian Reservation. This is the first lawsuit of its kind to try to recover lost tobacco revenues.

381. Beelman, Maud S., Duncan Campbell, Maria Teresa Ronderos, and Erik J. Schelzig. *Major Tobacco Multinational Implicated in Cigarette Smuggling, Tax Evasion, Documents Show*. Part 1. International Consortium of Investigative Journalists, Center for Public Integrity. January 31, 2000. www.public-i.org (accessed August 2, 2004).

The International Consortium of Investigative Journalists (ICIJ) has conducted a six-month investigation into the global smuggling activities of British American Tobacco (BAT). The ICIJ reviewed approximately eleven thousand company documents (out of eight million), selected by region and subject matter, covering the years 1990–1995. Overall, the investigators concluded that top-ranking BAT executives incorporated smuggling into their global strategy, used smuggling to increase market share, and controlled the distribution pipeline from manufacturing to final markets. In their documents, BAT used euphemisms such as "duty not paid" (most commonly used), "parallel market," and "second channel" to disguise their activities. The report focuses on smuggling activities particularly in Brazil, Colombia, and Venezuela.

382. Beelman, Maude S., Duncan Campbell, Maria Teresa Ronderos, and Erik J. Schelzig. *Global Reach of Tobacco Company's Involvement in Cigarette Smuggling Exposed in Company Papers*. Part 2. International Consortium of Investigative Journalists, Center for Public Integrity. February 2, 2000. www.publici.org (accessed August 2, 2004).

This is the second part of the International Consortium of Investigative Journalists (ICIJ) investigation into the global smuggling activities of British American Tobacco (BAT). This report focuses on Asia and the Third World, with special emphasis on Vietnam. Documents reviewed cover the years 1990–1994. In Asia, BAT predominantly referred to its smuggling activities as "GT," meaning "General Trade." One marketing plan by the company's UK and Export Ltd. subsidiary categorized markets as "domestic," "duty free," and "General Trade (GT);" it also noted that over 25 percent of its British cigarette production is destined for the GT market. Singapura United Trading, Ltd., in Singapore, served as one of BAT's major Asian distribution centers and sold cigarettes to other distributors or wholesalers. The company handled duty-free, duty-paid (legal), and general trade cigarettes.

383. DTZ Pieda Consulting. *The Black Market in Tobacco Products*. May 2000. London: DTZ Pieda Consulting, 2000. tma.pr24x7.com/index.php?MRM_pmid=66# (accessed September 28, 2004).

Prepared for the Tobacco Manufacturers' Association (United Kingdom), this report emphasizes the negative impact of black market cigarettes and hand-rolling tobacco on manufacturers, retailers, and the government. The black market for these products reaches a wide segment of the British population, especially among the unemployed and lone-parent households, and creates higher crime rates. British cigarette prices dwarf those charged in other European Union (EU) member states. In 1999, the government estimates, black market tobacco sales cost £2.5 billion; smugglers are estimated to obtain a profit of £500 million annually. Policy remedies recommended to address these problems include reducing British tobacco taxes vis-à-vis other EU nations and stiffening the penalties for tobacco smuggling.

384. Drozdiak, William. "European Union Sues Philip Morris, R. J. Reynolds." *Washington Post*, November 7, 2000: A9.

The European Union's (EU) executive commission is suing Philip Morris and R. J. Reynolds for activities related to smuggling cigarettes in the European Union. The EU filed the suit in New York's U.S. District Court. The suit seeks to recover three times the estimated annual $1.7 billion lost customs duties and sales taxes due to smuggling. This is the European Union's first attempt to use the U.S. courts to seek damages against American companies.

385. Alliance Against Contraband. *Smuggling, Counterfeiting and Piracy: The Rising Tide of Contraband and Organised Crime in Europe*. January 2001. Bates 525921715/1775. legacy.library.ucsf.edu/tid/pts60d00 (accessed March 8, 2004).

Six product categories, including pharmaceuticals, music, and cigarettes, are analyzed for the economic impact and contraband activities of organized crime. Section 5 describes the European contraband cigarette market. Contraband cigarette activities are most prevalent in Italy, Britain, Germany, and Spain. Major routes used for transporting contraband cigarettes are through the Balkans into Europe, Germany via Eastern Europe, Britain via the Baltics, and Spain via northern Europe.

386. Forster, Nikolaus, and Sead Husic. "Investigators Probe Montenegro's Role at Centre of Illegal Cigarette Trade." *Financial Times*, August 10, 2001: 7.

A Yugoslavian trade embargo imposed by the United Nations served as the impetus for a dramatic increase in smuggling across the Balkans and into Europe. At the heart of the activities is Montenegro, which serves as the "capital" for cigarette smuggling. Cigarettes flowed into Montenegro through various offshore companies. It is estimated that tax revenue losses over the last two years cost the European Union nearly £2.5 billion. Philip Morris, R. J. Reynolds, and British American Tobacco manufactured the cigarettes.

387. World Health Organization. *Coveting Iran: The Infiltration and Exploitation of Iran by Global Cigarette Companies*. September 2001. www.emro.who.int/TFI/ IranReport.doc (accessed January 19, 2004).

Documents supplied by Philip Morris, R. J. Reynolds (RJR), and British American Tobacco in a lawsuit by the state of Minnesota against the industry are used to paint a picture of smuggling operations into and out of the Islamic Republic of Iran. Iran is viewed as a major market up for grabs, with transit (i.e., smuggled cigarette) trade ranging between 62 and 68 percent of the market. RJR viewed the Iranian market as "numerous and promising"; documents indicate smuggling is integral to the company's success in the country. Smuggling routes run from Dubai into the southern ports of Iran, from Cyprus through Turkey into Iran, and possibly Kish Island. Tobacco companies refer to "umbrella operations" using legal tax-free and imported cigarette sales to mask transit operations.

388. Günther, Ernst. "The Catch of the Day." *Tobacco Journal International*, no. 2 (March/April 2002): 78, 80.

On January 29, 2002, the Hamburg (Germany) police busted an international cigarette smuggling ring comprising individuals from countries Russia, Latvia, Poland, France, and Britain. The authorities confiscated 198 million untaxed cigarettes and approximately $6 million (in euros) cash. Of the sixty-eight people taken into custody, some held jobs as public employees and haulers.

389. Schapiro, Mark. "Big Tobacco: Uncovering the Industry's Multibillion-Dollar Global Smuggling Network." *Nation* 274, no. 17 (May 6, 2002): 11–13, 15–20.

The Nation, the Center for Investigative Reporting, and the PBS newsmagazine show *NOW with Bill Moyers* have completed a six-month investigation into the international smuggling operations of the tobacco industry. The author describes how the industry smuggled cigarettes into Columbia via the free trade zones of Panama and Aruba, the port of Portette, and the town of Maicao. The author also describes how the tobacco industry used political connections to water down the definition of money laundering in the Patriot Act, which President Bush signed on October 26, 2001. The watered-down language denied foreign countries and other plaintiffs legal standing in cases involving smuggling and money-laundering charges.

390. Stecklow, Steve, and Alix M. Freedman. "Despite Restraints, Iraq Gets Winstons; Who's to Blame?" *Wall Street Journal*, October 30, 2002: A1, A13.

U.S. and European Union legal authorities are investigating R. J. Reynolds Tobacco International and Japan Tobacco about both companies' possible involvement in the appearance of billions of Winston cigarettes in Iraq. Any direct or indirect marketing of cigarettes in Iraq must be approved by the U.S. government (for cigarettes produced in the United States) and also abide by United Nations sanctions. Cigarettes flooded into Iraq during the 1991 Persian Gulf War and also, especially, from 1997 to 2001. The cigarettes allegedly flowed into Iraq through Cyprus and Turkey.

391. Levin, Myron. "Cigarettes, Greed and Betrayal: An Insider's Saga." *Los Angeles Times*, November 10, 2002: A1, A10–A11.

During the 1990s, Les Thompson worked for RJR-Macdonald, the Canadian subsidiary of R. J. Reynolds. According to this report, he assisted the company in its efforts to enter the contraband market and sidestep the high taxes exacted by the Canadian government. Reynolds's entrance into the contraband market netted it profits of over $100 million on revenues totaling more than $600 million. After serving a prison term of two years, Thompson is working with U.S. and European Union authorities in their investigations. The article reveals Thompson's role in the contraband operations.

392. Farah, Douglas. "R. J. Reynolds Accused of Money Laundering." *Washington Post*, November 14, 2002: A20.

In a lawsuit filed in the Eastern District of New York, the European Union has accused R. J. Reynolds Tobacco Holdings and its subsidiaries with using such devices as offshore tax havens and money laundering to smuggle cigarettes into countries like Iraq, Russia, and Colombia. Working with various criminal organizations, the companies accepted payments for cigarettes and, in return, had the organizations sell, and establish a demand for, the cigarettes. Also, the companies allegedly played "musical banks," using different banks to receive payments from the smugglers. Another alleged illegal activity involved selling cigarettes in Iraq despite U.S. and United Nations sanctions. The company allegedly used Cyprus as the main distribution point and falsified paperwork indicating the final destination as Russia instead of Iraq.

393. "Philip Morris Sues Retailers of Counterfeit Cigarettes." *NPN: National Petroleum News* 94, no. 13 (December 2002): 9.

Philip Morris USA is suing fifty-five retailers in California, Louisiana, New York, and Washington to stop sales of contraband cigarettes and from illegally using Philip Morris's trademarks. The illegal sales include counterfeit and illegally imported cigarettes. Philip Morris's brand integrity department is working to fight against these illegal sales.

394. Demirsar, Metin. "Suspicion of Smuggling." *Tobacco Journal International*, no. 1 (January/February 2003): 70–71.

A report appearing in the Turkish newspaper *Hürriyet* describes the smuggling activities of European Tobacco. The tobacco company has supposedly smuggled cigarettes into the country from its warehouse facilities in the Mersin Port Free Zone. The Turkish market for counterfeit or smuggled cigarettes is estimated to account for up to 5 percent (2.5–6 billion cigarettes) of annual cigarette consumption.

395. Campaign for Tobacco-Free Kids. *Illegal Pathways to Illegal Profits: The Big Cigarette Companies and International Smuggling*. February 28, 2003. University of California eScholarship Repository, the Center for Tobacco Control Research & Education, Reports on Industrial Activity, Paper TFK2. repositories.cdlib.org/tc/reports/TFK2 (accessed August 25, 2003).

Published reports and internal documents show that tobacco companies are actively involved in the global cigarette smuggling market. This articles provides a detailed analysis of company activity in Bangladesh and Cameroon (British American Tobacco), Colombia (Philip Morris), and Spain (R. J. Reynolds Tobacco). The analysis covers the stages of "strategic planning, manufacture and packing specifically for smuggling, setting quantities and prices for the contraband, overseeing shipping and route choices, assessing candidates for onward sale of the smuggled goods, and efforts to disguise the illegal activity." The Campaign for Tobacco-Free Kids offers recommendations for corralling global cigarette smuggling.

396. Levin, Myron. "1,500 Retailers Face Suits over Fake Smokes." *Los Angeles Times*, June 8, 2003: B3.

Philip Morris has filed trademark-infringement claims against 1,500 Los Angeles–area merchants for selling counterfeit Marlboro cigarettes. The district court case also includes charges against five import businesses for attempting to ship about forty-three million counterfeit Marlboros from South Korea and China. U.S. Customs recently seized these shipments. To this point, Philip Morris has filed lawsuits against 566 California retailers; another sixty lawsuits cover non-Californian retailers and distributors.

397. Levin, Myron. "Counterfeit Cigarettes Force Tobacco Firms to Fight Back." *Los Angeles Times*, November 24, 2003: A1, A21.

Counterfeit cigarettes, also known as "fakes" or "knockoffs," are estimated to total 200 billion annually and are causing headaches for both the tobacco industry and governments. Counterfeits rob governments of much needed tax revenues, perhaps $30 billion annually, and deny revenues to the tobacco manufacturers. Also, counterfeits could potentially strip companies of loyal customers should the smokes not be to their liking. Container ships are the prime means of moving counterfeits into the United States. About 425,000 packs, or 8.5 million cigarettes, can be stuffed into a forty-foot container. China is the global counterfeit kingpin. The tobacco industry and governments are working both separately and jointly to combat counterfeit cigarettes.

398. McKay, Michael A. "The Risks of Not Remembering." *World Tobacco*, no. 197 (November 2003): 70–71, 74.

Organized crime is playing an increasing role in the contraband and counterfeit cigarette trade. Organized crime takes sizeable revenues; the risks of being caught or penalized by governments are very low. Tax increases imposed by governments, by the Master Settlement Agreement, and through the Framework Convention on Tobacco Control are adding to the problem.

399. Paersch, Emily. "Proactive Measures Indispensable." *Tobacco Journal International*, no. 6 (December/January 2003): 99–100.

Strong measures must be undertaken to combat the global epidemic of cigarette counterfeiting. Governments and the public must be persuaded to become involved in the process. Companies must consider such countermeasures as hiring experts in the law enforcement field, undertaking forensic authentication, implementing digital watermarking, and performing "fingerprint" chemical analysis of tobacco.

400. Thompson, Frances. *Imperial Tobacco, Imasco, and the Smuggling of Cigarettes into Canada*. Non-Smokers' Rights Association, Smoking and Health Foundation, Toronto 2003. www.nsra-adnf.ca (accessed October 1, 2004).

Using company documents, the author makes a case for linking cigarette smuggling in Canada during the early 1990s with Imperial Tobacco, Imasco (the holding company for Imperial Tobacco), British American Tobacco, and also Philip Morris. One of the author's findings is that Imperial Tobacco reentered the "general trading" portion of the export market during 1993; in 1992, the company had tried unsuccessfully to get the Canadian government to repeal the cigarette export tax. During

1992, Imperial stopped supplying "smuggling channels," without any apparent effect on legitimate U.S. exports.

401. Thompson, Francis. *Rothmans, Benson & Hedges and the Smuggling of Cigarettes into Canada*. Non-Smokers' Rights Association, Smoking and Health Foundation, Toronto 2003. www.nsra-adnf.ca (accessed October 1, 2004).

    Using Philip Morris documents filed with the Securities and Exchange Commission, the author makes a case for linking cigarette smuggling in Canada during the early 1990s with activities undertaken between Philip Morris USA; Philip Morris International; Rothmans, Benson & Hedges (RBH); Rothmans International; and Tobacco Exporters International (TEI), a subsidiary of Rothmans International B.V. Shipments by RBH to the United States would be "destined for duty-free accounts with no verifiable U.S. retail sales." Faced with having to pay an export tax, Rothmans prepared an offshore cigarette manufacturing contingency plan to supply Canadian cigarettes to Philip Morris USA and TEI.

402. World Health Organization. *The Cigarette "Transit" Road to the Islamic Republic of Iran and Iraq: Illicit Tobacco Trade in the Middle East*. Cairo: WHO, 2003. www.emro.who.int/tfi/TFIiraniraq.pdf (accessed January 19, 2004).

    The report provides background information on the key elements of global tobacco smuggling, benefits accrued to the industry, and euphemisms used to disguise or camouflage tobacco smuggling. Information culled from such sources as articles published in tobacco periodicals, industry documents from British American Tobacco and Brown & Williamson, and lawsuits filed by the European Union describes the importance of establishing a foothold in the Islamic Republic of Iran and in Iraq. Also, the report points to the tobacco companies in identifying Iran as a smuggling distribution channel into other countries; the complicated distribution routes that have been created through such points as Valencia (Spain), Cyprus, and Beirut to move contraband into Iran and Iraq; and the industry's complicity in these activities.

403. Cienski, Jan. "Poland Marks New Frontier for Illegal Cigarette Trade." *Financial Times*, January 20, 2004: 9.

    Poland's northern and eastern borders became an enticing target for cigarette smuggling once the nation became a member of the European Union in May 2004. A lack of employment opportunities and tourist trade has helped to fuel the smuggling activities. "Ants," or small-time traders, conduct the Russian-Polish smuggling trade. Smugglers employ creative means of transporting contraband, such as filling tires with cigarettes and stuffing inaccessible door and engine spaces with cartons of cigarettes. Officials intercept only about 10 percent of contraband cigarettes.

404. "Cigarette Ring Stubbed Out, U.S. Says." *Los Angeles Times*, January 29, 2004: A21.

    U.S. federal agents have halted an El Paso–based cigarette smuggling ring and confiscated brand-name and counterfeit cigarettes valued at $18.1 million. The ring smuggled legally imported duty-free cigarettes from El Paso and Miami to New York and California. Also, the group shipped Chinese and Taiwanese counterfeit cigarettes into the country in containers marked "toys" or "plastic goods."

405. Levin, Myron. "Searching for Truth behind the Smoke." *Los Angeles Times*, February 15, 2004: C1, C4.

  In Eastern European markets, Japan Tobacco International is fighting a mysterious "JTI" company that is profiting from the shipment of counterfeit Monte Carlo cigarettes. The false "JTI" created three business names registered in Yugoslavia, obtained cigarettes from factories in such countries as Greece and Dubai, and Monte Carlo packaging from an Italian printer. Japan Tobacco International is also engaged in a fierce battle in Yugoslavia for ownership of the Monte Carlo trademark.

406. United Kingdom Department of Trade and Industry. "British American Tobacco." Press release, P/2004/118, March 26, 2004. www.dti.gov.uk (accessed June 7, 2004).

  The secretary of trade and industry, Patricia Hewitt, in a letter to Parliament, has announced that the department has dropped its investigation of smuggling allegations by British American Tobacco. No material evidence has been uncovered to justify a criminal investigation of the company.

407. Tobar, Hector, and Andres D'Alessandro. "A Counterfeit Industry Cheats Legitimate Trade." *Los Angeles Times*, April 4, 2004: A3.

  The Paraguayan government is fighting the production and distribution of counterfeit cigarettes within its borders and also to its neighbor Brazil. Local markets openly sell counterfeit products, including cigarettes. *Sacoleiros,* or bag carriers, use the Bridge of Friendship, which connects the countries, to smuggle cigarettes into Brazil. Due to the destructive counterfeit activities, British American Tobacco closed its Paraguayan cigarette factories. In 2002, approximately forty-eight billion counterfeit cigarettes sales occurred in Brazil.

408. U.S. General Accounting Office. *Cigarette Smuggling: Federal Law Enforcement Efforts and Seizures Increasing.* GAO-04-641. May 28, 2004. Washington, D.C.: GAO, 1998. www.gao.gov/new.items/d04641.pdf (accessed October 1, 2004).

  Cigarette smuggling siphons off federal and state excise-tax revenues, attracts criminal organizations (including terrorist groups), and poses a public health risk. Immigration and Customs Enforcement, Customs and Border Protection, and the Bureau of Alcohol, Tobacco, Firearms, and Explosives (ATF) are the main federal law enforcement agencies charged with fighting domestic and international cigarette smuggling, including the distribution of counterfeit cigarettes. Congressional legislation introduced to combat smuggling would give greater enforcement powers to the ATF.

409. "Belgium: Cigarette Case Settled." *New York Times*, July 10, 2004: C3.

  The European Union and Altria Group have settled all contraband lawsuits and civil litigation filed against Altria for alleging smuggling activities. Altria's Philip Morris International subsidiary will make thirteen payments over twelve years, for a total of $1.25 billion. Both parties will work to fight cigarette counterfeiting throughout the European Union.

410. "Tobacco Company Seeks Protection." *Los Angeles Times*, August 26, 2004: C3.

  Japan Tobacco's JTI-Macdonald Corporation filed for creditor protection after being slapped with a $1.05 billion tax bill by Revenue Quebec. Revenue Quebec claims the

Canadian subsidiary owes the money for cigarettes exported to the United States and then smuggled into the country during the 1990s. JTI-Macdonald made the move under the Companies' Creditors Arrangement Act to protect 40 percent of its national revenue.

MILITARY

411. Moore, Molly. "Cigarette Gift Has Some at Pentagon Fuming." *Washington Post*, October 5, 1990: A23.

    Free cigarettes donated by Philip Morris and R. J. Reynolds found way their to U.S. troops stationed in Saudi Arabia and serving in Operation Desert Shield. Approximately ten thousand cartons shipped from Pope Air Force Base (North Carolina) to the soldiers violated the Defense Department's four-year-old policy prohibiting distribution of such products "in promotional programs aimed primarily at military personnel."

412. Trueheart, Charles. "Magazines' Cover Blown." *Washington Post*, December 21, 1990: D1, D4.

    The Defense Logistics Agency halted a R. J. Reynolds donation of magazines to troops stationed in Saudi Arabia. The delay occurred because the magazine wrappers promoted Camel cigarettes and lacked the required military tobacco disclaimer, which reads "This [form of media] does not express or imply an endorsement of the sponsor or its products or services by the U.S. Army or any other part of the federal government nor has it been paid for or sponsored by the U.S. Army or any part of the federal government." The disclaimer was then hand-stamped on each magazine cover.

413. Shen, Fern. "The Military Courts a New Kind of Ally." *Washington Post*, May 27, 1991: B3.

    A 1988 Department of Defense policy allows the military to review unsolicited proposals from tobacco and alcohol companies to sponsor recreational activities. Activities include picnics, musical shows, fairs, and antidrug rallies. Sponsors may use advertising tools such as banners and T-shirts; a disclaimer must accompany each advertisement that the government does not endorse the company's products expressly or implicitly. R. J. Reynolds served as a sponsor at a Fort Bragg (North Carolina) Fair. Tobacco companies are not permitted to distribute free cigarettes.

414. Fontanez, Jose. "Marlboro Music 1993 Military Tour." June 25, 1993. Bates 2041952940/2941. legacy.library.ucsf.edu/tid/ezj52e00 (accessed March 8, 2004).

    The Marlboro Music tour has had an impact on military and military cigarette sales. The Morale, Welfare, and Recreation fund of each base receives all proceeds. Philip Morris's Military Sales unit has developed excellent relationships with commissary and exchange managers. For 1993, the tour's objectives included reaching the young adult male audience, increasing shelf space, and increasing sales with in-store pack promotions.

415. R. J. Reynolds Tobacco. "Military Sales Manual." September 1995 (revised). Bates 514317016/7134. legacy.library.ucsf.edu/tid/fub76d00. (accessed March 23, 2004).

    R. J. Reynolds's marketing and sales efforts for the military include promotional programs and military merchandising plans. Military outlets include the

Defense Commissary Agency, Army Air Force Exchange Service, and the Navy Exchange.

416. Schmitt, Eric. "Tobacco Lobby Fights for Military Subsidy." *New York Times*, October 20, 1996: sec. 1: 28.

    On August 23, 1996, the Pentagon issued a proposal, effective November 1, that would increase the price of cigarettes sold at military commissaries. The main goals were to decrease the number of soldiers who smoke and to end the tobacco subsidy. The annual tobacco subsidy is a minimum of $30 million and represents a 30 to 60 percent price discount over the commercial market. The tobacco industry is fighting the proposal; legislators contend the unilateral price increase requires congressional approval and violates federal law to price products at "the lowest practical price."

417. Jowers, Karen. "Tobacco Firms Sought Increase First." *Navy Times*, October 21, 1996: 13.

    In June 1996, Philip Morris and other tobacco companies proposed to the Pentagon officials an increase in prices for tobacco products sold in commissaries. Philip Morris proposed "a pricing structure that links [commissary] prices more closely with the civilian sector." The company stated that additional funds generated by the price increase "would go to the Defense Commissary Agency or the resale system." Pentagon officials believe that the companies would have kept the money. On August 23, 1996, when the Pentagon announced its intention to raise commissary tobacco prices, the tobacco industry objected and called the proposal illegal.

418. Department of Defense. Office of the Inspector General. *Economic Impact of the Use of Tobacco in DoD*. Report 97-060. December 31, 1996. Arlington, Va.: Department of Defense, 1996. www.dodig.osd.mil (accessed June 21, 2004).

    The Department of Defense (DoD) identified current tobacco retail practices as inconsistent with the military goal of reducing the active-duty smoking rate to 20 percent by 2000. Prices of tobacco products sold in commissaries enjoyed a maximum 76 percent discount vis-à-vis their commercial counterparts. On November 1, 1996, DoD erased this price differential by matching commissary tobacco prices to the prices offered at exchanges. In fiscal year 1995, DoD estimated health costs due to tobacco usage at $930 million. For the same period, commissary sales totaled $747 million and $103 million in gross profits and surcharge revenues, respectively. The inspector general recommended two approaches to reaching an active-duty smoking rate of 20 percent: raising commissary tobacco prices to match "local commercial retail outlet prices" and adopting commercial market tobacco promotional practices to deglamorize tobacco sales.

419. Graham, Bradley. "Pentagon Steps Up Effort to Limit Promotion, Sale of Tobacco in Military." *Washington Post*, June 19, 1997: A18.

    The Pentagon has implemented rules banning tobacco promotional practices at military commissaries and payments for placing tobacco products in favorable store locations. Also, tobacco products have been accorded less shelf space. The Pentagon is not expected to take as much political heat from Congress for this move as it did for the tobacco subsidy cut of November 1, 1996. The Pentagon views as a retaliatory measure an effort by the House National Security Panel on Morale, Welfare, and

Recreation to abolish the position held by Stephen Rossetti, Jr., whose duties include implementing the Pentagon's new cigarette policies.

NEW AND EMERGING GLOBAL MARKETS

420. Fisher, Marc. "Tobacco Firms Smell Smoke, Profit in E. Germany." *Washington Post*, August 29, 1990: G1, G4.

    Eyeing East Germany as a new virgin market for their products, Western tobacco companies have moved full force into the neophyte democracy. Philip Morris, R. J. Reynolds, and Reemtsma have purchased cigarette plants and guaranteed the jobs of all the employees. American Tobacco Company attracts East Germans to its Lucky Strike brand with free trips to the United States and by heavily promoting its "One-to-One Exchange" program. Smokers trade in their old brand, Cabinets, for fresh Lucky Strikes. Reemtsma follows a dual strategy of touting its best-selling West brand with a "Test the West" promotion and selling a reformulated and repackaged Cabinet cigarette.

421. Ramirez, Anthony. "Two U.S. Companies Plan to Sell Soviets 34 Billion Cigarettes." *New York Times*, September 14, 1990: A1, D5.

    A severe cigarette shortage in the Soviet Union and resulting demonstrations and riots have led the Soviet government to contract with Philip Morris and RJR Nabisco for a total of thirty-four billion cigarettes. Payment will be made with hard currency and marketable "counter-trade" goods. In 1989 dollars, the thirty-four billion cigarettes are valued at $1.9 billion. The shortage was caused by bureaucratic snafus that led to the closure of eleven of twenty cigarette plants. In addition, Philip Morris signed agreements to supply cigarettes over the next five years and to assist in upgrading old Soviet cigarette factories.

422. "More Cigarettes In RJR-Soviet Deal." *New York Times*, September 22, 1990: 33.

    RJR Nabisco has supplied an additional 3.2 billion cigarettes to the Soviet Union. This is in addition to the fourteen billion the company agreed to supply on September 14, 1990.

423. Levin, Mike. "U.S. Tobacco Firms Push Eagerly into Asian Market." *Marketing News* 25, no. 2 (January 21, 1991): 2, 14.

    The tobacco industry is moving swiftly to conquer the Asian cigarette market. The estimated annual $90 billion market is being flooded with mass-marketing techniques such as Western models and glamorous lifestyle images. Countries such as Japan, South Korea, and Taiwan are purchasing sportswear and fashion accessories emblazoned with tobacco logos. Tobacco sponsorship of sporting and cultural events is a big hit. Philip Morris sponsors motor sports and the arts, R. J. Reynolds sponsors tennis and rock concerts, and British American Tobacco sponsors the arts and track and field events. Cinematic events are also a prime opportunity to display products.

424. Bird, Laura. "Even Overseas, Tobacco Has Nowhere to Hide." *Adweek's Marketing Week* 32, no. 14 (April 1, 1991): 4–5.

Tobacco companies hungry to expand markets in Japan and Southeast Asia are being met with a brand of U.S.-style activism. This has not stopped the companies from deeply penetrating these markets. Philip Morris's Lark brand has become the number-one import brand in Japan. Pitchman James Coburn appears on television commercials and beckons potential smokers with the slogan "Speak Lark." In Malaysia, tobacco companies circumvent television ad restrictions by emphasizing images. "Salem High Country" and "Marlboro Country Tour" blanket the television screen. Activists squashed an R. J. Reynolds-sponsored rock concert in Taiwan, to which admission would have cost five empty packs of Winstons. Ten empty packs could have purchased a Winston sweatshirt.

425. Connolly, Gregory N. "Western Cigarettes and Celebrities in Asia." *Priorities* (Spring 1992): 17–20.

Over two billion Asian customers constitute a lucrative target for Western tobacco companies seeking to expand their global reach. Despite media restrictions implemented by many Asian nations, the tobacco companies are pursuing this hot market through entertainment, cinema, and "brand stretching" venues (attaching brand names to nontobacco products). Taped U.S.- and European-produced sporting events and rock concerts are altered so as to make it seem the companies had sponsored the events. The Salem Tennis Open and the Lucky Strike Challenge Motorcycle Racing Team are examples of sponsored sporting events. In cinema, Philip Morris sponsored ads in movies such as *License Revoked* and the radio program *Marlboro American Music Hour*. Nontobacco products include Benson & Hedges Gold Jewelry, Winston Clothing, and Kent Travel Holidays.

426. U.S. General Accounting Office. *International Trade: Advertising and Promoting U.S. Cigarettes in Selected Asian Countries*. GAO/GGD-93-38. December 31, 1992. Washington, D.C.: GAO, 1992. archive.gao.gov/d36t11/148468.pdf (accessed June 21, 2004).

At the request of various members of Congress, the General Accounting Office (GAO) has examined areas related to the tobacco industry's advertising and marketing activities in selected Asian countries. The GAO took a close look at the conflict arising out U.S. efforts to combat smoking at home while supporting exports to other countries. Secondly, the GAO reviewed the industry's advertising and promotional activities in Japan, Taiwan, South Korea, Thailand, Hong Kong, Malaysia, and Indonesia. The GAO notes that, for all these countries combined, Philip Morris, R. J. Reynolds, and Brown & Williamson spent more funds on sporting events (e.g., auto races) than on cultural events. The report also includes advertising restrictions and infractions, as well as examples of magazine advertisements and television commercials used in the region.

427. Sesser, Stan. "Opium War Redux." *New Yorker* 69, no. 29 (September 13, 1993): 78–82, 84–89.

The tobacco companies are engaged in a full-court press to blanket Southeast Asia, in particular China, with their advertising, marketing, and selling. China bans advertisements displaying or mentioning a cigarette; nevertheless, Philip Morris's Marlboro brand sponsors the *American Music Hour*. Backed by the theme song from *The Magnificent Seven*, a Chinese announcer proclaims, "Jump and fly a thousand miles. Raise the whip so the horse will fun faster. This is the world of Marlboro. Ride through the rivers and mountains with courage. Be called a hero throughout the thousand miles. This is the world of Marlboro." The Marlboro Man is used as a marketing icon to represent freedom, youth, fitness, and pride. In Manila, "jump boys," teenagers ten to fifteen years old, dash in and out of traffic to hawk cigarettes by the pack and by the individual cigarette. Manila does not restrict cigarette marketing by teenagers. Philip Morris sponsored the Marlboro tour '93 bicycle race throughout several Philippine islands. The companies are also applying their trade in Taiwan, Hong Kong, Malaysia, and Thailand.

428. Shenon, Philip. "Asia's Having One Huge Nicotine Fit." *New York Times*, May 15, 1994: sec. 4: 1, 16.

Asian markets offer the tobacco multinationals prime profit potential, especially in the face of growing hostility in Western markets. Asians view smoking as fashionable and as imparting status and cachet. Tobacco companies are tapping into the gold mine. In Hong Kong, R. J. Reynolds (RJR) operates a Salem Attitudes Boutique, where the upscale clothing bears the Salem logo. Philip Morris targets the age forty-and-under female market, of which only 2 percent are smokers, with Virginia Slims cigarettes and the slogan "You've come a long way, baby." In China, RJR continues to manufacture Camel and Winston cigarettes, while the government-controlled China National Tobacco Corporation has agreed to manufacture Philip Morris's brands. In the Philippines, Winston cigarettes are advertised as "The Taste of the U.S.A." A local Philippine cigarette maker has attempted to draw a link between tobacco and the Virgin Mary, by juxtaposing their symbols on wall calendars.

429. Banerjee, Neela. "Western Cigarettes Are Smoking in Russia." *Wall Street Journal*, August 14, 1995: A6.

Philip Morris, R. J. Reynolds Tobacco International (RJR), and British American Tobacco (BAT) have stormed into the newly emerging capitalist Russian economy and quickly established dominance. The trio has purchased more than 50 percent of shares in local tobacco factories. This presence, combined with the marketing of local favorites and premium foreign brands, has given the tobacco companies a dominant market share. BAT's Lucky Strike Man, RJR's Camel Man, and Philip Morris's Chesterfield logo appear on billboards on St. Petersburg's Moskovsky Prospekt. Philip Morris's eight-story-tall Marlboro Man adorns the side of a Moscow building. The "Lucky Strike Girls" haunt Moscow bars and lure people with sample cigarettes.

430. Flint, Anthony. "Hot Sales: Smoking's Big Guns Go Global." *Boston Globe*, June 9, 1996: 1, 30.

Facing trouble in the United States, the tobacco companies are establishing new beachheads in Russia, Eastern Europe, and, especially, China. The tobacco presence in China is quite evident despite advertising restrictions. Marlboro has its logos on café umbrellas, billboards, clothing, and sponsors radio, sports, and automobile races. Young women wearing short skirts and white vinyl jackets distribute free Salem cigarettes. In the city of Shenzhen, the Sueng Hung Restaurant is a marketing mecca for Salem cigarettes; Salem swizzle sticks, clocks, menu holders, and ashtrays adorn the restaurant. Tobacco brands impart status and cachet with young people. Placing a pack of Western cigarettes, especially Marlboro, on a table tells onlookers that the smoker has "made it."

431. Rupert, James, and Glenn Frankel. "In Ex-Soviet Markets, U.S. Brands Took on Role of Capitalist Liberator." *Washington Post*, November 19, 1996: A1, A18.

The giant global tobacco companies—Philip Morris and R. J. Reynolds Tobacco—have solved the Soviet Union's "tobacco rebellion" by supplying thirty-four billion cigarettes in exchange for barter goods and cash. This act of goodwill has opened the door to the Soviet Union, the bloc countries of Eastern Europe, and a host of advertising opportunities. Billboards for Marlboro dot many Soviet cities, featuring sunsets romanticizing the Old (American) West. In Bucharest, Camel logos adorn every yellow traffic light; the government agreed to this in exchange for a year's supply of traffic lights. In Kiev, Reynolds has sponsored gala parties and made videotapes of affluent, nightclub partygoers; the videotapes capture images of Camel posters and a dance group of girls dressed scantily in Camel attire. To fend off impending advertising restrictions in the Ukraine, Philip Morris has issued packets featuring a picture of crushed tobacco leaves reading "$400 million"—to drive home the point that acceptance of the proposed restrictions would cost the Soviet republic that much money over five years. Ukranians defeated the proposal.

432. Frankel, Glenn, and Steven Mufson. "Vast China Market Key to Smoking Disputes." *Washington Post*, November 20, 1996: A1, A22.

China, with its 350 million smokers and rising per capita cigarette consumption, is a big lure for tobacco companies. Though the state-owned China National Tobacco Corporation has a stranglehold on the sale of foreign cigarettes, it has entered into joint ventures with Philip Morris, British American Tobacco (BAT), and R. J. Reynolds. As a result, Philip Morris's and BAT's advertising expenditures have risen to approximately $20 million. BAT heavily promotes its State Express 555 brand through Beijing's Nightman Disco club. Cigarettes are distributed for free by slender Chinese women decked out with the 555 logo. Crowds dance beneath banners declaring "Be free from worldly cares."

433. Perlez, Jane. "Fenced In at Home, Marlboro Man Looks Abroad." *New York Times*, June 24, 1997: A1, A9.

Under siege at home, tobacco companies are setting their sites on the wide-open marketing and profitable tobacco vistas of Eastern Europe, Asia, and the Middle East. To establish a presence in these markets, they have purchased state-owned cigarette factories, with an eye toward turning them into modern and efficient plants. So far, the tobacco companies have invested over $3 billion to this end. In the former Soviet bloc, Philip Morris's market share skyrocketed to 70 percent (1996) from 51 percent (1992). Philip Morris employees in Warsaw discotheques snatch smokers' cigarettes and replace them with a Philip Morris brand. One of the local Polish government's brands, Mars, has been replaced as a favorite with British American Tobacco's Sobieski brand, named after a seventeenth-century Polish warrior king.

434. Pritchard, Chris. "Cigarette Giants Battle over Africa." *Marketing Magazine* 102, no. 40 (October 27, 1997): 8, 10.

Developing countries with few advertising restrictions, such as in Africa, loom as enticing cigarette markets for the transnational tobacco companies. The Kenyan cigarette market, worth $200 million (in shillings) and still growing, represents the prototype battleground for greater market control and greater profits. R. J. Reynolds, the newest entry, battles British American Tobacco and its entrenched market grip. Both companies aggressively use marketing techniques; their feverish competition includes sponsorship of music concerts and sporting events such as soccer, and tough strategies to garner the loyalty of retailers. The tobacco companies are penetrating other markets in east and central Africa with similar marketing techniques.

435. "U.S. Tobacco Firms Expand in Russia." *Chicago Tribune*, March 8, 1998: sec. 5: 8. (Associated Press).

The Russian government bans many forms of advertising, but Philip Morris and R. J. Reynolds are exploiting lax enforcement by using billboards to promote their brands with such slogans as "Total Freedom" and "Rendezvous with America," backed by imagery likes skyscrapers and white sandy beaches. At shows and presentations sponsored by R. J. Reynolds, young women stroll through crowds distributing free cigarettes. The company states that young adults age eighteen and under are not admitted at its disco events.

436. Lamb, David. "Vietnam: A Smoker's Paradise." *Los Angeles Times*, April 18, 1998: A2.

Tobacco is a booming business in Vietnam. Vietnamese are smoking more cigarettes, due to increasing discretionary income, and tobacco exports are up. The industry employs over a hundred thousand people. Western tobacco companies view Vietnam as an emerging cigarette market. State-owned companies are joining with Philip Morris, R. J. Reynolds, and British American Tobacco to produce such brands as Globe and Tourism. These Western-sounding brands must compete with Vinataba, the leading brand, produced by the state-owned Saigon Cigarette Factory.

437. Hwang, Suein L. "How Philip Morris Got Turkey Hooked on American Tobacco." *Wall Street Journal*, September 11, 1998: A1, A8.

Throughout the 1980s, Tekel, the state-run tobacco monopoly, retained the right to control the marketing, pricing, and distribution of all foreign and domestic cigarettes in Turkey. Philip Morris used the political influence of Turkish businessman Sakip Sabanci to change this situation. In 1991, the company won access and began to implement its marketing, distribution, and ingenuity muscle to outsmart and outmaneuver the state monopoly. Philip Morris implemented such techniques as using salespeople dressed like cowboys and driving Marlboro-covered vans, sponsoring parties at nightclubs and contests, selling Marlboro Classics jeans, and advertising the "Adventure Team '98" in the Turkish news magazine *Tempo*.

438. Collins, Glenn. "U.S. Tobacco Industry Looks Longingly at Chinese Market, but in Vain." *New York Times*, November 20, 1998: A16.

American tobacco companies are eyeing the Chinese market to boost declining U.S. sales and profits. The tobacco companies are allowed to advertise in bars and nightclubs, sponsor music and sporting events, and use posters and billboards. Popular brands are British American Tobacco's State Express 555 and Philip Morris's Marlboro. However, the China National Tobacco Corporation government monopoly thwarts expansion efforts by imposing a 230 percent tax rate on foreign cigarettes.

439. Srivastava, Ambika. *The Role and Responsibility of Media in Global Tobacco Control*. Geneva: World Health Organization, January 2000. www.who.int/entity/tobacco/media/en/AMBIKA2000X.pdf (accessed February 19, 2004).

India and other subcontinental countries, including Bangladesh, Nepal, and Pakistan, provide a sizeable target for the tobacco industry, seeking to expand its reach into emerging markets. In India, British American Tobacco commands a market share of approximately 80 percent, with Philip Morris owning some 12 percent. As the citizens switch from smoking bidis to cigarettes, consumption is expected to explode. The author presents solutions to control the tobacco industry and enlist the media as a global partner.

440. Kirk Don. "British American Tobacco Finds Opening in South Korea." *New York Times*, August 9, 2001: W1.

British American Tobacco has built a new cigarette factory in Sacheon City, South Korea. The new factory represents a multiyear investment of over a billion dollars. The long-term investment is prompted by the South Korean government's plan to impose a 10 percent tariff stating July 1. As of 2004, the tariff increased to 40 percent.

441. Stacchini, Alexis. "Philip Morris Investing Heavily in Key Markets." *World Tobacco*, no. 196 (September 2003): 34, 36.

Philip Morris International (PMI) is targeting emerging and developing markets to expand its global reach through acquisitions and investments in factories. In the Ukraine's Kharkiv region, the company has constructed a new cigarette manufacturing facility at a cost of over $100 million. Its Russian Philip Morris Izhora subsidiary has expanded its manufacturing capabilities, with a $240 million investment, to become the country's largest tobacco manufacturer. The company acquired a controlling stake in the Serbia and Montenegro–based Duvanska Industrija Nis. In Beijing, PMI has created a "tobacco-related consultancy company" at a cost of $15 million. In 2002, the company opened its $50 million South Korean cigarette manufacturing plant—the first by a foreign-owned tobacco company.

442. "KT&G and Imperial to Build in Turkey." *World Tobacco*, no. 198 (January 2004): 3.

Korea Tomorrow & Global Corporation's new plant in Tire began construction in mid-January 2004. The cost is estimated to be $200 million. Imperial Tobacco has a new cigarette manufacturing plant constructed in Manisa; it has been in operation since January 2005. These companies join British American Tobacco, JT International, and Philip Morris, which also have cigarette manufacturing facilities in Turkey.

443. Min-hee, Kim. "KT&G Strives to Join World's Top Five Tobacco Makers by 2008." *Asia Africa Intelligence Wire*, February 9, 2004: n.p. Infotrac OneFile (accessed October 25, 2004).

Korea Tomorrow & Global is planning to increase sales overseas and hopes to become one of the top five global cigarette companies by 2008. The company has been penetrating new markets in China and Turkey and has increased in global exports from 30.9 billion cigarettes (2003) to 35 billion in 2004. The company currently commands an 80 percent market share in South Korea.

444. Gilmore, A. B., and M. McKee. "Tobacco and Transition: An Overview of Industry Investments, Impact and Influence in the Former Soviet Union." *Tobacco Control* 13, no. 2 (June 2004): 136–42.

With the opening of markets in central and eastern Europe and the former republics of the Soviet Union, the transnational tobacco companies moved to establish a prominent economic and political presence through foreign direct investment, production capacity, brand development, and advertising. Russia, Ukraine, Latvia, Estonia, and Lithuania have all received varying degrees of direct investment. The tobacco companies have employed their marketing and advertising prowess, created new brands, and assumed control over local brands.

445. Gilmore, A. B., and M. McKee. "Moving East: How the Transnational Tobacco Industry Gained Entry to the Emerging Markets of the Former Soviet Union—Part I: Establishing Cigarette Imports." *Tobacco Control* 13, no. 2 (June 2004): 143–50.

This paper chronicles British American Tobacco's (BAT) moves to establish a beachhead in the republics of the former Soviet Union through cigarette imports. BAT noted factors in favor of entering this market, such as an expanding population growth, a younger population, and potential women smokers. BAT initiated a number of steps: getting known within the various countries, employing "pull" (brand awareness) and "push" ("limiting investments in distribution and channel management strategies and opportunistic use of declining state distribution assets") strategies for creating brand awareness, targeting women and younger "opinion leaders," and developing the import market through counter trade, smuggling, and money obtained by the republics through aid packages.

446. Gilmore, A. B., and M. McKee. "Moving East: How the Transnational Tobacco Industry Gained Entry to the Emerging Markets of the Former Soviet Union—Part II: An Overview of Priorities and Tactics Used to Establish a Manufacturing Presence." *Tobacco Control* 13, no. 2 (June 2004): 151–60.

This paper chronicles British American Tobacco's (BAT) moves to establish a cigarette-manufacturing presence in the former republics of the Soviet Union. Initially, BAT created the "New Business Development" unit to identify, assess, and prepare proposals for investment opportunities in the region. BAT felt a need to move quickly to take advantage of advertising opportunities, the absence of marketing restrictions, and competitive moves from others in the industry, as well as to avoid having to bid for properties. BAT employed numerous strategies to gain favorable entry: making a commitment to invest in the region, licensing the manufacture of company brands to build brand awareness, supporting that awareness by advertising, and winning the confidence of local managers. Also, BAT sold the benefits of privatization, its ability to collect excise taxes, and its expertise in leaf and manufacturing know-how.

PRISONS AND JAILS

447. Skolnick, Andrew. "While Some Correctional Facilities Go Smoke-Free, Others Appear to Help Inmates to Light Up." *JAMA: The Journal of the American Medical Association* 264, no. 12 (September 26, 1990): 1509, 1513.

Even in light of the antitobacco movement, state and local government entities continue to distribute cigarettes for free or at subsidized cost to incarcerated minors and prisoners. Cooperative prisoners housed in Suffolk County, Massachusetts, jails are rewarded with free cigarettes. Minors in New York City jails can purchase deeply discounted cigarettes. The Michigan Department of Corrections has distributed cigarettes statewide and to other states from a manufacturing plant at its Scott Correctional Facility. The product, Northern Lights, sells for sixty cents per pack (including state and federal taxes). The Illinois Department of Corrections' cigarette plant at its Menard State Prison produces two brands: Pyramid and Southern Lights. The cigarettes are sold for between thirty-two and thirty-five cents per pack, excluding state and federal taxes. In 1987, the state of Oregon halted the expenditure over a hundred thousand dollars per year to provide prisoners free cigarettes.

448. Glass, Chris. "Cigarettes for Convicts." *Tobacco Reporter* 124, no. 3 (March 1997): 30, 32.

To counter the state of Florida's lawsuit to recover Medicaid tobacco payments, the tobacco companies have filed papers showing that Florida has been involved in the manufacture and distribution of cigarettes to convicts. This practice began during 1972 at a correctional facility in Raiford. The annual cost totaled $501,000. Local governments purchased the cigarettes for distribution through their city jails. Yearly sales yielded a profit of $73,200. Even state facilities, such as the South Florida State Hospital, purchased the cigarettes, with the state pocketing annual profits of $9,660. The state's involvement in manufacturing cigarettes ended in the late 1970s.

449. Lankenau, Stephen E. "Smoke 'Em If You Got 'Em: Cigarette Black Markets in U.S. Prisons and Jails." *Prison Journal* 81, no. 2 (June 2001): 142–61.

The author studies the development of and interrelationships between prison economies, inmate behavior patterns, and cigarette policies at sixteen correctional institutions in eight states. Six jails and four prisons banned cigarette smoking; four jails and two prisons placed restrictions on cigarette usage within the institution. The author focuses on the transformation of "gray markets" (cigarettes used as currency) into "black markets" (cigarettes viewed as valued commodities) when cigarette bans are imposed on the inmates.

450. O'Connell, Vanessa. "Bans on Smoking in Prison Shrink a Coveted Market." *Wall Street Journal*, August 27, 2003: A1, A6.

Smoking in prisons is still permitted in thirty-one states and also throughout the 103 federal prisons. Within this "institutional market" of incarcerated people, an estimated 70 to 80 percent are smokers. In past and current years, this has translated into major profits for state governments and the tobacco industry. Vermont banned prison sales starting in January 2004, but as of June 25, 2003, tobacco sales grossed about $3.4 million, with profits totaling about $1.1 million. The state Department of Corrections used this money to purchase such items as recreation equipment and to fund long-distance trips by relatives of prisoners. In twelve states, Brown & Williamson sponsored a Captive Audience Prison Program and provided five-cent discount coupons for its Viceroy brand. In seven states, Lorillard Tobacco started the

Play Ball with Newport program. Prison officials collected empty packs of Newport cigarettes and traded them for weightlifting equipment, basketballs, and board games. In a related program called Great Newport Sneaker Deal, the company accepted three or four hundred empty Newport packs in exchange for running shoes or high-tops. Back covers of the prison magazine *Prison Life* have ads for Newport cigarettes.

RETAIL AND WHOLESALE

451. Love, Barbara. "Cigarettes Battle for Check-Out Space." *Folio: The Magazine for Magazine Management* 19, no. 3 (March 1990): 21, 32.

    R. J. Reynolds is paying supermarket chains to supplant magazines with Reynolds's tobacco products at checkout counters. On a yearly basis, for each magazine pocket, payments range from eight hundred to a thousand dollars. Magazine publishers pay forty dollars per pocket.

452. "Philip Morris Aims to Pack 'Em in for the '90s." *Candy Wholesaler* 43, no. 2 (March 1990): 112–14.

    Philip Morris's strategic goals include targeting increased sales of single packs of cigarettes and marketing niche-based cigarette brands. The company will encourage mass merchandisers like supermarkets to increase their usage of hardware designed to promote single packs. Also, the company will emphasize that single pack sales account for 29 percent of all sales and 28 percent of all front-end sales, and contribute 24 percent profit margins.

453. Felgner, Brent H. "Are New Incentive Programs Really Working?" *Candy Wholesaler* 43, no. 4 (May 1990): 31–32, 35–37.

    Reward programs implemented by the major tobacco manufacturers aim to prod wholesalers into upgrading their internal and external operations. Internal operations include developing business plans, formulating market strategies, and identifying strengths and weaknesses. External operations cover such variables as direct sales and community citizenship. The major tobacco programs are Masters in Distribution Excellence (Philip Morris), Winners-Partnership in Performance (R. J. Reynolds Tobacco), Achievement through Distribution and Display (American Tobacco), and MVP (Brown & Williamson). The programs assist wholesalers to improve their businesses and to increase return on investment.

454. Valero, Greg. "Untaxed Cigarettes Cost Wholesalers Millions." *U.S. Distribution Journal* 221, no. 3 (March 15, 1994): 6, 8.

    Cigarettes sold through Indian reservations are regulated by each state's laws and are not subject to state excise taxes. Overall, wholesalers and convenience store operators that must collect the taxes are at a disadvantage, especially when located near a reservation. In New York, revenue losses from untaxed cigarettes are estimated to be $205 million. In Montana, revenue losses are estimated to be between $750,000 and $1.5 million. In Washington State, sales from reservations account for $23 million in lost sales and excise taxes.

455. Warner, Fara. "P-M Wholesaler Program Aimed to Net Greater Share." *Brandweek* 35, no. 13 (March 28, 1994): 1, 6.

   Philip Morris is introducing a new "voluntary" incentive program for wholesalers, titled Wholesale Masters. The tobacco giant will reward wholesalers for increased sales and sharing of sales figures for competitor brands. "Volunteers" will be eligible for large cash rewards; all others would be eligible for a smaller slice of the financial pie.

456. Freudenheim, Milt. "Pharmacies in a Quandary over Tobacco." *New York Times*, April 25, 1994: D1, D11.

   Nationwide, independent drug stores are voluntarily pulling tobacco products from their shelves. Drug stores in Michigan, Minnesota, and South Carolina have joined the effort. Though tobacco sales constitute a very small percentage of overall sales, pharmacists are deciding that it is in their best interest to pull the products. Customers have responded by spending more on other product lines.

457. Fucini, Suzy. "A Smoke for Every Niche." *U.S. Distribution Journal* 221, no. 9 (September 15, 1994): 19, 21–22.

   Wholesalers, the author argues, should consider distributing specialty and imported cigarettes in addition to the major cigarette brands. These cigarettes offer profit potential, appeal to various demographic submarkets, and appear to deflect the antitobacco sentiment plaguing the industry leaders. Specialty cigarettes are available in three categories: luxury (such as Dunhill), ethnic (for example, Mild Seven), and "general distribution" (such as Dunhill Lights). These cigarettes are targeted to international travelers and ethnic groups.

458. Margulis, Ronald A. "Tobacco: How It Figures in Distributors' Future." *Candy Wholesaler* 48, no. 7 (September 1994): 36–40.

   Tobacco wholesale distributors are pursuing strategies to maintain their sales volume, maintain profit margins, and counter the effects of "Marlboro Friday." Distributors participate in manufacturers' incentive programs, perform marketing and merchandising duties formerly provided by the manufacturers, increase their presence to compensate for tobacco supplies no longer provided by non-convenience-store distributors, and market private-label cigarettes.

459. Turcsik, Richard. "A Pack of Trouble." *Supermarket News* 44, no. 50 (December 12, 1994): 31–32.

   Cigarette specialty stores aggressively court purchasers of cigarette cartons. According to Sam Hendrix, vice president of Trade Marketing at R. J. Reynolds Tobacco, these outlets account for 6 percent of industry volume. Some stores are as large as 20,000 to 30,000 square feet. Revenues from cigarette sales range from 50 percent up to 80 percent.

460. Weisz, Pam. "Smokes 'R' Us." *Brandweek* 36, no. 10 (March 6, 1995): 20–24.

   Cigarette specialty stores are seen as the future distribution channel for tobacco products. The stores are predicted to siphon away sales from supermarkets and drugstores. They offer a vast array of tobacco products, including obscure and foreign brands, at deeply discounted prices and offer price advantages vis-à-vis their competitors.

461. "CEO to CEO: R. J. Reynolds Turns over a New Leaf." *Candy Wholesaler* 49, no. 4 (May 1995): 43–45.

R. J. Reynolds Tobacco's (RJR) James Schroer has stated that his company's marketing strategies concentrate on building strong equity in a few brands, emphasizing the Doral brand, growing and maintaining its full-price brand franchise, and improving working relationships with its wholesale distributors and retail businesses. RJR's partnership program with its tobacco distributors seeks to provide cash incentives for increased product improvement through retail channels and increases in market share. Distributors pass along information electronically from their databases to RJR and enhance the implementation of "ECR," or Efficient Consumer Response. ECR entails automated order replenishment and electronic funds transfer to reduce manual operations and administrative costs.

462. Glass, Chris. "No One under 18." *Tobacco Reporter* 122, no. 8 (August 1995): 16.

Philip Morris's campaign, Action Against Access (AAA), seeks to prevent youths from having access to cigarettes. Through AAA, free cigarette samples will no longer be distributed through sample surveys or through the U.S. mail. Cigarette packages will be marked "Underage Sale Prohibited." The company will fight unauthorized use of its brand names or logos on items marketed to minors or on video games. Retailers found to be selling to minors will be barred from its retail incentive program. Also, a program called Ask First/It's the Law will be started to assist retailers in meeting the AAA goals.

463. "Philip Morris: Mastering the Market." *Distribution Channels* 49, no. 7 (September 1995): 50–52.

Philip Morris's Wholesale Masters program, started in April 1994, covers all the company's brands and incorporates pay-for-performance and geographically based share targets involving all their direct buying accounts (both wholesale and retail). Wholesalers provide Philip Morris with raw shipment data on disk or tape, including store names and addresses, brand descriptions, and quantities; Philip Morris transforms the data into meaningful information and shares it with wholesalers. Working with their retail clients, the wholesalers provide value-added consulting services in such areas as category management and space management.

464. "RJR: Focus on Partners." *Distribution Channels* 49, no. 7 (September 1995): 53–55

R. J. Reynolds Tobacco's (RJR) Partners is a performance-based program that rewards direct account buyers based on targeted increases in market share. RJR gathers information electronically from its direct buying accounts (both wholesalers and retailers). This data is used to uncover sales trends in a given geographical area or for specific brands, analyze the effectiveness of brand promotions, and design local and regional marketing programs. Distributors analyze the data and work with their retail accounts to determine the proper brand mix, brands to phase out due to declining sales, and brands that respond best to promotions.

465. Whalen, Jeanne. "Philip Morris Wants Exclusive Store Deals." *Advertising Age* 66, no. 43 (October 23, 1995): 54.

In early 1994, Philip Morris implemented its Retail Masters convenience store program. Dealer participants sign exclusive contracts to advertise and display the company's cigarettes. Though store dealers are allowed to stock competing cigarette brands, dealers are required to advertise only Philip Morris cigarettes on permanent display fixtures, such as sales racks. No competing brands are allocated advertising space on permanent fixtures. In return for this maximum level of participation, Philip Morris has increased payments for these displays and offered "access to special promotions." In 1992, Philip Morris began the Retail Masters Program as a financial enticement to increase advertising and prominently promote Philip Morris cigarette brands.

466. Harris, Ken. "An Industry on the Ropes? Think Again." *Brandweek* 36, no. 41 (October 30, 1995): 16.

Tobacco companies may have the last laugh over President Clinton's proposed tobacco marketing advertising regulations. The tobacco companies are redeploying their marketing budgets toward direct-mail marketing and the backing of "category killer" tobacco stores. The Houston-based Kroger chain has opened "The Tinder Box," a "store within a store," offering domestic and foreign tobaccos, cheeses, and fine wines.

467. Leovy, Jill. "Rise of Discount Cigarette Stores Vexes Health Officials." *Los Angeles Times*, January 27, 1996: A1, A17.

Discount tobacco outlets, such as Cigarettes Cheaper! and The Cigarette Stores, are appearing all over California. These stores, which sell only cigarettes, discount prices up to 20 percent. Cigarettes Cheaper! and Philip Morris have a contract whereby the discount outlet places heavier emphasis on selling Marlboro cigarettes and dedicates all permanent displays and signs to promote Philip Morris's stable of brands. For outlets meeting "maximum level of participation" conditions, Philip Morris provides substantial allowances and promotions as both a wholesaler and retailer.

468. "Computerised Distribution System Is Highly Prized." *World Tobacco*, no. 152 (May 1996): 20.

To protect its high market share, Czech-based Tabak has overhauled its distribution system for the Czech and Slovak markets. Tobacco is distributed from the factory to one of sixteen depots and then to the retailers. The logistical arrangement helps prevent shortages of Tabak cigarette brands and allows the company to quickly receive and deposit payments for goods. Tabak received the European Logistics Association's top prize for best consumer-goods distribution system.

469. Pool, Jessica Johns. "Self-Service Helps Combat Cigarette Sales Losses." *Distribution Channels* 50, no. 5 (June 1996): 34–36.

Convenience store operators are discovering new ways to increase tobacco sales and combat the threat of discount tobacco outlets. Lassus Handy Dandy Food Stores has created U-shaped tobacco shelving for single packs and cartons. A Florida-based chain, not identified due to the company's request for anonymity, employs a free-standing rack, placed near the cashier, with three sides devoted to selling single-pack cigarettes. Southwest Louisiana–based Shop Rite uses one-sided, open-face racks and counter displays for single-pack cigarettes.

470. Margulis, Ronald. "The State of Tobacco." *Distribution Channels* 50, no. 7 (September 1996): 48–51.

    Throughout the distribution channel, tobacco manufacturers and their distributors cooperate and compete in marketing and merchandising cigarettes. For national brands and their manufacturers, distributors prepare carton and pack add-ons, study the market and prepare market information, and arrange signs. At the retail level, distributors have limited clout, due to competition from manufacturers' representatives. Representatives make frequent visits to retail shops and attempt to limit and even undermine the distributors' merchandising and product placement of private-label cigarettes and franchised, branded discount lines. Marketing private labels (e.g., Focus from R. J. Reynolds) and franchised brands (such as Checkers from King Maker Marketing) give distributors the opportunity to provide complete service, control inventory, rack locations, and handle signs.

471. Szymanczyk, Michael. "The Premium Story." *Tobacco Reporter* 123, no. 11 (November 1996): 18, 20.

    Despite the current antitobacco environment, Michael Szymanczyk, Philip Morris USA executive vice president of marketing and sales, is upbeat on the industry. He states that sales of premium and discount brands are robust; continuity programs such as Marlboro Unlimited, Virginia Slims Wear, and Merit Awards are reinforcing strong brand equity; and the company's Retail Masters Program is in place to assist retailers enhance cigarette sales. The Retail Masters Program is based on five key principles: maximizing retail space for the top-selling brands, recognizing potential volume increases for premium and discount categories, ensuring proper category visibility, matching sales with inventory levels, and emphasizing the fact that consumer tobacco purchases focus mainly on cigarette packs.

472. Bentley, Stephanie. "Supermarkets Offload Cigarette Brands in Bid to Avoid Litigation." *Marketing Week* 20, no. 2 (April 10, 1997): 7.

    Major tobacco companies are taking over cigarette brands owned by British supermarkets. The stores are attempting to avoid litigation and negative media attention. R. J. Reynolds will take over ownership of Tesco's brand Bennington. In October 1995, the British Medical Association lambasted the supermarket for introducing the brand and purveying a "healthy image" for it in advertising. JT International Europe (Japan Tobacco) owns the Sainsbury supermarket brand Statesman.

473. Ono, Yumiko. "Tobacco Ruling May Hit Makers of Store Racks." *Wall Street Journal*, April 30, 1997: B1, B7.

    The point-of-purchase industry faces a squeeze-out due to a federal judge's ruling supporting the Food and Drug Administration and its battle against the purchase of cigarettes by underage youth. This will affect usage of store displays such as racks, signs, neon clocks, and shopping carts. Many small and medium-sized companies are dependent for the income on providing this equipment. In 1996, the point-of-purchase industry sold about $700 million of these items to the tobacco industry. Items sold include a yellow-and-purple model "Joe's" sports car dispensing packs of Camel, an open Camel "suitcase" filled with cigarettes, and a Lucky Strikes "gravity feed" dispenser feeding the consumer one cigarette pack at a time. Industry representatives argue that point-of-purchase items are come-ons and advertising tools, with a vastly different purpose than vending machines.

474. Feder, Barnaby J. "Tough Climate May Benefit Smoke Shops." *New York Times*, August 5, 1997: C1, C5.

On the heels of the proposed tobacco settlement, cigarette shops are popping up and diverting traffic from other types of outlets, including convenience stores and gas stations. Cigarette shops mushroomed from 400 in 1992 to 4,500 in 1996. The stores cater to adults only. While the proposed tobacco agreement bars most stores from displaying tobacco promotional items, cigarette shops are exempted if they can bar minors from entering. These shops can be very competitive. offering lower prices for cartons, moving more volume on a weekly basis, hiring fewer employees, working on lower profit margins, displaying a wider variety of brands, promoting the product more frequently, and extending a "welcoming attitude" to adult smokers.

475. Lee, Louise. "Tobacco Pact Founders, but Stores Stash Away Smokes." *Wall Street Journal*, September 30, 1997: B1, B13.

In anticipation of a vote in Congress in favor of the proposed tobacco settlement and its provisions for advertising restrictions, retailers are taking the lead in the reinvention of the marketing of tobacco products in their stores. The merchandising emphasizes visual and sight-oriented themes. San Antonio gas-station convenience store operator Ultramar Diamond has arranged cigarette cartons in a "waterfall" pattern on racks behind the counter. Mimicking its in-store processing centers, Kmart has created "tobacco convenience centers" with a service counter. Kroger Company and Family Express, a regional convenience store chain, both offer adults-only tobacco "store-within-a-store" services.

476. Rigby, Leslie. "Smokers: Stop Here." *Distribution Channels* 51, no. 9 (November 1997): 46–51.

Discount cigarette stores come in all sizes and are a growing trend in the cigarette industry. Convenience stores view them as a threat to their business, but manufacturers are drawn to their sales potential and ability to deal with the regulatory environment. The discount stores' characteristics include low maintenance, inventory turnover, access restrictions to minors, and prompt and accurate service. Some pharmacies, supermarkets, and national chains have decided to abandon the tobacco business, and this means spillover business for the new discount stores. Manufacturers provide such benefits as payments for shelf space, three-for-two offers on packs, and brand accessories such as T-shirts. Major players include Butt Hut of America and Cigarettes Cheaper!

477. "Electronics the Future of Vending Machines." *Tobacco Journal International*, no. 6 (November/December 1997): 48.

Vending machines are a critical venue for distributing cigarettes in Germany. In 1996, the machines accounted for nearly 33 percent of all cigarettes purchased. At a product fair for vending machines, cigarette machine manufacturers demonstrated models with sixteen and twenty-one cigarette shafts. Presently, the machines have thirteen shafts.

478. Dessoff, Alan. "The Uphill Battle of Small Tobacco." *Distribution Channels* 52, no. 9 (November 1998): 62–63.

"Small" tobacco companies such as S&M Brands struggle to get their products distributed to outlets. S&M Brands manufactures the Bailey. Financing slower-moving brands, "lockups" (financial incentives), and contractual arrangements with the major tobacco companies to devote shelf space and signage to their brands are some of the obstacles. The small tobacco companies respond by building customer demand, having sales forces build personal relationships with retailers, getting the product on the shelves, and creating demand pressure on wholesalers.

479. Chunxiang, Lü, and Xu Beili. "Spring Is Very Much in the Air: A Report on the Concourse of the Famous Brand Cigarette of the Tobacco Companies in Dalian." *Sino-World Tobacco* 42, no. 4 (December 31, 1998): 6–8, 10–11.

The Dalian Municipal Tobacco Company has constructed fourteen cigarette supermarkets, each building covering a thousand square meters. One part is a self-serve operation, with over a hundred Chinese brands, and the other part features smoking paraphernalia. Dalian promotes the supermarkets and services by providing a pleasant shopping environment, keeping the shelves stocked with reasonably priced merchandise, and offering discounts.

480. Segal, David. "Philip Morris, Leader of the Packs." *Washington Post*, September 15, 1999: E1, E9.

In November 1998, Philip Morris started its Retail Leaders program, offering retail outlets incentives for placing its product in favorable positions in cigarette racks. Philip Morris offers incentives ranging as high as a thousand dollars per month and requires placement of competitors brands in less favorable rack locations. R. J. Reynolds has alleged that Philip Morris does not allow retailers to offer competitor brands at a discount during quarterly price promotions. In June 1999, a court injunction froze certain aspects of the Retail Leaders program.

481. Beirne, Mike. "B&W's Divorce of Convenience." *Brandweek* 41, no. 30 (July 24, 2000): 1, 47.

Brown & Williamson will be drastically reducing cash payments to retailers for devoting shelf space and signage to the B&W cigarettes brands, such as Kool, Lucky Strike, and GPC. Retailers displaying signage will see their payments drop to $125 a month, from $400. Retailers not using signage will receive only $85 per month. The new program is in line with the company's policy of allowing retailers to make their own decisions regarding the cigarette brand mix for their stores.

482. Fairclough, Gordon. "BAT Division Will Start Taking Phone, Fax Orders for Cigarettes." *Wall Street Journal*, October 12, 2000: B16.

   British American Tobacco's American subsidiary, Brown & Williamson, will soon allow customers to order cigarettes by phone, fax, mail, and online. BWT Direct, which will direct these activities, will begin the campaign by distributing a fourteen-page cigarette catalog to customers in its direct-mail database. The catalog's cover page is emblazoned with the phrase "Great Prices! Fast & Easy! Always Fresh! Guaranteed!" Ideally, the new sales avenues will stem sales declines of approximately a million dollars due to price increases and retailers' preference for the major cigarette brands.

483. Fairclough, Gordon. "BAT Unit Sues to Block New York Law Banning Sale of Cigarettes over the Web." *Wall Street Journal*, October 16, 2000: B16.

   Brown & Williamson is contesting a New York State law banning the use of mail order, telephone, and the Internet to sell cigarettes. New York legislators addressed health issues, access by children, and nonpayment of state cigarette excise taxes. They perceived the sale of cigarettes through these electronic media as a "serious threat" to public health and sought to stop it.

484. Clark, Philip B. "Marlboro Man Rounds Up Its Retailers." *B to B* 85, no. 18 (November 6, 2000): 1. ABI/Inform (accessed December 19, 2003).

   Philip Morris is the first tobacco company to launch an Internet business-to-business initiative. The company will be deploying a product called RetailersMarketXchange (RMX) to create links with convenience stores and gas stations/snack shops. Philip Morris wants retailers to order signage, check prices, and review promotional activities through RMX and thereby to become comfortable using technology to transact business. Philip Morris sales representatives will then be able to spend less time on paperwork and more on marketing activities.

485. Beirne, Mike. "Big Tobacco Gets Tough." *Brandweek* 42, no. 20 (May 14, 2001): 28–30, 32, 34.

   Operating in the post-1998 Master Settlement Agreement environment, the major tobacco companies are turning to more in-store price promotions and merchandising contracts to maintain or increase market share, tie in to national marketing programs, such as sweepstakes, and put the squeeze on rivals. Shelf placement, signage, window decals, and permanent displays are valuable commodities up for grabs in retail outlets. Philip Morris uses its Retail Leaders program, and R. J. Reynolds uses its Everyday Low Pricing program for these purposes.

486. Pristin, Terry. "Court Strikes Down State Ban on Sale of Cigarettes Online." *New York Times*, June 9, 2001: B4.

   On June 8, 2001, Federal District Court of Manhattan judge Loretta A. Preska ruled that New York State's law prohibiting cigarette Internet and mail-order sales unconstitutional. The law's intent was to prohibit cigarette sales to minors, but Judge Preska found that the state had failed to pursue other avenues, such as verifying the customer's age and requiring Internet retailers to remit cigarette excise taxes.

487. Bloom, Paul N. "Role of Slotting Fees and Trade Promotions in Shaping How Tobacco Is Marketed in Retail Stores." *Tobacco Control* 10, no. 4 (December 2001): 340–44.

Since the signing of the Master Settlement Agreement in 1998, the major tobacco companies have emphasized "relationship marketing" and have worked more closely with retailers. The companies pay retailers "slotting fees" (cash, allowances, free cases) to display and promote tobacco products and to display products in certain ways (with respect to shelf facings, shelf height, location). The slotting fees could affect smoking in society in four ways: lowering prices more than normal, encouraging pilfering or enticing minors (where self-service displays are used), encouraging smoking or enticing minors with tobacco-friendly environments, and transforming retailers into political allies at all levels of government.

488. Dipasquale, Cara B., and Ira Teinowitz. "Store Wars." *Advertising Age* 73, no. 2 (January 14, 2002): 4, 18, 20, 22.

Philip Morris (PM), R. J. Reynolds (RJR), and Brown & Williamson (B&W) are battling each other for dominance in one of the last bastions available for advertising—the retail store. The fight is waged over shelf space, signage, and promotional funds spent by each company. The current point of contention is Philip Morris's Retail Leaders merchandising program. In a lawsuit, RJR and B&W contend that PM's program ties payment of promotional money to reservation of prime retail display space for the PM brands. The big issue is that PM retailers are to allocate store space "equal to its share of market in that store." A B&W representative referred to the "Marlboro monopoly"—the brand's control of almost forty share points—implying that PM is using this as a weapon to "foreclose retailers." RJR's and B&W's merchandising programs are Retail Partners and Retail Alliance Millennium Program, respectively.

489. Kling, Folker. "Keeping Up with Modern Times." *Tobacco Journal International*, no. 1 (January/February 2002): 30–32.

In Germany, tobacco wholesalers operate the network of cigarette vending machines, approximately 820,000 units. The German government is attempting to restrict teens sixteen and under from purchasing these cigarettes. To meet this potential goal, the tobacco wholesalers would implement a system whereby cigarettes may be purchased only with an age-verified eurocheque card. The wholesalers want to have customers use the card to verify their age and then use coins to purchase cigarettes.

490. Lipsith, Gavin. "Lucky Strike: Burning the Brand." *Travel Retailer International* (June 2002): 21–22, 24.

On July 4, 2001, in Amsterdam, British American Tobacco (BAT) opened its first retail venture, called Lucky Strike 451° F. The store is a mixture of "overt branding and pleasing design." Customers may purchase from among BAT's cigarette brands and competitor brands such as Marlboro. The store is stocked not with Lucky Strike merchandise but with 451° items like mugs, postcards, and key chains. The second floor combines "urban accessories" (recycled bags, microtools) and a lounge to reflect the values of the Lucky Strike brand and provide a unique shopping experience.

491. Lofstock, John. "Adult Smokers Wanted." *Convenience Store News* 38, no. 11 (August 26, 2002): 77. Ebsco Business Source Premier (accessed June 5, 2004).

Discount tobacco-only stores are growing significantly nationwide in terms of stores and sales volume. According to the trade publication *Tobacco Outlet Business*, ten thousand shops became operational by the end of 2002. On a weekly basis, the shops are selling an estimated nine million cartons. The stores control access to minors, operate on reduced hours, and save money for the store owners vis-à-vis convenience stores, supermarkets, drug stores, and mass merchandisers. These "adult-only concept" stores cater to upscale customers, with men accounting for 51 percent and women 49 percent. Major national tobacco-only shops include Cigarettes Cheaper!, based in Benicia, California, and Smoker Friendly International, based in Denver, Colorado.

492. van Kolfschooten, Frank. "Netherlands Introduces Child-Proof Cigarette Vending Machines." *Lancet* 360 (November 16, 2002): 1576.

As of January 1, 2003, smokers seventeen and over can purchase cigarettes from vending machines using an "AgeKey" smart card. Post offices provide an electronic chip for the smart card; the offices also verify the requester's age. British American Tobacco (BAT) Netherlands is one of three parties creating the new system. BAT owns 69 percent of the country's vending machines.

493. Tedeschi, Bob. "Pressure Grows from States to Restrict and Tax a Smoker's Haven—the Internet." *New York Times*, February 24, 2003: C7.

Eleven states are seeking to regulate Internet sales of cigarettes, protect children from accessing tobacco products, and preserve excise tax revenues. In 2003, California legislators enacted a law requiring online sellers to accept payment by check or credit card only and to match customer information, such as date of birth, with government records to verify that a buyer is eighteen or older. A second new California law requires that the outside portion of Internet and mail-order tobacco packages include, if applicable, a notification that the purchaser owes state sales taxes and that the sale has been reported to the state. A New York state federal appeals panel (the Second Circuit Court of Appeals) recently upheld a state law banning Internet, telephone, and mail sales of tax-free cigarettes.

494. U.S. General Accounting Office. *Internet Cigarette Sales: Limited Compliance and Enforcement of the Jenkins Act Result in Loss of State Tax Revenue*. GAO-03-714T. May 1, 2003. Washington, D.C.: GAO, 2003. www.gao.gov/new.items/d03714t.pdf (accessed October 1, 2004).

The General Accounting Office (GAO) has investigated Internet cigarette vendor compliance with the Jenkins Act. The act requires vendors conducting interstate commerce in cigarettes to report the sales to the buyer's state tobacco-tax administrator. GAO determined that vendors are subject to the act's provisions, though most do not comply with it. GAO recommends that federal enforcement authority be transferred from the Federal Bureau of Investigation to the Bureau of Alcohol, Tobacco, and Firearms.

495. Beirne, Mike. "Cigarette Companies Raise Stakes in Discount Battle." *Brandweek* 44, no. 23 (June 9, 2003): 13.

Due in part to the Master Settlement Agreement and the impact of discount cigarettes, R. J. Reynolds (RJR) is making sweeping structural changes in how promotional money is paid to retailers. The company will eliminate company-supplied displays and cash payments for shelf space and signage. Also, RJR will offer cash incentives to discount only core brands and instead offer discount coupons on promoted and nonpromoted brands that are due to expire within three months. Philip Morris will fight discount brands by using its Wholesale Leaders program to tie together wholesaler discounts and by meeting increased market-share targets.

496. Feighery, E. C., K. M. Ribisi, P. I. Clark, and H. H. Haladjian. "How Tobacco Companies Ensure Prime Placement of their Advertising and Products in Stores: Interviews with Retailers about Tobacco Company Incentive Programmes." *Tobacco Control* 12, no. 2 (June 2003): 184–88.

Through interviews with twenty-nine tobacco retailers sprinkled throughout twenty-one states, the authors gathered insights into retail incentive programs conducted by the tobacco industry. The interviews took place during the spring of 2001. They found that tobacco retailers are courted aggressively by the industry, with fierce competition taking place between Philip Morris and R. J. Reynolds. Incentive programs are promoted through contracts and "buydowns." Contracts cover items such as volume discounts, display allowances, product placement, and space allocation. Buydowns, or price reductions benefiting customers, require the usage of industry supplied special displays and signage. Retailers must follow strict requirements, such as product placement or advertising, to accept volume discounts and buydowns. Finally, retailers participating in incentive programs are easily recognizable.

497. Carter, S. M. "New Frontier, New Power: The Retail Environment in Australia's Dark Market." *Tobacco Control* 12, Suppl III (December 2003): iii95–iii101.

In Australia, cigarette manufacturers operate within a "dark market" where "above-the-line" marketing activities are restricted, leaving a need for "below-the-line" strategies. Within the retail sector, cigarette manufacturers look to build strong relationships and maintain loyalty with all retailers, especially with the larger companies. This is accomplished through five channels: trade promotional expenditures, in-store display hardware and assistance with point-of-sale marketing, corporate advertising and alliance building, brand advertising direct to retailers, and a new, innovative electronic distribution system.

498. Porter, Eduardo. "Tribes Go Online to Sell Cigarettes, and Fury Erupts." *New York Times*, September 26, 2004: sec. 1: 1, 26.

Internet tax-free cigarettes sales are booming for American Indian tribes, especially for the Seneca Nation of western New York. Price disparities between Internet sales and sales from commercial operations are substantial, and they are costing governments and businesses huge revenues. Indian reservations rely on treaties exempting them from state taxation, although states can collect taxes from non-Indian purchasers. Other non-Indian parties are taking advantage of the Internet to sell tax-free cigarettes. Sales originating from low-tax states and also duty-free sales from foreign Web operators pose problems.

3
Political Aspects

CALIFORNIA AND THE TOBACCO INDUSTRY

499. Bal, Dileep G., Kenneth W. Kizer, Patricia G. Felten, Harold N. Mozar, and Dearell Niemeyer. "Reducing Tobacco Consumption in California." *JAMA: The Journal of the American Medical Association* 264, no. 12 (September 26, 1990): 1570–74.

    The authors provide background information about California's Proposition 99, the Tobacco Tax and Health Promotion Act of 1988. The law raised cigarette excise taxes from ten to twenty-five cents per pack. The act provides funding for five main areas: health education, hospital services, physician services, research, and public resources. The authors describe how the California Department of Health Services used the funds to implement a statewide antitobacco use campaign, beginning with the April 1990 $28.6 million campaign to deglamorize smoking.

500. Price, Charles. "How Tobacco Courts California." *California Journal* 22, no. 8 (August 1991): 343–46.

    The tobacco industry is extensively involved in California legislative activities. The industry lobbies legislators and the public, makes political contributions, and advertises its positions in order to defeat or weaken pending or passed legislation. The industry lost in its drive to defeat Proposition 99. The industry spent over $21 million versus $2 million spent by the measure's proponents. California is instrumental in establishing national political and social trends and is for the industry a critical battleground in which to combat smoking initiatives.

501. Samuels, Bruce, and Stanton A. Glantz. "The Politics of Local Tobacco Control." *JAMA: The Journal of the American Medical Association* 266, no. 15 (October 16, 1991): 2110–17.

    Smoking initiatives developed at the local level have attracted the tobacco industry's complete attention. "Front" organizations, "grassroots" movements, referendum campaign organizations, and petition- and letter-writing campaigns are some of the tools used by the industry to mobilize smokers against antismoking ordinances.

The authors analyze these strategies with three California case studies and note the responses made by the health community.

502. Jacobs, Paul. "Tobacco Lobby Works Smoke-Filled Rooms." *Los Angeles Times*, September 20, 1992: A3, A32–33.

    Big-name tobacco lobbyists are working behind the scenes to defeat or weaken antismoking legislation. The tobacco representatives speak with legislators in the Capitol corridors, avoiding public hearings. The industry supports bills recognizing a civil right to smoke in nonworking hours and preventing antismoking ordinances from taking root at the local level. Philip Morris showers lawmakers with perks, such as meals and tickets to professional sports events.

503. Traynor, Michael P., Michael E. Begay, and Stanton A. Glantz. "New Tobacco Industry Strategy to Prevent Local Tobacco Control." *JAMA: The Journal of the American Medical Association* 270, no. 4 (July 28, 1993): 479–86.

    The tobacco industry uses four tactics to combat antismoking ordinances in California localities: monitoring the ordinances, organizing and directing pro-smoking efforts, organizing referendum petition drives, and financing election campaigns to overturn antismoking ordinances. The authors analyze this statewide four-pronged strategy as played out in nine cities and four counties.

504. Boyarsky, Bill. "Playing the Smoke and Mirrors Game in the Capitol." *Los Angeles Times*, August 22, 1993: B1, B3.

    The Los Angeles County supervisors recently worked with the tobacco industry to undermine the city's restaurant smoking ban. The supervisors agreed to support the industry's efforts to ban local antismoking ordinances. In return, the tobacco industry agreed to a cigarette tax increase, with Los Angeles County as the main beneficiary. Public backlash forced the parties to abandon the deal.

505. Begay, Michael Evans, Michael Traynor, and Stanton A. Glantz. "The Tobacco Industry, State Politics, and Tobacco Education in California." *American Journal of Public Health* 83, no. 9 (September 1993): 1214–21.

    The authors review Proposition 99, the implementation of its tobacco education and prevention programs, and the responses of the tobacco industry. In the 1991–1992 election cycle, the tobacco industry contributed $7.6 million in California. The industry's political activities have risen substantially since the passage of Proposition 99.

506. Adelson, Andrea. "A Campaign Aimed at Teen-agers Is at the Forefront of California's $499 Million Battle against Smoking." *New York Times*, April 5, 1994: D21.

    Proposition 99 created California's antismoking program. The program includes the use of television and billboard ads. Annually, about $14.5 million is spent on these ads. The television ads are paid; they are broadcast on the MTV and FOX networks. In the last five years, the program is credited with reducing cigarette sales by $1.6 billion and cigarette consumption by 1.1 billion packs.

507. Glantz, Stanton A., and Michael E. Begay. "Tobacco Industry Campaign Contributions Are Affecting Tobacco Control Policymaking in California." *JAMA: The Journal of the American Medical Association* 272, no. 15 (October 19, 1994): 1176–82.

The authors present evidence for a correlation between the tobacco industry's political contributions to California legislators and the legislators' policies toward the industry. Pro-tobacco legislators received greater contributions. During 1991 and 1992, twelve pro-tobacco bills and twenty-seven anti-tobacco bills came before the legislature; pro-tobacco sponsors received almost 2.5 times the amount of tobacco political monies contributed to the anti-tobacco bill sponsors.

508. Macdonald, Heather R., Michael P. Traynor, and Stanton A. Glantz. *California's Proposition 188: An Analysis of the Tobacco Industry's Political Advertising Campaign*. San Francisco: Institute for Health Policy Studies, School of Medicine, University of California, November 1994.

The November 1994 ballot included the California Uniform Tobacco Control Act, better known as Proposition 188. The measure was backed by the Californians for Statewide Smoking Restrictions (CSSR), a coalition formed by Philip Morris, the tobacco industry, and California hotels and restaurants. The group touted the proposal as one that would "enforce tough statewide smoking restrictions." Antismoking forces held that the proposal would weaken a smoke-free-workplace law that became effective in January 1995. Tobacco companies donated almost all of the $18.3 million spent by CSSR.

509. Lehrman, Sally. "Budget Hits 'Political' Research Funded by Tobacco Tax." *Nature* 382 (July 4, 1996): 6.

Under a rule adopted by California legislators working on the new budget, research of "a partisan political nature" would be prohibited from using Proposition 99 funds allocated for research. Overriding the peer-review process, the rule requires that research be reviewed first by the Department of Finance. The Tobacco Education and Research Oversight Committee would be consulted for advice. Antitobacco activists charge that the rule is aimed at tobacco researcher Stanton A. Glantz, of the University of California at San Francisco.

510. Claiborne, William. "California Puts 'No Smoking' behind Bars." *Washington Post*, December 20, 1997: A3.

In 1995, the California Assembly passed Assembly Bill 13. The bill banned workplace smoking but exempted bars and casinos until January 1, 1998. The law caused unrest among many business owners and smokers.

511. Macdonald, Heather, Stella Aguinaga, and Stanton A. Glantz. "The Defeat of Philip Morris's 'California Uniform Tobacco Control Act.'" *American Journal of Public Health* 87, no. 12 (December 1997): 1989–96.

The authors review the background and eventual defeat of Proposition 188, backed by Philip Morris and the tobacco industry. Proposition 188 attempted to weaken an already-passed antismoking law and restricted local communities from passing anti-tobacco ordinances. The authors examine the origins, petition drive, and strategies used by both the tobacco industry and antitobacco forces over the measure. In November 1994, California voters rejected the proposition by 71 to 29 percent.

512. Schwartz, John. "Unlikely Allies Opposed Anti-Smoking Campaign." *Washington Post*, January 20, 1998: A3.

A memo from the Tobacco Institute provides insight into the tobacco industry's efforts to prevent Proposition 99 money from being spent on hard-hitting ads, redirecting it to other programs in need of the funds. The memo encouraged actions through allies, such as business and minority organizations, so as to keep the industry out of the limelight. In 1992, Republican governor Pete Wilson halted the advertising campaign; the ads have recently reappeared but in a toned-down form.

513. Claiborne, William. "Unfiltered Defiance." *Washington Post*, February 17, 1998: A3.

California bar owners are openly defying a statewide law banning smoking in their establishments. The National Smokers Alliance, a tobacco industry–sponsored organization, provides bar owners with posters protesting the law and also coasters to be signed and sent to the legislature. The group distributes the *Prohibition News Update* and *The Resistance* newsletters, published biweekly and monthly, respectively.

514. Levin, Myron, and Dan Morain. "An Inside Look at Battles of Big Tobacco." *Los Angeles Times*, July 11, 1998: A1, A22.

A new treasure trove of tobacco documents covering the years 1977 to 1994 point to an industry obsession with attacking antismoking ordinances and laws in California. The documents include the industry's efforts battling Proposition 99 and backing Proposition 188. The industry felt overwhelmed by the number of local hearings; one response centered on developing working ties with groups usually not known to support the industry.

515. Feighery, Ellen C., Kurt M. Ribisi, Dale D. Archabal, and Tyzoon Tyebjee. "Retail Trade Incentives: How Tobacco Industry Practices Compare with Those of Other Industries." *American Journal of Public Health* 89, no. 10 (October 1999): 1564–66.

One hundred thirty-three randomly sampled retail venues in Santa Clara County, California, participated in the authors' survey regarding incentive programs. The authors sought to compare incentives offered by the tobacco industry versus other consumer products, such as candy, snack foods, soft drinks, and beer and wine. The incentives included slotting allowances, point-of-purchase display allowances, and trade allowances. The authors collected the data during November and December 1997. On average, tobacco industry payments for slotting fees and display allowances each month proved substantial. Trade allowances provided by the tobacco industry ranked behind those for soft drinks and those of beer and wine. The tobacco industry was more likely than the soft-drink industry to offer both slotting and display allowances (and promotional allowances) by a margin of two to one, and by six to one over beer and wine.

516. Glantz, Stanton A., and Edith D. Balbach. *Tobacco War: Inside the California Battles*. Berkeley: University of California Press, 2000. ark.cdlib.org/ark:/13030/ft167nb0vq (accessed March 15, 2004).

The authors document the California public health movement to battle the tobacco industry in the previous thirty years. Activities undertaken by the nonsmokers' rights movement period laid the groundwork for the present situation. The authors document the passage and implementation of Proposition 99, responses of the tobacco industry to the tobacco control movement, local tobacco control ordinances, preemption, and the use of polls by both sides to shape public opinion. The book includes a timetable of important tobacco control events.

517. Magzamen, Sheryl, and Stanton A. Glantz. "The New Battleground: California's Experience with Smoke-Free Bars." *American Journal of Public Health* 91, no. 2 (February 2001): 245–52.

    The California Legislature's Assembly Bill 13 (AB13), which requires that indoor workplaces be smoke-free (with some exceptions), like other smoke-free legislation, draws the ire of the tobacco industry. AB13 drew an unusual response from the industry, including numerous attempts to repeal the legislation, implementing a massive campaign to have the voters enact Proposition 188, and initiating a massive public relations campaign. The authors examine the tactics and strategies used by both protobacco and antitobacco forces in regard to AB13.

518. Morain, Dan. "Burning the Tobacco Windfall." *Los Angeles Times*, July 24, 2002: A1, A18.

    California legislators are eyeing tobacco to help plug a projected $24 billion shortfall. The legislature and Governor Gray Davis have proposed increasing cigarette taxes by $650 million, pulling $46 million from the anti-tobacco advertising campaign, and selling to investors the entire future stream of payments due the state under the master tobacco settlement. The lump-sum receipt from the sale would generate approximately $4.5 billion and would be placed in the state's general fund.

519. California. Office of the Governor. "AB384 by Assembly member Tim Leslie (R-Tahoe City), Tobacco Products: Correctional Facilities." Press release, Legislative Update, September 27, 2004. www.governor.ca.gov/state/govsite/gov_homepage.jsp (accessed October 1, 2004).

    California governor Arnold Schwarzenegger has signed legislation sponsored by Republican assemblyman Tim Leslie banning smoking in all of California's prisons. Starting in 2005, prisoners and staff will be forbidden from smoking at the state's youth and adult prisons. Indian religious ceremonies and staff housing (prisoners must not be present) are exempt from the new rules. (The bill, AB384, may be accessed at www.leginfo.ca.gov/cgi-bin/postquery?bill_number=ab_384&sess=CUR [September 27, 2004]).

INTERNATIONAL

520. Bonn, Dorothy. "New Zealand: Who's for Cricket?" *Lancet* 337 (June 8, 1991): 1402.

    Tobacco companies sponsoring sporting events are forbidden to advertise the events. However, the 1992 cricket cup, sponsored by Benson & Hedges, received an exemption, hastily passed by Parliament.

521. Colford, Steven W. "Senate Probes Ad Subsidies to Marketers." *Advertising Age* 63, no. 12 (March 23, 1992): 1, 45.

    The U.S. Senate Agriculture Committee will soon hear testimony regarding the U.S. Department of Agriculture's Market Promotion Program and whether the program should be scaled down or eliminated. The program provides funds for companies, organizations, and commodity groups to promote U.S. products in overseas markets. Major companies such as McDonalds, Pillsbury, and M&M/Mars have benefited from the program. According to Jeff Tenenbaum, aide to Representative Peter Kostmeyer (D-Pa.), "The U.S. Tobacco Associates got $3.5 million to promote U.S. tobacco abroad, which would seem to be a contradiction vis-à-vis the Department of Health & Human Services stance on smoking here at home."

522. Dean, Malcolm. "Margaret Thatcher's Tobacco Temptation." *Lancet* 340 (August 1, 1992): 294–95.

The *Sunday Times* (United Kingdom) reported that Philip Morris is courting the services of former prime minister Margaret Thatcher. Philip Morris supposedly believes that she would serve corporate interests in Vietnam, China, South Africa, and Russia. The company may use her skills to combat worldwide tobacco tax increases, government antismoking programs, and foreign ownership issues.

523. *Omnibus Budget Reconciliation Act of 1993*. Public Law 103-66, *U.S. Statutes at Large* 107 (August 10, 1993): 318, 330–31.

Title I (Agricultural Programs), Subtitle A (Commodity Programs), section 1106 changes the Agricultural Adjustment Act of 1938 to require domestic cigarette manufacturers to manufacture cigarettes with at least 75 percent tobacco grown in the United States. For each calendar year, the manufacturers must certify the numbers with the Secretary of the U.S. Department of Agriculture. Also, Title I, Subtitle C (Agricultural Trade), section 1302 Market Promotion Program, (b)(3) Tobacco states, "No funds made available under the market promotion program may be used for activities to develop, maintain, or expand foreign markets for tobacco."

524. Janofsky, Michael. "A Curb on Imported Tobacco Aids Farms and Philip Morris." *New York Times*, September 29, 1993: A1, D2.

A budget bill passed by Congress includes a provision requiring that cigarette tobacco include at least 75 percent American-grown tobacco. Senator Wendell Ford (D-Ky.) and Representative Charles Rose (D-N.C.) supported the measure. The measure favors Philip Morris, because of its manufacturing presence in foreign countries. R. J. Reynolds Tobacco opposed the measure.

525. *Agriculture, Rural Development, Food and Drug Administration, and Related Agencies Appropriations Act, 1994*. Public Law 103-111, *U.S. Statutes at Large* 107 (October 21, 1993): 1073–74.

Title I (Agricultural Programs), Title V (Foreign Assistance and Related Programs), "Foreign Agricultural Service" includes the statement, "None of the funds in the foregoing paragraph shall be available to promote the sale or export of tobacco or tobacco products." (Subsequent to the law's passage, the Foreign Agricultural Service stopped funding the tobacco component for two USDA programs. See entry 536.)

526. Nash, Nathaniel C. "In Europe, Philip Morris Beats the Drum against Government Regulations on Smoking." *New York Times*, November 28, 1995: D8.

Philip Morris Europe is taking the lead in championing the industry's position against any push by the central government, and perhaps any of the regional governments, toward regulating smoking in public places. Full-page print and billboard ads scream against infringing upon the personal liberty to smoke and rail against massive smoking regulations. One campaign ad uses the caption, "What sort of policy forces these people outside?" to depict smokers standing in the rain to enjoy a smoke.

527. Calian, Sara. "Philip Morris Tries to Snuff Out Curbs on Overseas Smokers." *Wall Street Journal*, June 5, 1996: B2.

Philip Morris Europe SA is paying for print ads to persuade the fifteen European Union governments not to adopt further restrictions on public smoking. Ads mention a "scientific study reference," data the company collected from reviewing research articles. The work states that secondhand tobacco smoke poses less risk than such "everyday activities" as drinking one to two glasses of milk daily, drinking chlorinated water, and eating cookies. One ad shows a restaurant scene of smokers and nonsmokers under the caption, "Doesn't it make sense for diners to decide whether smoking's on the menu?"

528. Flint, Anthony. "Aid to Cigarette Sales Abroad Stirs Debate." *Boston Globe*, June 11, 1996: 1, 28.

In stark contrast to its proposed domestic strict antitobacco measures, the U.S. federal government actively supports the sale of tobacco products in foreign countries. The Commerce Department and the Office of the U.S. Trade Representative (USTR) implemented this policy. The USTR does not object to foreign governments' imposition of tobacco controls such as health-warning labels and bans on vending machines; however, these restrictions must be applied equally to local companies and not act as phantom trade restrictions.

529. Moffett, Matt. "In Southern Brazil, a Town That Cigarettes Built." *Wall Street Journal*, July 21, 1997: B1, B10.

Santa Cruz do Sul is a major Brazilian center of tobacco influence. Tobacco's expansion and economic effects have helped substantially raise the per capita income. Tobacco's monetary contributions have helped to restore a Gothic-style cathedral, boost tax revenues, and provide employment. The industry plays a major role in the area's banking and agriculture industries, provides desperately needed technical expertise, and assists in purchasing materials for the area's university library.

530. *Departments of Commerce, Justice, and State, the Judiciary, and Related Agencies Appropriations Act, 1998: Act Making Appropriations for the Departments of Commerce, Justice, and State, the Judiciary, and Related Agencies for the Fiscal Year Ending September 30, 1998, and for Other Purposes.* Public Law 105-119, *U.S. Statutes at Large* 111 (November 26, 1997): 2519.

This law contains language prohibiting any U.S. embassy from promoting the sale or export of tobacco or tobacco products. The language appears under Title VI, General Provisions: "Sec. 618. None of the funds provided by this Act shall be available to promote the sale or export of tobacco or tobacco products, or to seek the reduction or removal by any foreign country of restrictions on the marketing of tobacco or tobacco products, except for restrictions which are not applied equally to all tobacco or tobacco products of the same type."

531. Robbins, Carla Anne, and Tara Parker-Pope. "U.S. Embassies Stop Assisting Tobacco Firms." *Wall Street Journal*, May 14, 1998: B1, B15.

    On February 14, 1998, American embassies around the world received a cable from the State Department directing them to halt all activities to promote "the sale or export of tobacco or tobacco products" overseas. Furthermore, local antismoking laws and regulations must be supported if the host country applies the rules "in a nondiscriminatory manner to both imported and domestic tobacco." This is in keeping with a provision inserted in Public Law 105-119 denying the usage of funds to promote the sale or export of tobacco or tobacco products. Philip Morris points out that the State Department continues to monitor "blatant" trade discrimination activities. In a recent case, the Thailand state tobacco monopoly marketed "Marble" cigarettes in packaging closely resembling a pack of Marlboro. The U.S. embassy assisted Philip Morris in battling this action.

532. Levin, Myron. "Tobacco Memos Show Overseas Price Fixing." *Los Angeles Times*, September 17, 1998: A1, A25.

    Tobacco internal documents obtained through Washington State's Medicaid lawsuit show Philip Morris and British American Tobacco entering into price-fixing deals to corner the markets in Latin America. A 1992 British American Tobacco (BAT) memo states that after the two company's Venezuelan affiliates engaged in a price war, both companies used Aruba and Colombia as vehicles to bring in smuggled cigarettes. A 1992 BAT memo dictated advertising expenditures and promotional activities for both company's brands in Costa Rica.

533. Fairclough, Gordon. "Philip Morris Notes Cigarettes' Benefits for Nation's Finances." *Wall Street Journal*, July 16, 2001: A2, A6.

    In the Czech Republic, a Philip Morris–sponsored "economic-impact study" is being circulated to government officials trumpeting the economic benefits of cigarette consumption. Arthur D. Little International produced the report for the company. The report argues that tax revenues and mortality-induced savings combined outweigh the costs of smoking. For 1999, Little states the net economic benefit is approximately $147.1 million; this includes savings from smoking-related deaths ranging between $23.8 million to $30.1 million.

534. Fairclough, Gordon, and Shelly Branch. "Tobacco Giants Prepare New Marketing Curbs Ahead of U.N. Treaty." *Wall Street Journal*, September 11, 2001: B1, B4.

    Work on a global tobacco treaty, the Framework Convention on Tobacco Control, is prompting Philip Morris, British American Tobacco, and Japan Tobacco to agree to voluntary marketing restrictions. One measure includes eliminating suggestive advertising where "smoking enhances popularity, or athletic, professional or sexual success." Also, youths will not be targeted by ads specifically "aimed" at them or by ads they will find particularly appealing. Billboard size will be reduced, outside covers or wrappings of magazines must not contain tobacco advertising, magazines carrying tobacco advertising must have youth readerships of less than 25 percent, and radio and television advertising will be banned.

535. Mapes, Timothy. "Big Cigarette Firm Fumes at Jakarta over a Trademark." *Wall Street Journal*, May 22, 2003: A12–A13.

United Kingdom–based Imperial Tobacco Group is seeking court relief to get its Davidoff cigarette trademark returned to the company. The Indonesian company Sumatra Tobacco Group claims the trademark. Sumatra's claim stems from a failed marketing agreement between Imperial's Reemtsma subsidiary and Indonesian tobacco company Gudang Garam. After the failure, Sumatra claimed the trademark and the right to market the product in Indonesia. Imperial proposed building a factory in Indonesia to manufacture the brand, employ hundreds of Indonesians, and conduct business with the nation's tobacco farmers. Over ten years, the manufacturing activities would have generated approximately $4 billion in revenues.

536. U.S. General Accounting Office. *Tobacco Exports: USDA's Foreign Agricultural Service Lacks Specific Guidance for Congressional Restrictions on Promoting Tobacco*. GAO-03-618. Washington, D.C.: GAO, May 30, 2003. www.gao.gov/new.items/d03618.pdf (accessed February 19, 2004).

The 1994 agriculture appropriations passed by Congress (Public Law 103-111) included language stopping the Foreign Agricultural Service (FAS) from promoting the "sale or export of tobacco or tobacco products" and restricting the tobacco-related activities of the U.S. Department of Agriculture. Subsequently, the FAS stopped funding the tobacco component of the Export Credit Guarantee Program and the Foreign Market Development Program. Similarly, the 1998 appropriations passed for the Commerce, Justice, and State departments (Public Law 105-119) placed restrictions on Commerce, State, and the Office of the U.S. Trade Representative. These offices are not barred from addressing foreign discriminatory trade practices. In this report, the General Accounting Office assesses how the agencies and then overseas personnel are working together to implement the restrictions and how the agencies are ensuring compliance.

537. "S. Korean Tobacco Firm KT&G Promotes New Image." *Asia Africa Intelligence Wire*, February 10, 2004: n.p. Infotrac OneFile (accessed October 25, 2004).

KT&G, the Korea Tomorrow & Global Corporation, is brandishing a new corporate image in hopes of changing the public's perception of the company. The new advertising theme, "The Glorification of Imagination," paints the company as "young and modern" and downplays the fact that it is a tobacco company. In effect since 1993, the advertising campaign costs $12.8 million annually. The ad campaign is having a positive impact; 43.8 percent of respondents polled during a December 2003 survey looked favorably on the company. This is an increase of 9.2 percent from last August, when 34.6 percent gave the company a good rating.

POLITICS, POLITICIANS, AND LOBBYISTS

538. Pytte, Alyson. "Tobacco's Clout Stays Strong through Dollars, Jobs, Ads." *Congressional Quarterly Weekly Report* 48, no. 20 (May 19, 1990): 1542–48.

Public pressure to place controls on the tobacco industry is also putting pressure on Congress to take action. Lawmakers also must grapple with the tobacco industry's immense impact on the economy and on politicians inside and outside the Beltway. Throughout the economy, the industry's tobacco strings can be traced to over one million jobs, government revenues exceeding $11 billion dollars, generous advertising revenues, and countless contributions to civic and charitable causes. Also, representatives run key congressional committees from the Tobacco Belt states.

539. Marshall, Eliot. "Tobacco Industry Does Slow Burn over EPA Advisor." *Science* 250 (October 12, 1990): 203.

The tobacco industry is objecting to the appointment of Associate Clinical Professor David Burns, University of California at San Diego, to the Environmental Protection Agency's Science Advisory Board. The board will review two draft documents related to tobacco smoke: whether tobacco is really a "class A" carcinogen and whether policy guidance should be issued for states to follow in regulating the smoke. Burns worked with the U.S. surgeon general on issues related to tobacco, and the industry regards him as "not open minded."

540. Williams, Marjorie. "Tobacco's Hold on Women's Groups." *Washington Post*, November 14, 1991: A1, A16.

Women's groups, associations, clubs, and foundations are receiving funding from Philip Morris, RJR Nabisco, and the Tobacco Institute. Critics claim the tobacco industry purchases "innocence by association," deters the groups from championing antitobacco causes, and associates smoking with independence. Women's groups contend that they encounter "glass ceilings" when it comes to fund-raising, that the amounts pale when compared to other funding vehicles used by the industry, equaling perhaps 5 to 10 percent of a group's total budget. Groups receiving tobacco funding include the Center for Women Policy Studies, Women's Research and Education Institute, and the National Women's Political Caucus.

541. Williams, Marjorie. "The Funding Habit Women's Groups Can't Resist." *Washington Post*, November 14, 1991: A16.

Philip Morris fully funded the twenty-five-thousand-dollar cost of the effort by Women's Campaign Fund, the National Women's Political Caucus, and Emily's List to poll the public's perceptions of women congressional and senatorial candidates. Over the past three years, RJR Nabisco has provided over two hundred thousand dollars for congressional fellowships through the Women's Research and Education Institute. Likewise, Philip Morris provides twenty-eight thousand dollars per year for two fellowships. Philip Morris underwrites the National Women's Political Caucus's *National Directory of Women Elected Officials,* to the tune of a hundred thousand dollars.

542. Morrissey, Matthew. "Tobacco Turns over a New (Green) Leaf." *National Journal* 24, no. 37 (September 12, 1992): 2073, 2075.

The tobacco companies established a stronger than usual presence in political affairs leading to the 1992 election. At the Republican National Convention in Houston, Philip Morris vice president Craig L. Fuller served as the general chairman. His employer contributed a hundred thousand dollars to sponsor the International Republican Institute's transportation of 250 foreign dignitaries to the convention. RJR Nabisco sponsored a brunch for Senator Robert Dole (R-Kans.). For the Democrats' New York City convention, delegates gathered atop the World Trade Center for a party cosponsored by Philip Morris.

543. Stone, Peter H. "A New Whiff of Tobacco's Influence." *National Journal* 25, no. 4 (January 23, 1993): 221.

Tobacco's clout in the federal government continued in the new Clinton administration. U.S. Trade Representative Mickey Kantor's law firm Manatt, Phelps, Phillips, and Kantor had Philip Morris Management Corporation as a client. Also, the firm worked with a Beverly Hills restaurant group to lobby against legislation placing restraints on smoking in public places. Commerce secretary designee Richard W. Riley reviewed applications for about three thousand subcabinet positions. Tobacco foes worried that Riley's client connections to Philip Morris through his law firm of Nelson, Mullins, Riley & Scarborough affected his judgment in filling these important positions, in such departments as Health and Human Services and Agriculture.

544. Novak, Viveca. "Kicking the Habits." *National Journal* 25, no. 16 (April 17, 1993): 912–16.

The Clinton administration proposed a raise in tobacco excise taxes two dollars per pack. The administration acted on a suggestion by the Coalition on Smoking OR Health. Over a five-year period, the tobacco tax increase was estimated to raise $90 billion. In response, the Council of State Governments issued a report, partially financed by Philip Morris, calling tobacco tax increases a "worn-out tax source." The president received a letter from twenty-five House members warning of serious economic consequences if tobacco taxes are increased sharply.

545. Stone, Peter H. "States of Siege." *National Journal* 25, no. 17 (April 24, 1993): 983–86.

Public-interest groups, legislators, and regulators are vigorously attacking the tobacco companies on the state level. High on the list of tools used is "preemption," attempts to get legislation enacted to preempt local antismoking ordinances, such as those restricting smoking in public places and banning cigarette vending machines. Tobacco companies are spending a great deal of money to support preemption. Tobacco political action committees distributed an average of $10,402 to California state legislators during the 1991–1992 session. Philip Morris hired Austin lobbyists Dick Brown, Stan Schlueter, and Neal T. Jones, Jr., to work against antismoking legislation introduced by Texas governor Ann Richards.

546. Janofsky, Michael. "Squaring Off over Cigarette Taxes." *New York Times*, June 5, 1993: 37, 49.

The antitobacco forces and the tobacco industry had completely opposite views of the effects of a proposed White House tobacco tax increase. Antitobacco groups pointed to the April 1993 price cuts by each company (following Philip Morris's forty cent price cut of Marlboros), a total of thirty-three price increases led to aggregate price increases in excess of 350 percent, higher profit margins, greater usage of cheaper foreign tobaccos, and cost savings due to technology. The price increases accounted for annual job losses of only 1.33 percent. The Tobacco Institute countered with a report written by Price Waterhouse and underwritten by the institute, stating that jobs losses in the growth, manufacturing, and distribution sectors would total 114,117 and payroll losses would total $3.33 billion with a forty-eight-cent tax increase. Job losses totaled 776,056 and payroll losses totaled $22.68 billion with a two-dollar increase.

547. Stone, Peter H. "Mobilizing against Tax." *National Journal* 25, no. 41 (October 9, 1993): 2438–39.

The tobacco industry is marshaling its forces to fight the president's proposed increase of seventy-five cents to a dollar in tobacco excise taxes. The Tobacco Institute employs lobbyist James C. Healey, who has met with House Ways and Means Committee chairman Dan Rostenkowski. Healey once worked for Rostenkowski. R. J. Reynolds's (RJR) fifteen regional network directors tap smokers' rights groups and train numerous members to lobby Congress. RJR's political consulting and advertising firm of Walt Klein & Associates operates an 800 number used to lodge antitax protests. Also, RJR has the Texas law firm of Akin, Gump, Strauss, Hauer & Feld and its partner, RJR board member Vernon E. Jordan, Jr., pressing tobacco's arguments with the Clinton administration.

548. Stone, Peter H. "Tobacco's Road." *National Journal* 26, no. 1 (January 1, 1994): 19–23.

The Tobacco Institute's impact and influence on national tobacco policy making took a turn downward with steep staff reductions and financial support from its major tobacco benefactors, Philip Morris and R. J. Reynolds (RJR). Still, the institute was able to employ former U.S. representatives Robin Tallon (D-S.C.) and Charles Whitley (D-N.C.) as in-house lobbyists. The institute's reduced role in lobbying politicians was covered in its entirety by Philip Morris and RJR. Philip Morris hired the stellar public relations firm Burson-Marstellar. The firm was expected to mount a public relations blitz in opposition to the president's proposal to fund his health care proposal by raising tobacco excise taxes from twenty-four cents to ninety-nine. RJR hired former Washington insiders Robert J. Leonard (Ways and Means Committee chief counsel), Thomas M. Ryan (House Energy and Commerce Committee aide), and William C. Oldaker (with connections to the Democratic Party).

549. Sharfstein, Joshua M., and Steven S. Sharfstein. "Campaign Contributions from the American Medical Political Action Committee to Members of Congress." *New England Journal of Medicine* 330, no. 1 (January 6, 1994): 32–37.

For the periods of 1989–1990 and 1991–1991, the authors examine the contributions of the American Medical Political Action Committee (AMPAC) to House members in connection with three health issues, including tobacco-export promotion. For 1989–1990, House members favoring the tobacco issue received an average AMPAC contribution of $6,018; opponents received an average of $4,833. For 1990–1991, House members favoring the tobacco issue received an average AMPAC contribution of $6,188; opponents received an average of $5,779. These figures belie AMPAC's official position of opposing all "efforts by the government or its agencies to actively encourage, persuade or compel any country to import tobacco products."

550. Shapiro, Eben. "Tobacco Firm Seeks Antismoking Network's Records." *Wall Street Journal*, March 30, 1994: B1, B8.

The Advocacy Institute has received a subpoena to relinquish the membership list, financial contributors, and meeting transcripts of its Smoking Control Advocacy Resource Network. The network is used to communicate antitobacco news and strategies to its two hundred members. The American Tobacco Company requested the data in response to a wrongful-death lawsuit filed against it and R. J. Reynolds Tobacco.

551. U.S. Congress. House. Committee on Energy and Commerce. Subcommittee on Health and the Environment. *Regulation of Tobacco Products: Hearings before the Subcommittee on Health and the Environment of the Committee on Energy and Commerce.* 103rd Cong., 2nd sess., Part 1, April 14, 1994.

The chief executive officers of the six major cigarette companies have testified against the claim their companies manipulated nicotine levels in their cigarette products. The six stated they did not believe nicotine is an addictive product. The officers included William I. Campbell (Phillip Morris), James W. Johnston (R. J. Reynolds Tobacco), Thomas E. Sandefur (Brown & Williamson), Andrew H. Tisch (Lorillard Tobacco), Donald S. Johnston (American Tobacco), and Edward A. Horrigan (Liggett Group).

552. Cloud, David S. "Tobacco Industry Losing Allies as Congress Eyes Health Tax." *Congressional Quarterly Weekly Report* 52, no. 16 (April 23, 1994): 985, 987, 989.

President Clinton's proposed seventy-five-cents-per-pack increase in the tobacco excise tax could generate $10 billion a year in revenue. The House Ways and Means Health Subcommittee's approved increase of $1.25 per pack could generate sixteen billion dollars per year. Even antitax tobacco allies find it hard to resist voting for an increase, no matter how large or small, to pay for health care reform.

553. Stone, Peter H. "It's All Done with Smoke and Some PR." *National Journal* 26, no. 22 (May 28, 1994): 1244–45.

The National Smokers Alliance (NSA) is a new national smokers' rights group. It is funded by Philip Morris and essentially operated by Burson-Marsteller, Philip Morris's public relations firm. The NSA's twenty-seven-member advisory board includes such political heavyweights as former U.S. representative Guy Vander Jagt (R-Mich.) and Republican National Committee cochairwoman Jeanie Austin. The group hires college students nationally to canvas bars, bingo parlors, and bowling alleys for new members age twenty-one and older. Each new member becomes a non-dues-paying member for three months. For the November 1994 ballot, the NSA worked to qualify a petition allowing Californians to vote for a single state smoking law and replace multiple local ordinances.

554. Valero, Greg. "Tobacco Tax Proposal Prompts 'Call to Action.'" *U.S. Distribution Journal* 221, no. 6 (June 15, 1994): 7–8.

Members attending the American Wholesale Marketers Association annual legislative conference have united in opposition to the Clinton administration's desire to raise tobacco excise taxes. The members argue that the tax increase will force many distributors out of business. They cite a 1992 Price Waterhouse study showing that such a tax increase will cause an estimated $8.006 billion in payroll losses and 273,902 job losses. These are the total losses affecting the growing, manufacturing, wholesale trade, retail trade, sector suppliers, and "expenditure-induced sectors." Tobacco wholesalers account for 62 percent of sales and 46 percent of gross profits.

555. Millman, Nancy. "Pro-Choice: Tobacco Company's Advocacy Campaign Lets the Average Person Be Heard." *Chicago Tribune*, August 23, 1994: sec. 5: 2.

R. J. Reynolds Tobacco is using a different method to express its views on the current antitobacco climate. In national newspaper advertisements, the company's views are preceded by the beliefs of ordinary citizens. The ads only reveal each person's first name, home state, and opinions about smokers' rights and government "intervention." The interviews and photographs occurred in Chicago. Each person received a dollar in payment, the legal amount required to be paid in such circumstances.

556. Tin, Annie. "Tobacco Conflict Smoldering as Critics Step Up Assaults." *Congressional Quarterly Weekly Report* 53, no. 29 (July 22, 1995): 2136, 2138–39.

The tobacco price-support program is under attack from two sides. Some Republicans believe the market should dictate whether the industry survives. Health advocates deplore the government support given to an industry chastised by the Food and Drug Administration and various surgeon generals. In 1994, federal financial support totaled $15 million for annual administrative costs and other promotion costs.

557. U.S. Congress. House. Committee on Appropriations. *Departments of Labor, Health and Human Services, and Education, and Related Agencies Appropriation Bill, 1996: Report of the Committee on Appropriations Together with Dissenting and Separate Views (to Accompany H.R. 2127)*. 104th Cong., 1st sess., July 27, 1995. H. Rep. 209.

Report includes language inserted by Representative John Porter's (R-Ill.) attempt to squelch a National Cancer Institute (NCI) grant to Professor Stanton Glantz, University of California at San Francisco, to study the effect of tobacco contributions on state lawmakers' ability to pass tobacco control legislation. The language appears on page 61. "*Study of campaign contributions*. The committee was disturbed to learn that NCI has funded a research grant studying tobacco industry campaign contributions to State legislators and voting records by those individuals on tobacco control initiatives. While the committee is not rendering judgment on the merits of the grant proposal, it feels strongly that such research projects do not properly fall within the boundaries of the NCI portfolio, especially when nearly three-quarters of approved research projects go unfunded. Accordingly, the committee does not provide any further funding for this research grant within the NCI appropriation."

558. Bird, Laura. "Cigarette Machine Operators Are Asking Clinton for Change." *Wall Street Journal*, August 14, 1995: A3–A4.

President Clinton proposed to ban the use of cigarette vending machines. The industry, led by the Amusement and Music Operators Association, voiced strong opposition to the proposal. The machines are banned in numerous municipalities; other localities restrict access to adult venues, such as bars. Each year, vending machines account for the sale of approximately three hundred million cigarette packs.

559. Cardador, M. Teresa, Anna R. Hazan, and Stanton A. Glantz. "Tobacco Industry Smokers' Rights Publications: A Content Analysis." *American Journal of Public Health* 85, no. 9 (September 1995): 1212–17.

The authors review the thematic content of articles printed in tobacco magazines from 1987 to 1992. This includes publications such as *Choice* (RJR) and *Philip Morris Magazine*, *American Smokers Journal*, and *Smoker's Rights Alliance* (Philip Morris). The authors identify four major themes: political and social action (e.g., letter writing, organizing, and circulating petitions), undermining the opposition (such as refuting scientific and medical evidence and discrediting the tobacco control movement), perceived threats (such as government interference and undermining American values), and creating legitimacy (such as accommodation and tolerance).

560. Marshall, Eliot. "Researchers Protest Attack on Tobacco Study." *Science* 270 (October 27, 1995): 573.

In 1993, the National Cancer Institute (NCI) awarded a three-year, six-hundred-thousand-dollar grant to Professor Stanton Glantz, University of California at San Francisco. A leading antitobacco proponent, Dr. Glantz proposed studying the interrelationship between the tobacco industry's contributions to state lawmakers and tobacco control measures. The grant caught the eye and ire of Representative John Porter (R-Ill.). Porter sought to have the funding stopped by attaching a paragraph in an appropriations report containing funding for the National Institutes of Health, the NCI's parent agency. The research community reacted angrily, blasting Porter in a newspaper ad.

561. Fisher, Ian. "On Tobacco Lobby List, Two Unlikely Names." *New York Times*, November 19, 1995: sec. 1: 41, 49.

Representatives Edolphus Townes (D-N.Y.) and Charles B. Rangel (D-N.Y.) both receive generous contributions from the tobacco industry. Both have opposed congressional antitobacco legislation and sided with the tobacco industry on many of its positions regarding tobacco issues. Rangel opposes higher excise taxes. Townes regards the tobacco industry as a job creator, taxpayer, and contributor to many charitable causes.

562. Freyman, Russ. "Butting In." *Governing* 9, no. 2 (November 1995): 55–57.

Antitobacco measures passed by cities and counties are being attacked vigilantly by the tobacco industry. The tobacco lobby is pushing state legislatures to pass "preemption" laws barring the local authorities from passing any type of tobacco regulation. Such laws are on the books in twenty-six states. Maine, Nevada, and North Carolina recently passed various types of preemption laws. The tobacco industry's attempt to overturn multiple ordinances in California failed miserably with the defeat of its Proposition 188.

563. Noah, Timothy, and Laurie McGinley. "Tobacco Industry's Figures on Political Spending Don't Reflect Gifts to Think Tanks, Other Groups." *Wall Street Journal*, March 25, 1996: A16.

Contributions to politicians are but one way the tobacco companies influence public policy. The companies also make contributions to conservative think tanks and liberal groups. Philip Morris gave $25,000 (1991) and the RJR Nabisco Foundation $30,000 (1993) to the Washington Legal Foundation. Philip Morris annually donates more than $10,000 to the Competitive Enterprise Institute. Philip Morris donated $91,800 (1991) to the Citizens for a Sound Economy. Both tobacco companies give money to the Progress and Freedom Foundation. The think tanks work to oppose the Food and Drug Administration's proposed regulation of the tobacco industry. The American Civil Liberties Union opposes tobacco advertising restrictions; it receives an annual tobacco contribution of between $50,000 and $7,000.

564. Sanger, David E. "For Helms, His Home State Is Source of Foreign Policy." *New York Times*, April 2, 1996: A1, A18.

The Durham, North Carolina, steakhouse Angus Barn set the stage for a R. J. Reynolds (RJR)–sponsored dinner honoring ambassadors from the seven countries constituting the Association for Southwest Asian Nations. The ambassadors met Senate Foreign Relations Committee chairman Jesse Helms (R-N.C.) and heard his pitch to promote tobacco exports to their countries. The Vietnamese ambassador, Le Van Bang, commented that "in Vietnam, we have a custom now of greeting each other by offering a cigarette." The ambassadors' three-day visit included a tour of RJR's Winston-Salem tobacco plant.

565. Stone, Peter H. "Blowing Smoke at Its Critics." *National Journal* 28, no. 16 (April 20, 1996): 884–87.

R. J. Reynolds (RJR) and Philip Morris are using grassroots operations, political connections, and think tanks to combat the antitobacco movement. The RJR-created Ramhurst Corporation (Winston-Salem, N.C.) has attacked the Food and Drug Administration's proposal to regulate cigarettes as a drug. Ramhurst consultant Karl Gallant's tax-fighting crusades have led him to work with the Washington, D.C., conservative think tank Citizens for a Sound Economy, which worked to oppose New Jersey governor Christine Todd Whitman's proposed increase in the tobacco excise tax. In 1993, Philip Morris contributed $4 million to form the smokers' rights group National Smokers Alliance. Senator Robert Dole's (R-Kans.) former think tank, Better America Foundation, received a hundred thousand dollars from both RJR and Philip Morris. The Dole Foundation, which focuses on providing for the disabled, received funds from Philip Morris, RJR, and the Tobacco Institute.

566. Levin, Myron. "Legal Weapon." *Los Angeles Times*, April 21, 1996: D1, D4.

Tobacco companies are using the Freedom of Information Act and similar state laws to launch massive document requests aimed at attacking and stalling the efforts of antismoking advocates and public health departments. Their main targets are usage of public funds to finance tax increase campaigns, smoking bans, and other antismoking programs and lobbying efforts. In Colorado, state health staff copied over thirteen thousand documents, including seven thousand documents never retrieved by the tobacco companies, at a cost to the taxpayers of from fifty to sixty thousand dollars. The Washington State health department staff copied over five thousand pages; this involved over 360 hours of staff time. Even surrogates with ties to the industry are filing requests. For example, one tobacco-client proxy, Fiscal Planning Services, filed document requests in all seventeen Project ASSIST (American Stop Smoking Intervention Study) states requesting a comprehensive list of ASSIST-funded groups.

567. Herbert, Bob. "Checking Out the House." *New York Times*, May 10, 1996: A33.

During a 1995 House summer session, Representative John A. Boehner (R-Ohio) distributed about six tobacco checks to certain colleagues. House Ethics Committee rules do not prevent the acceptance or distribution of "voluntary" donations. Boehner abstained from distributing donations after fellow Republicans, such as Steve Largent (R-Okla.), objected to the practice.

568. Simpson, Glenn R. "A Cloudy Trail of Cigarette-Industry Money Winds Its Way to Democrats' Campaign Coffers." *Wall Street Journal*, July 5, 1996: A8.

The Democratic Party quietly accepts funds from tobacco companies while labeling the GOP as a "wholly owned subsidiary" of the tobacco industry. Money contributed to the Democratic National Committee (DNC) is forwarded to state parties. The Nevada State Democratic Party received twenty-five thousand dollars via Philip Morris and deposited it in a "coordinated campaign" account. The money is available to support the president and Nevada Democrats. Courtesy of R. J. Reynolds Tobacco (RJR), the California, Colorado, Nevada, and New Jersey state organizations each received ten thousand dollars. RJR made the contributions based on a list of states supplied by the Democratic National Committee. DNC spokesman David Eichenbaum stated the committee had given RJR the list for informational purposes only. In addition, the California Democratic Party (CDP) rejected a ten-thousand-dollar DNC contribution received from RJR. The DNC redirected the funds to the CDP-affiliated, San Francisco–based group Agenda for the '90s.

569. Cockburn, Alexander. "The Democrats' Anti-Tobacco Stance Goes Up in Smoke." *New Statesman* 125 (July 26, 1996): 26.

Contrary to his antitobacco persona, President Clinton has stated that he "pleaded guilty to smoking six cigars a year." During the early 1990s, Philip Morris, Brown & Williamson, RJR Nabisco, Lorillard Tobacco, and the Tobacco Institute filled Clinton's political coffers. Vice President Al Gore once farmed tobacco and benefited from the government's tobacco support program. Horace Liebengood, a family friend of his father and lobbyist for the Tobacco Institute, leaned on Gore, Jr., to water down a tough antitobacco bill offered by Representative Henry Waxman (D-Calif.). Gore's amendments kept the words "death" and "addiction" out of Waxman's legislation.

570. Frisby, Michael K. "Tobacco Companies Are Low-Key in San Diego." *Wall Street Journal*, August 15, 1996: A12.

At the Republican National Convention in San Diego, tobacco companies shunned the spotlight and dodged antismoking protestors. Philip Morris and U.S. Tobacco hosted small groups on boats docked in the site's marina. RJR Nabisco hosted a party for House Commerce Committee chairman Thomas J. Bliley (R-Va.). Philip Morris donated five hundred thousand dollars to support the convention, hosted parties for the Connecticut and New York delegations, and sponsored a trip to the Nixon Library. For the Democratic convention in Chicago, Philip Morris was the only tobacco company hosting events. Kraft Foods, Inc., a subsidiary of Philip Morris, donated a hundred thousand dollars to support the convention.

571. Martz, Michael. "Watchdog Group Hid Tobacco Link: Philip Morris Financed Key Study." *Richmond Times-Dispatch*, December 1, 1996. LexisNexis Academic (accessed May 19, 2004).

Contributions Watch, a nonprofit arm created in 1996 by the public relations firm State Affairs, issued a report in July 1996 titled "Off the Radar Screen." This report noted that from January 1995 through March 1996, $11.6 million in political contributions flowed from trial lawyers to federal candidates. A follow-up study in September 1996 tracked contributions to state and federal candidates from early 1985 through 1989. In announcing the results, Contributions Watch failed to note that Philip Morris financed the reports. Officers in State Affairs have connections to Burson-Marstellar, Philip Morris's public-relations firm, the Democratic and Republican parties, and Senator Charles S. Robb.

572. Hilts, Philip J. *Smokescreen: The Truth behind the Tobacco Industry Cover-Up*. Reading, Mass.: Addison-Wesley, 1996.

New York Times reporter Hilts uses tobacco industry secret documents to paint a picture of deceit, denial, and political influence. The industry denied scientific evidence and internal research showing that smoking is dangerous and nicotine is addictive. Also, the documents point to an industry clearly targeting the youth market with advertising that paints smoking as cool and as rebellion against authority. In addition, tobacco money is used as a weapon to corral politicians and keep them on the industry's side. The author explores the stories of industry whistle-blowers Jeffrey Wigand and Merrill Williams.

573. Kluger, Richard. *Ashes to Ashes: America's Hundred-Year Cigarette War, the Public Health, and the Unabashed Triumph of Philip Morris*. New York: Alfred A. Knopf, 1996.

Kluger's eight-hundred-page tome provides an encyclopedic wealth of knowledge about the tobacco industry's history. He explores such issues as the medical case built against smoking, the story behind the surgeon general's 1964 report that smoking is dangerous to health, how the industry used cigarette warning labels to ward off lawsuits, the rise and power of marketing to sell the glamor of cigarette smoking, Philip Morris's rise in power at the expense of American Tobacco and R. J. Reynolds, and the movement to conquer new and emerging markets.

574. Pincus, Walter. "House Sweeps Checks Off Floor." *Washington Post*, February 14, 1997: A19.

Both Democrats and Republicans help freshman representatives improve their financial cash-on-hand numbers toward the end of reporting periods. During one week in June 1995, Representative John A. Boehmer (R-Ohio) distributed at least six Brown & Williamson (B&W) checks, each worth five hundred dollars, to his colleagues on the House floor. These six checks came from a total of fifty-nine checks written by B&W to members of both parties; B&W wrote checks to certain lawmakers at the behest of Boehner. To prevent similar episodes, in January 1997, the House voted to ban such distributions on the House floor, the speaker's lobby, and the cloakrooms of both parties.

575. "Tobacco Lobby Hosts Lawmakers at Golf Resort." *Boston Globe*, February 18, 1997: A9. (Associated Press).

The Tobacco Institute has sponsored a three-day conference at the Scottsdale, Arizona, golf resort The Phoenician. Over one hundred congressmen and congressional aides attended the conference; the Tobacco Institute paid the tab, except for golf matches. Legislators are permitted to accept privately funded "fact-finding" and/or educational travel if the purpose is in the best interest of their constituents.

576. Elliston, Jon. "Philip Morris Front Group Exposed." February 1997. parascope.com/articles/0297/smoke.htm (accessed May 29, 2004).

In 1996, State Affairs Company created Contributions Watch to serve as a nonprofit organization, with a mission documenting trial lawyers' political contributions to state and federal candidates. In September 1996, news surfaced that Philip Morris served as the funding sponsor for the organization's reports. These documents include a State Affairs Company's report entitled "Lobbying and Public Affairs of Philip Morris and R. J. Reynolds." The State Affairs report examines both companies' activities in the areas of state and federal lobbying, public affairs, litigation support, and corporate philanthropy.

577. Crenshaw, Albert B. "Freddie Mac Sells Its Tobacco Bonds." *Washington Post*, April 18, 1997: G1–G2.

On April 17, 1997, the Federal Home Loan Mortgage Corporation, better known as "Freddie Mac," announced that the stockholder-owned company has sold Philip Morris bonds valued at $340 million. Freddie Mac had purchased the securities with money borrowed at favorable interest rates. House Banking Committee chairman James Leach (R-Iowa) had discovered the investment and pressured Freddie Mac to sell the bonds. Leach claimed the investment breached the company's mission to provide low-cost mortgage funds for housing purchases and constituted "an abuse of privilege."

578. Mintz, John. "17-State Federal Program Cuts Smoking, Draws Fire." *Washington Post*, April 19, 1997: A1, A14.

The American Stop Smoking Intervention Study is a federally funded program in seventeen states. The National Cancer Institute operates the program, which started in 1993 and is funded annually at $25 million. The key strategies used to reduce smoking are advocating higher cigarette taxes, restricting smoking in public venues through regulations, and restricting teen access to cigarettes. Antitobacco advocates point to the program's successes, such as a 10 percent drop in aggregate per capita cigarette consumption and a reduction of eight hundred million cigarettes packs.

Tobacco advocates such as the Tobacco Institute and some Republication congressional members, such as Representative Ernest J. Istook, Jr. (R-Okla.), want the program dismantled, claiming its funds are used on political activities such as lobbying state legislatures and municipalities and having the American Cancer Society lobby on behalf of the program.

579. Kerwin, Ann Marie. "Tobacco Ad Debate Played Part in Condé Nast Launch Shakeup." *Advertising Age* 68, no. 18 (May 5, 1997): 3, 67.

Condé Nast has fired Deanna Brown as publisher of the soon-to-be-issued magazine *Condé Nast Sports for Women*. The company stated that her inexperience disqualified her to handle a $40 million budget. Insiders, however, speculate that the company fired Brown for refusing to accept tobacco advertising. Tobacco advertising is accepted by all other Condé Nast publications.

580. Ingersoll, Bruce, and Laurie McGinley. "First Smoking-Related Veterans Claims Are Handled and Potential Flood Is Seen." *Wall Street Journal*, July 16, 1997: A2, A6.

Veterans afflicted with smoking-related diseases and veterans' families impacted by smoking-related deaths are expected to flood the Department of Veteran Affairs (VA) with compensation claims. The onslaught is tied to a legal opinion issued by VA general counsel Mary Lou Keener. The May 13, 1997 ruling stated that postservice smoking illnesses directly related to the development of in-service dependence on tobacco are entitled to compensation claims. Surviving spouses and other parties directly affected by veterans' dependence on tobacco are also entitled to be compensated. In response, the VA floated the idea that Congress should pass legislation narrowing tobacco-related compensation claims to active-duty veterans.

581. Boncompagni, Tatiana S., and Jill Abramson. "Tobacco-Funded Group Gives Legislators Free Trips." *Wall Street Journal*, August 4, 1997: A20.

A little-known nonprofit group called the New York Society for International Affairs is very active in the political scene. Members of the Council of State Governments and the National Governors Association are recruited for trips sponsored by the society. The group recently sponsored a junket to Costa Rica for a select group of House and Senate members. The society paid all the costs for the five-day trip, including the stay at a posh hotel and a jungle boat safari. The society received the majority of its funding from Philip Morris. In 1996, it received $370,000 in contributions, with Philip Morris providing the lion's share.

582. Siegel, Michael, Julia Carol, Jerie Jordan, Robin Hobart, Susan Schoenmarklin, Fran DuMelle, and Peter Fisher. "Preemption in Tobacco Control." *JAMA: The Journal of the American Medical Association* 278, no. 10 (September 10, 1997): 858–63.

The authors review the tobacco industry's influence in preempting the rights of local communities to enact tobacco control measures. Overall, the tobacco industry employs a three-pronged strategy to repeal local tobacco control. First, the industry influences legislators to add language to tobacco control bills that bans local communities from enacting tobacco control legislation. Secondly, the industry tries to sway legislators with the idea that meeting the provisions of the Synar Amendment (Public Law 102-321) to regulate sales of tobacco to underage youth requires the preemption of local controls. Third, the industry pushes legislators to enact "superpremption" bills to take the rights from *all* local communities to enact tobacco control legislation. The authors conclude that public health advocates must get involved in fighting the tobacco industry's influence on state legislators to enact preemption legislation.

583. Carey, John. "Big Tobacco's Hidden War." *Business Week* (November 10, 1997): 139–40.

The tobacco industry and antismoking advocates are waging fierce battles over tobacco legislation passed or pending at the county, city, and town levels. The tobacco industry uses front groups like the Californians for Scientific Integrity, the National Smokers Alliance, and the Minnesota Coalition of Responsible Retailers to defeat, overturn, or water down passed or pending tobacco legislation. Court fights, "antitobacco" legislation, and the Freedom of Information Act are additional tools used by these groups. The antitobacco forces push ahead to have legislation passed to prevent youth access to tobacco, raise cigarette taxes, ban cigarette vending machines, and mandate clean-indoor-air ordinances targeting restaurants and workplaces.

584. Levin, Myron. "Big Tobacco's Dollars Douse Push for Fire-Safe Cigarettes." *Los Angeles Times*, January 1, 1998: A1, A22–A23.

Smoldering in the background of the tobacco settlement is an issue not very well-known to the public. Cigarettes rank as the nation's number-one cause of fire deaths. Each year, over a thousand people die as a result of fires ignited by cigarettes. Tobacco companies counter that a fire-safe cigarette is not economically feasible. The companies attack the technical merits of such a cigarette by underwriting research performed by scientists and consultants hired internally and externally. Fire organizations are enlisted to oppose state legislation mandating fire-safe cigarettes. Furthermore, the companies shift the public focus to manufacturers' need to create fire-safe products such as mattresses and pajamas.

585. Carr, Rebecca. "Smoking Program Hits Bureaucratic Wall." *Congressional Quarterly Weekly Report* 56, no. 2 (January 10, 1998): 72.

The American Stop Smoking Intervention Program is a $25 million federally funded program designed to implement smoking cessation and public policy programs in seventeen states. The National Cancer Institute oversees the program. It is estimated that the program costs the tobacco industry $100 million in revenues, or fifty million cigarette packs each month; Representative Ernest Istook (R-Okla.) is questioning the authenticity and legitimacy of the program.

586. Taylor, Andrew. "Clinton's Fancy Budget Work Upstages Skeptical GOP." *Congressional Quarterly Weekly Report* 56, no. 6 (February 7, 1998): 287–91.

President Clinton's fiscal year 1999 budget included two provisions related to the tobacco industry. One provision was for $66 billion in new taxes related to the pending tobacco industry settlement. The taxes were projected over a five-year period. The second provision reversed a Department of Veterans Affairs decision to allow veterans to claim compensation for all smoking-related illnesses and thus "book" $17 billion in savings. The VA altered its former policy of allowing compensation only for smoking during a veteran's term of service.

587. Levin, Myron. "Smoker Group's Thick Wallet Raises Questions." *Los Angeles Times*, March 29, 1998: A21.

In August 1993, the National Smokers Alliance came to life through the efforts of Philip Morris and its public relations firm Burson-Marsteller. The group received $7 million in seed money. Records show that Philip Morris provided most of this money. Since that time, the organization's executives state, dues paid by the more than three million members and corporate contributions have kept the organization running. Contributions from other tobacco companies assist in supporting the group. The organization portrays itself as "a nonprofit, grassroots membership organization."

588. Walker, Adrian. "Crusading AG Holds Stock in Tobacco." *Boston Globe*, April 22, 1998: B1, B6.

Mutual fund's with holdings in tobacco companies are part of a stock portfolio owned by a candidate for governor, Attorney General Scott Harshbarger. The two mutual funds are Fidelity Puritan and Fidelity Equity Income II. Together, Philip Morris stock equals 8.6 million shares with a current market value of $1 billion. Furthermore, the attorney general and his wife manage trust accounts for their children. Fidelity Magellan and Fidelity Equity shares are part of these accounts. The two funds own Philip Morris stock valued at $788 million. Harshbarger's spokesman, Edward Cafasso, defended the holdings by noting that owning mutual funds with tobacco holdings has not hindered the attorney general's determination to bring Big Tobacco to justice.

589. Harwood, John, and Brian Duffy. "Democratic Leaders Are Sending Mixed Message on Accepting Tobacco-Industry Campaign Funds." *Wall Street Journal*, April 30, 1998: A20.

Congressional and Senate Democrats are swearing off tobacco political donations and look forward to completely severing ties. Other Democrat organizations, however, are accepting tobacco funds. At the Democratic National Committee headquarters in Washington, D.C., Representative Martin Frost (D-Tex.), chairman of the Democratic Congressional Campaign Committee, states that the committee does "accept tobacco money." Frost accepted a thirty-two-thousand-dollar donation from the Tobacco Institute, on the grounds that the party accepts funds from a wide variety of politicians, including those of tobacco-producing states.

590. Marcus, Ruth, and Ceci Connolly. "Tobacco Money Still Filters into Campaigns." *Washington Post*, May 8, 1998: A1, A28.

Many Republicans and Democrats are avoiding taking funds directly from Philip Morris, R. J. Reynolds, or other tobacco companies. However, politicians are accepting campaign contributions from corporate subsidiaries' political action committees and indirectly from donations made to state parties and House and Senate campaign committees. Philip Morris's Kraft subsidiary gave money to fund a Republican Women's Leadership Forum hosted by Republicans Jennifer Dunn (R-Wash.) and Deborah Pryce (R-Ohio). Senator Tom Daschle (D-S.D.) collected a total of two thousand dollars from three tobacco industry lobbyists attending his fund-raising breakfast. Later, Daschle's political director returned these funds, stating they had been received "in error."

591. Greenblatt, Alan. "Road Bill Conferees May Grab Money from Ill Veterans Who Smoked." *Congressional Quarterly Weekly Report* 56, no. 19 (May 9, 1998): 1205.

House and Senate conferees reviewing HR2400, the surface transportation bill, are looking for ways to help pay for the more than $200 billion cost. One possibility being examined is to eliminate nonmilitary-service-related smoking illness benefits. The Congressional Budget Office estimates that over a five-year period, the savings would be approximately $10.5 billion. On May 5, 1998, the White House approved this plan.

592. Fletcher, Michael A. "Tobacco's Ties to Minority Groups Put Their Leaders in a Bind." *Washington Post*, May 17, 1998: A8.

During the past two years, Philip Morris and R. J. Reynolds (RJR) contributed to minority politicians and business groups. RJR contributed over $800,000, and in just the past year Philip Morris contributed nearly $24 million. The Congressional Hispanic Caucus, Congressional Black Caucus, black-run newspapers, and Democratic and Republican politicians all received money. Philip Morris and RJR employ a high percentage of minority employees. Minority leaders support smoking-cessation programs and want to be careful that minority businesses, social services, and arts programs do not lose the tobacco financial support all at once.

593. Abrams, Jim. "Veterans Protesting Transportation Bill." *Washington Post*, May 21, 1998: A17. (Associated Press).

The White House and members of the House are working together to eliminate benefits paid to veterans for smoking-related illnesses and apply the funds for road building. They suggest this move could save approximately $10.5 billion that could be applied to a transportation bill moving through Congress. The Veterans Administration estimates that $17 billion would be paid over five years.

594. Abramson, Jill. "Tobacco Industry Gave Big to Parties in States Where It Faced Attack." *New York Times*, June 8, 1998: A16.

Over the last three years, the tobacco industry showered Republican and Democratic state central political committees with $1.8 million in political donations. This is evident in twenty-six states that filed lawsuits against the industry seeking to recover the health costs attributable to smoking. Florida, New York, and Washington received the largest amounts, with Florida receiving nearly 50 percent of the money. Philip Morris contributed nearly 62 percent of the $1.8 million, of which Republicans received 70 percent. The tobacco industry's stated aims include support to legislation and "people who think along similar lines" with the industry's views on issues.

595. *Transportation Equity Act for the 21st Century*. Public Law 105-178, *U.S. Statutes at Large* 112 (June 9, 1998): 492–93, 495.

Title VIII, "Transportation Discretionary Spending Guarantee and Budget Offsets," Subtitle B, "Veterans' Benefits," limits veterans' rights to claim benefits related to smoking-related illnesses that began during their military service. The Department of Veterans Affairs is restricted in granting service-connected compensation. Also, the legislation directs the attorney general or the secretary of veterans affairs to seek to recover from the tobacco companies costs incurred in treating smoking-related illnesses. The specific language appears in "Sec. 8202. Prohibition on Establishment of Service-Connection for Disabilities Relating to Use of Tobacco Products" and "Sec. 8209. Sense of the Congress Concerning Recovery From Tobacco Companies of Costs of Treatment of Veterans for Tobacco-Related Illnesses."

596. "Hypocritical Oath: Some Docs Profit from Growing Tobacco While Warning Patients That Smoking Kills." *Modern Healthcare* 28, no. 26 (June 29, 1998): 70. Infotrac General BusinessFile ASAP (accessed October 9, 1998).

A study of tobacco-quota owner data provided by the U.S. Department of Agriculture reveals that at least 760 doctors and other health care workers appear on the list. The researchers checked the names against medical licensing records in Florida, Georgia, Indiana, Kentucky, Missouri, North Carolina, Ohio, South Carolina, Tennessee, Virginia, West Virginia, and Wisconsin. Over seven million pounds of tobacco can be traced to their collective ownership of tobacco quota. This equates to 193 million packs of cigarettes. Based on 1997 prices, the market value of this equaled $13 million. Quota owners include "a longtime regional medical director for the American Cancer Society," an orthopedic surgeon in Kentucky, a family practitioner from South Carolina, and a cardiovascular surgeon from Tennessee.

597. Nagourney, Adam. "Ferraro to Donate Tobacco Fee." *New York Times*, July 1, 1998: B2.

In February 1997, Geraldine Ferraro accepted a twenty-thousand-dollar honorarium from Philip Morris. Ms. Ferraro attended and participated in a debate at a meeting in Palm Beach, Florida. This surfaced when her Senate campaign opponent, Mark Green, raised the issue. In return, Ms. Ferraro noted that in 1993 Mr. Green accepted a fifty-dollar check from Philip Morris. Mr. Green responded by donating fifty dollars to the Campaign for Tobacco-Free Kids. Ms. Ferraro donated ten thousand dollars to the Marymount Manhattan College. The after-tax value of the Philip Morris contribution filled a scholarship fund established in the name of her mother.

598. Hardin, Peter. "Spying on Foes of Smoking: Philip Morris Files Detail Tobacco Industry's Opposition." *Richmond Times-Dispatch*, July 12, 1998. LexisNexis Academic (accessed May 29, 2004).

Philip Morris planted an informant at a 1991 meeting of the Colorado chapter of the American Stop Smoking Intervention Study (ASSIST) to gather information as to whether the group misspent taxpayer money. Also, in a January 1992 memo, the company identified such tactics as congressional investigations and antitax groups as ways to impede the progress of ASSIST.

599. U.S. House. Committee on Government Reform and Oversight. Minority Staff Report. *Air Tobacco: Campaign Travel on Tobacco Industry Jets*. July 20, 1998: 4488–501. In U.S. Congress. House. Committee on Government Reform and Oversight. *Investigation of Political Fundraising Improprieties and Possible Violations of Law, Interim Report: Sixth Report by the Committee on Government Reform and Oversight, Together with Additional and Minority Views, v. 4*. 105th Cong., 2nd sess., November 5, 1998, H. Doc. 829.

This report analyzes reports filed with the Federal Election Commission (FEC) covering political contributions made to congressional leaders and national parties for the period January 1, 1997, through May 31, 1998. The report identified a total of eighty-four separate disbursements made by the tobacco industry for campaign travel. Because FEC regulations require reimbursement to contributors for only the cost of a first-class ticket, the benefits received over this threshold have greatly benefited the Republican National Committee, the National Republican Senatorial Committee, the National Republican Congressional Committee, and the Republican congressional leaders and their political action committees.

600. *Internal Revenue Service Restructuring and Reform Act of 1998*. Public Law 105-206, *U.S. Statutes at Large* 112 (July 22, 1998): 865–66.

"Section 9014, "Corrections to Veterans Subtitle," amends "Sec. 8202 Treatment of Tobacco-Related Illnesses of Veterans" contained in Public Law 105-178, *Transportation Equity Act for the 21st Century*. U.S. Code Title 38, Chapter 11 is amended by inserting "Section 1103. Special provisions relating to claims based upon effects of tobacco products":

"(a) Notwithstanding any other provision of law, a veteran's disability or death shall not be considered to have resulted from personal injury suffered or disease contracted in the line of duty in the active military, naval, or air service for purposes of this title on the basis that it resulted from injury or disease attributable to the use of tobacco products by the veteran during the veteran's service.

"(b) Nothing in subsection (a) shall be construed as precluding the establishment of service connection for disability or death from a disease or injury which is otherwise shown to have been incurred or aggravated in active military, naval, or air service or which became manifest to the requisite degree of disability during any applicable presumptive period specified in section 1112 or 1116 of this title."

601. Sharfstein, Joshua. "1996 Congressional Campaign Priorities of the AMA: Tackling Tobacco or Limiting Malpractice Awards?" *American Journal of Public Health* 88, no. 8 (August 1998): 1233–36.

During 1996, the American Medical Association's (AMA) political action committee (PAC) spent in excess of $4.1 million. This study examined the PAC's 1996 contributions to 101 pro-tobacco and 91 antitobacco members of the House of Representatives. Also, the authors compare the AMA's contributions to pharmaceutical companies, health insurance firms, hospitals/nursing homes, health service industry, non-AMA physicians, nonphysician professionals, and the tobacco industry. For pro-tobacco legislators, the AMA contributed a mean contribution of $5,382 versus $11,285 for the tobacco industry and $32,744 for all medical PACs. For antitobacco legislators, the AMA contributed a mean contribution of $2,103 versus $290 for the tobacco industry and $26,510 for all medical PACs.

602. "Cancer Study Criticism Tied to Tobacco Money." *Washington Post*, August 5, 1998: A2. (Associated Press).

In 1993, scientists engaged in a letter-writing campaign and submitted manuscripts to journals in an attempt to debunk the link between secondhand smoke and lung cancer. A published report exposed the fact that the tobacco companies and the

Tobacco Institute had paid these scientists over $156,000 to conduct this campaign. For example, in 1993 the *Journal of the American Medical Association* published a letter from American University's Nathan Mantel; this biostatistician had received a ten-thousand-dollar payment from the Tobacco Institute. The publication's editors did not know about these payments, except when authors revealed their links to the tobacco industry when submitting their manuscripts.

603. Snook, Dennis W. *Veterans and Smoking-Related Illnesses: Congress Enacts Limits to Compensation.* Report 98-373. August 13, 1998. Washington, D.C.: Congressional Research Service, 1998.

This "Short Report for Congress" summarized the legislative history and issues behind the enactment of Public Law 105-178, the Transportation Equity Act for the 21st Century. This public law prohibits veterans from claiming compensation for smoking-related illnesses related to military service. In 1993, the Veterans Administration (VA) general counsel had ruled, in a finding affirmed in 1997 by the VA undersecretary for Health, that diseases linked to tobacco use that began during military service are service-connected disabilities. President Clinton's fiscal 1998 and 1999 budgets recommended overturning this ruling and incorporating the estimated savings of $16.9 billion (over five years) into the budget.

604. Hardin, Peter. "Warner Praised in Quick Stock Sale: Senator's Portfolio Included Philip Morris." *Richmond Times-Dispatch*, September 24, 1998. LexisNexis Academic (accessed May 24, 2004).

Even during the raging debates over the proposed tobacco settlement, Senator John W. Warner (R-Va.) owned one hundred Philip Morris shares. In September 2004, when the issue was raised by a *Times-Dispatch* reporter, the senator sold his shares. Representatives from the American Cancer Society and the Campaign for Tobacco-Free Kids praised him as an honorable man and called his actions noteworthy and commendable.

605. Torry, Saundra. "Philip Morris's Smoke Signals Are Questioned." *Washington Post*, March 29, 1999: A3.

Philip Morris has created a Youth Smoking Prevention department and provided $100 million to fund a national campaign aimed at reducing underage smoking. Seven thirty-second commercials created by the department are airing on national television, the first tobacco company ads since a 1971 industry agreement banning all television advertisements. Also, Philip Morris is providing a $4.3 million grant to the National 4-H Council to develop local community antismoking programs. The 4-H, six million strong, provides a "wholesome image" setting. Various council leaders object to the organization's accepting the grant and have pledged not to participate. Other anti–teenage smoking programs include Brown & Williamson's work with the U.S. Junior Chamber of Commerce (Jaycees) and R. J. Reynolds's antismoking efforts with schools.

606. Van Natta, Don, Jr., and Jill Abramson. "Tobacco Largess Is Touchy Subject for Gore and Bush." *New York Times*, August 29, 1999: sec. 1:1, 34.

Vice President Al Gore and Texas governor George W. Bush are attempting to distance their political campaigns from the tobacco industry's largesse. However, both candidates have hired political consultants with ties to the industry and have accepted contributions from individuals with tobacco connections. For example, Mr. Gore hired Carter Eskew as his top media advisor; Mr. Eskew's advertising leadership helped defeat last year's congressional antitobacco legislation. Governor Bush hired a former Philip Morris consultant as his chief political strategist. Tobacco executives have donated over fifty thousand dollars to the Bush presidential campaign. While the Democratic National Committee does not accept tobacco donations, soft tobacco money has been accepted by state Democratic Party organizations.

607. Fisher, Brandy. "Opening Up." *Tobacco Reporter* 126, no. 11 (November 1999): 28, 30.

In response to the antitobacco movement, Philip Morris has announced a campaign to develop better communication channels with the press and public. The company plans to inform the public that it is more than just a tobacco company, that it is quite active in the fight against hunger, domestic violence, education, environmental issues, and the arts. Philip Morris participated in assisting victims of Hurricane Floyd and earthquake victims in Turkey. This "groundbreaking" strategy is taking place in the United States and is eventually to be rolled out worldwide.

608. Cogan, Douglas G., ed. *Tobacco Divestment and Fiduciary Responsibility: A Legal and Financial Analysis*. January 2000. Washington, D.C.: Investor Responsibility Research Center, 2000.

This report addresses a number of areas dealing with tobacco divestment and fiduciary responsibility. In connection with the history of tobacco divestment, the report focuses on actions taken by foundations and health groups, universities and health insurers, and state and municipal pension funds. Legal analysis of tobacco divestment covers such areas as taxable employers, church plans, and governmental plans. Other topics include financial analysis of tobacco investment and shareholder activism on tobacco issues. An appendix includes the results of survey of institutions (e.g., public pension funds) regarding tobacco investment policies.

609. U.S. Congress. *Bond Amendment No. 2913: Sense of the Senate against Federal Funding of Smoke Shops*. 106th Cong., 2nd sess. *Congressional Record* 146, no. 42, daily ed. (April 6, 2000): S2333–S2334.

Senator Christopher Bond (R-Mo.) has offered an amendment to Senate Concurrent Resolution 101. The senator seeks to stop the government from providing funds to the Department of Housing and Urban Development (HUD) for the purpose of providing grants or other assistance to build discount cigarette stores known as "smoke shops," in particular on Indian reservations. Over the last three years, $4.2 million obtained through HUD's Community Development Block Grant program helped construct six smoke shops. The Senate voted eighty-one to nineteen to defeat the amendment. Senator Bond voted against his own amendment.

610. Benson, Mitchel. "California Teachers' Pension Fund Votes to Divest Itself of Tobacco Stocks." *Wall Street Journal*, June 8, 2000: A16.

The California State Teachers' Retirement System will be selling its tobacco stock, valued at $237 million. California state treasurer and board member Philip Angelides states that last year's $600 million drop in market value helped in the decision. The treasurer will try to convince the California Public Employees' Retirement System to sell its nearly $600 million tobacco portfolio.

611. Briggs, Jonathon E. "Convention to Refuse Tobacco Firms' Money." *Los Angeles Times*, July 6, 2000: A9.

Noelia Rodriguez, chief executive of LA Convention 2000, announced that the committee would not accept tobacco company contributions to fund the Democratic National Convention. At a press conference, she signed a document titled "A Public Promise from LA Convention 2000." The Republican National Convention local committee has already accepted a $250,000 contribution from Philip Morris.

612. Kaufman, Marc. "Tobacco Exports Get Aid in Bill Set for House Vote." *Washington Post*, September 12, 2000: A20.

A bill providing American exporters with annual subsidies of $4 to $6 billion is scheduled for a House vote. The bill would provide a $100 million annual subsidy for tobacco exports. The subsidy is supported by the Clinton administration but panned by the industry's critics. Representative Lloyd Doggett (D-Tex.), along with such antitobacco groups as the American Medical Association and the Campaign for Tobacco-Free Kids, tried unsuccessfully to strip the subsidy for the tobacco industry when the House Ways and Means Committee reviewed the bill. (The export subsidies passed into law as the *FSC Repeal and Extraterritorial Income Exclusion Act of 2000*. Public Law 106-519, *U.S. Statutes at Large* 114 [November 15, 2000]: 2423.)

613. Fairclough, Gordon. "Governments Can Be Addicted to Cigarettes." *Wall Street Journal*, October 2, 2000: A1.

Governments from around the globe will be discussing a global tobacco treaty in Geneva. Such an accord will be difficult, since many governments are highly dependent on tobacco revenues. Marlboros sold in the European Union generate a revenue stream equal to 70 percent or more of the average retail price. The Brazilian government's revenue from tobacco sales is about 65 percent of sales. Tobacco sales in Germany generate about 6 percent of revenues for the government. Thirteen percent of revenue generated from cigarette sales in China is derived through the Chinese government's tobacco monopoly.

614. Groves, Martha. "Tobacco Firm's Gift Viewed as a Marketing Smoke Screen." *Los Angeles Times*, November 29, 2000: A3, A16.

During the first six months of 2000, Philip Morris donated fifteen million textbook jacket covers to schools across the country. The covers are designed for the kindergarten through twelfth-grade levels. For the year, the company will distribute 125 million jackets. Tobacco critics decry the donation as a marketing ruse and an opportunity to attract future customers.

615. Kaufman, Marc. "3 Nominees Helped Tobacco." *Washington Post*, January 21, 2001: A6.

President Bush's cabinet nominees John D. Ashcroft, Gale A. Norton, and Tommy G. Thompson have close ties with the tobacco industry. In 1998, the Senate Commerce Committee debated a bill to restrict the industry's national marketing activities. Attorney general nominee Ashcroft voted against the bill. As Colorado attorney general, Interior secretary nominee Norton worked against calls for lawsuits to recover health care costs. Tommy G. Thompson, the Health and Human Services secretary-designate, has accepted campaign contributions from Philip Morris, developed close business ties with the company (which is a major employer in Wisconsin), and as governor of that state vetoed a state bill requiring that expenditure of the state's share of the national settlement follow the federal Centers for Disease Control and Prevention's guidelines for tobacco control programs. Also, Governor Thompson accompanied Philip Morris top officials on trips over the years to Australia, southern Africa, and England.

616. Bialous, Stella Aguinaga, Brion J. Fox, and Stanton A. Glantz. "Tobacco Industry Allegations of 'Illegal Lobbying' and State Tobacco Control." *American Journal of Public Health* 91, no. 1 (January 2001): 62–67.

The American Stop Smoking Intervention Study (ASSIST), established in 1991 and lasting for seven years, was a federally funded project to implement tobacco control across the seventeen participating states. The program formed a partnership with the American Cancer Society and other health-related state and private organizations. Philip Morris attempted to undermine this program by claiming the organizers used federal funds for "illegal lobbying." Their strategy is detailed in the document "Counter Assist Plan." The authors examine the perceived effects of Philip Morris's efforts on the ASSIST program and also how the program responded to the allegations.

617. Cooper, Helene, and Gordon Fairclough. "U.S. Effort to Stall Tax on Tobacco Draws Ire of Cigarette Opponents." *Wall Street Journal*, June 27, 2001: A2.

The White House is attempting to sidetrack a move by South Korea to impose a 40 percent tariff on tobacco imports. White House spokesman Ari Fleischer has stated that the administration's actions are "a straight trade issue." The tobacco industry supports the move to abort what it refers to as a discriminatory trade practice.

618. Kessler, David A. *A Question of Intent: A Great American Battle with a Deadly Industry*. New York: PublicAffairs, 2001.

Former Food and Drug Administration (FDA) head Dr. David Kessler describes the genesis and course of the battle against the tobacco industry during the 1990s. Dr. Kessler was initially reluctant to expend FDA resources, time, or money tackling a formidable and powerful opponent, which controlled tobacco lawyers, politicians in Congress, and the message transmitted to the public. After enlisting the support of President Clinton, however, Dr. Kessler and the FDA sought to regulate the industry, document the industry's knowledge that nicotine is an addictive drug, and prove that cigarettes are devices used to deliver nicotine. Dr. Kessler details his case through interviews with key players in the struggle and through researching the literature and tobacco industry documents.

619. Hall, Kerry. "NBA, Lorillard Blame Publicity." *News & Record*, August 22, 2002: B8. LexisNexis Academic (accessed May 29, 2004).

On July 19, under pressure from the American Cancer Society, American Heart Association, American Lung Association, and Campaign for Tobacco-Free Kids, the National Basketball Association dropped Lorillard Tobacco as a sponsor of its Hoop-It-Up basketball tournament. Lorillard's sponsorship had targeted teens with an antitobacco message. The company supported the three-on-three tournament, with its "Tobacco is whacko if you're a teen" slogan emblazoned on T-shirts and basketballs.

620. VandeHei, Jim. "GOP Whip Quietly Tried to Aid Big Donor." *Washington Post*, June 11, 2003: A1, A6.

Of all the tobacco companies, Philip Morris would have been a largest beneficiary of language almost included in the Department of Homeland Security bill. The newly appointed GOP majority whip, Representative Roy Blunt, quietly tried to erect barriers against Internet-based tobacco sales and contraband cigarettes. John Scruggs, Altria Group's vice president of government affairs, referred to the provisions as "pretty important" to the company. Philip Morris has contributed campaign money to Blunt. Philip Morris employs his son Andrew B. Blunt as a lobbyist to the Missouri legislature.

621. Smith, Elizabeth A., and Ruth E. Malone. "Thinking the 'Unthinkable': Why Philip Morris Considered Quitting." *Tobacco Control* 12, no. 2 (June 2003): 208–13.

Starting in the late 1980s, executives at Philip Morris understood the company faced an image problem. Items like the antitobacco movement, litigation, increased government regulation, and a declining demand for tobacco underlay these perceptions. Institutional investors began divesting corporate stock, and employee morale started to drop. Company executives considered two options: to extricate the firm from the tobacco business or seek to create a better business environment. As of April 1994, the company considered a spin-off of its tobacco business but withdrew the proposal on the advice of legal counsel. Meanwhile, such image-enhancement ideas came to fruition as "Philip Morris in the 21st Century," which included the "Youth Smoking Prevention Project," and a change of the corporate name to "The Altria Group," in order to "sever its image from tobacco without severing its financial ties."

622. Jalonick, Mary Clare, and Kate Schuler. "Tobacco Producers Offering Once Unheard-of Concessions." *CQ Weekly* 61, no. 31 (August 2, 2003): 1972–73.

The seventy-year-old federal tobacco price-support program may be ending, under legislation introduced by Senator Mitch McConnell (R-Ky.). A deal hammered out between protobacco and antitobacco senators would provide farmers $13 billion over six years, implement new marketing and safety warning rules, authorize the Food and Drug Administration to regulate tobacco products, and give Congress the right to eliminate nicotine from tobacco products.

623. Wong, Edward. "An Iraqi Factory Reflects U.S. Recovery Effort." *New York Times*, February 15, 2004: sec. 1: 10.

The American military helped to reopen and now operates a five-story cigarette manufacturing factory in Baghdad. The base where the factory is located is referred to as "Camp Marlboro," employs 850 Iraqis, and is currently producing three to four hundred cases daily of the popular Sumer cigarette brand. The factory is capable of producing two thousand cases daily. A case sells for forty dollars. At full capacity, the factory can generate sixty-four thousand dollars revenue daily. The military hopes the goodwill and revenues generated by the factory will improve its relations with the Iraqi people.

624. White, Jenny, and Lisa A. Bero. "Public Health under Attack: The American Stop Smoking Intervention Study (ASSIST) and the Tobacco Industry." *American Journal of Public Health* 94, no. 2 (February 2004): 240–50.

The authors have searched through various tobacco industry Web archives for materials related to the American Stop Smoking Intervention Study (ASSIST) program. The tobacco industry viewed ASSIST as a movement to undermine its power at the state legislature level and empower tobacco control advocates at the local level. After the launching of ASSIST in October 1991, the tobacco industry formulated six strategies to combat the program. These strategies included gathering information on the program and monitoring its activities, building and using alliances and networks, and launching investigations of the program in Congress and in state legislatures.

625. Jalonick, Mary Clare. "Philip Morris, Tobacco Foes on Shaky Common Ground." *CQ Weekly* 62, no. 23 (June 5, 2004): 1316–17, 1321–22.

Philip Morris and its adversaries (such as the American Heart Association and the Campaign for Tobacco-Free Kids) have been negotiating for months to find common ground and acceptable wording in proposed federal regulation of the tobacco industry. Bills introduced in Congress include such regulatory features as larger warnings on cigarette packages, magazine ads in black and white only, and a ban on flavored cigarettes. Other tobacco companies, such as Lorillard Tobacco, oppose regulation on the grounds that it would merely lock in market share for Philip Morris and freeze out small tobacco competitors.

626. Kaufman, Marc. "Tobacco Buyout Favors Big Growers." *Washington Post*, June 22, 2004: A2.

The House of Representatives approved a taxpayer-financed buyout of the tobacco subsidy program. The corporate-tax bill contained a $9.6 billion buyout of tobacco growers and quota owners. According to a study conducted by the Environmental Working Group, 463 companies, individuals, and estates were set to receive at least a million dollars. One North Carolina company was expected to receive over $8 million. Over a five-year period, a thousand dollars was paid to each of 354,000 recipients, out of a total of 437,000 eligible recipients. House members never debated the tobacco plan before voting on the measure. *See also* entry 631.

627. O'Connell, Vanessa. "New Worry for Cigarette Makers: New York Fire-Safety Law." *Wall Street Journal*, June 23, 2004: B1, B11.

Starting June 28, 2004, the tobacco industry began selling "fire-safe" cigarettes in lieu of regular cigarettes. Designed to self-extinguish quickly, the new cigarette's wrapper contains a "speed bump," ultra-thin paper melded into the regular paper and designed to extinguish the cigarette when not in use. Fire-safe cigarette packages are marked with a distinguishing feature, such as an asterisk or a diamond, to set them apart from regular cigarettes. Tobacco companies fear that without a federal standard they will eventually have to deal with a multitude of differing state laws on fire-safe cigarettes.

628. "Tobacco Buyout Benefits Lawmakers." *Washington Post*, July 10, 2004: A10. (Associated Press).

A recently passed House measure to end the tobacco subsidy program would also benefit various House members, according to the Environmental Working Group. Representative Bill Jenkins (R-Tenn.) and his wife, Kathryn, would get $55,000. Jenkins chairs a subcommittee that deals with tobacco-farming issues. Representative Bobby R. Etheridge (D-N.C.) would get $30,900. A brother of Representative Lincoln Davis (D-Tenn.) would receive $29,700. *See also* entry 631.

629. Hulse, Carl. "Senate Approves Tobacco Buyout and New Curbs." *New York Times*, July 16, 2004: A1, A20.

By a vote of seventy-eight to fifteen, the Senate has passed a bill calling for the regulation of the tobacco industry and providing for a $12 billion, ten-year buyout of the nation's tobacco growers. The Food and Drug Administration would regulate the sale, distribution, and advertising of cigarettes. Words such as "lite" and "ultra-lite" could not be used on cigarette packages unless the government certified them. Color magazine advertisements would be prohibited. As for the tobacco buyout, tobacco manufacturers and importers would be assessed a fee, and the money would be paid to the tobacco quota owners. Tobacco companies, including R. J. Reynolds, oppose the bill. *See also* entry 631.

630. Alamar, B. C., and S. A. Glantz. "The Tobacco Industry's Use of Wall Street Analysts in Shaping Policy." *Tobacco Control* 13, no. 3 (September 2004): 223–27.

The authors present two cases in which Wall Street analyst David Adelman of Morgan Stanley worked with Philip Morris USA on issues of prime importance to the tobacco industry. During an April 1998 Senate Judiciary Committee hearing to discuss the McCain tobacco bill and the potential impact of cigarette smuggling, Adelman presented testimony favorable to the industry, arguing that if the provisions of the bill were implemented, tobacco prices would spike and create a haven for cigarette smuggling. Adelman never mentioned his work with Philip Morris's John Hoel in preparing for the meeting. Also, in 1991, when presenting testimony to the Florida Task Force on Tobacco Settlement Revenue Protection, Adelman spoke of the positive financial state of the tobacco industry and its positive aggregate industry stock performance. The task force later issued a report recommending against securitizing tobacco revenues due under the state's 1997 agreement with the industry, and also against purchasing insurance for this revenue stream.

631. U.S. Congress. *American Jobs Creation Act of 2004*, Public Law 108-357, *U.S. Statutes at Large* 118 (October 22, 2004): 1521–36.

The public law allocates $10.1 billion to end the tobacco price-support program, in place since the Depression era. The major tobacco companies will be assessed fees to pay for the buyout. The law does not provide for regulating the tobacco industry. The Senate had approved such language, but the House did not, and House-Senate conferees agreed to strip the language from the final legislation, in Title VI, "Fair and

Equitable Tobacco Reform." Contract payments are to be made from fiscal year 2005 through fiscal 2014.

632. Wander, Nathaniel, and Ruth E. Malone. "Selling Off or Selling Out? Medical Schools and Ethical Leadership in Tobacco Stock Divestment." *Academic Medicine* 79, no. 11 (November 2004): 1017–26.

The divestiture by academic institutions of tobacco holdings in stocks and bonds began during the early 1990s. Harvard University divested its holdings in March 1990, and the City University of New York took that action in May 1990. The board of trustees at Johns Hopkins University (JHU) voted to divest its holdings in February 1991. When JHU began its discussions in April 1990, Philip Morris met with school officials and made numerous arguments against such action. The arguments included the implied threat to halt the granting of research dollars to the university and also that JHU would be aiding the antismoking movement's goal of a complete ban on smoking. Philip Morris used similar arguments to fend off Yale University's discussion of divesting tobacco investments; in February 1991, that school decided not to take such action.

TOBACCO LITIGATION

633. Collins, Glenn. "Huge Tobacco Lawsuit Is Thrown Out on Appeal." *New York Times*, May 24, 1996: A1, A20.

A group of New Orleans judges struck down a massive class-action lawsuit against the tobacco industry. The three judges from the federal appeals panel, "decertified" the *Castano* lawsuit and overturned a 1995 decision in favor of the plaintiffs; the lawsuit may continue but can represent only the original four plaintiffs. The four plaintiffs had filed the lawsuit on behalf of as many as fifty million smokers claiming the tobacco industry knew about the negative effects of nicotine, kept smokers hooked on nicotine through adjusting the levels in cigarettes, and kept this information from the public.

634. Hwang, Suein L., and Ann Davis. "Secondhand-Smoke Case May Kindle New Suits." *Wall Street Journal*, October 13, 1997: B1, B10.

The four largest tobacco manufacturers settled a six-year-old class-action lawsuit filed against it by flight attendants claiming that secondhand smoke had exposed them to various illnesses. A three-year research project on smoking illnesses will be funded by the companies at $300 million. The companies have avoided paying punitive damages but will pay, if the agreement is approved, $49 million to the plaintiffs' lawyers. Individual flight attendants may sue the industry but will receive only compensatory damages if each should win his or her lawsuit. The settlement may encourage others to file lawsuits based on smoke exposure in confined workplaces.

635. Rubin, Alissa J. "President Targets Tobacco Industry in Massive Lawsuit." *Los Angeles Times*, January 20, 1999: A14.

In his 1999 State of the Union address, President Clinton announced that the Justice Department would file a lawsuit against the tobacco industry. The government would seek to recover money paid for tobacco-related illnesses. This would include funds expended by Medicare, the Department of Veterans Affairs, and the Defense Department. The government is still considering the possible use of the Medical Care Recovery Act to recover expenditures caused by the negligence of a third party.

636. Meier, Barry. "Cigarette Producers Face a Fresh Threat in Individuals' Suits." *New York Times*, February 12, 1999: A1, A20.

The number of lawsuits filed by individuals against the tobacco industry has been steadily increasing since even before the Master Settlement Agreement. In one verdict, a California jury ordered the tobacco industry to pay $1.5 million compensatory damages and $50 million punitive damages to plaintiff Patricia Henley. Ms. Henley claimed that smoking Marlboros for over thirty-five years had caused her lung cancer.

637. Stout, David. "Justice Dept. Plans Tobacco Suit Seeking Billions in Health Costs." *New York Times*, September 22, 1999: A1, A25.

The tobacco industry was hit with another lawsuit, this one filed by the Justice Department. The government accused the industry of civil racketeering, charged it with covering up the dangers of cigarette smoking, and sought to recoup medical-related expenses. President Clinton first proposed the lawsuit in January 1999. The tobacco industry launched an advertising campaign against the lawsuit. Earlier, the Justice Department fought off an attempt by members of Congress to stop funding of the department's lawsuit.

638. Greenhouse, Linda. "High Court Holds F.D.A. Can't Impose Rules on Tobacco." *New York Times*, March 22, 2000: A1, A23.

In a five-to-four ruling, the Supreme Court ruled that the Food and Drug Administration (FDA) does not have the right to regulate the advertising, marketing, and promotion of tobacco products to children and teenagers. The justices ruled that the FDA could not use the Food, Drug, and Cosmetic Act (1938) as its authority to regulate tobacco. The FDA had claimed that the law's reference to "drugs" and "devices" gave the agency the authority to regulate nicotine (drugs) and cigarettes (devices). The case, *Food and Drug Administration v. Brown & Williamson*, upheld a 1998 decision by the U.S. Court of Appeals for the Fourth Circuit striking down the regulations.

639. Bragg, Rick. "Tobacco Lawsuit in Florida Yields Record Damages." *New York Times*, July 15, 2000: A1, A11.

A Miami jury has assessed the tobacco industry with a $144.8 billion punitive damage penalty in a class-action lawsuit. The punitive damages are in addition to a court-ordered $12.7 million compensatory-damage penalty. The punitive damages rank as the highest amount ever assessed a plaintiff in a U.S. court. The court ordered Philip Morris, R. J. Reynolds, Brown & Williamson, Lorillard Tobacco, and Liggett Group to pay $73.96 billion, $36.28 billion, $17.59 billion, $16.25 billion, and $790 million, respectively.

640. Zegart, Dan. *Civil Warriors: The Legal Siege on the Tobacco Industry*. New York: Delacorte, 2000.

The author has six years of experience covering the tobacco wars and provides an insider's viewpoint. Zegart traveled with lawyer Ron Motley and gained firsthand

641. Day, Sherri. "Philip Morris Is Convicted of Fraud in Marketing." *New York Times*, March 22, 2003: A6.

Judge Nicholas Byron, Third Circuit Court of Illinois, has ruled in favor of 1.1 million Illinois smokers involved in a class-action lawsuit against Philip Morris. The judge found that Philip Morris failed to notify the smokers that its Marlboro or Cambridge light cigarettes, purchased by the plaintiffs from 1971 through February 2001, "were not less harmful that full-tar cigarettes." The judge awarded the plaintiffs $7.1 billion in compensatory damages. Also, the judge assessed Philip Morris with $3 billion in punitive damages and $1.78 billion in lawyers' fees. Philip Morris had claimed that it informed purchasers about the dangers of smoking through the surgeon general's warning. The company needs to post a $12 billion bond to appeal the verdict.

642. Roig-Franzia, Manuel. "$145 Billion Award in Tobacco Case Voided." *Washington Post*, May 22, 2003: E1, E12.

Florida judge David M. Gersten, Third District Court of Appeals, has voided a $145 billion punitive damage award assessed against the major tobacco companies. The judge cited inflammatory racial comments made by the plaintiff's lawyers, the need to adjudicate tobacco cases on an individual basis and not in a class-action lawsuit, a "grossly excessive" award given by a "runaway jury," and the intent of the award to bankrupt companies, in violation of Florida law prohibiting such awards. First filed in 1994, the class-action lawsuit had been filed by six Florida smokers on behalf of over seven hundred thousand statewide smokers.

643. Pittman, Rhashad. "Cigarette Makers Lose Suit." *Los Angeles Times*, July 23, 2003: B6.

A district judge has dismissed a lawsuit filed by the R. J. Reynolds Tobacco Company and Lorillard Tobacco claiming that tax revenues spent on antitobacco ads violated the companies' business interests and poisoned court cases and potential jurors. Judge Lawrence K. Karlton ruled that the state government might continue to spend the money "within legal limits." Both companies plan to file an appeal to the U.S. Court of Appeals for the Ninth Circuit.

644. "R. J. Reynolds Forced to Pay Damages to Fla. Smoker." *Los Angeles Times*, August 28, 2003: C5.

Floyd Kenyon, a retired Florida schoolteacher, became only the second litigant paid by a tobacco company over the last three years when he received a $195,602.87 check for compensatory damages from R. J. Reynolds. Reynolds paid the damage award, first issued in December 2001, after a Florida appeals court turned down its request to dismiss the judgment. In 2001, Grady Carter became the first person suing the industry to receive a check in damages, $1.1 million, from Brown & Williamson.

645. "Court Slashes $12 Billion Bond for Philip Morris." *Los Angeles Times*, September 17, 2003: C3.

The Illinois Supreme Court ruled that Philip Morris needed to post a term note of $6 billion and a deposit of $800 million, not a $12 billion bond, to appeal an Illinois verdict finding the company guilty of deceiving smokers about the safety of its "light" cigarettes. The highest state court altered the appeal process and heard the case without it first being adjudicated by the state appellate court.

646. "Appellate Ruling Pares Damages in Tobacco Case." *Los Angeles Times*, September 27, 2003: C2.

In the case of *Henley v. Philip Morris*, the plaintiff's original award of $50 million in punitive damages dropped to $9 million in a ruling handed down by a San Francisco state appeals court. The court took into account a U.S. Supreme Court opinion limiting punitive damage awards to six times the amount awarded for compensatory damages. Philip Morris plans an appeal to the California Supreme Court.

647. "Court Upholds Fine against R. J. Reynolds." *Los Angeles Times*, October 31, 2003: C3.

A California appeals court upheld a judgment rendered against R. J. Reynolds for distributing free cigarettes on public grounds, in violation of a California law prohibiting this action at events attended by minors.

648. "Judge Says U.S. May Go After Long-Ago Tobacco Profits." *Los Angeles Times*, March 11, 2004: C10.

U.S. district judge Gladys Kessler ruled in favor of the U.S. Justice Department in a motion filed by the tobacco industry. The government is seeking to obtain tobacco profits earned before 1970 by using the federal racketeering law. The tobacco industry sought to have this motion overturned.

649. O'Connell, Vanessa. "U.S. Suit Alleges Philip Morris Hid Cigarette-Fire Risk." *Wall Street Journal*, April 23, 2004: A1, A8.

As part of its racketeering lawsuit against the tobacco industry, the Justice Department alleges that Philip Morris knew cigarettes sold under the Merit brand name did not meet the company's claims of reducing fire risks if left unattended. In 2000, Philip Morris patented the banded-paper technology used to manufacture the cigarettes; the company spent a total of $100 million for research, development, and changes to equipment used to manufacture the paper. The company spent $20 million on marketing, placing a "PaperSelect" logo on the cigarette packages, and including information about the new design in each pack. Thereafter, acting on customer complaints about "coal dropoff," Philip Morris instructed scientist Dr. Michael Lee Watkins to investigate the problem. Dr. Watkins found that the new banded-paper technology could harm individuals. Citing various other reasons, Philip Morris fired Dr. Watkins, who brought the information to the Justice Department.

650. O'Connell, Vanessa, and Christina Cheddar Berk. "Worst May Not Be Over for Tobacco Industry." *Wall Street Journal*, May 10, 2004: C1, C3.

The Supreme Court of Florida, without further comment, decided to accept jurisdiction of the class-action Engle lawsuit brought against the tobacco industry. The court will review and possibly reinstate the case. In 2003, the $145 billion suit had been decertified, giving hope that the worst would be behind the industry and its investors.

651. Kaufman, Marc. "Tobacco Racketeering Trial to Proceed." *Washington Post*, May 25, 2004: A15.

U.S. district judge Gladys Kessler has ruled in favor of the federal government's efforts to proceed with its lawsuit seeking $280 billion from the tobacco industry. The government is seeking the disgorgement of industry profits by claiming that for decades the industry knew about the dangers of smoking and that nicotine is addictive. The tobacco industry may appeal the ruling before the case goes to trial.

652. DeGraff, Nate. "Suit: Lorillard Targeted Blacks." *News & Record*, June 29, 2004: B6. LexisNexis Academic (accessed August 7, 2004).

Willie Evans, on behalf of his late mother, Marie R. Evans, has filed suit against Lorillard Tobacco claiming the tobacco company targeted black teenagers and children by giving them its Newport cigarettes. As a child, Ms. Evans had lived in a Roxbury, Massachusetts, housing project. Lorillard had provided free cigarettes to her and other black children at events in the surrounding area. The lawsuit, filed in Suffolk Superior Court in Massachusetts, noted that Newport ads appearing in *Jet* and *Ebony* influenced Ms. Evans's decision to smoke these cigarettes. The lawsuit is expected to go to court in 2007.

653. Lichtblau, Eric. "Judge Fines Philip Morris for E-Mail Loss." *New York Times*, July 21, 2004: C5.

U.S. district court judge Gladys Kessler has slapped a $2.75 million fine on the Altria Group and its tobacco subsidiary Philip Morris USA. The fine, related to the U.S. Department of Justice's pending case *United States of America v. Philip Morris USA*, penalizes the companies for "reckless disregard and gross indifference" in destroying e-mails covering more than two years; in October 1999, Judge Kessler had ordered the tobacco giant to preserve all case-related documents and records.

654. O'Connell, Vanessa. "Secret Memo Sought by U.S. in Tobacco Suit." *Wall Street Journal*, September 13, 2004: B1, B3.

In the U.S. government's pending case against the tobacco industry, British American Tobacco (BAT) and its Australian subsidiary are attempting to prevent a document known as the Foyle Memorandum from being presented as evidence against the company and the industry as a whole. In this 1990 memorandum, lawyer Andrew Foyle of the London law firm of Lovells, commenting on document requests related to tobacco litigation, noted that "document destruction had been taking place." BAT is claiming attorney-client privilege. The U.S. government believes the memorandum will bolster its claim that the industry knew of the negative health effects of cigarettes and attempted to keep this from public view through the destruction and suppression of internal documents.

655. Rayburn, Kelly. "U.S. Opens Tobacco Industry Suit." *Wall Street Journal*, September 22, 2004: A10.

On September 21, 2004, Judge Gladys Kessler, U.S. District Court (District of Columbia), began hearing oral arguments in the U.S. government's $280 billion case against the tobacco industry. The tobacco defendants include Philip Morris USA (a subsidiary of Altria Group), R. J. Reynolds Tobacco, Brown & Williamson,

British American Tobacco, Liggett Group (a subsidiary of Vector Group Ltd.), and Lorillard Tobacco (a subsidiary of Loews Corporation). The government's case rests on illegal conduct committed under RICO, the Racketeer Influenced and Corrupt Organizations Act.

656. Levin, Myron. "State High Court Backs Damages in Smoker's Case." *Los Angeles Times*, September 17, 2004: C2.

    The California Supreme Court has upheld an appeals court's ruling against Philip Morris. The company had appealed the awarding of $1.5 million in compensatory damages and $9 million in punitive damages to the plaintiff Patricia Henley; a San Francisco appeals court had previously lowered the punitive damage award to $9 million from $25 million. Philip Morris may file an appeal with the U.S. Supreme Court.

657. Altria Group, "Appeals Court Rules Blue Cross Insurer Cannot Sue Philip Morris USA under New York's Deceptive Practices Law." Press release, October 19, 2004. www.altria.com (accessed October 20, 2004).

    In an appeal of the case *Empire Health Choice*, formerly known as *Empire Blue Cross and Blue Shield*, the New York State Court of Appeals has ruled in favor of the tobacco industry and against the insurance company. The insurance company cannot attempt to recover medical costs for smoking by invoking a New York state consumer-protection law. The ruling overturns a 2001 verdict against the major cigarette companies awarding $17.8 million to the insurance company.

658. Altria Group, "Henley Case," October 27, 2004, www.altria.com/media/03_06_04_09_00_Henley.asp (accessed October 28, 2004).

    The U.S. Supreme Court agreed to review a decision handed down by the California Supreme Court against Philip Morris. The California court ordered the tobacco company to pay $10.5 million to plaintiff Patricia Henley. Philip Morris's petition for certioari (i.e., corrective action brought against the California court's judgment) was due December 14, 2004.

659. Rayburn, Kelly. "U.S. Court Crimps Big Tobacco Suit." *Wall Street Journal*, November 3, 2004: A2, A8.

    The U.S. Court of Appeals has ruled in favor of British American Tobacco (BAT) regarding a memorandum written by lawyer Andrew Foyle. The court ruled that BAT may claim attorney-client privilege in its efforts to keep the memorandum from being introduced as evidence in the U.S. Department of Justice's case against the tobacco industry. The government responded that it might pursue a "crime-fraud exception" in its efforts to get BAT to turn over the document. (The court case may be accessed at pacer.cadc.uscourts.gov/docs/common/opinions/200411/04-5207a.pdf [accessed November 3, 2004].)

TOBACCO SETTLEMENT AGREEMENTS, 1997–1998

660. Broder, John M. "Cigarette Maker Concedes Smoking Can Cause Cancer." *New York Times*, March 21, 1997: A1, A12.

The Brooke Group's subsidiary, Liggett Group, has become the first tobacco company to admit that smoking is addictive and causes cancer. In settling lawsuits filed by twenty-two states, Chairman Bennett LeBow also acknowledged that tobacco advertising and marketing targets youth, agreed to submit internal documents, and committed the company to attach a warning label on its cigarette packages proclaiming that smoking is addictive. The company will pay an annual fine of 25 percent of pretax profits and up to $25 million, over the next twenty-five years.

661. Freedman, Alix M., and Suein L. Hwang. "Philip Morris, RJR and Tobacco Plaintiffs Discuss a Settlement." *Wall Street Journal*, April 16, 1997: A1, A8.

Philip Morris, RJR Nabisco, various state officials, and anti-tobacco representatives are engaged in secret negotiations to resolve all liability litigation against the industry. In return, the industry would pay as much as $300 billion over the next twenty-five years to fund smokers' compensation claims, would agree to be regulated by the Food and Drug Administration, would end the use of cigarette billboards, and would stop using human figures such as the Marlboro Man to promote its products. Congress would need to review and approve the plan. The White House wants the negotiators to address its own plan on regulating the industry and to substantially increase the compensation fund.

662. Sack, Kevin. "For the Nation's Politicians, Big Tobacco No Longer Bites." *New York Times*, April 22, 1997: A1, A12.

The tobacco industry's political support vanished with the revelation of secret meetings with tobacco plaintiffs to discuss a sweeping national settlement. Since 1994, reports of the tobacco industry's practices have dramatically impacted public opinion and spilled over to the political arena. Disclosures include the health impact of secondhand smoke, the exposure of internal documents by whistle-blowers, the 1994 congressional testimony of tobacco executives denying that cigarettes are addictive, and the first state tobacco lawsuit, filed by Mississippi attorney general Michael C. Moore.

663. McGraw, Dan. "Junkyard Dogs for Hire." *U.S. News & World Report* 122, no. 21 (June 2, 1997): 46–47.

State attorneys general, national political organizations, and two hundred private law firms have forged a close relationship through the twenty-nine state Medicaid lawsuits filed against the tobacco industry. Texas attorney general Dan Morales has received $150,945 in campaign contributions from the five law firms hired to battle the tobacco industry. The national Democratic Party and Texas Democrats have received contributions from Texas lawyers hired by the state. During 1995 and 1996, the law firms of two lawyers hired by Attorney General Morales made political contributions totaling $434,600.

664. Broder, John M. "Cigarette Makers in a $368 Billion Accord to Curb Lawsuits and Curtail Marketing: Major Concessions." *New York Times*, June 21, 1997: 1, 8.

In a landmark settlement with forty-six states, the tobacco industry has agreed to a multitude of new rules and regulations. The settlement terms include the payment of $368.5 billion over twenty-five years, an up-front payment of $10 billion, a ban on punitive damage awards for past behavior, a ban on class-action lawsuits, and caps on individual lawsuit awards of $5 billion a year. Also, the industry will fund anti–youth smoking and smoking-cessation programs, cease using human and cartoon characters (like the Marlboro Man and Joe Camel), ban billboard advertisements, end advertising and marketing geared toward underage smokers, agree to a ban on Internet and movie advertising, end sponsorship of sporting events and outdoor concerts, end the merchandising of products bearing cigarette logos, and agree to the Food and Drug Administration's regulation of nicotine as a drug.

665. Elliott, Stuart. "Industry Still Has Many Weapons Available." *New York Times*, June 21, 1997: 10.

Despite an agreement to ban the Marlboro Man and Joe Camel, the tobacco industry still has plenty of advertising and marketing tools left in its arsenal. An example is grabbing smokers' attention with soothing landscapes. Semiotician Marshall Blonsky, who studies the meaning of symbols, argues that the allure of cigarette advertising rests with visual connotations of brand imagery. Humans are not needed to get across the message that smoking is cool and relaxing. An ad for Philip Morris's Benson & Hedges brand, labeled "Rest & Relaxation," shows a cigarette, in the shape of a human being, perched in a hammock.

666. Meier, Barry. "Philip Morris to Pay Most of First Bill." *New York Times*, June 25, 1997: C1, C6.

Under terms reached with the state attorneys general for the proposed national tobacco settlement, the initial $10 billion industry payment will be based on the five companies' market capitalization (outstanding shares multiplied by closing stock prices). Using the June 24, 1997 closing prices, Philip Morris would pay $6.5 billion, British American Tobacco (the parent of Brown & Williamson) $1.7 billion, Lorillard Tobacco $720 million, and RJR Nabisco $571 million.

667. Meier, Barry. "Acting Alone, Mississippi Settles Suit with 4 Tobacco Companies." *New York Times*, July 4, 1997: A1, A12.

Mississippi attorney general Michael Moore has announced that the state has settled its Medicaid lawsuit against the tobacco industry. The parties agreed to a $3.4 billion settlement to be paid over twenty-five years, with an initial payment of $170 million. This is the first settlement of a lawsuit to recover smoking-related costs between a state and the industry. Philip Morris, RJR Nabisco, Brown & Williamson, and Lorillard Tobacco signed the agreement.

668. Freedman, Alix M., and Suein L. Hwang. "How Seven Individuals with Diverse Motives Halted Tobacco's Wars." *Wall Street Journal*, July 11, 1997: A1, A8.

Seven individuals played essential roles in bringing the tobacco industry to the negotiating table and ultimately to the $368 billion settlement. They produced the ideas and creative strategies to fight the once impregnable tobacco industry. These individuals are Jeffrey Nesbitt, Michael T. Lewis, Jeffrey Wigand, Walt Bogdanich, Dick Morris, Bennett LeBow, and Grady Carter.

669. Taylor, Jeffrey. "Tobacco Farmers Lobby for Slice of Settlement to Protect Them against a Decline in Demand." *Wall Street Journal*, July 16, 1997: A24.

Tobacco farmers are lobbying the White House and Congress for a piece of the pie in the proposed national tobacco settlement. They are seeking protection for falling demand and to offset losses. One idea tossed around is for the industry to allocate $6 billion to help farmers seek alternative crops. Another idea is to have the U.S. tobacco companies manufacture cigarettes with a larger portion of U.S.-grown tobacco.

670. Stone, Peter H. "Lobbyists Come Out Smokin'." *National Journal* 29, no. 31 (August 2, 1997): 1555–56.

Asbestos-products manufacturers are forming a coalition to press for a share of the proposed $368.5 billion tobacco settlement. They are proposing the earmarking of $15 billion for asbestos victims. The coalition proposes that Congress create a commission to determine the amount. Owens Corning, Armstrong World Industries, Consolidated Rail Corporation, Owens-Illinois, and W. R. Grace & Company form the coalition.

671. *Taxpayer Relief Act of 1997*. Public Law 105-34, *U.S. Statutes at Large* 111 (August 5, 1997): 1098–99.

Title XVI (Technical Amendments Related to Small Business Job Protection Act of 1996 and Other Legislation), section 1604(f)(3), amends subsection (k) of section 9302 of the Balanced Budget Act of 1997 (Public Law 105-33, 111 Stat. 251). The law now grants the tobacco industry a $50 billion tax credit against the $368.5 billion proposed tobacco settlement agreement. The amended language reads: "(k) Coordination with Tobacco Industry Settlement Agreement.—The increase in excise taxes collected as a result of the amendments made by subsections (a), (e), and (g) of this section shall be credited against the total payments made by parties pursuant to Federal legislation implementing the tobacco industry settlement agreement of June 20, 1997."

672. Neergaard, Lauran. "Deal Seen to Give Big Profits for Tobacco." *Boston Globe*, August 17, 1997: A1, A21. (Associated Press).

The Treasury Department has conducted an internal audit of the proposed $368.5 billion tobacco settlement and determined that the tobacco companies could "profit handsomely" from the deal. The audit concludes that the tobacco industry would receive revenues of $15 billion even by raising the per-pack price of cigarettes by fifty cents and with a 5 percent decrease in consumption. Even if the industry raised the per-pack price by sixty-two cents and consumption dropped 7 percent, the industry would still generate profits after making payments under the settlement provisions.

673. Mintz, John. "How a $50 Billion 'Orphan' Was Adopted." *Washington Post*, August 17, 1997: A1, A18.

In June 1997, the Senate passed a fifteen-cent cigarette tax–increase bill sponsored by Edward M. Kennedy (D-Mass.) and Orrin G. Hatch (R-Utah). The $50 billion raised by the tax measure would be targeted for a children's health program. Alarmed by this development and reeling from the $368.5 billion proposed tobacco agreement, tobacco lobbyists approached twenty House members about providing the industry a $50 billion credit. The House members passed the idea to Senate majority leader Trent Lott (R-Miss.) and House speaker Newt Gingrich (R-Ga.). On July 28, during a House-Senate conference session to negotiate final language for a balanced-budget and tax-cut bills, Lott and Gingrich persuaded White House administrators, including Treasury secretary Robert E. Rubin and White House chief of staff Erskine B. Bowles, to add the credit. The final tax cut bill included the language. White House spokesman Michael McCurry stated, "It was necessary to have that [credit] provision there in order to get the [cigarette tax-financed] children's health program."

674. "Black Farmers Ask for Fair Share of Monies in Tobacco Settlement." *Jet* 92, no. 13 (August 18, 1997): 27.

The tobacco industry is being asked to include minority farmers in the proposed tobacco settlement with the state attorneys general. Of the $7 billion allocated for tobacco farmers, John W. Boyd, leader of the National Black Farmers Association, is asking for $290 million. In addition, he is requesting $100 million to be allocated among land grant research institutions ($75 million) and minority scholarships ($25 million).

675. Stone, Peter H. "Smokin' Lobbyists." *National Journal* 29, nos. 34–35 (August 23, 1997): 1684–87.

The lineup of lobbyists ready to do battle in Washington, D.C., on both sides of the proposed tobacco settlement is taking shape. The tobacco industry has hired the Washington law firm of Barbour Griffith & Rogers (of which former GOP chairman Haley Barbour is a principal). The industry's law firm, Verner, Liipfert, Bernhard, McPherson and Hand, has hired former Democratic senator George Mitchell (D-Me.). The state attorneys general have hired John D. Raffaelli, partner in the Washington Group, to serve as the group's campaign coordinator. The National Center for Tobacco-Free Kids has hired former representative Vin Weber (R-Minn.). Public health groups, insurance companies, and labor-management health plans are also hiring lobbyists.

676. Meier, Barry. "Cigarette Makers Agree to Settle Florida Lawsuit." *New York Times*, August 26, 1997: A1, A10.

Tobacco manufacturers have agreed to settle a smoking-related lawsuit filed against it by the state of Florida. The $11.3 billion settlement requires the companies to dismantle all product billboard promotions and transit advertisements, discontinue use of vending machines except in businesses catering to adults, and support stiffer penalties levied against retailers selling cigarettes to underage smokers. Mississippi, the first state to settle its own lawsuit with the industry, will benefit from concessions agreed to by the industry in the Florida settlement and other state settlements.

677. Teinowitz, Ira. "Fla. Tobacco Deal Triggers Outdoor Cuts and Anti Ads." *Advertising Age* 68, no. 35 (September 1, 1997): 14.

The $11.3 billion settlement between Florida and the tobacco industry provides for a two-year antismoking campaign. The industry would fund this "pilot" project with $200 million. The money will cover expenditures for advertisements, enforcement, and education. The settlement terms state that the advertising "shall not be directed against the tobacco companies or any particular company or companies or any particular brand of tobacco products." Also, the agreement allows the industry to post sponsorship notices at entertainment and sporting events and to display signs outside stores.

678. Collins, Glenn. "Cigarette Makers Increasing Prices a Record Amount." *New York Times*, September 3, 1997: A1, C8.

Tobacco companies substantially raised the per-price pack of cigarettes for the second time since March 1997. The wholesale price increase of 7.6 percent equated to a seven-cent increase at retail. Based on projected sales of 23.5 billion packs, the increase generated $1.6 billion in revenues during 1998. The companies raised retail prices by five cents per pack in March 1997, four cents per pack in April 1996, and three cents per pack in May 1995. Increases in the federal excise tax boosted cigarette prices. The tax rose by ten cents (from twenty-four cents) on January 1, 2000, and an additional five cents on January 1, 2002.

679. Phillips, Michael M., and Suein L. Hwang. "Why Tobacco Pact Won't Hurt Industry." *Wall Street Journal*, September 12, 1997: A3, A8.

The proposed national tobacco settlement has the major tobacco companies agreeing to pay $368.5 billion over twenty-five years, but the industry can afford the cost, for a variety of reasons. Tobacco demand is inelastic (that is, consumption will drop only slightly even when prices rise), smokers have no substitutes for cigarettes, an antitrust provision would give cover to the companies' raising of prices in unison, future lawsuits will be muted by provisions granting broad liability protection, a decline in consumption will help reduce the annual payments, the payments are tax deductible, less money will be required for advertising and marketing, and the costs are spread out over twenty-five years versus an immediate lump-sum payment.

680. Carlson, Margaret. "Where There's Smoke . . . ." *Time* 150, no. 13 (September 29, 1997): 29.

Two Republican Party officials have identified Haley Barbour, former chairman of the Republican National Committee, as the individual responsible for asking the Senate majority leader, Trent Lott (R-Ms.), and House speaker Newt Gingrich (R-Ga.) to include a provision in a balanced-budget bill before Congress granting the tobacco industry a $50 million tax break. The tax break came to light through the efforts of Senators Richard Durbin (D-Ill.) and Susan Collins (R-Me.).

681. Federal Trade Commission. *Competition and the Financial Impact of the Proposed Tobacco Industry Settlement*. September 1997. Washington, D.C.: Federal Trade Commission, Bureaus of Economics, Competition, and Consumer Protection, 1997. www.ftc.gov/reports/tobacco/ndoc95.pdf (accessed September 23, 1997).

Prepared for the Congressional Task Force on Tobacco and Health, this report is an analysis of the potential economic impact of the proposed tobacco settlement on cigarette prices, industry profits, and government revenues. It addresses the likely extent of any price rises and how much the public and private sectors will benefit from the increased revenue flows. The tobacco companies may act in concert to raise prices substantially above the "pass-through" threshold (the increase needed per pack to meet the settlement terms). Antitrust language contained in the agreement would allow the tobacco companies to "jointly confer, coordinate, or act in concert." The commission is concerned the language may clear the way for the companies to retard competition, increase per-pack prices, and generate substantial profits. Overall, more effective coordination would result in the tobacco companies' keeping about two-thirds and the public sector one-third of the financial benefits. Advertising and marketing restrictions contained in the national proposal would serve as barriers to new entrants or maverick firms seeking to compete with new products, lower-priced products, or new brands to gain market share and would also lead to higher prices. Nonparticipatory firms in the national settlement would have to pay 50 percent higher annual payments over twenty-five years, raising marginal costs for small firms and new entrants. This would restrict competition with the established companies.

682. Navarro, Mireya. "After Tobacco Settlement, Florida Battles Its Lawyers." *New York Times,* October 5, 1997: sec. 1: 22.

Florida's contract with its lawyers provides for a 25 percent contingency fee "of the total sum of monies recovered" by "any final judgments, court orders or negotiated settlement." Five out of the eleven lawyers working on the lawsuit have filed suit claiming $190 million in fees from the tobacco industry's first payment of $750 million. The state asserts that according to the June 20, 1997 proposed national settlement, a panel of independent arbitrators would determine "reasonable attorneys' fees."

683. Lorillard Tobacco Company, Philip Morris Companies, R. J. Reynolds Tobacco Company, and UST, Inc. *Impact of the Proposed Resolution on the U.S. Cigarette Industry*. Submitted to the Senate Democratic Task Force on the Tobacco Settlement. October 8, 1997.

This is the tobacco industry's response to the Federal Trade Commission's (FTC) September 1997 report. The report addresses the FTC's per-pack price, sales, and revenue projections. In nominal terms, including the effect of inflation, the tobacco industry projects that the retail price of a pack of cigarettes will increase by $1.52 in the year 2007. Cigarette sales are projected to decline annually by 2.5 percent. As for industry profits, the tobacco companies state that any additional revenues generated beyond the "pass-through" level will go to parties other than the manufacturers. The FTC, they argue, had failed to consider or give sufficient weight to various factors that would diminish future profits, including current profit margins, fixed costs, and a shift toward discount brands.

684. Kempster, Norman. "Pentagon Seeks Share of Tobacco Deal." *Los Angeles Times*, October 15, 1997: A12.

The Department of Defense (DoD) has become the first federal agency to seek reimbursement for smoking-related medical expenses under the proposed tobacco settlement. The DoD estimates that it has spent $584 million annually and $15 billion over the past twenty-five years to treat smoking-related illnesses in military personnel.

685. Schwartz, John. "U.S. Wants Share of State Tobacco Deals." *Washington Post*, November 5, 1997: A19.

A letter from Sally K. Richardson, director of the Health Care Financing Administration's Center for Medicaid and State Operations, has informed state Medicaid officials that the federal government, under the Social Security Act, is to be compensated for Medicaid money received by the states. The letter targets money that would be received under the $368.5 billion proposed tobacco settlement. Although not all the funds are Medicaid related, Richardson writes, state Medicaid officials should discuss appropriate amounts that would be sent back to the federal government.

686. Wallison, Ethan. "VA Urged to Take Piece of Tobacco Pie." *Chicago Tribune*, November 9, 1997: sec. 4: 3.

Representatives Lane Evans (D-Ill.) and Bob Filner (D-Calif.) have sent a letter to acting Veterans Administration secretary Hershel Gober faulting the administration for not requesting a share of the $368.5 billion proposed tobacco settlement. Evans serves on the House Veterans' Affairs Committee, as its top-ranking Democrat.

687. Federal Trade Commission. *Evaluation of the Tobacco Industry Analysis Submitted to Congress on October 8, 1997*. November 10, 1997. www.ftc.gov/os/1997-11/tobacco.htm (accessed November 17, 1997).

The Federal Trade Commission (FTC) has determined the tobacco industry's response did not identify any significant errors or omissions that undermine the commission's findings. The tobacco industry estimated that in nominal terms (inflation-adjusted), cigarette retail prices would increase by $1.52 in the year 2007. The FTC calculated its estimate in real terms (i.e., constant 1997 dollars) to be seventy-two cents. Recalculating the industry's estimate in real terms yields, at most, seventy-nine cents. The tobacco industry's projected annual decline in cigarette sales is overstated, due to a higher estimate of the elasticity of demand. Also, the impact on industry profits is inaccurate, due to the inconsistent use of adjustments for inflation; some of the figures used by the tobacco industry are adjusted for inflation but others are not. Finally, the tobacco industry's report did not address other items reviewed by the commission: antitrust exemption language, industry coordination to raise prices beyond that necessary to "pass through" to consumers the annual settlement payments, and the increase in industry profits due to the ability to raise prices substantially.

688. Schwartz, John. "States Want U.S. Out of Tobacco Deals." *Washington Post*, November 12, 1997: A21.

In a November 7, 1997 letter sent to President Clinton, state attorneys general requested the federal government to drop its claim to at least 50 percent of all state tobacco settlement money. The letter is in response to the Health Care Financing Administration's claim that each state must remit a pro rata share of all Medicaid-related money. Mississippi attorney general Michael Moore states that the attorneys general have worked with the White House to resolve this issue. The states would keep and spend the funds on children's healthcare. Moore stated, "It's kind of hard for us to figure out why another agency of the Federal government tried to reach out and take these funds."

689. "Arbitration on Florida Fees." *New York Times*, November 13, 1997: A25.

Private lawyers who worked for the state of Florida in reaching a settlement with the tobacco industry have filed a lawsuit demanding the state abide by its contract in compensating the lawyers. A Florida judge has ruled that their figure of $2.8 billion is "patently ridiculous" and has ordered that the fees be determined through arbitration.

690. *An Act Making Appropriations for the Departments of Labor, Health and Human Services, and Education, and Related Agencies for the Fiscal Year Ending September 30, 1998, and for Other Purposes.* Public Law 105-78, *U.S. Statutes at Large* 111 (November 13, 1997): 1519.

    Title V (General Provisions), section 519 repeals a $50 billion tax credit afforded the tobacco industry regarding the June 20, 1997, $368.5 billion tobacco settlement agreement. The language reads as follows: "Sec. 519. Subsection (k) of section 9302 of the Balanced Budget Act of 1997, as added by section 1604 (f)(3) of the Taxpayer Relief Act of 1997, is repealed."

691. Schwartz, John. "Administration Isn't Seeking Fight with States over Tobacco Funds, Aide Says." *Washington Post*, December 9, 1997: A13.

    Administration officials have released a letter written by President Clinton addressing the dispute surrounding the government's attempt to recover Medicaid funds from the states' tobacco settlement. The document became available during a hearing conducted by the House Commerce Subcommittee on Health and the Environment. In his letter, addressed to Governor George V. Voinovich of Ohio, the president stated that he "would prefer to see the allocation of tobacco funds between federal and state government resolved through legislation." Indiana attorney general Jeffrey A. Modisett had labeled the Health Care Financing Administration's recent letters "an eleventh-hour raid on the state settlement funds."

692. Williams, Mike. "Accusations Tarnish Florida Tobacco Deal." *Atlanta Journal and Constitution Journal*, January 7, 1998: A4.

    On August 25, 1997, the tobacco industry agreed to a $11.3 billion settlement with the state of Florida. Since then, the deal has been tarnished by accusations of unsavory dealings. It is alleged that one of Florida's attorneys lent twenty-four thousand dollars to Harold Lewis. Lewis served as the inspector general under Governor Lawton Chiles. Lewis had served as a key state representative working with state-hired private attorneys.

693. Meier, Barry. "Philip Morris Considered Proposing Ad Curbs in '93." *New York Times*, January 7, 1998: A9.

    In the June 20, 1997 proposed tobacco settlement, Philip Morris agreed to implement advertising restrictions that the company discussed implementing on its own back in 1993. An internal document titled "Philip Morris Corporate Affairs Strategic Plan for 1993" indicated that company officials had discussed separating from the industry trade group, the Tobacco Institute, implementing provisions to protect nonsmokers, and seeking legislation to "modify, restrict, or reform" advertising to young people. The company had discussed pursuing the moral high ground, neutralizing issues surrounding the tobacco controversy, and becoming a model corporate citizen.

694. Lewis, Neil A. "U.S. May Fill in for Tobacco Sponsorships." *New York Times*, January 12, 1998: A17.

Reflecting language of the provisions of the proposed tobacco settlement, Senators Edward M. Kennedy (D-Mass.) and John McCain (R-Ariz.) have each introduced a bill to allow funds from a final tobacco settlement to be used to sponsor sports and artistic events. Kennedy's legislation would allow states to subsidize sporting events with block grants. McCain's bill would allow groups dependent on tobacco money to tap into a fund established by the secretary of Health and Human Services. As in Kennedy's bill, these funds would be used to subsidize sponsorship of various events. Both bills refer to these acts as "alternative event sponsorship" and "substitute sponsorship."

695. "Official Says U.S. Accepts Split on Tobacco Funds." *Washington Post*, January 13, 1998: A7. (Associated Press).

Mississippi attorney general Michael Moore has reported that the states would receive $196 million from the proposed national tobacco settlement negotiated by the states. Last week, Moore met with White House officials to discuss this matter. Congress must approve the $368.5 billion proposed settlement and the allocations made to the states.

696. Meier, Barry. "Tobacco Concerns Settle Texas Case for $14.5 Billion." *New York Times*, January 16, 1998: A1, A14.

The five major tobacco companies agreed to settle the Texas lawsuit and avoid a courtroom trial. The $14.5 billion agreement will end the state's lawsuit seeking to recover funds spent on tobacco-related illnesses. A major battle, however, could be brewing over how to spend the funds. Texas legislators argue that any specific allocations would violate the legislature's right to make such decisions. A maximum of 15 percent of the proceeds could be awarded to the state's private lawyers negotiating the deal.

697. Torry, Saundra. "Billions of Dollars in Lawyers' Fees Become Hot Issue in Tobacco Settlement." *Washington Post*, January 17, 1998: A9.

In a motion filed with the presiding judge overseeing Texas's settlement with the tobacco industry, the state's private attorneys have requested $2.2 billion in fees. They are seeking to enforce the 15 percent contingency fee terms contained in their contract. The lawyers are opposed to having the fees determined by an arbitration panel and then paid separately by the tobacco companies.

698. Torry, Saundra. "Tobacco Funds Allocation Adds Settlement Pressure." *Washington Post*, February 3, 1998: A8.

The proposed national tobacco settlement was under congressional review, and President Clinton was counting on nearly $10 billion to fund new program initiatives contained in his fiscal 1999 proposed budget. The White House hoped this would place the Congress, and especially the Republicans, under public pressure to come to terms. The president's budget included $4 billion for the federal government to spend on science research and to implement youth smoking–prevention programs; the states' allocation of $2.4 billion funded child care and Medicaid programs. A variety of other programs including smoking-cessation programs were funded with $3.4 billion.

699. Verhovek, Sam Howe. "Fat Fees in Tobacco Deals Signal New Foe for States: The Lawyers." *New York Times*, February 9, 1998: A1, A10.

One hundred fifty lawyers, representing the state of Texas in its $15.3 billion settlement with the tobacco industry, are requesting the state to honor its contractual terms and remit them 15 percent of the total settlement. Governor George W. Bush thinks the payment is "outrageous" and has filed a court motion to block the payment. Texas attorney general Dan Morales accuses Bush of playing politics and seeking future funds from the tobacco industry for a possible presidential bid.

700. Marshall, Eliot. "Science Funding: Up in Smoke?" *Science* 279 (February 13, 1998): 974–75.

President Clinton's proposed fiscal 1999 budget includes increased spending of $10 billion, tied to the first installment received from Congress's pending enactment of the comprehensive tobacco settlement. Federal research would be a major beneficiary, receiving $3.6 billion. The National Institutes of Health would benefit with an increased FY99 budget of 8.4 percent; over five years, the cumulative increases would total 48 percent. Congressional leaders such as Representative John Porter (R-Ill.) and Senator Arlen Specter (R-Pa.) favor increased allocations for federal research but are opposed to making them dependent on funds allocated from the tobacco settlement.

701. Pringle, Peter. "The Great Smoke-Out: Minnesota Chases Big Tobacco." *Nation* 266, no. 6 (February 23, 1998): 11–14.

The author discusses Minnesota's quest to recover documents from the tobacco companies, especially British American Tobacco, for the state's Medicaid lawsuit. The tobacco companies included a paragraph in the tobacco settlement being negotiated with the states—Title VI, B 6, "Payment Protection." Pringle cites the statement "Obligation for annual payments responsibility only of entities selling into the domestic market" as placing full payment for the proposed settlement in doubt, since it releases the parent tobacco companies from liability. Harvard Law School professor Lynn LoPucki notes that, excluding Brown & Williamson, the "identifiable assets" of the other four tobacco companies "tobacco segments" equaled approximately the first three years' payments under the proposed tobacco settlement.

702. Levin, Myron. "Tobacco Deal Spurs Bonanza for Lobbyists." *Los Angeles Times*, March 1, 1998: A1, A11–A12.

Forces other than the major cigarette manufacturers and anti-tobacco groups are girding for a battle over the proposed national tobacco settlement. Companies and associations are arming themselves with the best lobbyists and legal representation possible. Because other tobacco companies, merchants, and other related parties will be subject to the settlement terms, smaller tobacco companies have hired J. Alex McMillan, former House member from North Carolina, as their lobbyist. These companies will fight settlement terms requiring all tobacco manufacturers to contribute payments based on market share; companies not signing the agreement would be subject to an additional 50 percent premium.

703. Taylor, Jeffrey. "Lawyers, Once Chary of Big Tobacco, Rush to Line Up Plaintiffs." *Wall Street Journal*, April 1, 1998: A1, A8.

Lawyers are blitzing the airwaves seeking tobacco victims. The lawyers are stepping up their campaign, encouraged by the revised proposed tobacco settlement passed by the Senate Commerce Committee. The new proposal strips tobacco companies of protection from class-action lawsuits and "immunity from punitive damages for past misconduct." Washington, D.C., lawyer Wayne Cohen seeks people inflicted with emphysema, lung, and throat cancer. His television ad shows him with his slogan "Tobacco Victims' Rights." Chicago lawyer Kenneth Moll seeks to represent every Illinois citizen who has used tobacco; also, he wants to consolidate all tobacco lawsuits filed in federal court.

704. Buckham, Tom. "Tobacco Bill Has Indians Fuming over Tax Clause." *Buffalo (New York) News*, April 7, 1998: 1B. LexisNexis Academic (accessed April 10, 1998).

States have been losing millions in cigarette taxes due to their inability to collect sales taxes on cigarettes sold to non–tribe members on reservations. It is estimated that New York, Washington, California, and Oklahoma lose a combined total of $235 million in lost cigarette taxes. The loss is also due to the tribes' immunity from state lawsuits. In the debates over a proposed national tobacco settlement, the Senate Commerce Committee voted ten to nine and approved a provision to require the collection of these taxes.

705. Goldstone, Steven F., Chief Executive Officer, RJR Nabisco Holdings Corporation. Luncheon Speaker. National Press Club, Washington, D.C., April 8, 1998.

Steven F. Goldstone, chief executive officer of RJR Nabisco, has announced that R. J. Reynolds and the other tobacco parties to the proposed national tobacco settlement are withdrawing from the agreement. Goldstone cites numerous reasons for this action. These include the growing litigation and punitive damages against the industry, an insatiable appetite for taxes and price increases to fund social programs, failure of the president to exert leadership, and language contained in the Senate Commerce Committee bill banning the trademark camel from cigarette packages.

706. Dorning, Mike. "Tobacco Revenue as Much as Spent." *Chicago Tribune*, April 10, 1998: sec. 1: 1, 14.

Although the compromise tobacco bill agreed to by the Senate Commerce Committee has been neither passed nor defeated by Congress, Senator Ernest Hollings (D-S.C.) says, the White House and Republicans have made commitments to spend money from the proposed settlement. President Clinton's budget spends the funds on programs such as hiring a hundred thousand new elementary school teachers ($7.3 billion) and improving child care and early development through state block grants ($7.5 billion). The Republicans' tax-cut initiatives would have to be funded from tobacco money.

707. Harwood, John, and Jeffrey Taylor. "Industry Tries to Turn Tobacco Debate into Tax Issue." *Wall Street Journal*, April 13, 1998: A24.

The tobacco industry has launched a broadside against Senator John McCain's (R-Ariz.) $516 billion tobacco legislation pending in Congress. The industry paid for a full-page ad printed in major newspapers. The ad charges that the legislation would increase taxes by $500 billion, prevent adults from purchasing tobacco products, create a tobacco black market, and establish seventeen new federal bureaucracies. Republican politicians are fearful of giving the opposition any opportunity to portray their party as being against reducing teenager smoking and as in the pocket of the tobacco industry.

708. U.S. General Accounting Office. *Tobacco: Issues Surrounding a National Tobacco Settlement*. GAO/RCED-98-110. April 15, 1998. Washington, D.C.: GAO, 1998. www.gao.gov/archive/1998/rc98110.pdf (accessed May 29, 2004).

This report identifies three major economic factors affecting the tobacco industry. First, the report identifies and summarizes published studies assessing the tobacco industry's regional and national impact. Money saved from declining tobacco consumption would be spent on other goods and services and result in only small losses in employment nationwide. Secondly, the study examines the effect of a tobacco settlement on state revenues generated from cigarette excise taxes. Assuming a decline in tobacco consumption, the General Accounting Office estimates that revenues could decline, based on current tax rates, in a range of from $673 million to $3 billion. The third is U.S. interstate and international cigarette smuggling. In the aggregate, states are losing hundreds of millions of dollars in tax revenues due to interstate smuggling. International smuggling also occurs as a means to avoid both state and federal taxes.

709. Connolly, Ceci. "Diverse Opposition to Tobacco Bill Builds to Hazardous Levels." *Washington Post*, April 20, 1998: A7.

The tobacco industry is implementing a plan to defeat Senator John McCain's (R-Ariz.) proposed $516 billion tobacco settlement bill. This plan calls upon its allies, such as the National Restaurant Association, the American Marketers Association, and friendly Wall Street analysts, to lobby against the bill. Also, the industry is bringing in such other parties as insurance groups, the American Civil Liberties Union, and the Chamber of Commerce. A national advertising campaign is under way, and town-hall meetings are being considered to create public resistance to the new tax and spending programs contemplated by the bill and the White House.

710. U.S. General Accounting Office. *Tobacco Settlements: States' Use of Settlement Proceeds*. GAO/HEHS-98-147R. April 22, 1998. Washington, D.C.: GAO, 1998. archive.gao.gov/paprpdf2/160536.pdf (accessed February 19, 2004).

This report reviews how Mississippi, Florida, and Texas are using the proceeds from their separate settlement agreements with the tobacco industry: how the proceeds are to be spent, how the parties are deciding how to spend the funds, and what programs and activities are to be funded. In addition, the report covers tobacco prevention or control efforts under way or planned in California, Maine, and Oregon. The report includes a table giving the terms of each state's settlement agreement.

711. Connolly, Ceci. "GOP's Tack on Tobacco: A Fight against Taxes." *Washington Post*, April 27, 1998: A1, A4.

Paralleling their position on the 1993 health care bill, the Republicans are attacking the McCain tobacco tax bill with antitax and antibureaucracy messages. They are attempting to convince House members and voters who support the GOP that the bill is not about controlling teenage smoking but raising taxes. GOP leaders leading the assault are House Speaker Newt Gingrich (R-Ga.), House Majority Whip Tom DeLay (R-Tex.), and Representative John Linder (R-Ga.). Other Republicans see a silver lining in raising tobacco tax money. House Budget Committee chairman John R. Kasich (R-Ohio) and Ways and Means Committee chairman Bill Archer (R-Tex.) are each contemplating including language raising tobacco revenue in future legislation.

712. Connolly, Ceci. "Big Tobacco to Fight Legislation with Ad Blitz, Lobbying Network." *Washington Post*, April 30, 1998: A6.

The tobacco industry is commencing a television and newspaper ad campaign to warn the public about the dangers inherent in Senator John McCain's (R-Ariz.) pending tobacco legislation. Chicago, New York, and up to forty-three other markets will air television commercials, and a print ad campaign will appear in about twenty national newspapers. Also, the industry is planning to plead its case by tapping the political expertise of professionals with links to U.S. senators.

713. U.S. Congressional Budget Office. *The Proposed Tobacco Settlement: Issues from a Federal Perspective*. April 1998. Washington, D.C.: Congressional Budget Office, 1998. www.cbo.gov (accessed February 20, 2004).

The Congressional Budget Office examines the June 20, 1997, $368.5 billion agreement between the tobacco industry and the state attorneys general, and its potential impact on consumers and the industry. The report examines the context of the proposed settlement (e.g., trends in cigarette consumption), impact of regulatory and public health provisions, the impact of required industry payments (such as price increases under the settlement), cigarette consumption and industry payments, and reduction of teen smoking.

714. Schwartz, John. "Tobacco Settles Minnesota Suit." *Washington Post*, May 9, 1998: A1, A10.

The five major tobacco manufacturers reached an out-of-court agreement to settle the lawsuit filed against it by the state of Minnesota. Minnesota will receive $6.1 billion over twenty-five years, and Blue Cross and Blue Shield of Minnesota will receive $469 million. The tobacco industry also agreed to disband its Council for Tobacco Research, stop advertising tobacco products in the movies, stop non-tobacco-product merchandising, end billboard advertising in the state, and agree to restrict minors' access to cigarettes in stores by having the products moved behind counters.

715. "Cigarette Makers Increase Prices." *New York Times*, May 12, 1998: D6. (Associated Press).

For the fourth time in fourteen months, Philip Morris and R. J. Reynolds Tobacco announced price increases for their cigarettes. The increase of five cents per pack follows price increases in March (five cents) and September (seven cents) of 1997 and January 1998 (2.5 cents).

716. Greenblatt, Alan. "Growing Ranks of Cigarette Tax Critics Invigorate Big Tobacco's Lobbying Effort." *CQ Weekly* 56, no. 20 (May 16, 1998): 1306, 1308.

Wholesalers, distributors, and convenience store operators are lobbying against provisions contained in Senator John McCain's (R-Ariz.) proposed tobacco legislation

(S. 1415). Over five years, the bill would boost per-pack fees by $1.10. Wholesalers would pay these increases immediately, face a substantial increase in the book value of inventory, and also incur increases in insurance costs and "shrinkage" (i.e., theft). Convenience store owners fear the loss of customers to "adults only" tobacco stores. Retail establishments face the loss of $2 billion in "slotting fees," paid by the tobacco companies for placing their products in prime display areas. In addition, the tobacco companies pay $250 million annually for point-of-sale displays. This money could disappear under the anti–tobacco bill provisions.

717. Marcus, Ruth. "Big Tobacco Quietly Tries to Grow Grass Roots." *Washington Post*, May 16, 1998: A1, A10.

The tobacco companies are waging a grassroots war against Senator McCain's tobacco bill. They are using various tools to generate support from ordinary citizens. The companies are employing telemarketing firms to contact names contained in their databases. Courtesy of Brown & Williamson (B&W), retailers are receiving petitions for customers to complete; the petitions are then express-mailed to their respective U.S. senators, with B&W paying the postage. They are sent in business-reply envelopes indicating, deceptively, that the specific senator paid for the postage. The National Smokers Alliance has blitzed Senator McCain's office with antitobacco legislation letters. Magazine ads appear courtesy of the Washington Legal Foundation, a conservative legal group that has received money from RJR Nabisco. Also, the industry established an 800 number whereby callers can request that a letter be sent to their U.S. senator or have their call redirected to the senator's office.

718. Harris, John F., and Saundra Torry. "White House, McCain Agree on Amendments to Tobacco Bill." *Washington Post*, May 16, 1998: A10.

Senator John McCain (R-Ariz.) and White House officials have issued a statement agreeing to specific amendments to the senator's tobacco bill pending before Congress. Parties and programs would receive allocations as follows: $26 billion to the states, $14.3 billion for federal medical research, $15.3 billion for such programs as smoking-cessation and antitobacco ads, and $10.4 billion for tobacco farmers. These are funds to be received over the first five years. The agreement also raises the liability cap to $8 billion and strengthens "look-back" provisions to reduce youth smoking.

719. Parker-Pope, Tara. "Philip Morris and RJR Nabisco Take Charges to Begin Paying Settlement." *Wall Street Journal*, May 18, 1998: A6.

Philip Morris and RJR Nabisco have announced that they will begin taking pretax charges for settling the lawsuit filed by the state of Minnesota. Philip Morris will charge pretax earnings for $806 million. This covers the first payment to Minnesota for $324.6 million, $148.4 million to Blue Cross and Blue Shield, $283.1 million for lawyers' fees covering the next two years, and $50 million for tobacco-control programs, such as youth smoking. RJR Nabisco will charge pretax earnings for $312 million. Each company will recoup these charges over time through price increases.

720. Torry, Saundra. "Fearing Gain for Trial Lawyers, Business Groups Fight Tobacco Bill Harder." *Washington Post*, May 19, 1998: A5.

The U.S. Chamber of Commerce funded a hundred-thousand-dollar anti–McCain tobacco bill blitz in Washington, D.C. The group, along with corporate America, fears that the legislation will enrich trial lawyers, encouraging them to forge new lawsuits against "politically incorrect" industries, make further inroads with Congress, and block legislation reforming the nation's liability laws.

721. U.S. Congress. Senate. *National Tobacco Policy and Youth Smoking Reduction Act.* S. 1415, 105th Cong., 2nd sess. *Congressional Record* 144, no. 64, daily ed. (May 19, 1998): S5034–S5084.

The bill is "to reform and restructure the processes by which tobacco products are manufactured, marketed, and distributed, to prevent the use of tobacco products by minors, to redress the adverse health effects of tobacco use, and for other purposes." This text is modified to incorporate the text of Senate Amendment 2420, which was submitted on May 18. This bill came to the Senate from the Senate Commerce Committee, chaired by Senator John McCain (R-Ariz.).

722. Meier, Barry, and Jill Abramson. "Tobacco War's New Front: Lawyers Fight for Big Fees." *New York Times*, June 9, 1998: A1, A14.

Lawyer fees for services in the fight against the tobacco industry are taking center stage in Florida, Texas, and the U.S. Senate. The size of the potential fees under the Florida and Texas agreements are being disputed. Approximately 160 law firms could receive $18 billion. The lone law firm hired by the state of Minnesota will receive $430 million. In Mississippi, a state court will decide the amount of money to be paid to the eleven law firms hired by the state. The U.S. Senate has debated and defeated an amendment to implement a $250 per hour fee for the plaintiff's lawyers.

723. Torry, Saundra, and Helen Dewar. "Big Tobacco's Ad Blitz Felt in Senate Debate." *Washington Post*, June 17, 1998: A1, A12.

On April 18, 1998, the tobacco industry commenced a television and radio ad campaign to drum up public support against Senator John McCain's (R-Ariz.) tobacco bill now being considered by Congress. The $40 million campaign includes time purchased on CNN and ads purchased in the *Washington Post*, *USA Today*, *Amsterdam News* (a New York–based African-American weekly), and the North Dakota newspaper *Argus Leader*.

724. Torry, Saundra, and Helen Dewar. "Senate GOP Kills McCain Tobacco Bill." *Washington Post*, June 18, 1998: A1, A18.

The sixty-vote standard parliamentary rule of the U.S. Senate proved to be the Achilles' heel in the downfall of the proposed tobacco regulation bill. Two procedural votes helped kill it. The first vote sought to place the discussion under time constraints and press the legislators to vote on the bill. This lost by fifty-seven to forty-two. The second and lethal vote lost by fifty-three to forty-six. The senators declined to keep the bill on the floor for debate; Majority Leader Trent Lott (R-Miss.) pulled the bill from the Senate floor.

725. Kurtz, Howard. "The Democrat Who Switched and Fought." *Washington Post*, June 19, 1998: A1, A14.

A former Democratic Party and consultant to Vice President Al Gore, Carter Eskew, is the man behind the tobacco industry's $40 million ad campaign to extinguish the McCain tobacco reform bill. For the "Project Blue" campaign, Eskew convinced the industry to put forth a "simple, straightforward message" and play the "Blame Washington" card. The ads portrayed the Washington tobacco bill as "tax and spend," a bureaucratic boondoggle creating seventeen new government agencies and hurting farmers, retailers, and small businesses. The ads, which contained an 800 number, prompted more than 150,000 people to call in support of the industry.

726. Redhead, C. Stephen. *The Tobacco Settlement: Issues*. CRS Issue Brief. August 28, 1998. Washington, D.C.: Congressional Research Service, Library of Congress, 1998.

The Congressional Research Service (CRS) has reviewed the June 20, 1997, proposed tobacco settlement agreement and its provisions to settle lawsuits brought against the industry, recover tobacco-related medical costs, and provide payments for tobacco control programs. The report provides background and analysis, a summary of the agreement's key points, and a review of the issues such as Food and Drug Administration regulation, public health, economics, attorneys' fees, and tobacco farmers.

727. Teinowitz, Ira. "Effect of Tobacco Makers' $60 Mil Effort Lingers On." *Advertising Age* 69, no. 38 (September 21, 1998): 18.

September 15, 1998 marked the end of the tobacco industry's six-month, $60 million advertising campaign to defeat the antitobacco McCain tobacco bill and any subsequent tobacco legislation. The industry used the print and television media to get its message across to the citizens. To counter these ads, the American Cancer Society launched its own television ad campaign to paint the tobacco industry's campaign as "a big lie." The society spent $5 million.

728. Teinowitz, Ira. "Tobacco Makers Likely Limited to 1 Sponsorship." *Advertising Age* 69, no. 45 (November 9, 1998): 3, 89.

The tobacco manufacturers and the state attorneys general are working on a settlement of all state lawsuits. It is anticipated that the companies will be limited in their sponsorship of sporting events. Philip Morris will likely continue its sponsorship of the Championship Auto Racing Teams (CART). This includes its sponsorship of Marlboro Team Penske. The company has withdrawn its sponsorship of women's tennis. R. J. Reynolds Tobacco will likely continue with its sponsorship of the National Association of Stock Car Auto Racing (NASCAR) and its Winston Cup Series. Its sponsorship of the National Hot Rod Association may be in jeopardy. Brown & Williamson will likely continue its sponsorship of its Team Kool Green entry in the CART tour.

729. Torry, Saundra, and John Schwartz. "Big Tobacco, State Officials Reach $206 Billion Deal." *Washington Post*, November 14, 1998: A1, A8.

Negotiations among eight state attorneys general and the tobacco companies had the potential to lead to an end of Medicaid lawsuits filed by most of the states. The parties agreed to a twenty-five-year $206 billion settlement. The final settlement—and how much money is to be paid to each state—depended on how many states signed on. November 20, 1998 was the deadline. The deal limited each tobacco company to one brand-name sponsorship, established a $1.45 billion national foundation (funded over five years) to support antismoking advertisements geared toward youth, and banned cartoon figures, billboards, transit ads, and brand-name merchandise bearing cigarettes logos. The tobacco industry was not accorded legal immunity.

730. Torry, Saundra, and John Schwartz. "States Approve $206 Billion Deal with Big Tobacco." *Washington Post*, November 21, 1998: A1, A7.

   Forty-six states, the District of Columbia, and the U.S. territories have given their approval to a $206 billion settlement with the tobacco industry. The agreement settles all state lawsuits, but individual and class-action lawsuits are still potential threats to the industry. The industry is still under investigation by the Justice Department.

731. Nasar, Sylvia. "The Ifs and Buts of the Tobacco Settlement." *New York Times*, November 29, 1998: sec. 4: 1, 10.

   The November 20, 1998 tobacco settlement was labeled as "damages" money to be paid by the major tobacco manufacturers. Analysts labeled the deal as a disguised tax hike, as tailormade for trial lawyers, and a sweetheart package for the smaller tobacco companies. Ninety-nine percent of the $206 billion deal was borne by smokers in the form of increased prices. On November 21, 1998, Philip Morris and R. J. Reynolds raised prices by forty-five cents a pack. All the trial lawyers involved shared from an $8 billion total payout. Damages were collectible only from Philip Morris, R. J. Reynolds, Brown & Williamson, and Lorillard Tobacco. Smaller companies, such as Liggett & Myers, were basically handed an annual subsidy of about $100 million, since they were not forced to raise cigarette prices.

732. Meier, Barry. "Lawyers in Early Tobacco Suits to Get $8 Billion." *New York Times*, December 12, 1998: A1, A10.

   The December 11, 1998 ruling by an arbitration panel awarded $8.2 billion in fees to lawyers representing Florida, Mississippi, and Texas in lawsuits against the tobacco companies. The Florida lawyers received $3.43 billion, the Mississippi lawyers received $1.43 billion, and the Texas lawyers received $3.3 billion. The large awards drew harsh words from the legal community. It appeared that, based on this ruling, legal fees stemming from the $206 billion agreement netted billions for the legal teams representing the states.

733. Mollenkamp, Carrick, Adam Levy, Joseph Menn, and Jeffrey Rothfeder. *The People vs. Big Tobacco: How the States Took on the Cigarette Giants*. Princeton, N.J.: Bloomberg, 1998.

   The authors document the events and negotiations leading to the June 20, 1997, $368.5 billion proposed settlement between state attorneys general and Philip Morris, RJR Nabisco, Brown & Williamson, and Lorillard Tobacco. Also, the authors discuss the stories behind Michael Lewis and his novel idea to sue the tobacco industry; the interrelationship between Michael Moore, Ricky Scruggs, and Merrill Williams; Bennett LeBow and his Liggett Group's lawsuit settlements; and the brokers behind the negotiations.

734. Pringle, Peter. *Cornered: Big Tobacco at the Bar of Justice*. New York: Henry Holt, 1998.

   Pringle explores the events shaping the background leading to the proposed 1997 $368.5 billion settlement agreed to by the state attorneys general and the tobacco industry. The author explores such areas as the state of Mississippi's suit against the industry, the *Castano* class-action lawsuit, Merrill Williams and the public disclosure of the Brown & Williamson document largesse, Liggett Tobacco's settlement with the state and its release of tobacco industry documents, and the negotiations leading to the national settlement agreement.

POST–TOBACCO SETTLEMENT AGREEMENTS, 1999–2004

735. Meier, Barry. "Tobacco Windfall Begins Tug-of-War among Lawmakers." *New York Times*, January 10, 1999: sec. 1: 1, 18.

    State lawmakers have begun deliberating how to spend money received from the $206 billion national tobacco settlement. States are not mandated to spend the funds on specific projects and will treat the funds as general revenues. Special-interest groups are jockeying to have funds spent on their projects. State leaders are proposing projects such as youth-related programs, rebuilding health facilities, paying state debt, plugging budget holes, and funding antismoking initiatives.

736. Torry, Saundra. "Clinton to Propose Higher Cigarette Tax." *Washington Post*, January 15, 1999: A8.

    President Clinton's fiscal year 2000 budget included a proposed fifty-five-cent cigarette tax hike. According to the bill, veterans, military personnel, and federal employees would be primary beneficiaries of $8 billion in annual projected revenues to fund the treatment of smoking-related illnesses. Congressional Republicans countered that the money would be used to fund different projects proposed by the administration. The administration planned to seek $5 billion per year, beginning in 2001, of the $206 billion tobacco agreement to compensate the government for funding state Medicaid programs. The administration agreed to relent on its claim if the states conceded to spend the funds on tobacco-related control programs.

737. "Tobacco Fund for Farmers." *New York Times*, January 22, 1999: A22. (Associated Press).

    Philip Morris, R. J. Reynolds, Lorillard, and Brown & Williamson have created a twelve-year, $5.15 billion trust fund for tobacco farmers. Markets for tobacco products are expected to decrease in the future due to decreasing demand and the $206 billion national tobacco settlement. Tobacco farmers will be compensated for these variables.

738. Warren, Peter M. "Debate Flares over Plans for Tobacco Funds." *Los Angeles Times*, April 16, 1999: A3, A33.

    Squabbling is already occurring on how to spend annual payments of $1 billion paid to the state by the tobacco industry as part of the $206 billion national settlement. Questions are being asked if there is a "moral and fiscal responsibility" to spend the funds on tobacco-related programs or on projects that would need to be funded with different revenue streams after the year 2025. Some ideas offered on how to spend the funds include addressing the bankruptcy debt of Orange County and the sidewalks of Los Angeles.

739. Torry, Saundra. "Giving the Medium a New Message." *Washington Post*, April 23, 1999: A3, A16.

Midnight on April 22, 1999 marked the demise of billboard advertising for the tobacco industry. The industry agreed to this provision as part of the November 1998 Master Settlement Agreement. The Marlboro Man's removal from Los Angeles's Sunset Boulevard and a Virginia Slims billboard removed from Washington, D.C.'s, New York Avenue symbolize the end of an era in advertising. Antitobacco billboards are taking their places.

740. *1999 Emergency Supplemental Appropriations Act*. Public Law 106-31, *U.S. Statutes at Large* 113 (May 21, 1999): 103–104.

The law contains language waiving any claim put forward by the federal government on any portion of the $206 billion Master Settlement Agreement. The language is contained in Section 3031, "Prohibition on Treating Any Funds Recovered from Tobacco Companies as an Overpayment for Purposes of Medicaid," paragraphs a, b, and c.

741. Liu, Betty W. "Farmers Reap State Tobacco Compensation." *Financial Times*, June 16, 1999: 6.

Georgia was not the only state ready to use tobacco money, due under the national settlement agreement, for purposes other than tobacco-control projects. Georgia's governor, Roy Barnes, announced that the state's tobacco farmers would receive about one-third of the total payments due the state. Forty percent of Nevada's total payments funded a college scholarship program. Settlement money paid to renovate a state morgue in North Dakota. State debt was pared in California and Louisiana. New York sold tobacco bonds and received the funds directly instead of over the next twenty-five years. The national settlement terms were not legally binding; thus, the states were not bound to spend funds on tobacco prevention programs.

742. Applebome, Peter. "Tobacco's Imprimatur Is Less Bold, but Still on Cultural Events." *New York Times*, June 21, 1999: E1, E4.

As part of the $206 billion national tobacco settlement, the tobacco industry agreed to phase out sponsorships of entertainment (e.g., concerts) and sporting events except for one event. The sponsorship may encompass one single event or a series of events, such as R. J. Reynolds's (RJR) sponsorship of the Winston Cup. RJR will switch its "Winston Blues Revival" to an adults-only venue. Brown & Williamson will eventually discontinue either the Team Kool Green auto racing team or the George Strait Music Festival. Philip Morris's Virginia Slims tennis, Merit bowling, and military base concerts are ending. The company will continue with its Marlboro Grand Prix and Marlboro 500 sponsorships. The agreement allows tobacco companies to sponsor events conducted in bars and clubs, so long as the programs are limited to adult smokers. The three companies are busily signing agreements with bars and clubs. Sponsoring all-adult events in these venues allows the companies to promote their products and distribute giveaways, such as napkins and ashtrays.

743. Lima, Julie C., and Michael Siegel. "The Tobacco Settlement: An Analysis of Newspaper Coverage of a National Policy Debate, 1997–98." *Tobacco Control* 8, no. 3 (Autumn 1999): 247–53.

The authors reviewed 117 articles appearing in the *Washington Post* to understand how the media reported the proposed tobacco settlement talks. The articles covered the period from January 1, 1997, through June 18, 1998. The analysis identified the major policy themes and how the media framed the issues. The major policy themes reported are public policy health aspects (e.g., Food and Drug Administration authority), financial aspects (such as generation of new revenues), and civil justice aspects (for example, ban on punitive damages). Media frames used included kids, "David v. Goliath," and outside intruder.

744. James, Joni. "Bush Plans Sale to Secure Tobacco Funds." *Wall Street Journal*, January 12, 2000: F1. ABI/Inform (accessed September 5, 2003).

A state budget shortfall of $71.2 million and a decline in projected 1999 tobacco settlement proceeds from $712.1 million to $640.9 million is prompting Florida governor Jeb Bush to propose "securitizing" part of the state's projected total tobacco settlement payments. Governor Bush has proposed selling $8.3 billion of the projected $17.4 billion tobacco settlement proceeds; it is estimated that current market conditions would value the sale at $2.4 billion. The money would be invested in the Lawton Chiles Tobacco Endowment for Children and Elders. State law mandates that the endowment's funds be used for social and health services.

745. Leung, Shirley. "So Far, California Is Being General on Tobacco Cash." *Wall Street Journal*, March 8, 2000: CA2. ABI/Inform (accessed September 5, 2003).

In 2000, the state of California deposited 50 percent of its billion-dollar payment from the tobacco industry in the general fund. The other money was funneled to the state's fifty-eight counties and to four cities, including Los Angeles. One-third of the other states also placed tobacco settlement money in their general funds.

746. Meier, Barry, and Emily Yellin. "Big Tobacco Is Lobbying the States for Help." *New York Times*, March 20, 2000: A20.

The tobacco industry persuaded legislators from two tobacco states, and two other states as well, to amend laws requiring the posting of cash or a bond while punitive damages were being appealed. Generally, corporations appealing punitive damages post cash or a bond, along with interest, equaling the jury's award. This also depends on the state where the corporation is domiciled. A Miami jury considered assessing the industry with stiff punitive damages, and this prompted the industry to take action. Virginia passed a law capping a bond payment at $25 million during the appeals process. Georgia passed a similar law, and the governor signed it. In Kentucky, the state senate began the process by passing a law capping an appeal bond at $100 million. Two of North Carolina's tobacco companies, R. J. Reynolds and the Liggett Group, pushed for an emergency session, since the state legislative session did not convene until May.

747. "North Carolina Acts to Protect Tobacco Companies." *New York Times*, April 6, 2000: A22.

North Carolina–based companies, and in particular the tobacco industry, received assistance on April 5, 2000, when the state legislature passed a law limiting to $25 million bonds paid to appeal any state's judgment involving punitive damages. Specifically, the legislature acted in response to a Florida class-action tobacco court case and the possibility that the jury will assess the tobacco defendants, including state-based R. J. Reynolds, Liggett Group, and Lorillard Tobacco Company, with a huge punitive damage penalty. If punitive damages are appealed in Florida, the defendant "must post a bond equal to 115 percent of an award once a judge enters that verdict."

748. "Deal Protects Florida's Tobacco Payments." *New York Times*, May 6, 2000: A10.

    Governor Jeb Bush signed a bill placing a $100 million cap on a bond needed to appeal a punitive-damage award. The tobacco companies are the beneficiaries in their fight against a Miami jury's award in a class-action lawsuit. The governor considered the bill to be "a great victory" that would help protect the state's $450 million annual payment due from the tobacco industry. The legislature passed the bill on its final business day for the session.

749. Fairclough, Gordon. "California Sues R. J. Reynolds Tobacco, Alleging Cigarette Mailings Violate Pact." *Wall Street Journal*, May 12, 2000: B8.

    In a lawsuit filed against R. J. Reynolds, California attorney general Bill Lockyer accused the company of mailing nearly one million multipack cigarettes to Californians last year. The mailings violated the terms of the 1998 tobacco settlement limiting the industry's ability to distribute free cigarettes in age-restricted venues, through coupon-style offers, and market-research tests. R. J. Reynolds responded that it had engaged in "consumer testing" and that its actions met the conditions set forth in the national settlement.

750. Fairclough, Gordon. "Are Cigarette Ads in Magazines Angling for Teens?" *Wall Street Journal*, May 17, 2000: B1, B4.

    The 1998 national tobacco settlement prevents the industry from taking "any action" to advertise and market cigarettes directly or indirectly to teens. The industry claims it has worked within the letter and spirit of the agreement. However, critics note that youths are being targeted indirectly through the industry's advertisements in such trade magazines as *Rolling Stone*, *Sports Illustrated*, and *Entertainment Weekly*. Philip Morris and Brown & Williamson are voluntarily abiding by the "15 percent" rule the Food and Drug Administration has attempted to implement. The rule prevents targeting magazines if 15 percent or more of the readers are under the age of twenty-one. Both companies follow data published by the market trackers Simmons and Mediamark. R. J. Reynolds uses the Simmons data to determine if a magazine's under-twenty-one readership is at least 50 percent of all the readers.

751. Fairclough, Gordon. "Philip Morris to Pull Some Cigarette Ads." *Wall Street Journal*, June 6, 2000: A4.

    By the end of September 2000, Philip Morris discontinued advertisements in magazines identified by the market research firm Simmons as having a high number of readers under the age of eighteen. It was decided that if the magazine's teen audience exceeded 15 percent or if more than two million people under the age of eighteen viewed the magazine, the company would stop advertising in that magazine. This impacted forty to fifty national magazines, including *Glamour, Vogue,* and *People*. Advertisements in *Rolling Stone* and *Sports Illustrated* have already been suspended.

752. Fairclough, Gordon. "Philip Morris Removed Slogan from Ad in Second Attempt to Respond to Critics." *Wall Street Journal*, June 13, 2000: A6.

Philip Morris executive Michael Szymanczyk said the company has dropped its slogan "Find your voice" from its Virginia Slims ads. In May 2000, Syzymanczyk ordered the removal after being questioned about it by attorney Stanley M. Rosenblatt in a Florida tobacco class-action lawsuit. Szymanczyk agreed with Rosenblatt that smokers suffering from throat cancer might be offended by the ad. Also, Rosenblatt said the Virginia Slims slogan "Don't let the goody-two-shoes get you down" suggested that the cigarette pack warnings be ignored. The Philip Morris executive responded that the ad would stop being used by the end of June 2000 and that future Virginia Slims ads would not be rebellious.

753. "RJR Unit Agrees to Limits on Mailing Cigarettes." *Wall Street Journal*, January 8, 2001: C13. ABI/Inform (accessed September 5, 2003).

R. J. Reynolds Tobacco (RJR) and California attorney general Bill Lockyer have settled the state's lawsuit charging RJR with violating the terms of the $206 billion national tobacco settlement. Adults agreeing to evaluate or test cigarettes will receive cigarettes through the mail for free. The number of free cigarettes sent to each person will be limited, and the total numbers mailed will be submitted to the state.

754. Edsall, Thomas B. "Lawyers Get Tobacco Fees Early." *Washington Post*, February 14, 2001: A14.

Lawyers from eleven law firms in four states have sold future tobacco fee payments for an up-front lump-sum payment. The lawyers sold a billion dollars in fees due them over the next eight years for $308.1 million. The fees stem from the 1998 Master Settlement Agreement. Institutional investors purchased the tobacco bonds for $308.1 million. Over the next eight years, the investors will receive payments based on the billion-dollar figure.

755. "California Lawyers to Get $637.5 Million from Tobacco Suits." *Wall Street Journal*, March 7, 2001: B2.

Four lawsuits brought against the tobacco industry by California lawyers have net them $637.5 million. The Tobacco Fee Arbitration Panel has awarded this fee as fair and just compensation. The lawyer fees paid are in addition to the money the state will receive from the tobacco industry as part of the $206 billion national tobacco settlement. In 2000, the panel awarded approximately $633 million in compensation to state tobacco case lawyers from Hawaii, Illinois, Oklahoma, New Mexico, South Carolina, and Utah.

756. Fairclough, Gordon. "Tobacco Deal Has Unintended Effect: New Discount Smokes." *Wall Street Journal*, May 1, 2001: A1, A6.

The $206 billion national tobacco settlement spawned unintended consequences, including the proliferation of small tobacco manufacturers, the creation of partnerships between these companies and the major tobacco companies, and a slowing of the decline of cigarette consumption. Patriot Tobacco and S&M Brands are satisfying a demand for lower-priced smokes by producing such brands as Patriot and Bailey's, respectively. One low-cost manufacturer, Star Scientific, has two-thirds of its brands manufactured by Brown & Williamson, prompting complaints that this violates the national tobacco agreement. The major tobacco companies benefit by provisions in the national tobacco agreement that allow them to reduce payments to the states based on their lower tobacco sales because of the increased sales of low-cost smokes. The major companies can cease making payments to fund antitobacco campaigns if the market share of the nonsigning manufacturers exceeds 0.95 percent in any year. This provision has been in effect since the year 2003. Companies not a party to the national settlement do not face restrictions on marketing their cigarettes.

757. Glanton, Dahleen. "Few States Use Money to Fight Smoking." *Chicago Tribune*, May 20, 2001: sec. 1: 11.

Though they promised to use the tobacco settlement proceeds for tobacco control programs, most states are instead using the funds to fill budget gaps. The U.S. Centers for Disease Control recommended using 20 to 25 percent of the initial settlement payments to fund tobacco programs. But the American Medical Association has reported that programs are only being funded with 8 percent of the payments. Seventeen states, including Arizona, California, Mississippi, and Massachusetts, have committed substantial funds for tobacco-control programs.

758. U.S. General Accounting Office. *Tobacco Settlement: States' Use of Master Settlement Agreement Payments*. GAO-01-851. June 29, 2001. Washington, D.C.: GAO, 2001. www.gao.gov/new.items/d01851.pdf (accessed February 19, 2004).

Covering fiscal years 2000 and 2001, the General Accounting Office (GAO) has reviewed Master Settlement Agreement (MSA) money paid to each of the forty-six states signing the national tobacco agreement and their budget allocation processes, and the funding of various smoking prevention and cessation programs with these payments. GAO reviewed only the MSA payments made to the states and excluded the District of Columbia and the U.S. territories.

759. Kuczynski, Alex. "Tobacco Companies Accused of Still Aiming Ads at Youths." *New York Times*, August 15, 2001: A1, C14.

The $206 billion national tobacco settlement prohibited advertisements in magazines whose under-eighteen readers account for 16 percent or more of the total readership or number more than two million. Philip Morris is following the document's language, but R. J. Reynolds, Brown & Williamson, and Lorillard regard it as a "guideline" and not legally binding. The three companies continue to advertise in *People*, *Sports Illustrated*, *ESPN Magazine*, and *Rolling Stone*. All four magazines have high teenage readerships. R. J. Reynolds spokesperson Jan Smith said that the company targets magazines if the teenage readership is less than 25 percent of the total readership. Lacking this data, the company looks to see if the median age of readers is around twenty-three years, reviews the editorial content, and sees if, for example, liquor or car companies advertise in the magazine. Interestingly, *People* publisher Peter Bauer states that the language restricting magazine advertising applies only to the tobacco companies and not to the magazine publishers.

760. King, Charles, III, and Michael Siegel. "The Master Settlement Agreement with the Tobacco Industry and Cigarette Advertising in Magazines." *New England Journal of Medicine* 345, no. 7 (August 16, 2001): 504–11.

The authors analyze trends in tobacco advertising expenditures (estimates) of "youth" (such as Marlboro) and "adult" (for example, Winston) cigarette brands in youth-oriented (like *Sports Illustrated*) and adult-oriented magazines over the years 1995–2000. Fifteen brands and thirty-eight magazines are covered. Expenditures in youth-oriented magazines far exceed their adult counterparts. The authors conclude that youth exposure to tobacco advertisements has changed very little in spite of the advertising restrictions of the 1998 Master Settlement Agreement.

761. Kaufman, Marc. "States Get a Surprise in Tobacco Settlement." *Washington Post*, March 9, 2002: A3.

The Council of State Governments notes that through April 2001, an 11 percent reduction in the tobacco settlement revenue flowed to the states versus initial projections. Through 2010, the revenue shortfalls are predicted to be approximately 20 percent, or about $14 billion. The decrease is attributed to the decline in cigarette consumption and rise in sales from companies not participating in the tobacco settlement.

762. Winter, Greg. "Tobacco Company Reneged on Youth Ads, Judge Rules." *New York Times*, June 7, 2002: A18.

The first legal test of youth marketing restrictions detailed in the national tobacco settlement has ended in R. J. Reynolds's being fined $20 million for flagrant disregard of the settlement. Judge Ronald S. Prager of the Superior Court in San Diego has ruled that the tobacco company advertised in magazines such as *Rolling Stone* and *Sports Illustrated* with high teenage readerships. The judge ordered R. J. Reynolds to adopt "reasonable measures" and advertise in magazines where there is a much lower level of teenage readership vis-à-vis adults. R. J. Reynolds stated that this ruling impinges the company's First Amendment rights. The company was sued by California State attorney general Bill Lockyer and attorneys general from New York, Connecticut, Maryland, and Pennsylvania.

763. Pierre, Robert E. "Tobacco Tempts States in Financial Need." *Washington Post*, June 30, 2002: A3.

Though state lawmakers view tobacco as a health and societal menace, state budget crises are forcing legislators to use tobacco as a tool to help bridge budget gaps. Cigarette taxes have been raised in eleven states, with over a dozen more considering the same action. Future claims on tobacco settlement payments are being "securitized" and money received through bond sales is used to boost general funds. Over a dozen states have taken this action, including Wisconsin, which received $1.59 billion on bond sales securitized to cover $5.9 billion in future tobacco payments. The bond funds are being used to close the state's budget gap. States are also raiding funds targeted for smoking-cessation programs and are spending settlement payments on nonsmoking matters.

764. U.S. General Accounting Office. *Tobacco Settlement: States' Allocations of Phase II Funds*. GAO-03-262R. December 3, 2002. Washington, D.C.: GAO, 2002. www.gao.gov/new.items/d03262r.pdf (accessed February 19, 2004).

This is the General Accounting Office's (GAO) first report on the National Tobacco Grower Settlement Trust agreement (also known as "Phase II") signed in July 1999. Over twelve years, the tobacco-producing states will receive a total of $5.15 billion.

Tobacco growers and quota owners will receive these funds to offset the Master Settlement Agreement's economic impact. GAO reports on the money distributed under the agreement and the allocation of funds by the states to the intended parties.

765. Derthick, Martha A. *Up in Smoke: From Legislation to Litigation in Tobacco Politics*. Washington, D.C.: CQ, 2002.

    The author traces the history of the tobacco political wars, with an initial review of its legislative and litigable origins. Derthick follows with a recounting of the Food and Drug Administration's (FDA) drive to regulate nicotine content, the industry's advertising and marketing agenda, and how these events turned the tide against the tobacco industry. Derthick traces the developments surrounding the 1997 settlement, the death of FDA's proposed regulations, the 1998 Master Settlement Agreement (MSA), and the MSA's impact on the industry and government.

766. Feldheim, David, and Stan Rosenberg. "California to Sell $3 Billion in Bonds." *Wall Street Journal*, January 13, 2003: C10.

    California's Golden State Tobacco Securitization Corporation will issue $3 billion of tax-exempt tobacco bonds. Future tobacco revenues to be received under the multistate national tobacco agreement back the bonds. The bond issue will comprise $2.625 billion of fixed-rate bonds and $375 million of auction-rate securities. The auction-rate, or variable-rate, bonds will have the interest rate adjusted every thirty-five days. This is the first such financing technique offered by any state securitizing future tobacco revenues. Legislators will apply the proceeds to the state's budget deficit.

767. U.S. General Accounting Office. *Tobacco Settlement: States' Allocations of Fiscal Years 2002 and 2003 Master Settlement Agreement Payments*. GAO-03-407. February 28, 2003. Washington, D.C.: GAO, 2003. www.gao.gov/new.items/d03407.pdf (accessed March 2, 2004).

    This report discusses the Master Settlement Agreement (MSA) payments received by each of the forty-six states during fiscal year 2002 and the MSA payments each state expected to receive during fiscal year 2003; fiscal-year 2002 and 2003 allocations made to fund various program categories and allocation formula changes made vis-à-vis previous years; and changes in states' decision-making frameworks for MSA funds since fiscal year 2001. This is the General Accounting Office's second report as mandated by the Farm Security and Rural Investment Act of 2002 (Public Law 107-171, section 10908).

768. Fairclough, Gordon, and Vanessa O'Connell. "Once Tobacco Foes, States Are Hooked on Settlement Cash." *Wall Street Journal*, April 2, 2003: A1, A11.

    Since the signing of the $206 billion national tobacco settlement, the public sector's reliance on the financial well-being of the tobacco industry has grown inextricably tight. State legislators have become hooked on tobacco payments to plug budget gaps and provide money for various other projects. This reliance is now in jeopardy due to the recent $12 billion punitive damage verdict issued by an Illinois judge against Philip Morris in which the judge ruled that the company mislead smokers into thinking that low-tar, or "light," cigarettes are less harmful than full-tar cigarettes. The fallout from the Illinois verdict is threatening the ability of such states as

Virginia, California, New York, and Kansas to issue tobacco-backed bonds. Other states have come to the industry's aid and passed laws limiting the bond that must be posted to appeal a lower-court punitive damage verdict. Sixteen states have passed such laws. Four of these states—Louisiana, Nevada, Oklahoma, and West Virginia—have limited this provision to the tobacco companies signing the national accord. Twenty-two states have passed legislation requiring smaller tobacco companies to make certain payments according to the provisions included in the national tobacco settlement.

769. "Tobacco Settlement Ties Up Loose Ends from '98 Agreement." *Wall Street Journal*, June 19, 2003: B7.

Tobacco companies and forty-six states have signed a separate $160 million agreement supplementing the 1998 national tobacco settlement agreement. The agreement tackles the manufacture of cigarettes for third-party companies and the relationship between the 1998 agreement and the companies' declining market shares.

770. Peltz, James F., and Myron Levin. "How Big Tobacco Got Its Way in California." *Los Angeles Times*, September 14, 2003: C1, C5.

During last-minute meetings to pass a state budget, the California legislature passed two measures favoring the tobacco industry. One law, panned by antitobacco critics, allows tobacco companies to post a maximum $150 million bond to appeal a lower-court judgment. The cap makes California the twenty-first state to pass such a law and the seventh to make it applicable only to the tobacco industry. The second law obligates the state to guarantee payments underlying securitized tobacco bonds should a tobacco company default or declare bankruptcy. Senate president pro tempore John Burton (D-San Francisco) and Republican senate leader James Brulte (R-Rancho Cucamonga) are identified as having inserted the proposals in legislation to be reviewed by the entire legislature.

771. Brinson, Brandy. "Rise of the Rebels." *Tobacco Reporter* 130, no. 10 (September 2003): 28, 30, 32, 34, 36.

The Master Settlement Agreement (MSA), has created unintended consequences. Problems include a decline in market share for the original participating manufacturers; the introduction of "fourth-tier" manufacturers; an increase in counterfeit, black market, and gray market cigarettes; and increasing sales through the Internet and American Indian reservations. Also, Florida, Minnesota, Mississippi, and Texas did not include language covering "compliant nonparticipating manufacturers" (NPMs) in their separate agreements with the tobacco industry. MSA escrow payments are not legally required from NPMs operating in these states.

772. McKinley, Andrew, Lee Dixon, and Amanda Devore. *State Management and Allocation of Tobacco Settlement Revenue, 2003*. Denver, Colo., and Washington, D.C.: National Conference of State Legislatures, September 2003. www.ncsl.org/programs/press/2003MSA.pdf (accessed October 25, 2004).

This report examines how each state allocated its tobacco settlement revenues in fiscal years 2000–2004. This includes the Master Settlement Agreement (MSA; forty-six states) and the separate agreements signed by Florida, Minnesota, Mississippi, and

Texas. The National Conference of State Legislatures uses nine categories: health services, long-term care, tobacco-use prevention, research, education, children and youth, tobacco farmers, endowments and budget reserve, and other (e.g., tax relief and debt reduction). Additional legislative analysis is provided for fiscal year 2004. Also, the report includes a review of the MSA, a table displaying state tobacco settlement revenues received from 2000 to 2003, a detailed analysis of each of the nine categories and the securitization of tobacco settlement revenues, and a table listing all the states securitizing the revenues and how they used the funds. This year, the tobacco companies paid the states $7.9 million under the terms of the MSA. Nearly half the funds found their way to the states' general funds, with only 3 percent earmarked for antismoking programs and 28 percent for health services. General-fund tobacco settlement allocations increased from 29 percent in 2003 to 47 percent in 2004.

773. Smith, K., M. Clegg, M. A. Wakefield, and M. Nichter. "Press Coverage of Public Expenditure of Master Settlement Agreement Funds: How Are Non-Tobacco Control Related Expenditures Represented?" *Tobacco Control* 12, no. 3 (September 2003): 257–63.

The authors analyze daily newspaper articles to determine how various state and local parties staked their claims to the money paid the states under the Master Settlement Agreement. The ninety-four articles reviewed cover the period of October 1, 2000, through September 30, 2001. Themes included funding priorities for issues, providing funds for "deserving" or "needy" parties, allocating a "greater share" of funds for the needy, using tobacco funds to garner additional federal funds, and obtaining long-term economic development benefits from capital outlays.

774. "Tobacco Ads Pulled from School Magazines." *Wall Street Journal*, November 11, 2003: D3.

Philip Morris USA, R. J. Reynolds Tobacco (RJR), and Brown & Williamson have reached an agreement with New York attorney general Eliot Spitzer to stop placing ads in school editions of *Time* and *Newsweek*. Philip Morris and RJR also agreed to stop advertising in school editions of *U.S. News and World Report*. The agreements become part of the 1998 Master Settlement Agreement.

775. Campaign for Tobacco-Free Kids. *Special Report: State Tobacco Settlement*. November 12, 2003. www.tobaccofreekids.org/reports/settlements (accessed June 11, 2004).

The organization assesses the status of state funding of tobacco prevention programs. The assessments are based on the Centers for Disease Control's (CDC) minimal funding recommendations for both settlement revenues and revenues generated from tobacco taxes and settlement money. For fiscal year 2004, in the aggregate, states spent $541.1 million on such programs versus the CDC's minimum recommendation of $1.6 billion. Using 2001 tobacco advertising expenditure data from the Federal Trade Commission, the Campaign for Tobacco-Free Kids estimated that the tobacco industry spends twenty dollars on marketing for every dollar spent by the states on prevention programs.

776. Cushman, John H., Jr. "Big Tobacco Pays This Foundation to Bash Tobacco." *New York Times*, November 17, 2003: F10.

As part of the 1998 Master Settlement Agreement, the major tobacco companies have provided $1.45 billion to the American Legacy Foundation®. The funds, covering the years 1999 to 2003, are used to produce "truth" ads aimed at getting young people to stop, or resist the temptation to start, smoking. After a flurry of spending, the foundation's funds are only about $800 million, insufficient to continue the current advertising pace. The foundation is looking to partner with groups such as government agencies and nonprofit groups in order to maintain the momentum.

777. Rosenberg, Stan. "New York Tobacco Bonds: Smokin'." *Wall Street Journal*, November 19, 2003: C12.

The New York State Tobacco Settlement Financing Corporation has securitized and sold $490 million of bonds backed by future funds to be received through the 1998 Master Settlement Agreement. This equals only about 25 percent of the $2 billion bond issue offered investors. The bonds are meeting investor resistance due to rating agency downgrades of both the tobacco companies and the securitized bonds. As with the tobacco bonds sold in June 2003, this bond issue also came with an "appropriation pledge"—if future tobacco payments fall short, the state would be obligated to use general revenue funds to pay the bondholders.

778. Becker, Jo. "Trying to Stunt the Growth of Little Tobacco." *Washington Post*, January 13, 2004: B1, B4.

States are seeking to protect their revenue streams from the 1998 Master Settlement Agreement (MSA) and protect the "Big Four" tobacco companies' market share. The Big Four companies—Philip Morris, R. J. Reynolds Tobacco, Brown & Williamson, and Lorillard Tobacco—are pushing states like Virginia to pass legislation revoking the right of non-MSA participating companies to receive a substantial refund of escrow payments if their products are distributed in a limited number of states. Three nonparticipating MSA "Little Tobacco" companies, such as S&M Brands of Keysville, Virginia, are seeking to protect their market share by filing a lawsuit in the federal district court of Louisiana to overturn this model legislation. The legislation has been approved by nineteen states.

779. Levin, Myron. "Reynolds Ads Targeted Youth, Court Agrees." *Los Angeles Times*, February 26, 2004: C2.

The California Fourth District Court of Appeals has affirmed the San Diego Superior Court's ruling that R. J. Reynolds violated the terms of the 1998 Master Settlement Agreement, wherein the industry agreed not to take "any action, directly or indirectly, to target youth" in its advertising. The district court ruled that Reynolds knew its 1999–2001 advertising would be exposed to youth as well as young adults. The court also ruled the original judgment of $20 million against Reynolds needed to be reevaluated in light of Reynolds's activities in California.

780. Marino, Jon. "Anti-Smoking Campaign at Issue." *Los Angeles Times*, March 17, 2004: A27.

Various public officials are urging the tobacco industry to continue funding antitobacco advertisements handled by the American Legacy Foundation®. The 1998 Master Settlement Agreement (MSA) committed the industry to provide $300 million each year to the MSA-created public-health group. Payments are contingent upon the industry maintaining a 99.05 percent market share. In 2004, the market share dipped to 92–93 percent. The tobacco companies stated they have fulfilled their obligation, but it is claimed the companies informally agreed to continue the funds when they signed the MSA.

781. U.S. General Accounting Office. *Tobacco Settlement: States' Allocations of Fiscal Year 2003 and Expected Fiscal Year 2004 Payments*. March 19, 2004. GAO-04-518. Washington, D.C.: GAO, 2004. www.gao.gov/new.items/d04518.pdf (accessed June 15, 2004).

The report provides fiscal year 2003 payments made by the tobacco industry to the forty-six states as part of the Master Settlement Agreement. Expected payments for fiscal year 2004 are also included. The report also includes information on changes in states' decision-making frameworks for these funds in comparison to prior years.

782. Barnes, Steve. "Texas: State Claims Cheating on Payments." *New York Times*, May 28, 2004: A14.

In a lawsuit filed against Brown & Williamson, Texas state attorney general Greg Abbott has accused the company of masking sales and underpaying the state money due under the national tobacco settlement. Abbott claims that the company did not report 7.5 billion cigarettes manufactured for Star Tobacco and Pharmaceuticals, representing $16 million not paid the state.

783. O'Connell, Vanessa. "Tobacco Makers Want Cigarettes Cut from Films." *Wall Street Journal*, June 14, 2004: B1, B4.

The $206 billion 1998 national tobacco settlement prohibits tobacco manufacturers from paying for product placement in movies or on television. Also, according to California state authorities, the agreement requires the companies to prevent unauthorized use in these mediums by taking "commercially reasonable" steps. Philip Morris requested that Paramount Pictures revamp its upcoming DVD release of the film *Twisted* and delete all references to Marlboro cigarettes. Earlier in the year, R. J. Reynolds requested Sony Pictures Entertainment to delete all references to Camel and Winston cigarettes before the national release of the film *Mona Lisa Smile*. Last year, Lorillard Tobacco's parent Loews Corporation complained to Warner Brothers about an "unauthorized use" of Newport cigarettes in the film *City by the Sea*. The cigarette companies contend that studios have "fair use" rights to use their brands per U.S. trademark laws.

784. O'Connell, Vanessa. "New Laws Help Tobacco Makers with Big Judgments." *Wall Street Journal*, July 19, 2004: A1, A4.

"Appeal-bond caps" limit payments plaintiffs must post to appeal massive dollar amounts assessed in lower-court cases. Tobacco companies are the major beneficiaries from such laws, passed in thirty states. Legislation passed in eleven states, including New Jersey, Oregon, and Pennsylvania, applies only to the tobacco companies. While the appeal-bond caps do not benefit plaintiffs, they benefit the states and their ability to continue to receive funds due them under the 1998

$206 billion national tobacco settlement. During the past year, fourteen states, including California (with a $150 million cap), have passed appeal-bond cap legislation.

785. "Attorneys General in New York, Maryland and Illinois Last Week Reached a Deal in Lawsuits against Brown & Williamson Tobacco over the Marketing of Kool Cigarettes." *Brandweek* 45, no. 36 (October 11, 2004): 3.

Brown & Williamson's agreement with the three attorneys general acknowledges that the Master Settlement Agreement, signed in 1998, has been breached by the company's recent Kool MIXX promotion. The fine of over $1.4 million will be funneled into youth smoking–prevention programs.

Appendix A
Statistical Tables

Table AA.1. Tobacco Farm Cash Receipts ($ thousands)

State	1990–1993	1994–1996	1997–1999	2000–2003	Total
North Carolina	4,185,719	3,012,941	2,954,120	2,832,622	12,985,402
Kentucky	3,377,838	2,235,244	2,391,514	2,114,953	10,119,549
Tennessee	908,495	672,217	668,412	597,175	2,846,299
South Carolina	741,029	584,134	501,969	553,920	2,381,052
Virginia	750,438	531,289	520,215	467,954	2,269,896
Georgia	637,712	460,679	420,230	481,577	2,000,040
Ohio	149,016	99,024	94,355	82,908	425,303
Florida	120,779	89,176	87,763	80,217	377,935
Indiana	124,433	72,998	81,093	67,378	345,902
Pennsylvania	117,217	55,152	54,389	62,103	288,861
Connecticut	142,374	36,778	40,201	40,115	259,468
Maryland	76,617	58,601	48,685	39,783	223,686
Wisconsin	84,293	27,041	22,571	20,435	154,250
Missouri	38,344	34,671	27,272	22,749	123,036
Massachusetts	43,882	10,137	24,447	25,970	104,436
West Virginia	23,843	16,053	12,141	13,455	65,492
Alabama	5,055	3,632	3,552	0	12,239
Totals	11,527,084	7,999,767	7,952,929	7,503,224	34,983,004

Source: U.S. Department of Agriculture, Economic Research Service. www.ers.usda.gov/Data/farmincome/finfidmu.htm.

Table AA.2. Cigarette Advertising and Promotional Expenditures ($ thousands)

Category	1990–1993	1994–1996	1997–1999	2000–2002	Total
Promotional Allowances	5,249,368	5,695,412	8,860,337	10,148,897	29,954,014
Retail Value Added	a	a	5,085,637	9,300,269	14,385,906
Coupons & Retail Value Added	7,801,463	3,905,982	a	a	11,707,445
Price Discounts	b	b	b	7,873,835	7,873,835
Specialty Item Distribution	1,587,162	2,060,328	1,204,117	884,844	5,736,451
Point-of-Sale	1,415,414	854,304	925,528	892,259	4,087,505
Coupons	a	a	1,707,753	1,829,655	3,537,408
Magazines	1,078,567	743,538	895,610	574,621	3,292,336
Outdoor	1,288,930	805,949	643,842	41,695	2,780,416
Public Entertainment	417,731	363,138	711,118	875,081	2,367,068
Direct Mail	182,685	104,508	189,692	338,168	815,053
Other[c]	236,963	128,048	166,449	281,071	812,531
Newspapers	191,073	57,332	97,376	108,866	454,647
Sampling Distribution	247,380	36,755	70,212	68,282	422,629
Transit	212,822	80,731	72,138	4	365,695
Internet	n/a	432	991	2,730	4,153
Telephone	b	b	b	679	679
Totals	19,909,558	14,836,457	20,630,800	33,220,956	88,597,771

Source: U.S. Federal Trade Commission. *Cigarette Report for 2002*, issued October 22, 2004, www.ftc.gov.
[a] Prior to 1997, Coupons and Retail Value Added were reported in a single category.
[b] Both categories first appeared in the 2002 report.
[c] Expenditures for audio-visual are included in the other category to avoid disclosure of individual company data.

Table AA.3. Advertising Expenditures: Selected Cigarette Brands ($ thousands)

Company/Brand	1990–1993	1994–1996	1997–1999	2000–2003	Total
Brown & Williamson					
Capri	62,390	54,094	19,642	59	136,184
Carlton	72,252	51,355	22,788	260	146,655
Kool	51,859	130,475	124,863	73,748	380,944
Misty Slims	43,398	48,478	25,677	2,290	119,843
Lorillard Tobacco					
Newport	166,476	64,302	51,357	54,839	336,974
Philip Morris					
Basic	7,817	60,840	73,617	60,193	202,467
Benson & Hedges	53,287	84,570	55,097	1,415	194,369
Marlboro	347,901	337,086	343,053	127,208	1,155,248
Merit	88,978	88,279	84,155	27,553	288,965
Parliament	23,728	17,026	31,020	70,132	141,906
Virginia Slims	108,559	82,655	85,944	70,512	347,670
R. J. Reynolds					
Camel	130,570	107,681	183,544	114,205	535,999
Doral	12,602	47,786	71,700	55,635	187,722
Salem	47,819	7,183	12,014	44,503	111,518
Winston	95,770	31,706	139,934	96,826	364,236
Totals	1,313,404	1,213,516	1,324,404	799,376	4,650,700

Source: Ad Dollar Summary, 1990–2003

Table AA.4. U.S. Cigarette Exports: Selected Countries (Thousands of Pieces)

Country/Destination	1990–1993	1994–1996	1997–1999	2000–2004[a]	Total
Japan	214,749,873	186,362,849	211,091,889	364,684,800	976,889,411
Belgium	206,147,297	205,067,623	108,852,662	13,186,610	533,254,192
Saudi Arabia	30,731,695	28,151,428	28,227,016	53,453,970	140,564,109
Hong Kong	61,188,492	20,148,237	11,266,848	12,506,786	105,110,363
Lebanon	12,500,398	30,477,153	27,011,432	20,637,794	90,626,777
Singapore	18,022,320	22,899,734	15,039,744	10,739,762	66,701,560
Russian Federation	14,151,162	27,858,033	18,303,440	5,820,459	66,133,094
Cyprus	7,995,728	23,516,493	21,435,014	12,781,841	66,729,075
Korea, South	15,860,661	17,650,036	11,204,574	15,731,614	60,086,885
United Arab Emirates	29,055,193	9,293,627	5,235,651	9,916,446	53,500,917
Israel	8,354,583	10,290,410	11,641,944	22,356,442	52,643,379
Turkey	26,685,804	3,431,368	6,708,422	2,610,774	39,436,368
Taiwan	12,595,852	6,916,008	6,767,409	9,230,670	35,509,939
Kuwait	5,097,767	5,658,023	5,655,660	9,098,012	25,509,462
Germany	2,740,551	9,723,976	6,399,611	5,644,548	24,508,686
Paraguay	8,426,332	6,096,206	5,514,123	1,455,908	21,492,569
Morocco	6,482,447	5,869,142	4,942,850	1,131,375	18,425,814
Panama	5,072,118	5,814,930	3,787,981	1,433,219	16,108,248
Netherlands	1,154,068	4,412,079	2,654,833	4,332,185	12,553,165
Mexico	2,123,613	6,379,876	1,511,432	808,501	10,823,422
Totals	689,135,953	636,017,231	513,252,535	577,201,716	2,415,607,435
World Totals	744,447,138	695,342,994	569,907,738	624,889,655	2,634,587,525

Source: U.S. Department of Agriculture, Foreign Agricultural Service. U.S. Trade Internet System. www.fas.usda.gov/ustrade.
[a] Through September 2004.

Table AA.5. U.S. Cigarette (Paper) Imports: Selected Countries (Thousands of Pieces)

Country/Origin	1990–1993	1994–1996	1997–1999	2000–2004[a]	Total
Canada	19,785,037	3,433,508	1,282,898	6,756,337	31,257,780
Colombia	180	310	0	18,820,642	18,821,132
Spain	1,497	338,715	4,276,378	7,745,714	12,362,304
India	740	302,554	1,927,979	7,492,097	9,723,370
Japan	241,088	884,645	3,313,388	5,283,534	9,722,655
China (PRC)	2,093	28,115	93,183	6,015,035	6,138,426
Korea, South	7,786	24,152	161,749	5,770,650	5,964,337
United Kingdom	1,636,650	1,352,256	1,260,267	1,373,543	5,622,716
Brazil	790	317	247	4,059,466	4,060,820
Greece	4,481	1,190	44,952	2,502,595	2,553,218
Panama	308,331	1,373,706	691,336	0	2,373,373
Philippines	5,220	0	335,604	1,824,408	2,165,232
Paraguay	0	0	0	1,545,950	1,545,950
Indonesia	23,276	173,352	341,779	901,234	1,439,821
Mexico	29,580	21,950	10,451	507,456	569,437
Netherlands	32,395	190,743	41,660	253,106	517,904
Belgium	5,834	1,437	3,150	253,527	263,948
Malaysia	645	1,218	2,178	167,081	171,122
France	21,778	33,468	37,505	62,606	155,357
Totals	22,107,402	8,161,816	13,824,704	71,334,981	115,428,903
World Totals	22,481,132	8,337,869	15,276,198	84,771,991	130,867,190

Source: U.S. Department of Agriculture, Foreign Agricultural Service. U.S. Trade Internet System. www.fas.usda.gov/ustrade.
[a] Through September 2004.

Table AA.6. Tobacco and Cigarette Retail Sales ($ thousands)

Year	All Retail Sales—Tobacco[a]	Supermarket Sales—Cigarettes[b]	Grocery Sales—Cigarettes
1990	30,904,073	11,708,770	15,206,206
1991	31,825,632	11,853,010	15,393,519
1992	34,234,390	10,803,815	14,030,929
1993	34,996,888	9,753,702	12,667,145
1994	33,517,610	8,607,279	11,178,284
1995	33,959,374	8,348,612	10,842,354
1996	34,072,380	8,014,668	10,400,419
1997	34,190,714	7,918,492	10,127,021
1998	34,491,448	8,013,514	10,258,725
1999	37,758,126	8,742,744	11,151,048
2000[c]	22,318,190	6,185,880	c
2001	26,400,610	6,037,580	c
2002	27,579,240	5,833,840	c
2003	25,832,710	5,305,740	c

Source: The annual *Consumer Expenditures Study* appears in the September 15 issue of *Supermarket Business* (1991-2002) and *Progressive Grocer* (2003-2004).
[a] Sales include cigars, lighter fluids and flints, lights, smoking accessories, and chewing and smoking tobacco.
[b] Supermarkets defined as grocery stores with annual sales over $2 million.
[c] Methodology changed to focus solely on supermarket sales; grocery sales data are no longer collected. Estimates of all retail sales based on ACNielsen Homescan Information.

Table AA.7. Military Commissary and Exchange Worldwide Cigarette Sales ($ thousands)

Commissary/Exchange	FY1990–1993	FY1994–1996	FY1997–1999	FY2000–2003	Total
AAFES (Army & Air Force Exchange)					
American Tobacco	26,643	6,045	—	—	32,688
Brown & Williamson	49,778	58,296[a]	320,930	275,718	704,722
Liggett Group	24,228	12,781	49,277	62,464	148,750
Lorillard Tobacco	33,554	27,214	61,071	94,182	216,021
Pegasus Tobacco[b]	—	—	—	75,166	75,166
Philip Morris	184,020	152,265	489,687	729,690	1,555,662
R. J. Reynolds Tobacco	80,119	52,754	208,404	201,410	542,687
Total	398,342	309,355	1,129,369	1,438,630	3,275,696
DeCA (Defense Commissary Agency)[c]					
American Tobacco	101,418	39,019	—	—	140,437
Brown & Williamson	129,546	280,444[a]	—	—	409,990
Liggett Group	75,481	88,179	—	—	163,660
Lorillard Tobacco	43,863	62,285	—	—	106,148
Philip Morris	379,505	492,639	—	—	872,144
R. J. Reynolds Tobacco	330,826	369,149	—	—	699,975
Total	1,060,639	1,331,715	—	—	2,392,354

NEXCOM (Navy Exchange Service Command)				
American Tobacco	20,188	2,609	—	22,797
Brown & Williamson	45,745	47,646[a]	75,876	192,331[b]
Lorillard Tobacco	14,299	11,089	12,483	228,075
Philip Morris	119,919	83,292	114,923	364,470
R. J. Reynolds Tobacco	69,156	35,576	33,168	475,344
Total	269,307	180,212	236,450	1,283,017
All Operations				
American Tobacco	148,249	47,673	—	195,922
Brown & Williamson	225,069	386,386	396,806	1,307,043
Liggett Group	99,709	100,960	49,277	280,569
Lorillard Tobacco	91,716	100,588	73,554	550,244
Pegasus Tobacco	—	—	—	75,166
Philip Morris	683,444	728,196	604,610	2,792,276
R. J. Reynolds Tobacco	480,101	457,479	241,572	1,718,006
Total	1,728,288	1,821,282	1,365,819	6,919,226

Sources: *Military Market*, 1991–2000; MilitaryMarket.com (July 15, 2001; site discontinued); *Exchange & Commissary News*, www.ebmpubs.com/ecn_web.html; NEXCOM.

[a] Brown & Williamson purchased American Tobacco in April 1995. Figures include sales from American Tobacco.
[b] Subsidiary of British American Tobacco.
[c] Operations started in October 1991. In 1996, AAFES assumed distribution and management of tobacco products in DeCA-run commissaries.

Table AA.8. Duty-Free and Tax-Free Worldwide Tobacco and Cigarette Sales ($ millions)

Category	1990–1993	1994–1996	1997–1999	2000–2003	Total
Tobacco Goods[a]					
Markets					
Africa	94.1	101.8	3,866.0	4,083.1	8,145.0
Americas	1,046.6	872.8	887.4	993.7	3,800.5
Asia & Oceania	1,421.5	1,505.9	588.5	657.8	4,173.7
Europe	6,065.7	5,201.6	2,929.8	3,466.8	17,663.9
Total	8,627.9	7,682.1	8,272.2	9,201.4	33,783.6
Channels					
Airlines	847.0	747.0	2,844.2	3,591.7	8,029.9
Airports & Shops	3,361.3	3,448.0	1,748.8	1,725.4	10,283.5
Ferries	1,598.4	1,537.3	1,722.8	1,387.9	6,246.4
Other Shops	2,821.2	1,949.8	1,956.4	2,496.4	9,223.8
Total	8,627.9	7,682.1	8,272.2	9,201.4	33,783.6
Product					
Cigarettes	7,500.0	6,667.0	6,992.0	7,709.0	28,868.0
Market Share of Category (avg.)	11.93%	11.23%	11.37%	9.73%	11.03%

Source: Generation Group, www.generation.se; Best & Most, 2004; Best & Most, 1991–2003.
[a] Category includes cigarettes, cigars, and other tobacco products.

Table AA.9. State Government Tobacco Sales Tax Collections ($ thousands)

State	1990–1993	1994–1996	1997–1999	2000–2003	Total
California	2,936,644	1,996,055	2,221,945	4,525,814	11,680,458
New York	2,292,375	2,119,213	1,999,584	3,816,157	10,227,329
Texas	2,268,209	1,779,049	1,839,262	2,238,992	8,125,512
Michigan	1,004,287	1,606,093	1,746,081	2,763,072	7,119,533
Florida	1,653,931	1,348,612	1,361,061	1,830,309	6,193,913
Illinois	1,268,647	1,262,321	1,394,372	2,009,469	5,934,809
Pennsylvania	1,096,579	992,406	998,454	1,839,801	4,927,240
New Jersey	1,003,762	763,103	1,005,752	1,846,959	4,619,576
Ohio	903,829	877,965	887,780	1,452,637	4,122,211
Massachusetts	625,233	704,315	866,959	1,276,498	3,473,005
Washington	569,490	712,207	832,735	1,235,311	3,349,743
Wisconsin	608,447	569,356	737,259	1,124,665	3,039,727
Minnesota	639,695	522,092	563,585	718,689	2,444,061
Maryland	353,301	409,298	387,183	904,688	2,054,470
Oregon	334,753	341,951	551,403	784,259	2,012,366
Connecticut	470,575	373,045	398,397	659,894	1,901,911
Arizona	204,933	333,117	501,189	703,299	1,742,538
Indiana	444,051	253,703	271,095	649,262	1,618,111
Missouri	315,258	328,576	340,797	435,124	1,419,755
Iowa	363,862	293,930	298,274	382,089	1,338,155
Total	19,357,861	17,586,407	19,203,167	31,196,988	87,344,423
All State Totals	23,885,385	21,402,597	23,403,227	37,414,479	106,105,688

Source: U.S. Department of Commerce, Bureau of the Census. *State Government Tax Collections, 1990–1991*; *State Government Tax Collections by State, 1992–2003*, www.census.gov/govs.

Table AA.10. Federal Tobacco Excise Taxes Collected[a] ($ thousands)

Fiscal Year	Domestic[b]	Cigarettes[b]	Imported
1990	4,267,013	n/a	n/a
1991	4,781,936	n/a	n/a
1992	5,072,322	5,087,048	79,946
1993	5,577,104	5,649,832	134,394
1994	5,713,810	5,755,422	89,389
1995	5,865,940	5,868,247	44,934
1996	5,809,297	5,759,424	43,867
1997	5,819,552	5,898,191	53,806
1998	5,608,259	5,583,318	64,649
1999	5,189,723	5,147,438	114,524
2000	7,019,884	6,684,265	196,141
2001	7,120,255	7,013,007	252,229
2002	7,879,499	7,643,220	404,308
2003	5,836,860	5,526,697	358,067
Totals	81,561,454	71,616,109	1,836,254

Source: SOI Bulletin: A Quarterly Statistics of Income Report, various issues; see also www.irs.gov/taxstats/article/0,,id=117514,00.html.
[a] Taxes displayed in table are before postfiling tax adjustments. Therefore, the statistics by type of tax for domestic products will not add to the total tax on domestic tobacco products, which is after these adjustments. In some instances, the figures for cigarettes are greater than the domestic (total tax) category.
[b] Domestic tobacco products includes cigarettes, cigars, papers/tubes, chewing tobacco and snuff, pipe/roll-your-own tobacco, and floor stocks. Cigarettes listed as a separate subcategory of total domestic tobacco products.

Table AA.11. 1998 Master Settlement Agreement (MSA): Original Allocations[a] ($ thousands)

State	1998–2003[b]	2004–2007	2008–2017	2018–2025	Total
California	4,140,713	3,575,948	9,117,290	8,173,016	25,006,967
New York	4,140,090	3,575,412	9,115,920	8,171,784	25,003,206
Pennsylvania	1,864,320	1,610,040	4,104,980	3,679,832	11,259,172
Ohio	1,634,202	1,411,308	3,598,290	3,225,616	9,869,416
Illinois	1,509,869	1,303,932	3,324,530	2,980,208	9,118,539
Michigan	1,411,801	1,219,240	3,108,600	2,786,640	8,526,281
Massachusetts	1,310,272	1,131,560	2,885,040	2,586,240	7,913,112
New Jersey	1,254,480	1,083,376	2,762,200	2,476,112	7,576,168
Georgia	796,242	687,640	1,753,200	1,571,640	4,808,742
Tennessee	791,842	683,840	1,743,530	1,562,952	4,782,164
North Carolina	756,609	653,412	1,665,950	1,493,408	4,569,379
Missouri	737,896	637,252	1,624,750	1,456,472	4,456,370
Maryland	733,307	633,288	1,614,640	1,447,416	4,428,651
Louisiana	731,652	631,860	1,611,000	1,444,144	4,418,656
Wisconsin	672,184	580,504	1,480,060	1,326,768	4,059,516
Washington	666,091	575,240	1,466,640	1,314,744	4,022,715
Virginia	663,329	572,856	1,460,560	1,309,288	4,006,033
Indiana	661,726	571,472	1,457,030	1,306,128	3,996,356
Connecticut	602,273	520,128	1,326,120	1,188,776	3,637,297
Kentucky	571,332	493,408	1,258,000	1,127,704	3,450,444
Total	25,650,230	22,151,716	56,478,350	50,628,888	154,909,184
Grand Totals[c,d]	32,440,676	28,016,000	71,430,000	64,032,000	195,918,676

Sources: National Association of Attorneys General, www.naag.org; annual payments schedule obtained in 1998 and no longer posted on the website; also available from the Center for Social Gerontology, www.tcsg.org/tobacco/settlement/totalfunds.htm (accessed September 3, 2004).

[a] MSA original annual payments to the forty-six states and five territories from 2000 to 2025 are adjusted for separate settlement agreements with Florida, Minnesota, Mississippi, and Texas. Other payments to be made are not reflected in the table: Strategic contribution fund payments, Base foundation payments (American Legacy Foundation), National Public Education Fund payments, National Association of Attorneys General administration payments, and Attorney general enforcement fund. See GAO-01-851, page 57, for these annual allocations.
[b] 1998 allocation is only for an "up-front" payment of over $2.4 billion. Payments not scheduled during 1999.
[c] Grand totals include payments to the District of Columbia, American Samoa, Guam, Northern Marianas, Puerto Rico, and the Virgin Islands.
[d] Numbers may not total evenly due to rounding.

Table AA.12. 1998 Master Settlement Agreement: Payments to the United States[a] ($ thousands)

State	FY00/01[b]	FY02	FY03	FY04[c]	Total
California[d]	895,178	474,992	474,066	399,372	2,243,608
New York[e]	651,845	399,000	498,300	334,000	1,883,145
Pennsylvania	664,190	433,530	416,918	360,528	1,875,166
Ohio	724,742	368,588	368,998	297,000	1,759,328
Illinois	669,603	312,276	341,498	269,247	1,593,124
Michigan	610,424	328,200	318,400	273,900	1,530,924
Massachusetts	566,526	304,500	300,037	250,700	1,421,763
New Jersey[f]	557,730	283,872	283,700	122,000	1,247,302
Tennessee	354,256	180,706	179,102	147,800	861,964
Georgia	353,121	184,650	178,041	146,124	861,936
North Carolina	327,137	175,836	169,201	155,479	827,653
Missouri	338,200	172,700	166,320	143,000	820,200
Maryland	325,210	164,247	171,300	149,000	809,757
Louisiana[g]	324,476	165,021	165,483	143,767	798,747
Wisconsin[h]	290,634	156,215	153,923	135,617	736,390
Washington[i]	295,401	150,000	150,655	124,000	720,056

Virginia	294,180	149,614	150,030	126,206	720,030
Indiana	293,465	149,200	148,000	127,600	718,265
Connecticut	260,406	140,000	137,914	113,000	651,320
Kentucky	247,028	132,777	130,829	109,100	619,735
Total—20 States	9,043,852	4,825,924	4,902,714	3,927,940	22,700,430
Total—All States[j]	11,781,916	6,138,393	6,305,730	5,156,128	29,382,168

Sources: U.S. General Accounting Office. *Tobacco Settlement: States' Allocations of Fiscal Years 2002 and 2003 Master Settlement Agreement Payments.* GAO-03-407. February 28, 2003. Washington, DC: GAO, 2003. www.gao.gov/new.items/d03407.pdf (accessed February 19, 2004); U.S. GAO. *Tobacco Settlement: States' Allocations of Fiscal Year 2003 and Expected Fiscal Year 2004 Payments.* March 19, 2004. GAO-04-518. Washington, D.C.: GAO, 2004. www.gao.gov/new.items/d04518.pdf (accessed June 15, 2004).

[a] The GAO reports do not cover payments received by American Samoa, District of Columbia, Guam, Northern Marianas, Puerto Rico, and the U.S. Virgin Islands. Also, the reports do not cover payments received by the states entering into their own separate agreements with the tobacco industry: Florida, Minnesota, Mississippi, and Texas.
[b] Covers payments received through April 2001.
[c] Estimated receipts.
[d] California also received $2,485,000,000 in securitized tobacco payments in FY03 and expects to receive $2,000,000,000 in FY04.
[e] New York expects to receive $4,200,000,000 in securitized tobacco payments in FY04.
[f] New Jersey also received $2,751,814,469 in securitized tobacco payments in FY03.
[g] Louisiana also received $1,069,510,894 in securitized tobacco payments in FY02.
[h] Wisconsin also received $1,275,002,400 in securitized tobacco payments in FY02.
[i] Washington also received $517,905,000 in securitized tobacco payments in FY03.
[j] Securitized tobacco payments also received by Alabama, Alaska, Arkansas, Iowa, Oregon, Rhode Island, South Carolina, and South Dakota.

Table AA.13. Tobacco Industry Political Contributions: Election Cycles[a] ($)

Company	1989–1992	1993–1996	1997–2000	2001–2004[h]	Total
Brown & Williamson[b]					
Individuals	5,050	20,250	13,302	3,591	42,193
PACs	124,143	615,700	762,371	258,324	1,760,538
Soft Money[i]	1,000	893,500	1,168,330	410,693	2,473,523
Lobbying[j]	n/a	n/a	34,348,029	5,960,000	40,308,029
527s[k]	n/a	n/a	55,000	398,030	453,030
Total	130,193	1,529,450	36,347,032	7,030,638	45,037,313
Liggett Group[c]					
Individuals	39,550	45,000	78,000	242,512	406,062
PACs	0	0	0	0	0
Soft Money[i]	0	15,000	81,090	521,000	617,090
Lobbying[j]	n/a	n/a	3,330,000	n/a	3,330,000
527s[k]	n/a	n/a	0	0	0
Total	39,550	60,000	3,489,090	763,512	4,352,152
Lorillard Tobacco[d]					
Individuals	30,950	21,340	3,900	91,000	147,190
PACs	0	50,000	153,550	152,100	355,650
Soft Money[i]	15,000	202,785	282,630	422,613	923,028
Lobbying[j]	n/a	n/a	8,650,000	7,400,000	16,050,000
527s[k]	n/a	n/a	5,000	321,585	326,585
Total	45,950	274,125	9,095,080	8,387,298	17,802,453
Philip Morris[e]					
Individuals	180,663	260,400	280,341	293,828	1,015,232
PACs	1,305,831	1,661,285	1,838,040	1,720,000	6,525,156

Soft Money[i]	806,580	3,758,961	4,820,356	2,745,698	12,131,595
Lobbying[j]	n/a	n/a	64,720,000	46,560,000	111,280,000
527s[k]	n/a	n/a	165,547	1,620,587	1,786,134
Total	2,293,074	5,680,646	71,824,284	52,940,113	132,738,117
R. J. Reynolds[f]					
Individuals	85,887	86,725	78,825	20,649	272,086
PACs	1,582,113	1,457,550	1,104,750	659,750	4,804,163
Soft Money[i]	875,305	1,974,083	1,565,324	397,631	4,812,343
Lobbying[j]	n/a	n/a	14,239,245	4,155,385	18,394,630
527s[k]	n/a	n/a	71,000	766,137	837,137
Total	2,543,305	3,518,358	17,059,144	5,999,552	29,120,359
Reynolds American[g]					
Individuals	n/a	n/a	n/a	113,350	113,350
PACs	n/a	n/a	n/a	708,000	708,000
Soft Money[i]	n/a	n/a	n/a	0	0
Lobbying	n/a	n/a	n/a	n/a	n/a
527s	n/a	n/a	n/a	n/a	n/a
Total	n/a	n/a	n/a	821,350	821,350
Totals—6 Companies					
Individuals	342,100	433,715	454,368	651,580	1,881,763
PACs	3,012,087	3,784,535	3,858,711	2,790,174	13,445,507
Soft Money	1,697,885	6,844,329	7,917,730	4,497,635	20,957,579
Lobbying	n/a	n/a	125,287,274	64,075,385	189,362,659
527s	n/a	n/a	296,547	3,106,339	3,402,886
Total	5,052,072	11,062,579	137,814,630	75,121,113	229,050,394
Totals—All Industry					
Individuals	782,204	1,047,064	1,243,004	1,418,940	4,491,212
PACs	4,570,729	5,423,735	5,184,391	4,549,065	19,727,920

(*continued*)

Table AA.13. Tobacco Industry Political Contributions: Election Cycles[a] ($) (continued)

Company	1989–1992	1993–1996	1997–2000	2001–2004[h]	Total
Soft Money	2,807,955	9,423,580	10,799,081	6,014,516	29,045,132
Lobbying	n/a	n/a	148,818,131	72,172,715	220,990,846
527s	n/a	n/a	946,000	3,070,839	4,017,639
Total	8,160,888	15,894,379	166,991,407	87,226,075	278,272,749

Source: Center for Responsive Politics, www.opensecrets.org; for the 2000–2004 lobbyist contributions, see Tobacco-Free Kids Action Fund and Common Cause, "Buying Influence, Selling Death: Campaign Contributions by Tobacco Interests, Quarterly Report," October 2004: 15. tobaccofreekids.org/reports/contributions; for the 527 contributions, see The Center for Public Integrity, www.publicintegrity.org/527/db.aspx?act=main. Database searched on October 25, 2004.

[a] An election cycle covers a two-year period. Each column covers two election cycles.
[b] Contributions are from Brown & Williamson and British American Tobacco and its subsidiaries.
[c] Contributions are from Brooke Group Ltd., Liggett Tobacco, Liggett Vector Brands, and Vector Corp.
[d] Contributions are from Lorillard Tobacco and Loews Corp.
[e] Contributions are from Philip Morris and Altria Group.
[f] Contributions are from R. J. Reynolds Tobacco and RJR Nabisco.
[g] Formed by the merger of R. J. Reynolds Tobacco Company and Brown & Williamson, effective July 31, 2004.
[h] 2003–2004 cycle includes data available through October 4, 2004.
[i] Soft money contributions to the national parties were not publicly disclosed until the 1991–1992 election cycle and were banned by the Bipartisan Campaign Finance Reform Act following the 2002 elections.
[j] Data through June 30, 1994, based on midyear federal lobby reports submitted through October 14, 2004.
[k] A 527 is a nonprofit organization formed under Section 527 of the Internal Revenue Code, which grants tax-exempt status to political committees at the national, state, and local level. The committees are formed for the purpose of influencing elections, but cannot directly contribute to federal candidates or use words that expressly advocate someone's election or defeat. See The Center for Public Integrity, www.publicintegrity.org/527/default.aspx?act=faq or the Tobacco-Free Kids Action Fund and Common Cause source cited above.

Appendix B
Tobacco Company Profiles

TOBACCO COMPANY PROFILE: ALTADIS S.A.[a]

Address:	Eloy Gonzalo 10
	28010 Madrid, Spain
Web:	www.altadis.com
Stock Exchange:	Paris and Madrid Stock Exchanges
Ticker Symbol:	AOF (Paris)
	ALT.MC (Madrid)
Subsidiaries (selected):	Altadis Belgium
	Altadis Korea
	Coretab (France)
Cigarette Brands (selected):	Ducados
	Fortuna
	Gauloises
	Gitanes
	Habanos
	News
	Royale
Fiscal year ending September 30, 2003:	
Economic Sales, company-wide (millions of Euros)	3,385
(51% of sales from cigarettes)	
Net Income (millions of Euros)	293
Market Share:	
France	18.6%
Cigarette sales (million units)	11,348
Gauloises Blondes (France)	7.9%
News (France)	5.0%
Spain	29.0%
Cigarette sales (million units)	22,175
Fortuna (Spain)	22.6%

Source: 2003 Annual Report, Altadis S.A. webpage, www.altadis.com.

a In 1999, Tabacalera S.A. (Spain) and SEITA (Societe Nationale d'Exploitation Industrielle des Tabacs et Allumettes, S.A.) (France) merged to form Altadis S.A.

TOBACCO COMPANY PROFILE: ALTRIA GROUP

Address:	120 Park Avenue New York, N.Y. 10017
Web:	www.altria.com
Stock Exchange:	New York Stock Exchange
Ticker Symbol:	MO
Subsidiaries (selected):	Philip Morris USA www.philipmorrisusa.com Philip Morris International www.philipmorrisinternational.com Rothmans, Benson & Hedges (40% ownership)
Cigarette Brands (selected):	
Philip Morris USA	Basic Benson & Hedges Marlboro Merit Parliament Virginia Slims
Philip Morris International	Apollo Soyuz Peter Jackson Philip Morris Red and White
Fiscal year ending December 31, 2003:	
Tobacco Revenues: Domestic (millions of dollars)	$17,001
Tobacco Revenues: International (millions of dollars)	$33,389
Net Income (all subsidiaries) (millions of dollars)	$9,204
Cigarette shipments worldwide (billion units)	923
World Ranking (based on cigarette units sold)	1
Market Share:	
United States	48.7%
International (excluding U.S. and duty-free)	14.2%
Marlboro (U.S.)	38.0%

Source: Form 10-K, Altria Group, Inc., available at www.sec.gov; Altria Group webpage, www.altria.com.

TOBACCO COMPANY PROFILE: BRITISH AMERICAN TOBACCO PLC

Address:	Globe House 4 Temple Place London WC2R 2PQ England

Web:	www.bat.com
Stock Exchange:	American Stock Exchange (ADR)[a]
Ticker Symbol:	BTI
Subsidiaries (selected):	British American Tobacco Central America S.A.
	Imperial Tobacco Canada, Ltd.
	Reynolds American (42% ownership through Brown & Williamson)
	Souza Cruz S.A. (Brazil; 75 percent ownership)
Cigarette Brands (selected):	Benson & Hedges
	Dunhill
	Kent
	Kool
	Lucky Strike
	Merit
	Pall Mall
	Peter Stuyvesant
	State Express 555
	Winfield
Fiscal year ending December 31, 2003:	
Revenues (millions of pound sterling)	25,622
Profit for the Year (millions of pound sterling)	631
Cigarette shipments worldwide (billion units)	792
World Ranking (based on cigarette units sold)	2
Market Shares:	
Australia	44.5%
Winfield Virginia 25s	21.9%
Germany	16.3%
Lucky Strike	5.1%
Malaysia	67.1%
Dunhill	46.1%

Sources: 2003 Annual Report; British American Tobacco webpage, www.bat.com; Maxwell, John C. "Global Market Shares of British American Tobacco," *Tobacco Reporter* 131, no. 6 (June 2004): 62.

[a] American Depository Receipt.

TOBACCO COMPANY PROFILE: GALLAHER GROUP PLC

Address:	Members Hill
	Brooklands Road
	Weybridge, Surrey KT13 0QU, England
Web:	www.gallaher-group.com
Stock Exchange:	New York Stock Exchange (ADR)[a]
Ticker Symbol:	GLH
Subsidiaries (selected):	Austria Tabak AG & Co. KG
	Liggett-Ducat CJSC (Confederation of Independent States)

Cigarette Brands (selected):	Benson & Hedges
	Dorchester
	Mayfair
	Memphis
	Reynolds
	Sovereign
	Sterling
Fiscal year ending September 30, 2003:	
Turnover (Sales) excluding duty (millions of dollars)	$6,517
Operating Profit (millions of dollars)	$904
Cigarette shipments worldwide (billion units)	160
World Ranking (based on cigarette units sold)	5
Market Share:	
United Kingdom	38.1%
Mayfair (UK)	10.4%
Benson & Hedges Metal (UK)	9.3%
Austria	46.5%
Memphis (Austria)	26.8%
Kazakhstan	30.0%
Sovereign (Kazakhstan)	14.8%

Sources: Form 20-F for the fiscal year ended December 31, 2003, available at www.sec.gov; Gallaher Group PLC Web page, www.gallagher-group.com.
[a] American Depository Receipt.

TOBACCO COMPANY PROFILE: P. T. GUDANG GARAM

Address:	Jl. Jendral A. Yani 79
	Jakarat 10510 Indonesia
Web:	n/a
Stock Exchange:	Indonesia Stock Exchange
Ticker Symbol:	GGRM.JK
Subsidiaries (selected):	n/a
Cigarette Brands (selected):	Clove Merah
	Djaja
	Filter International
	Surya
Fiscal year ending December 31, 2002:	
Sales, Cigarettes (millions of IDR)	204,392
Operating Income, Cigarettes (millions of IDR)	3,344
Market Share: 2002	
Indonesia	34%

Sources: Worldscope, LexisNexis Academic (accessed November 1, 2004); IndoExchange.com, www.indoexchange.com/jsx/ggrm/financial/spreadsheet-annual-index.html.

TOBACCO COMPANY PROFILE: IMPERIAL TOBACCO GROUP PLC

Address:	Upton Road
	Bristol BS99 7UJ England
Web:	www.imperial-tobacco.com
Stock Exchange:	New York Stock Exchange (ADR)[a]
Ticker Symbol:	ITY
Subsidiaries (selected):	Reemtsma Cigarettenfabriken GmbH, Germany
	Tobaccor S.A., France
Cigarette Brands (selected):	Cabinet (Germany)
	Davidoff
	Lambert & Butler (UK)
	Peter Stuyvesant (Germany)
	Richmond (UK)
	West
Fiscal year ending September 30, 2003:	
Turnover (Sales) excluding duty (millions of dollars)	$5,318
Profit attributable to shareholders (millions of dollars)	$700
Cigarette shipments worldwide (billion units)	222
World Ranking (based on cigarette units sold)	4
Market Share:	
United Kingdom	44.6%
United Kingdom Duty-Free market	38.3%
Cabinet brand family	8.0%
Davidoff brand family (Germany)	1.1%
Lambert & Butler brand family (September 2003)	16.2%
Richmond brand family (September 2003)	12.2%
Davidoff brand family (Germany) (fiscal 2003)	1.1%

Sources: Form 20-F for the fiscal year ending September 30, 2003, available at www.sec.gov; Imperial Tobacco Group PLC Web page, www.imperial-tobacco.com.

[a] American Depository Receipt.

TOBACCO COMPANY PROFILE: JAPAN TOBACCO, INC.

Address:	2-1, Toranomon 2-chrome,
	Minato-ku, Tokyo 105-8422, Japan
Web:	www.jti.co.jp/JTI_E
Stock Exchange:	Tokyo Stock Exchange
Ticker Symbol:	TYO
Subsidiaries (selected):	JT International S.A. (Switzerland)
	(International Headquarters)
	www.jti.com/english
	JT International USA Inc. (New Jersey)
	JTI-Macdonald, Inc. (Canada)

Cigarette Brands (selected): Camel
Mild Seven
Monte Carlo
Russian Style
Salem
Seven Stars
Winston

Fiscal year ending March 31, 2004:	
Net Sales-Tobacco Business (billions of yen)	4,237
Operating Income-Tobacco Business	
Yen (billions)	238.4
U.S. (billions of $)[a]	$36.5
Net Loss for all businesses (billions of yen)	7.6
Cigarette shipments worldwide (billion units)	423.5
World Ranking-publicly-traded companies (based on cigarette units sold)	3
Market Share:	
Japan (overall)	73.1%
Japan, excluding the distribution of Marlboro	63.8%
Mild Seven brand family (Japan)	32.6%
Seven Stars brand family (Japan)	8.4%

Source: Annual Report 2004 for the year ended March 31, 2004, available at the Japan Tobacco Web page, www.jti.co.jp.gov/JTI_E; Japan Tobacco International Web page, www.jti.com/english.

[a] Converted at Yen 116.00 to U.S. $1

TOBACCO COMPANY PROFILE:
KOREA TOMORROW & GLOBAL CORPORATION (KT&G)

Address:	100 Pyeongchon-dong
	Daedeok-gu 306-712 Korea (South)
Web:	www.ktng.com
Stock Exchange:	Korea Stock Exchange
Ticker Symbol:	n/a
Subsidiaries (selected):	USA KT&G
Cigarette Brands (selected):	Carnival
	Cima
	Esse
	Lumen
	Pleasure
	Time
Fiscal year ending December 31:	
Revenues, 2003 (millions of won)	2,453,254
Net Income, 2002 (millions of won)	460,099
Cigarette shipments worldwide, 2003 (billion units)	30.9
Market Share: 2003	
Korea	80%

Sources: Worldscope, LexisNexis Academic (accessed November 1, 2004); Shibui Markets, www.shibuimarkets.com/perl/company.pl?cid=114991&page=Financials (accessed November 23, 2004), Min-hee, Kim. "KT&G Strives to Join World's Top Five Tobacco Makers by 2008." *Asia Africa Intelligence Wire*, February 9, 2004: n.p.

TOBACCO COMPANY PROFILE: LORILLARD TOBACCO COMPANY

Address:	714 Green Valley Road
	Greensboro, N.C. 27408-7018
Web:	www.loews.com
	Lorillard is a subsidiary of the Loews Corp.
	www.lorillard.com
Stock Exchange:	New York Stock Exchange
Ticker Symbol:	CG
	Carolina Group is the tracking stock created by Loews Corp. to track the performance of Lorillard Tobacco.
Subsidiaries:	n/a
Cigarette Brands (selected):	Kent
	Maverick
	Newport
	Old Gold
	True
Fiscal year ending December 31, 2003:	
Revenues (millions of dollars)	$3,295.4
Net Income (millions of dollars)	$587.6
Cigarette shipments (U.S.; billion units)	34.4
Market Share:	
United States	9.27%

Sources: Form 10-K, December 31, 2003, Loews Corporation, available at www.sec.gov; Loews Corp. Web page, www.loews.com.

TOBACCO COMPANY PROFILE: REYNOLDS AMERICAN[1]

Address:	401 North Main Street
	Winston-Salem, N.C. 27102-2866
Web:	www.reynoldsamerican.com
Stock Exchange:	New York Stock Exchange
Ticker Symbol:	RAI
Subsidiaries (selected):	R. J. Reynolds Tobacco Co.
	Santa Fe Natural Tobacco Company, Inc.
Cigarette Brands (selected):	Doral
	Camel
	Kool
	Lucky Strike
	Pall Mall

	Salem Winston
Fiscal year ending December 31, 2003:	
Pro Forma Net Sales (millions of dollars)	$8,365
Pro Forma Net Loss (millions of dollars)	$3,549
Market Share:	
United States—R. J. Reynolds Tobacco (2003)	22.5%
United States—Brown & Williamson (2003)	9.76%
United States—Pro Forma as Reynolds American, Inc.	32.28%
Cigarette shipments (2003; billion units)	371.4

Sources: Amendment No. 1 to Form S-4, March 8, 2004, Reynolds American, Inc., available at www.sec.gov; Reynolds American webpage, www.reynoldsamerican.com.

1. Effective July 30, 2004, R. J. Reynolds Tobacco Holdings and Brown & Williamson merged to form Reynolds American, Inc.

TOBACCO COMPANY PROFILE: ROTHMANS, INC.

Address:	1500 Don Mills Road
	Toronto, Ontario M3B 3L1
Web:	www.rothmansinc.ca
Stock Exchange:	Toronto Stock Exchange
Ticker Symbol:	TSX
Subsidiary:	Rothmans, Benson & Hedges (60% ownership)
Cigarette Brands:	Belmont Milds
	Belvedere
	Benson & Hedges
	Canadian Classics
	Craven A
	Dunhill
	Mark Ten
	Number 7
	Rothmans
	Viscount
Fiscal year ending March 31, 2004:	
Revenues (millions of dollars)	$620.1
Earnings (millions of dollars)	90.3
Market Share (Canada):	24.4%
Premium cigarette category	14.6%

Source: 2004 Annual Report; Rothmans, Inc. Web page, www.rothmansinc.com.

TOBACCO COMPANY PROFILE: P. T. HANJAYA MANDALA SAMPOERNA TERBUKA

Address:	Jalan Rungkut Industri Raya No 14-18
	Surabaya 60293, Indonesia

Web:	n/a
Stock Exchange:	Jakarta Stock Exchange
Ticker Symbol:	HMSP
Subsidiaries (selected):	n/a
Cigarette Brands (selected):	"A" Mild
	"A" Mild Menthol
	Filter International
	Surya
Fiscal year ending December 31, 2002:	
Sales, Cigarettes (millions of rupiahs)	204,392
Operating Income, Cigarettes (millions of rupiahs)	3,344
Market Share: 2004	
Indonesia	19.1%

Sources: Worldscope, LexisNexis Academic (accessed November 1, 2004); "Review-Private Enterprise: Stocks an Option," www.laksamana.net/print.cfm?id=7569 (October 25, 2004).

TOBACCO COMPANY PROFILE: VECTOR GROUP LTD.

Address:	100 S.E. Second Street
	Miami, Fla. 33131
Web:	www.vectorgroupltd.com
Stock Exchange:	New York Stock Exchange
Ticker Symbol:	VGR
Subsidiaries (selected):	Liggett Group, Inc.
	Vector Tobacco, Inc.
Cigarette Brands (selected):	Eve
	Jade
	Omni
	Quest
	Pyramid
Fiscal year ending December 31, 2003:	
Revenues, company-wide (thousands of dollars)	$536,683
Net Loss (thousands of dollars)	$15,610
Cigarette shipments-U.S. (billion units)	9.8
Market Share:	
United States	2.6%
Deep-discount category	9.4%
Premium cigarette market	.2%

Sources: Form 10-K for the fiscal year ended December 31, 2003, available at www.sec.gov; Vector Group Ltd. Web page, www.vectorgroupltd.com.

Appendix C
Tobacco Litigation: Selected Court Cases

Tobacco Litigation: Selected Court Cases

Case/Defendants[a]/Type	Jurisdiction	Damage Award	Status
Broin v. Philip Morris Companies, Inc. et al. PM, RJRT, B&W, LOR/Flight Attendants	Dade County Circuit (Miami, Fla.)	$300 million	Settled

Class-action suit was filed in October 1991; trial began on June 2, 1997. On September 7, 1999, the settlement and judgment became final. Case filed on behalf of all flight attendants in U.S. airplanes alleged to be suffering from diseases or ailments caused by exposure to secondhand smoke in airplane cabins. Damages paid in three installments of $100 million, allocated among the companies by market share, to fund research on early detection and cure of diseases associated with tobacco smoke. The settlement allowed individual flight attendants one additional year to file lawsuits seeking compensatory damages for any injuries they may have suffered from exposure to environmental tobacco smoke in airline cabins. The settlement bars the award of punitive damages to any individual flight attendant who is successful in recovering compensatory damages at trial.

Blue Cross and Blue Shield of New Jersey v. Philip Morris, Inc. PM, RJRT, BW/Health Care Cost Recovery	U.S. District Court, Eastern District	$17.8 million/compensatory	Ongoing

Suit filed by Empire Health Plan of New York to seek damages for money allegedly spent to provide medical treatment to injured smokers. On September 16, 2003, the U.S. Court of Appeals for the Second Circuit reversed the verdict on one of two claims the jury had returned in favor of the plaintiff. The Second Circuit reversed the decision on the second claim, pending guidance from the New York Court of Appeals on two issues of New York law. Oral argument was scheduled for September 7, 2004. On October 19, 2004, the New York State Court of Appeals struck down the case.

Engle v. R. J. Reynolds Tobacco Company et al. PM, RJRT, BW, LOR, BRK/Class Action	Circuit Court, Dade County (Miami, Fla.)	$12.7 billion/compensatory $145 billion/punitive	Ongoing

On May 21, 2003, Florida's Third District Court of Appeals reversed the trial court's final judgment and remanded the case to the Dade County Circuit Court with instructions to decertify the class. On July 16, 2003, the plaintiffs filed a motion for rehearing, which was denied on September 22, 2003. Mandate issued on October 8, 2003. The plaintiffs filed a notice seeking review by the Florida Supreme Court. On May 12, 2004, the Florida Supreme Court agreed to review the case. Oral argument was scheduled for November 3, 2004.

Henley v. Philip Morris, Inc. PM/Individual Smoking and Health	Superior Court of the City and County of San Francisco	$1.5 million/compensatory $50 million/punitive	Ongoing

This was the first California case where a smoker recovered a verdict from a cigarette manufacturer. Original verdict issued in February 1999. The California Court of Appeals vacated the $25 million punitive damage award and ordered that Philip Morris USA should be granted a new trial on punitive damages unless the plaintiff agreed to accept a reduction of the punitive damage award to $9 million. On January 23, 2004, plaintiff accepted the reduced punitive damages award ordered by the California Court of Appeals. Philip Morris USA filed a petition for rehearing on February 9, 2004. On April 28, 2004, the California Supreme Court granted Philip Morris USA's request for review of the California Court of Appeals' decision. On September 17, 2004, the California Supreme Court upheld an appeals court's ruling against Philip Morris. On October 28, 2004, the U.S. Supreme Court agreed to review the California Supreme Court's ruling against Philip Morris.

Price v. Philip Morris, Inc.   Circuit Court, Third $7.1 billion/compensatory   Ongoing
PM/Class Action, Lights/Ultra Lights   Judicial District (Ill.) $3 billion/punitive

The trial began on January 21, 2003. On March 21, 2003, the trial judge entered compensatory and punitive damages against Philip Morris. Based on Illinois law, the bond required to stay execution of the judgment was initially set at $12 billion. On April 14, 2003, the trial judge reduced the amount bond and ordered the bond secured by $800 million, payable in four equal quarterly installments beginning in September 2003, a preexisting $6 billion long-term note to be placed in escrow pending resolution of the case. On July 14, 2003, the appeals court ruled that the trial judge had exceeded his authority in reducing the bond and ordered the trial judge to reinstate the original bond. On September 16, 2003, the Illinois Supreme Court ordered that the reduced bond be reinstated and agreed to hear Philip Morris's appeal without the need for intermediate appellate court review.

Scott v. American Tobacco Company, Inc. et al.   District Court, New Orleans, La. $591 million   Ongoing
PM, RJRT, BW, LOR, TI/Class Action

On November 5, 1998, a Louisiana state appeals court affirmed the certification of medical monitoring of smoking cessation of Louisiana residents who had been smokers on or before May 24, 1996. On July 28, 2003, the jury returned a verdict in favor of the defendants on the plaintiffs' claim for medical monitoring and found that cigarettes were not defectively designed (phase I). The jury found that smoking cessation programs existed and had clinical value (phase II). On May 21, 2004, in phase II, the jury returned a verdict in the amount of approximately $591 million on the class's claim for a smoking cessation program. Post-trial motions pending. Legislation in Louisiana limits the amount of a bond to prevent execution upon such a judgment to $50 million collectively for signatories of the Master Settlement Agreement (MSA).

United States of America v. Philip Morris, Inc. et al.   U.S. District Court (D.C.)   —   Ongoing
PM, RJRT, BW, LOR, LGT, AMT/ Health Care Reimbursement

Originally filed on September 22, 1999, the case began on September 21, 2004, U.S. District Judge Gladys Kessler presiding. The Department of Justice's suit (1) sought medical cost recovery for federal funds spent to treat alleged tobacco-related illnesses and (2) asserted federal Racketeer Influenced and Corrupt Organizations Act (RICO) violations. Judge Kessler ruled against the medical claims, but the RICO claims continued.

Sources: Form 10-K for the fiscal year ended December 31, 2003, Altria Group, Inc.; Amendment No. 1 to Form S-4 filed March 8, 2004, Reynolds American, Inc.; U.S. Department of Justice, Litigation against Tobacco Companies, www.usdoj.gov/civil/cases/tobacco2/index2.htm; Tobacco Control Resource Center, www.tobacco.neu.edu.
[a]PM = Philip Morris; RJRT = R.J. Reynolds Tobacco Co.; BW = Brown & Williamson; LOR = Lorillard Tobacco Company;
LGT = Liggett Group; BRK = Brook Group Ltd; TI = Tobacco Institute; AMT = American Tobacco Company.

Appendix D
Tobacco Websites

Action on Smoking and Health
www.ask.org (U.S.)
www.ash.org.uk (UK)

Advertising and Sponsorship of Tobacco Products
European Union Directive 2003/33/EC
europa.eu.int/scadplus/leg/ens03000.htm

Advocacy Institute
www.advocacy.org

British American Tobacco Documents Archive
www.bat.library.ucsf.edu

British-American Tobacco Guildford Depository Document Collection
www.library.ucsf.edu/tobacco/batco

Brown & Williamson document website
www.bwdocs.com

Campaign for Tobacco-Free Kids
www.tobaccofreekids.org

Centre for Tobacco Control Research. UK Tobacco Advertising Documents Database
www.tobaccopapers.com

European Union
europa.eu.int

Generation AB
www.generation.se

Legacy Tobacco Documents Library
legacy.library.ucsf.edu/

Lorillard Tobacco Company Document Site
www.lorillarddocs.com

Manufacture, Presentation, and Sale of Tobacco Products
European Union Directive 2001/37/EC
europa.eu.int/scadplus/leg/en/s03000.htm

Master Settlement Agreement and Amendments
www.naag.org

National Association of Attorneys General
www.naag.org

National Conference of State Legislatures
www.ncsl.org

Non-Smokers' Rights Association
www.nsra-adnf.ca

Philip Morris USA, Inc., document site
www.pmdocs.com

Present at the Creation: The Marlboro Man
www.npr.org/programs/morning/features/patc/marlboroman

TobaccoArchives.Com
www.tobaccoarchives.com

Tobacco Advertising and Promotion Act 2002 (United Kingdom)
www.legislation.hmso.gov.uk/si/si2003/20030258.htm

Tobacco Advertising and Promotion (Point of Sale) Regulations 2004 (UK)
www.legislation.hmso.gov.uk/si/si2004/20040765.htm

Tobacco Control
tc.bmjjournals.com

Tobacco Control Archives
www.library.ucsf.edu/tobacco

Tobacco Documents Online
tobaccodocuments.org

Tobacco Journal International
www.tobaccojournal.com

Tobacco Litigation Documents
www.library.ucsf.edu/tobacco/litigation

Tobacco.org: Tobacco News and Information
www.tobacco.org

Tobacco Outlet Business
www.tobonline.com

Tobacco Reporter
www.tobaccoreporter.com

Tobacco Settlement Agreement, Proposed (1997)
news.findlaw.com/cnn/docs/tobacco; also reproduced in Carrick Mollenkamp, *The People vs. Big Tobacco: How the States Took on the Tobacco Giants* (Princeton, N.J.: Bloomberg), 1998

Tobacco State Settlement Documents: Florida, Minnesota, Mississippi, and Texas
news.findlaw.com/cnn/docs/tobacco

Tobacco: World Markets and Trade
www.fas.usda.gov/tobacco_arc.html

United Kingdom Department of Health
www.dh.gov.uk/Home/fs/en

University of California eScholarship Repository
repositories.cdlib.org/escholarship

U.S. Centers for Disease Control and Prevention
www.cdc.gov/tobacco/industrydocs

World Health Organization. Framework Convention on Tobacco Control
www.who.int/tobacco/areas/framework/en

Index

Note: Numbers denote entries and not pages.

Abbott, Greg, 782
Abrams, Jim, 593
Abramson, Jill, 581, 594, 606, 722
Accord cigarettes, 78
Achabal, Dale D., 515
An Act Making Appropriations for the Departments of Labor, Health, and Human Services, and Education and Related Agencies for the Fiscal Year Ending September 30, 1998, and for Other Purposes (Public Law 105-78), 690
Action on Smoking and Health, 269, 306
Adelman, David, 630
Adelson, Andrea, 506
Advance cigarettes, 82; lights, 88
Advertising Standards Authority, United Kingdom, 145
Advocacy Institute, 38, 550
Afghanistan, 332, 366
Africa, 434
African Americans, 174, 215–16, 226, 232–33
Agenda for the '90s, 568
Agricultural Adjustment Act of 1938, 523
Agriculture, Rural Development, Food and Drug Administration, and Related Agencies Appropriations Act, 1994 (Public Law 103-111), 525
Aguinaga, Stella, 511
Ahmad, S. M., 366
Ahrens, A. Bridget, 191
AIDS, 247, 252

AIDS Nutrition Services Alliance, 254
airports: Athens International, 230; Barajas, Madrid, 230
Akin, Gump, Strauss, Hauer, & Feld, 547
Akwesasne Indian Reserve, 330, 336, 338, 340, 343, 380
Alamar, B. C., 630
Alexander, Robert, 279, 282
Ali, Syed Rashid, 332
Alley-Cats Scramble, 288
Alliance Against Contraband, 385
Alliance for Sponsorship Freedom, 286
Altadis cigarettes, duty-free, 322, 326
Altria Group, 620, 657–58; arts sponsorship, 246; cigarettes, smuggling, 409; public relations, 621
Alvin Ailey Dance Theater, 233
The American Achievers (book), 102
American Ballet Theater, 232, 234
American Brands, 52, 145; promotions, 138
American Cancer Society, 155, 260, 268, 287, 578, 596, 604, 619, 727
American Civil Liberties Union, 563, 709
American Heart Association, 155, 619, 625
American Jobs Creation Act of 2004 (Public Law 108-357), 631
American Journal of Respiratory Cell and Molecular Biology, 260
American Journal of Respiratory and Critical Care, 260
American Legacy Foundation, 776, 780

217

American Lung Association, 155, 260, 263, 619
American Marketing Association, 709; Effies Awards, 141
American Medical Association (AMA), 258, 263, 601, 612, 757; political action committee, 549, 601
American Smokers Journal, 559
American Stop Smoking Intervention Study (ASSIST), 566, 578, 585, 598, 616, 624
American Thoracic Society, 260
American Tobacco Company, 52, 102, 550, 573; congressional testimony, 551; international markets, emerging, 420; litigation, tobacco, 655; partnership programs, 453
American University, 602
American Wholesale Marketers Association, 554
Amigo cigarettes, packaging, 29
Amsterdam News magazine, 723
Amusement and Music Operators Association, 558
Anderson Cancer Center, 262
Andorra, 369
Angelides, Philip, 610
Angus Barn, 564
"ants," smuggling, 403
Antwerp, Belgium, 358, 361–62, 374
appeal-bond caps, 645, 746–48, 768, 770, 784
Applebome, Peter, 742
Arcellaschi, Augusto, 362
Archer, Bill, 711
Areddy, James T., 98
Argentina, 68, 121, 143–44, 150
Argus Leader newspaper, 723
Ariva lozenges, 84
Armstrong World Industries, 670
Army Air Force Exchange Service (AAFES), 415
aromathcrapy, 169
Arthur D. Little International, 533
Arts Forward Fund, 234
arts sponsorship, 103, 121, 130, 217, 231–46, 275, 286, 423, 425, 427
Aruba, 532
As Four (fashion team), 217
As the World Turns (soap opera), 239
Ashcroft, John D., 615
Asia, 382
Asian markets, 423–28, 433
Aspen cigarettes, 69

ASSIST. *See* American Stop Smoking Intervention Study
Association for Southwest Asian Nations, 564
attorneys' fees, 634. *See also* litigation, tobacco; Tobacco Settlement; Master Settlement Agreement
attorneys general, 221
Audits & Surveys Worldwide, 153
Austin, Jeanie, 553
Australia, 181, 259, 615
Australian Tobacco Research Foundation, 259

Bailey's cigarettes, 66, 478
Baird, Roger, 160
Baker, Donald P., 66, 78
Bal, Dileep G., 499
Balanced Budget Act of 1997 (Public Law 105-33), 671
Balbach, Edith D., 215, 516
Balkans, 386
Baltic Imports, 376
Banderas, Antonio, 143
Banerjee, Neela, 429
Bangladesh, 395, 439
Barbeau, Elizabeth M., 215
Barbieri, Kelly, 244
Barbour, Griffith, & Rogers, 675
Barbour, Haley, 675, 680
Barford, Michael F., 47, 348
Barnes, Steve, 782
Barr, Josh, 277
Barrington, Stephen, 21
Bartlett, Bruce, 371
Basic cigarettes, 99, 134
Bastos NY 25s cigarettes, 46
Bateh, Freddie, 1
Bates, James, 212
Bauer, Peter, 759
Beardi, Cara, 184–87, 189, 192, 195
Becker, Jo, 778
Beelman, Maud S., 381–82
Begay, Michael E., 503, 505, 507
Beili, Xu, 479
Beirne, Mike, 93, 95, 161, 188, 197, 222, 224, 481, 485, 495
Belluck, Pam, 76
Beltrame, Julian, 18
Bennington cigarettes, 472
Benson & Hedges cigarettes: 100mm, 125; "Creative Solutions," 225; DeNic, 41; Formula One, 306; gays and lesbians, 216;

New Zealand, 520; promotions, 145, 150, 157, 167; slogans and themes, 26, 125, 665; special editions, 26; Special Kings, 116; sports sponsorship, 293, 297
Benson, Mitchel, 610
Bentley, Stephanie, 472
Berk, Christina Cheddar, 650
Bernstein, Viv, 302
Bero, Lisa A., 207, 624
Berry, Michele, 232
Better America Foundation, 565
Bevel Flair cigarettes, 71
Bhatti, Jabeen, 30
Bhutan, 324
Bialous, Stella Aguinaga, 267, 616
Bible, Geoffrey C., 50, 51
bidis cigarettes, 65, 439
"Big Tobacco," 91, 179, 251, 277, 389, 485, 514, 583–84, 588, 659, 662, 701, 703, 712, 716–17, 723, 729, 733–34, 746, 776
Bird, Laura, 38, 109, 424, 558
Bistoon cigarettes, 43
Black History Month, 233
black market. *See* cigarettes, smuggling
Blair, Tony, 285
Bleek, Memphis, 195
Bliley, Thomas J., 570
Bloch, Michele, 232
Blonsky, Marshall, 665
Bloom, Paul N., 487
Blue Cross and Blue Shield (Minnesota), 719
Blue Cross and Blue Shield of New Jersey v. Philip Morris, 657
Blumenstyk, Goldie, 268
Blunt, Andrew B., 620
Blunt, Roy, 620
Boehner, John A., 567, 574
Bogdanich, Walt, 668
Boncompagni, Tatiana S., 581
Bond Amendment No. 2913: Sense of the Senate Against Federal Funding of Smoke Shops, 609
Bond, Christopher, 609
Bonn, Dorothy, 520
Bonner, Raymond, 361–63, 370
Bosna cigarettes, 339
Boston Medical University, 258
Bowles, Erskine B., 673
Boyarsky, Bill, 504
Boyd, John W., 674
Boys and Girls Club of America, 242

Bragg, Rick, 639
Branch, Shelly, 256, 534
brand: coloring, 32, 157; stretching, 105–6, 121, 139, 142, 157, 160, 162, 423, 425, 430, 471, 714
Brat, Da, 195
Bravo cigarettes, 70, 73
Brazil, 59, 64, 171, 359, 381, 407, 529, 613
Breach, Michael L., 191
Brenner, Sydney, Dr., 261
Brierley, David, 279
Briggs, Johnathon E., 611
Brigham and Women's Hospital, 262
Brinson, Brandy, 32, 227, 327, 771
Bristol City Council Trading Standards, 228
British American Racing, 290, 294, 303, 309
British American Tobacco (BAT), 52, 63–64, 75; advertising, 534; airports, 204; brand stretching, 157, 160; British American Racing, 290, 294, 303, 309; China, 432, 438; cigarettes, duty-free, 317, 319, 356; cigarettes, smuggling, 356, 381–82, 386, 395, 400, 406–7; *Discover* magazine, 204; Formula One, 283–84, 290, 294, 307, 309; Foyle memorandum, 654, 659; India, 439; international markets, emerging, 423, 433; Internet cigarettes sales, 482; Kenya, 69, 434; Korea, South, 440; litigation, tobacco, 654–65, 659; Lucky Strike, 451; packaging, 3, 26, 28, 34; philanthropy, 253; price-fixing, 532; promotions, 167, 199, 212, 229, 309; research sponsorship, 264–66; Russia, 429, 444–46; sports sponsorship, 106, 274, 283, 304; Turkey, 442; vending machines, 492; Vietnam, 436; World Cup, 203, 300. *See also* Lucky Strike cigarettes; tobacco industry
British Labor Party, 285
British Medical Association, 472
Broder, John M., 660, 664
Broin v. Philip Morris Companies, 634
Bronx Museum of Art, 246
Brooke Group, 77, 79, 660. *See also* Liggett Group
Brooklyn Academy of Music, 235
Brown & Williamson, 88, 97; Alliance Millennium program, 488; CART, 280; cigarette displays and racks, 481; "Circuit Breaker," 148; congressional testimony, 551; *Details* magazine, 222; *Flair* magazine, 178; hip-hop, 222, 226, 785;

international markets, emerging, 426; Internet cigarettes sales, 482–83, 486; litigation, tobacco, 639, 644, 655; lozenges, nicotine, 84; Master Settlement Agreement (MSA) (1998), 226, 729, 731, 750, 756, 774, 782, 785; *One World* magazine, 196, 222; packaging, 1, 14, 25; partnership programs, 453; political contributions, 567, 574; prisons and jails, 450; promotions, 111, 138, 156, 169–70, 175, 184, 187–88, 192–93, 195, 197, 208; *Real Edge* magazine, 178–79, 190; *Simple Living* magazine, 179; sports sponsorship, 296, 728; Tobacco Settlement, Florida (1997), 676; Tobacco Settlement, Minnesota (1998), 714; Tobacco Settlement, Mississippi (1997), 667; Tobacco Settlement, proposed (1997), 664, 666, 717, 733–74; Tobacco Settlement, Texas (1998), 696; youth smoking prevention program, 605. *See also* Kool cigarettes; tobacco industry
Brown, Deanna, 579
Brown, Dick, 545
Brown, Jonathan, 323, 325
Brown, Richard, 373
Brulte, James, 770
Buckby, Simon, 266
Buckham, Tom, 704
Burnett, Leo, 216
Burns, David, 539
Burritt, Chris, 250
Burson-Marstellar, 548, 553, 571, 587
Burton, John, 770
Bush, George W., 389, 606, 615, 699
Bush, Jeb, 744, 748
Butalla, Laura, 213
Butterfield, Deborah, 237
Butt Hut of America, 476
"buttlegging," 360
buydowns, 496
Byrne, Martha, 239
Byron, Nicholas, 641

Cabinet cigarettes, international markets, emerging, 420
Caesar's Palace, 208
Cafasso, Edward, 588
Calian, Sara, 527
California, 704, 741; antismoking legislation, 501–4, 507, 513, 516, 543, 643; Assembly Bill 13, 510, 517; Assembly Bill 384, 519; Golden State Tobacco Securitization Corporation, 766; Internet cigarette sales, 493; Master Settlement Agreement (MSA) (1998), 738, 745, 749, 753, 755, 762, 766, 770, 779; political contributions, 500, 505, 507, 545; preemption, 553; prisons and jails, 519; Proposition 99, 499, 500, 505–6, 509, 512, 514, 516; Proposition 188, 508, 511, 514, 517, 562; Tobacco Settlement, Proposed (1997), 710
California Democratic Party, 568
California Department of Health Services, 499
Californians for Scientific Integrity, 583
Californians for Statewide Smoking Restrictions, 508
California Office of the Governor, 519
California Public Employees Retirement System, 610
California State Teachers' Retirement System, 610
California Supreme Court, 646, 656
California Uniform Tobacco Control Act (Proposition 188), 508, 511
Cambridge cigarettes, "lights," 641
Cambridge University, 264–66
Came, Barry, 343
Camel cigarettes, 178, 198, 783; "99s," 42; cigarettes, duty-free, 320; Joe Camel ads, 109, 129, 144, 153–54, 473, 664; limited editions, 93; marketing, trend influence, 126, 200; Midnight Madness, 93; military, 412; movies, 191; packaging, 19; promotions, 104, 115, 117, 121, 139, 149, 159, 173, 199, 243; slogans and themes, 89, 109, 129, 149, 159, 176; "smoking lounge," 230; Turkish Gold, 83, 89; Turkish Jade, 83, 86, 89; Turkish Royal, 89; Wides, 42
Cameroon, 395
Camilleri, Louis, 209
"Camp Marlboro," Baghdad, 623
Campaign for Tobacco-Free Kids, 395, 597, 604, 612, 619, 625, 775
Campbell, Bill, 53
Campbell, Duncan, 381-82
Campbell, William I., 119, 551
Canada, 18, 21, 236, 244, 336–38, 340, 342–44, 349–51, 368, 371, 380, 391, 400–1
Canadian Government, duty-free cigarettes, 311
Cancer Research Campaign, 264–66
Cancer Research Foundation, 242

Capri cigarettes: promotions, 169; slogans and themes, 188; Superslims, 188
Cardador, M. Teresa, 559
Carey, John, 583
Carl Edelmann GmbH, 10
Carlson, Margaret, 680
Carlton cigarettes; promotions, 169, 170, 196; slogans and themes, 170, 196
Carlyle, Joshua, 309
Carol, Julia, 582
Carr, Rebecca, 585
CART. *See* Championship Auto Racing Team
Carter, Grady, 644, 668
Carter, S. M., 220, 497
Cartier cigarettes, duty-free, 316
Castano v. American Tobacco, 633, 734
Celadon Corporation, 62
Center for Investigative Reporting, 389
Center for Public Integrity, 381–82
Center for Women Policy Studies, 540
Chadha, K. K., 103
Championship Auto Racing Team (CART), 280, 301, 728
Cheaper Cigarettes!, 491
Checkers cigarettes, 55, 470
Chesterfield Brown cigarettes, 68; promotions, 150
Chesterfield cigarettes, 77, 79
Chidley, Joe, 236
Chiles, Lawton, 692
China, 17, 33, 143, 167, 274, 282, 292, 307, 328, 353, 355–56, 379, 396–97, 404, 427, 430, 432, 438, 441, 479, 522, 613
China National Tobacco Corporation, 356, 428, 432, 438
Chinese cigarettes, 479
Choice magazine, 559
Chretien, Jean, 342, 344
Christian of Denmark cigarettes, duty-free, 323
Chunxiang, Lü, 479
Ciba-Geigy, 207
Cienski, Jan, 403
cigalettes, 84
"cigarette boys," 181
"cigarette girls," 114, 181, 214, 219, 429–30, 432, 435
The Cigarette Stores, 467
cigarettes: Afghanistan, 366; Canada, 311, 338, 351; China, 328, 355, 396, 397, 404; counterfeit, 22, 54, 409; discount, 45, 47, 50, 91, 209, 495, 456; displays and racks, 322; duty-free, 7, 315, 317, 323, 326–27, 347; European Union, 373; fire-safe, 81, 189, 584, 627, 649; gray market, United States, 364, 377–78; Great Britain, 314; international, 397–99; Korea, South, 396; Malaysia, 329; nicotine-free, 90; Pakistan, 366; paper, 189, 584, 649; South Africa, 329; specialty, 457; supermarket, 472; tipping paper, 227; Turkey, 394; United States, 408
Cigarettes Cheaper!, 377, 467, 476
cigarettes, smuggling: Afghanistan, 332, 366; Andorra, 369; Antwerp, Belgium, 374; Asia, 382; Balkans, 386; Bangladesh, 395; Brazil, 359, 381; California, 347; Cameroon, 395; Canada, 330, 336–38, 340, 342–44, 349–51, 368, 371, 380, 391, 401, 410; China, 353, 356, 379; Columbia, 375, 381, 389, 392, 395; Cyprus, 387, 392; Dubai, 387; "duty not paid," 381; East Germany, 331; Eastern Europe, 367; Europe, 385; European Union, 352, 358, 369, 370, 373, 384, 403, 409; "general trade," 382; Germany, 385; Great Britain, 371, 385; Hong Kong, 372; international, 354, 361, 365, 374, 388, 398; Iran, 387, 402; Iraq, 390, 392, 402; Italy, 334–35, 341, 348, 362, 379, 385; Kish Island, 387; Latin America, 381, 532; Lebanon, 402; Malaysia, 345, 371; Montenegro, 386; Pakistan, 332, 366; Paraguay, 371, 407; "parallel market," 381; Poland, 403; prison and jails, 449; Russia, 392, 403; Sarajevo, 339; "second channel," 381; South Africa, 371; Spain, 369–70, 385, 395; Surinam, 359; Sweden, 367; Switzerland, 362; Taiwan, 333, 404; Third World, 382; "transit trade," 402; Turkey, 387, 394; United Kingdom, 349, 383; United States, 336, 346, 357, 360, 368, 379, 408, 630, 708; Venezuela, 381; Vietnam, 382
cigarettes, tax-free: Native-American reservations, 357, 454, 609; United States, 357
"Circuit Breaker," 148
Citizens for a Sound Economy, 563, 565
City by the Sea, 783
City University of New York, 632
Claiborne, William, 510, 513
Clark, Philip B., 484
Clark, P. I., 496
Clarke, Liz, 289

Clinton administration, 543–44, 547, 554, 612, 661, 669, 673, 688, 691, 695, 709, 718
Clinton, Bill, 54, 273, 466, 543–24, 552, 558, 569, 586, 603, 618, 635, 637, 688, 691, 698, 700, 706, 736
Cloud, David S., 552
CML magazine, 178–79
"coal dropoff," 649
Coalition on Smoking OR Health, 544
Coburn, James, 424
Cockburn, Alexander, 569
Cogan, Douglas G., 608
Cohen, Jon, 261–62
Cohen, Wayne, 703
Coleman, Tim, 70, 168, 365
Colford, Steven W., 102, 521
Collin, Jeff, 309
Collins, Glenn, 438, 633, 678
Collins, Susan, 680
Colorado, 140, 566
Columbia, 375, 381, 389, 392, 395, 532
Combs, Sean, 217
Communist Party, 98
Companies' Creditors Arrangement Act (Canada), 410
Competitive Enterprise Institute, 563
Conde Nast, 579
Condeé Nast Sports for Women, 579
Confederate Tribes (Chehalis Reservation), 76
Congressional Black Caucus, 592
Congressional Budget Office. *See* U.S. Congressional Budget Office (CBO)
Congressional Hispanic Caucus, 592
Congressional Record, 609, 721
Congressional Research Service (CRS), 603, 726
Connolly, Ceci, 590, 709, 711–12
Connolly, Gregory N., 425
Consolidated Rail Corporation, 670
Consumer Analyst Group of New York, 51
contraband cigarettes. *See* cigarettes, smuggling
Contributions Watch, 571, 576
convenience stores, 476; cigarette displays and racks, 469
Cookson, Clive, 266
Cooper, Helene, 617
Corn, David, 100
Cosmopolitan, 188
Costa Rica, 532, 581
Council for Tobacco Research, 258, 262, 714
Council of State Governments, 544, 581, 761

Country America, 134
Crenshaw, Albert B., 577
Crescenti, Marcelo G., 6–8, 59
Croatia, 158
Cummings, K. M. (K. Michael), 24
Curtis, James, 211
Cushman, John H., Jr., 776
Cyprus, 387, 390, 392, 402
Czech Republic, 238, 468, 533

Dagnoli, Judann, 42, 102, 107, 111
Dakota cigarettes, 38, 54; slogans and themes, 37
D'Alessandro, Andres, 407
Dalian Municipal Tobacco Company, 479
Dalton, Madeline A., 191
Daniels, Chris, 288
Darby, Ian, 177, 294
"dark market," 220, 497
Daschle, Tom, 590
Dave's cigarettes, 56
Davidoff cigarettes: duty-free, 316; slogans and themes, 199
Davidoff Classic cigarettes: packaging, 12; trademarks, 535
Davis, Gray, 518
Davis, Lincoln, 628
Day, Sherri, 641
D.C. Central Kitchen, 252
Dean, Malcolm, 522
Death cigarettes, slogans and themes, 44, 67
Death Cigarettes, Ltd., United Kingdom, 44
DeBakey, Michael, 102
Defense Commissary Agency (DeCA), 415, 417
Defense Logistics Agency, 412
DeGraff, Nate, 652
DeLay, Tom, 711
Demirsar, Metin, 394
Democratic National Committee (DNC), 568, 589, 606
Democratic National Convention, 542, 570, 611
Democratic Party, 568, 571, 663
Deng Xiaping, 98
Departments of Commerce, Justice and State, the Judiciary, and Related Agencies Appropriations Act of 1998 (Public Law 105-119), 530–31
Derby cigarettes, 59
Derthick, Martha A., 765

Dessoff, Alan, 478
Details (magazine), 222
Devore, Amanda, 772
Dewar, Helen, 723–24
Dewhirst, T. (Timothy), 301
Dillman, D. Gene, II, 138
Dipasquale, Cara B., 25, 88–89, 206, 208–9, 488
Diplomat cigarettes, 203
di Robilant, Maurizo, 6
Discover magazine, 204
divestment, tobacco, 608, 610, 632
Dixon, Lee, 772
doctors, 596
Doggett, Lloyd, 531, 612
Dohrmann, George, 273
Dole Foundation, 565
Dole, Robert, 542, 565
Doolittle, David E., 120
Doral & Co., 86, 198
Doral cigarettes, 86, 461; promotions, 134–35, 161, 172; slogans and themes, 135, 198
Dorning, Mike, 706
Doroba, Steve, 166
Dow Chemical, 207
Drew, Christopher, 361
Drozdiak, William, 384
DTZ Pieda Consulting, 383
Duailibi Petit Zaragoza Propoganda, 171
Dubai, 387, 405
Duffy, Brian, 589
Duke University, 250, 264
du Maurier cigarettes; promotions, 219, 236, 244
DuMelle, Fran, 582
Dunhill cigarettes: duty-free, 316; lights, 114; sports sponsorship, 288; World Cup, 300
Dunn, Jennifer, 590
Durbin, Richard, 680
Dwek, Robert, 151

East Germany, 331
Ebony, 215, 652
Eccelstone, Bernie, 285
Ecenbarger, William, 121
Eclipse cigarettes, 60, 250; promotions, 183, 185, 221; slogans and themes, 185
Edsall, Thomas B., 754
Efron, Sonni, 143
Eichenbaum, David, 568
Electronic Arts, 104

Elliott, Stuart, 115, 122, 125, 131, 141, 156, 176, 255, 665
Elliston, Jon, 576
embassies, U.S., 530
Embassy cigarettes, 69
Emily's List, 541
Empire case. *See Blue Cross and Blue Shield of New Jersey v. Philip Morris*
Empire Health Choice, 657
Emro, Inc., 107
Engle v. R. J. Reynolds Tobacco Co., 639, 642, 650, 746–47, 752
entertainment industry, 201
Entertainment Weekly, 750
Environmental Working Group, 626, 628
Equinox cigarettes, slogans and themes, 317
Escher, Sandra, 15
Eskew, Carter, 606, 725
ESPN Magazine, 759
Essence, 174, 215, 233
Estonia, 444
Etheridge, Bobby R., 628
Europe, 385; central, 444; eastern, 167, 367, 430, 433, 444
European Commission, UCLAF (Unité de Coordination de la Lutte Anti Fraude) (UCLAF), 373
European Community Committee of Inquiry into the Community Transit System, 358
European Logistics Association, 468
European Single Market Act of 1993, 349, 365
European Tobacco, 394
European Union, 352, 369–70, 373, 384, 403, 409; bans and restrictions, smoking, 526, 527; dependence on tobacco industry, 613; directives, 27, 32, 157, 227, 284, 308, 310, 316
Evans, Lane, 686
Evans, Marie R., 652
Evans, Willie, 652
Export A cigarettes; smuggling, 376
Export Credit Guarantee Program, 536
export programs, tobacco, 528, 530–31, 536, 555, 612

Fairclough, Gordon, 18, 83–84, 87, 91–92, 198, 482–83, 533–34, 613, 617, 749–52, 756, 768
fake cigarettes. *See* cigarettes, counterfeit
Family Express, 475
Farah, Douglas, 375, 392

Farah, George, 328
Farley, Christopher John, 239
farmers, tobacco, 669, 737, 741; minority, 674
Feder, Barnaby J., 474
Federal Bureau of Investigation (FBI), 494
Federal Election Committee (FEC), 599
Federal Home Loan Mortgage Corporation, 577
Federal Trade Commission (FTC), 153, 155, 681, 683, 687
Federation Internationale de Football Association (FIFA), 203, 300
Federation Internationale de l'Automobile (FIA), 299, 305
Federation of Italian Tobacconists, 341
Feighery, E. C., 496, 515
Feldheim, David, 766
Felgner, Brent H., 453
Felten, Patricia G., 499
Fennell, Tom, 340
Ferraro, Geraldine, 597
FHM magazine, 306
FIA International Research, Ltd., 378–79
Fidelty Investments, 588
fiduciaries, 608
Field & Stream magazine, 135
Filipov, David, 75
Filner, Bob, 686
Finora, Joseph, 86
First Nations Development Institute, 254
Fiscal Planning Services, 566
Fisher, Brandy, 607
Fisher, Ian, 561
Fisher, Marc, 420
Fisher, Peter, 582
Fitzgerald, Mike, 257
Flair magazine, 178–79
Fleenor, Patrick, 357
Fleischer, Ari, 617
Fletcher, Michael A., 592
Flint, Anthony, 354, 430, 528
Florida, 744, 748
Florida Task Force on Tobacco Settlement Revenue Protection, 630
Fontanez, Jose, 414
Food and Drug Administration (FDA), 84, 124, 273, 473, 556, 563, 565, 618, 622, 625, 629, 661, 664, 750, 765; litigation, tobacco, 638
Food and Drug Administration v. Brown & Williamson (2000), 638
Foodchain Network of Food Rescue, 254
Food, Drug, and Cosmetic Act (1938), 638
Ford, Wendell, 524
Foreign Agricultural Service, 525, 536; Market Promotion Program, 521, 523
Foreign Market Development Program, 536
Formula One (F1), 279, 282–83, 284–85, 290, 294, 298, 301, 303, 305–8, 310, 328
Formula One Constructors Association, 284
Forster, Nikolaus, 386
Fort Bragg, North Carolina, 413
Fortuna cigarettes, duty-free, 326
Fortune Tobacco Company, 55
Forward Publishing, 151
Foundation for Independent Higher Education, 249
Fowler, Geoffrey A., 307
Fox, Barry, 23
Fox, Brion J., 616
Foyle, Andrew, 654, 659
Foyle memorandum, 654, 659
Framework Convention on Tobacco Control, 299, 305, 307, 324, 327, 398, 534, 613
Frankel, Glenn, 431–32
Freddie Mac, 577
Freedman, Alix M., 113, 390, 661, 668
Freedom of Information Act (FOIA), 566, 583
Freedom Tobacco, 214, 217
free trade zones, 364, 375, 389
Freudenheim, Milt, 456
Freyman, Russ, 562
Friedland, Jonathan, 144
Frisby, Michael K., 570
Frontier Pure cigarettes, 71
Frost, Martin, 589
FSC Repeal and Extraterritorial Income Exclusion Act of 2000 (Public Law 106-519), 612
Fucini, Suzy, 457
Fuller, Craig R., 542
Full-Flavor cigarettes, 76
Fumarillo cigarettes, 70
Fushion cigarettes, packaging, 28
Fuyuno, Ichiko, 94

Gallaher Group: magazine (Silk Cut), 151; packaging, 28; promotions, 133, 150, 177, 229; sports sponsorship, 297
Gallant, Karl, 565
Gasior, Rebecca J., 215
Gauloises cigarettes, duty-free, 326
gays and lesbians, 116, 216, 247

General Accounting Office. *See* U.S. General Accounting Office (GAO)
Genre magazine, 116, 216
Georgia, 746
Germany, 19, 150, 160, 199, 385, 477, 489, 613
Gersten, David M., 642
Gilmore, A. B., 444–46
Gingrich, Newt, 673, 680, 711
Glamour, 174, 188, 751
Glanton, Dahleen, 757
Glantz, Stanton A., 200–2, 205, 232, 501, 503, 505, 507–9, 511, 516–17, 557, 559–60, 616, 630
Glass, Chris, 158, 164, 252, 276, 448, 462
GlaxoSmithKline, 303
Globe cigarettes, 436
Glogan, Tim, 20
Gober, Hershel, 686
Gold Coast cigarettes, 46
Golden American cigarettes, 46
Golden, Daniel, 258
Golden State Tobacco Securitization Corporation, 766
Goldstein, Carl, 106
Goldstone, Steven F., 705
Goodlad, John I., 249
Gore, Al, Jr., 569, 589, 606, 725
GPC cigarettes, 134
GQ, 208
Graham, Bradley, 419
Graham, Robert, 334–35
Great Britain, 308, 371, 385; cigarettes, duty-free, 314
Great Wall cigarettes, packaging, 17
Greece, 405
Green, Mark, 597
Greenblatt, Alan, 591, 716
Greenhouse, Linda, 638
Griffiths, John, 278, 284
Groves, Martha, 614
Guevara, Che, 30
Günther, Ernst, 388

Habitrol, 207
Hachette Filipacchi, 146, 179
Haladjian, H. H., 496
Hall, Kerry, 619
Hanaggi, Michael, 370
Hanson, Gayle M. B., 241
Hardin, Peter, 598, 604

Harley-Davidson cigarettes, 58
Harley-Davidson Company, 58
Harman, Alan, 337
Harris, John F., 718
Harris, Ken, 466
Harshbarger, Scott, 588
Harvard Medical School, 258
Harvard University, 632
Harverson, Patrick, 278
Harwood, John, 589, 707
Hatch, Orrin, 673
Häusel, Hans-Georg, Dr., 218
Hays, Constance L., 178
Hazan, Anna R., 559
HB cigarettes: HB907, 63; packaging, 3; slogans and themes, 63
HCFA. *See* Health Care Financing Administration (HCFA)
Headden, Susan, 162
Healey, James C., 547
Health Canada, 21
Health Care Financing Administration (HCFA), 685, 688, 691
Hearn, Wayne, 263
Hearst Publishing, 179
Heatherton, Todd F., 191
Heathrow Airport, 204
Heineken (company), 34
Helms, Jesse, 247, 564
Hendrix, Sam, 459
Henley, Patricia, 636, 646, 656, 658
Henley v. Philip Morris, 636, 646, 656, 658
Herbert, Bob, 567
Herman, Dick, 61
Hewitt, Patricia, 406
Hilts, Philip J., 572
Hirschhorn, Norbert, 267
Hitpold, Irene, 15
Hobart, Robin, 582
Hoel, John, 630
Holiday cigarettes, 72
Holland, 160
Hollings, Ernest, 706
Hollós, Mihály, 238
Hollywood cigarettes, slogans and themes, 64, 171
Hong Kong, 372, 426–27
Horan, J. K., 24
Horne, Barbara, 4, 59, 60
Horovitz, Bruce, 110
Horrigan, Edward A., 551

House of Prince, cigarettes, duty-free, 323
Hulse, Carl, 629
Hundley, Lars, 61
Hungary, 121, 238, 253
Hunter, A., 301
Hurricane Floyd, 607
Hürriyet newspaper, 394
Hurt, Richard D., 309
Husic, Sead, 386
Hwang, Suein L., 80, 155, 163, 377, 437, 634, 661, 668, 679

Icebox cigarettes, 67; packaging, 5
Icon magazine, 133
ICON Research and Consulting, 10
Idaho, 140
IEG, Inc., 296
Illinois, 785
Illinois Department of Corrections, 447
Illinois Supreme Court, 645
Imasco, 400
Imperial Tobacco Canada, Ltd., 74; arts sponsorship, 236, 240, 244, 286; cigarettes, duty-free, 311; cigarettes, smuggling, 400; marketing, database, 194; promotions, 219; *Real Edge* magazine, 190; "smokers' lounges," 194; sports sponsorship, 286
Imperial Tobacco Group, United Kingdom: cigarettes, duty-free, 321–22, 325; Formula One, 321; packaging, 28; promotions, 151, 220, 228; sports sponsorship, 293; trademarks, 535
India, 275, 282, 439
Indian Tobacco Company (ITC), India, 55; sports sponsorship, 275
Indonesia, 426, 535
Indy League Racing (IRL), 271–73, 295
Ingersoll, Bruce, 580
INTAR Hispanic American Arts Center, 235
Internal Revenue Service Restructuring and Reform Act of 1998 (Public Law 105-206), 600
International Republican Institute, 542
Internet cigarette sales, 136, 493–94, 498, 620; slipcases, 30
investments, tobacco, state pension funds, 608
Iran, 387, 402
Iranian Revolution (1979), 43
Iranian Tobacco Organization, 43
Iraq, 390, 392, 402, 623

Istook, Ernest, Jr., 578, 585
Italy, 36, 334–35, 341, 348, 362, 379, 385
Ives, Nat, 97

Jacobs, Paul, 502
Jagt, Guy Vander, 553
Jalonick, Mary Clare, 622, 625
The Journal of the American Medical Association (JAMA), 602
James, Joni, 744
Janofsky, Michael, 524, 546
Japan, 1, 34, 424, 426
Japan Tobacco, Inc., 40, 71, 94, 333; arts sponsorship, 103; advertising, bans and restrictions, 534; Iraq, 390
Japan Tobacco International, 442, 472; cigarettes, counterfeit, 405; cigarettes, duty-free, 20; cigarettes, supermarket, 472; "smoking lounge," 230; Turkey, 442
Jenkins Act (1949), 494
Jenkins, Bill, 628
Jet magazine, 215, 652
Jing, Zou, 353
Joffrey Ballet, 232
John, Glenn A., 333
Johns Hopkins University, 632
Johnson, Danny R., 233
Johnson, Lyndon B., 54
Johnson, Robert, 234
Johnston, Donald S., 551
Johnston, James W., 38, 551
Jones, Neal T., Jr., 545
Joossens, Luk, 352, 374
Jordan, Jerie, 232, 582
Jordan, Vernon, Jr., 547
Jowers, Karen, 417
Joy, Robin, 316
JTI-Macdonald Corporation, 410
"jump boys," 427

Kahnawake Indian Reserve, 330, 336, 343
Kanesatake, Mohawks of, 343
Kantor, Mickey, 543
Kaplan, Andrew, 55
Karp, Jonathan, 275
Kasich, John R., 711
Kaufman, Marc, 612, 615, 626, 651, 761
Keenan, Faith, 274
Keener, Mary Lou, 580
Kelly, Keith J., 146
Kempster, Norman, 684

Kennedy, Edward M., 673, 694
Kennedy, John F., 54
Kent cigarettes: packaging, 1; promotions, 204
Kentucky, 746
Kenyon, Floyd, 644
Kerwin, Ann Marie, 579
Kessler, David A., 618
Kessler, Gladys, 648, 651, 653–55, 659
Kevin Berg and Associates, 126
"kiddie packs," 72
Kiley, David, 101
Kimelman, John, 52
King, Charles, III, 760
King Maker Marketing, 55, 470
Kirk, Don, 440
Kish Island, 387
Kizer, Kenneth W., 499
Kleinman, Mark, 204, 210, 297, 299, 303, 306
Kling, Folker, 489
Kluger, Richard, 573
K-Mart, 475
Knight, Patrick, 359
"knockoffs." *See* cigarettes, counterfeit
Koeppel, Dan, 40
Koerner, Brendan I., 67
Koerner, Manfred, 331
Kondro, Wayne, 342
Konrad, Walecia, 112
Kool cigarettes: African Americans, marketing toward, 226; hip-hop, 195, 222, 785; packaging, 14, 25; promotions, 104, 111, 187; slogans and themes, 25, 111, 156, 187; "Smooth Fusions," 97, 222
Korea, South, 282, 426, 441, 617
Korea Tobacco & Ginseng Corporation, World Cup, 203
Korea Tomorrow & Global Corporation, 537; China, 443; Turkey, 442–43
Kostmeyer, Peter, 521
KPMG Peat Marwick Thorne, 330
Kraft Foods, 256; arts sponsorship, 237; philanthropy, 252, 254–55; political contributions, 570, 590
kretek cigarettes, smuggling, 345
Kroger's supermarket, 466, 475
KT&G. *See* Korea Tomorrow & Global Corporation
Kucharsky, Danny, 190
Kuczynski, Alex, 179, 759
Kurtz, Howard, 725

L&M cigarettes, 46, 59, 77, 79; slogans and themes, 143
Labous, Jane, 320
LA Convention 2000, 611
Ladies' Home Journal, 193
L'Aimable, Guy, 341
Lakson Tobacco (India), 203
L.A. Link, 287
Lamb, David, 436
Lambert & Butler cigarettes, duty-free, 325
Lankenau, Stephen E., 449
Largent, Steve, 567
Lark cigarettes, 77, 79; slogans and themes, 424
Lassus Handy Dandy Food Stores, 469
Latin America, 381
Latina magazine, 174
Latino Americans, 174, 232
Latvia, 444
Lavack, Anne M., 304
Lawson Mardon Packaging Flexibles, 11
Lawton Chiles Tobacco Endowment for Children and Elders, 744
Lawton, Christopher, 203
LBL Importing, 376
Leach, James, 577
"leaners." *See* "cigarette girls"
Lebanon, 402
LeBow, Bennett S., 660, 668, 733
Lee, Louise, 475
Legal cigarettes, promotions, 214, 217
Lehrman, Sally, 509
Leo, John, 152
Leonard, Robert J., 548
Leovy, Jill, 467
Lerner, Sharon, 251
Leslie, Tim, 519
Letcher, T., 26
Leung, Shirley, 745
Levy, Adam, 733
Levin, Mike, 237
Levin, Myron, 391, 396–97, 405, 423, 514, 532, 566, 584, 587, 656, 702, 770, 779
Levy, Adam, 733
Lewis, Harold, 692
Lewis, Jay, 22
Lewis, Michael T., 668, 733
Lewis, Neil A., 694
Liberal Party, Canada, 342
License Revoked, 425
Lichtblau, Eric, 653

Liebengood, Horace, 569
Liggett Group, 77, 79, 733; appeal-bond caps, 746–47; congressional testimony, 551; litigation, tobacco, 639, 655, 660; Master Settlement Agreement (MSA) (1998), 729, 731
Lima, Julie C., 743
limbic branding, 218
Linder, John, 711
Lindquist, Avey, Macdonald, Baskerville, 346, 351
Ling, Pamela M., 200, 202, 205
Link, Emily, 12, 28, 82, 90
Lipman, Joanne, 116
Lipsith, Gavin, 319, 328, 490
Lithuania, 444
litigation, tobacco, 163, 363, 376, 380, 384, 392, 409, 640; attorneys' fees, 663; *Broin* case, 634; California, 643, 647, 753, 779; *Castano* case, 633; *Empire* (*Blue Cross*) case, 657; *Engle* case, 639, 642, 650; *FDA v. B&W*, 638; *Henley* case, 636, 646, 656, 658; Kenyon, Floyd, 644; Mississippi, 662, 667; *Price* case, 641, 645, 768; Texas, 782; *U.S.A. (DOJ)* case, 635, 637, 648–49, 651, 653–54, 655, 659. *See also* tobacco Settlement; Master Settlement Agreement
"Little Tobacco," 91, 478, 756, 778; Tobacco Settlement, Proposed (1997), 702
Liu, Betty W., 741
Liu Wenbo, 355
lobbyists, 675, 702, 709, 716
Lockyer, Bill, 749, 753, 762
Loews Corporation, 655, 783
Lofstock, John, 491
Logan, Rob, 257
Lolita cigarettes, 62
LoPucki, Lynn, 701
Lorillard Tobacco, 35, 250, 746; appeal-bond caps, 746–47; congressional testimony, 51; federal regulation, 625; Harley-Davidson, 58; litigation, tobacco, 639, 643, 652, 655; Master Settlement Agreement (MSA) (1998), 729, 731, 759, 783; National Basketball Association (NBA), 619; political contributions, 569; prisons and jails, 450; sports sponsorship, 296; Tobacco Settlement, Florida (1997), 676; Tobacco Settlement, Minnesota (1998), 714; Tobacco Settlement, Mississippi (1997), 667; Tobacco Settlement, Proposed (1997), 664, 666, 683, 733; Tobacco Settlement, Texas (1998), 696
Los Angeles County, 504
Lott, Trent, 673, 680, 724
Louisiana, 741, 768
Love, Barbara, 451
Lovells law firm, 654, 659
Lucia cigarettes, 94
Lucky Strike cigarettes, 294, 490; duty-free, 319; Formula One, 309; international markets, emerging, 420; movies, 191; packaging, 28, 34; promotions, 121, 148, 167, 184, 187, 196, 199, 473; slogans and themes, 52, 184, 196

Macdonald, Heather R., 508, 511
M cigarettes, slogans and themes, 87
magazines, 86, 133, 146, 151, 178–79, 190, 196, 198, 204, 222, 559, 760
Magna cigarettes, 107
Magzamen, Sheryl, 517
Maine, Tobacco Settlement, Proposed (1997), 710
Malaysia, 121, 282, 329, 345, 371, 424, 426–27
Malone, Ruth E., 216, 225, 621, 632
Manatt, Phelps, Phillips, and Kantor, 543
Mandel-Campbell, Andrea, 68
Mandela, Nelson, 101
Mantel, Nathan, 602
Mapes, Timothy, 535
"Marble" cigarettes, 531
Marcus, Ruth, 590, 717
Margulis, Ronald A., 50, 53, 62, 458, 470
Marino, Jon, 780
Market Promotion Program (USDA), 521, 523
Market Tracking International, Ltd., 361
marketing, database, 108, 112, 124, 127, 193–94
Marketing Hall of Fame, 141
Marlboro cigarettes, 94, 118, 247, 467, 490, 760, 783; "72," 95, 123; advertising: television, 295; "Camp Marlboro," Baghdad, 623; China, 438; counterfeit, 396, 531; duty-free, 7; smuggling, 375; "Friday," 45, 47, 50–51, 53, 123, 458; Hall of Fame, 141; Lights, 641; limbic branding, 218; "Man," 48, 154, 427, 429, 661, 664, 739; Mediums, 48, 110, 112; Milds, 80, 181; military, 414; movies, 191, 201; packaging, 7; promotions,

104, 113, 121, 130–32, 137, 140, 152, 163, 165, 199, 206; slogans and themes, 39, 48, 110, 182, 427; special editions, 20; "Thursday," 209; Ultra Lights, 163
Marlboro Friday (April 2, 1993), 45, 47, 50–51, 53, 123, 458
Marlboro Man, 48, 154, 427, 429, 661, 664, 739
"Marlboro Thursday," 209
Mars company, 521
Mars cigarettes, 433
Marsh, Ann, 140
Marsh, Harriet, 167
Marshall, Eliot, 539, 560, 700
Martha Graham Dance Company, 241
Martial, Luc R., 350
Martin, Michele, 133
Martz, Michael, 571
Maryland, 785
Marymount Manhattan College, 597
Massachusetts Suffolk Superior Court, 652
Master Settlement Agreement (MSA) (1998), 91, 170, 176, 193, 226, 295, 377, 398, 485, 487, 495, 518, 615, 636, 728–30, 765, 769, 782; advertising, bans and restrictions, 759–60, American Legacy Foundation, 776, 780; appeal-bond caps, 768, 784; attorneys' fees, 731, 754, bars and clubs, 742; California, 738, 745, 749, 753, 770; Clinton, Bill, 736; "fourth-tier" manufacturers, 209, 771; GAO reports, 758, 767, 781; marketing, restrictions on, 785; media coverage, 773; movies, 783; nonparticipating manufacturers, 756, 771, 778; original participating manufacturers, 771; Phase II, 737, 764; Public Law 106-31, 740; securitization, 754, 763, 766, 770, 777; sports sponsorship, 742; state expenditures, 735–36, 741, 757–58, 767, 772–73, 775; state revenues, 761; teenage smoking, 750–51; television, 783; Tobacco Fee Arbitration Panel, 755; youth marketing restrictions, 762, 774
Matinee cigarettes, 240; Ultra Mild, 194
The Matrix, 212
Maxim magazine, 306
McCain, John, 694, 707, 709, 711–12, 716–18, 721, 723–24
McCain tobacco bill (S. 1415). *See* Tobacco Settlement, Proposed (1997)

McCarthy, Michael J., 104
McCollister, Tom, 272
McConnell, Mitch, 622
McCurry, Michael, 673
McDonald's, 521
McGillion, Alice T., 247
McGinley, Laurie, 563, 580
McGraw, Dan, 663
McIvor, Greg, 367
McKay, Michael A., 398
McKee, M., 444–46
McKinley, Andrew, 772
McMillan, J. Alex, 702
Mediamark Research, 750
Medical Care Recovery Act, 635
Medical Research Council, 265
Mehegan, Sean, 5, 14, 147
Meier, Barry, 81, 183, 285, 636, 666–67, 676, 693, 696, 722, 732, 735, 746
Mekemson, C., 201
Menard State Prison, Illinois, 447
Menn, Joseph, 733
menthol cigarettes, 80, 83, 86, 95
Mercer cigarettes, 74
Merit cigarettes: bowling tour, 742; fire-safe, 81, 189, 649; DeNic, 41; slogans and themes, 189
Merlo, Ellen, 131, 174
Mersin Port Free Zone, 394
Mesquita, Lućio, 314
Michigan Department of Corrections, 447
microsmoke cigarettes, 5, 61, 67
Middle East, 433
Midnight Madness cigarettes, slogans and themes, 93
Mild Seven cigarettes: Prime Super Lights, 94; slogans and themes, 40, 94
military, 231; exchanges, 414; commissaries, 414, 416–19; Iraq, 623; United States, 742
Miller Brewing, 247; philanthropy, 249, 255
Millman, Nancy, 555
Min-hee, Kim, 443
Ministry of Sound, 167
Minnesota, 701
Minnesota Coalition of Responsible Retailers, 583
Mintz, John, 578, 673
Mitchell, George, 675
Modisett, Jeffrey A., 691
Moffett, Matt, 529

Molecular Sciences Institute, 261
Molins (company), 23
Moll, Kenneth, 703
Mollenkamp, Carrick, 733
Mona Lisa Smile, 783
money laundering, 389, 392
monopolies, tobacco, 531
Monte Carlo cigarettes, 59, 405
Montenegro, 386
Montreal International Jazz Festival, 286
Montreal La Press newspaper, 219
Moonlight Tobacco Company, 5, 61, 67
Moore, Michael C., 662, 667, 688, 695, 733
Moore, Molly, 411
Moore, Pamela, 54
Morain, Dan, 514, 518
Morales, Dan, 663, 699
More cigarettes, direct sales, 180
Morgan Stanley, 630
Morley, C., 24
Morocco, 282
Morris, Dick, 668
Morrissey, Matthew, 542
Moser, Tom, 283
Motluk, Alison, 264
movies, 201, 425
Moyers, Bill, 389
Mozar, Harold N., 499
Mrlilli, Denise, 280
MS cigarettes, Mundial, 36
Mufson, Steven, 431
Muggli, Monique E., 309
Murphy, David, 157
Murray, Barbra, 73
Murray, Keith B., 232
Murray, R. William, 261
Museum of Modern Art, 241
Myerson, Allen R., 45, 124, 243

Nagourney, Adam, 597
Nasar, Sylvia, 731
NASCAR. *See* National Association of Stock Car Auto Racing (NASCAR)
Nash, Nathaniel C., 526
The Nation, 389
National 4-H Council, 605
National AIDS Fund, 254
National Archives and Records Administration, 100
National Association for the Advancement of Colored People (NAACP), 248

National Association of Stock Car Auto Racing (NASCAR), 164, 271–73, 276–77, 281, 289, 302, 728
National Basketball Association (NBA), 619
National Black Farmers Association, 674
National Cancer Institute (NCI), 557, 560, 578, 585
National Center for Tobacco-Free Kids, 675
National Conference of State Legislatures, 772
National Council of La Raza, 248
National Governors Association, 581
National Hot Rod Association (NHRA), 270–73, 728
National Institutes of Health (NIH), 560, 700
National Interagency Council on Smoking and Health, 207
National Meals-on-Wheels Foundation, 254
National Press Club, 705
National Republican Congressional Committee, 599
National Republican Senatorial Committee, 599
National Restaurant Association, 709
National Smokers Alliance (NSA), 513, 553, 565, 583, 587, 717
National Tobacco Grower Settlement Trust (Phase II), 737, 764
National Tobacco Policy and Youth Smoking Reduction Act (S. 1415), 716, 721
National Urban League, 248
National Women's Political Caucus, 540–41
Native Americans, 357, 454; Internet cigarette sales, 498; tobacco retail outlets, 609; Tobacco Settlement, Proposed (1997), 704
Navarro, Mireya, 682
Navy Exchange Service Command (NEXCOM), 415
Neergaard, Lauran, 672
Nelson, Mullins, Riley & Scarborough, 543
Nepal, 439
Nesbitt, Jeffrey, 668
Netherlands, 492
Neubauer, Bernd, 16
Nevada, 768
Nevada State Demographic Party, 568
New England Journal of Medicine, 260
New Jersey, 784
Newport cigarettes, 35; prisons and jails, 450; promotions, 152, 652
Newsweek, 185; school edition, 774
Newton, Jon, 336

New West cigarettes, slogans and themes, 49
New York City, 235
New York Society for International Affairs, 581
New York State, 704, 741, 785; cigarettes, fire-safe, 627; Internet cigarette sales, 483, 486, 493
New York State Court of Appeals, 657
New York State Tobacco Settlement Financing Corporation, 777
New Zealand, 520
Next DeNic cigarettes, 41
NHRA. *See* National Hot Rod Association
Nicholson, Marjorie, 349
Nichter, M., 773
Nicklin, Julie L., 249
Nicoderm, 287
Nicorette, 207, 287
nicotine, 265, 618; lozenges, 84; replacement therapies, 207, 287, 303
Niemeyer, Dearell, 499
1999 Emergency Supplemental Appropriations Act (Public Law 106-31), 740
NiQuitin, 303
Noah, Timothy, 563
Nobleza Picardo SA, 144
North Carolina, 746–47
North Dakota, 741
Northern Brands, 376
Northern Lights cigarettes, 447
Norton, Gale A., 615
Novak, Viveca, 544
Now cigarettes, direct sales, 180
NOW with Bill Moyers television program, 389

Ocean's Eleven, 212
O'Connell, Vanessa, 214, 217, 450, 627, 649–50, 654, 768, 783–84
Ogilvy & Mather, 101
Oklahoma, 704, 768
Oldaker, William C., 548
Omaha Indians, 76
Omni cigarettes, 88
Omnibus Budget Reconciliation Act of 1993 (Public Law 103-66), 523
100 Black Men of America, 195
OneWorld magazine, 196, 222
Ono, Yumiko, 473
On-Premise Marketing, 166
Operation Desert Shield, 411
Oregon, 784; Tobacco Settlement, Proposed (1997), 710

organized crime, 351, 358, 362, 368, 371, 378–79, 385, 398
Overlooked Opinions, 116
Owens Corning, 670
Owens-Illinois, 670
Oxford University, 264

packaging, 4, 6, 10, 13, 15–16, 24, 34; art, 17, 33; brand coloring, 32; Canada, 18, 21, 351; China, 17, 33; cigarettes, counterfeits, 22; clam-shell, 317; European Union, 27, 32; Evo Flask, 28; facsimile, 7; FlavorSeal, 2; health warnings, 4, 18, 21, 23, 27, 30, 31; hinge-lid, 1, 3, 8, 12, 28; overwrapping, 7, 11; PaperSelect, 649; side-slide, 12; slide-box, 28; slide-pack, 317; slipcases, 30; soft packs, 8; special editions, 19, 20, 26, 29; 25 pack, 46. *See also* individual brand names and individual company names
Paersch, Emily, 31, 96, 399
Pakistan, 203, 275, 332, 366, 439
Pall Mall cigarettes, 52; Export, 158; Lights, 158; promotions, 192, 193, 197; slogans and themes, 192
Panda cigarettes, 98
Paraguay, 371, 407
Paramount Pictures, 783
Paris Opera Ballet, 234
Parker-Pope, Tara, 145, 531, 719
Parliament cigarettes, promotions, 143
Patriot Act, United States, 389
Patriot cigarettes, 756
Patriot Tobacco, 756
Peltz, James F., 770
Pennsylvania, 784
Penteado, Claudia, 64
People magazine, 751, 759
People Weekly magazine, 215
People's Princess Charitable Foundation, 242
Perlez, Jane, 433
Perrone, Vinnie, 277
Perry, Tony, 237
Peter Stuyvesant cigarettes: packaging, 16; promotions, 220
pharmacies, 456, 476
Philadelphia, 35
philanthropic sponsorships, 247–56
Philip Morris & Company, 39, 41, 48, 50, 59, 77–80, 95, 99, 118, 154, 183, 270, 347, 543–44, 573, 577; Accommodation Program, 225; advertising, 125, 132, 225;

African Americans, marketing toward, 233; *American Smokers Journal* magazine, 559; arts sponsorships, 130, 231, 233–35, 237, 241–42; ASSIST, 598, 616; bans and restrictions, smoking, 526–27, 534; Bill of Rights Centennial celebration, 100–1; brand stretching, 105–6, 139, 142, 160, 162; California, 502, 553, Proposition 188, 508, 511, 553; CART, 280; China, 432, 438; cigarette displays and racks, 452, 467, 496; cigarette pricing, 45, 47, 51; cigarettes, counterfeit, 393, 396, 531; cigarettes, discount, 45, 47, 56; cigarettes, duty-free, 7, 312–33; cigarettes, fire-safe, 81, 189, 649; cigarettes, smuggling, 334–35, 363, 375, 384, 386, 395, 400–1; congressional testimony, 551; "Creative Solutions," 225; Czech Republic, 533; distribution system, 484; divestment, 632; economic impact study, 533; family branding, 128; federal regulation, 625; Formula One, 282, 285; gays and lesbians, marketing toward, 116, 216; India, 439; international markets, 522; international markets, emerging, 420, 423–28, 430–31, 433; Internet cigarettes sales, 136; legislation, federal, 524; litigation, tobacco, 636, 639, 641, 645–46, 655–58; lobbying, 620; lobbyists for, 548; marketing, database, 108, 112; marketing, research, 202; Master Settlement Agreement (MSA), 1998, 729, 731, 737, 742, 750–51, 759, 774, 783; military, 231, 411, 414, 417; movies, 201, 425; National Smokers Alliance (NSA), 553, 565, 583, 587, 717; nicotine replacement therapies, 207; packaging, 7, 12, 15, 46, 87, 313; partnership programs, 453; philanthropy, 199, 247, 249, 251–52, 254–56, 607; *Philip Morris Magazine*, 559; political contributions, 540–42, 563, 565, 568–71, 576, 581, 590, 592, 594, 597, 611, 615, 620; price-fixing, 532; price increases, 715, 731; promotions, 110, 113, 119–20, 123–24, 128, 137–40, 145, 147, 162, 165, 168, 182, 199, 206, 209, 214, 665; public relations, 256, 607, 621, 693; research sponsorship, 257, 261, 267; Retail Leaders program, 480, 485, 488; retail stores, 485, 496; Retailers Masters program, 113, 119, 147, 465, 471; Russia, 429, 435, 444; schools, donation to, 614; *Smoker's Rights Alliance* magazine, 559; Soviet Union, 421, 431; special editions, 20, 42; sports sponsorship, 103, 106, 143, 269, 271–72, 274, 292, 296, 471, 728; Tobacco Settlement, Florida (1997), 676; Tobacco Settlement, Minnesota (1998), 714, 719; Tobacco Settlement, Mississippi (1997), 667; Tobacco Settlement, Proposed (1997), 630, 661, 664, 666, 683, 733; Tobacco Settlement, Texas (1998), 696; Turkey, 437, 442; *Unlimited* magazine, 146, 178–79; Vietnam, 436; Wholesale Leaders program, 495; Wholesale Masters program, 53, 455, 463; Woman Thing Music, 239; youth smoking prevention programs, 462, 605, 621. *See also* Benson & Hedges cigarettes; Marlboro cigarettes; Merit cigarettes; Parliament cigarettes; tobacco industry

Philip Morris International, 71, 94; China, 441; cigarettes, duty-free, 328; cigarettes, smuggling, 401, 409; Formula One, 328; international markets, emerging, 441; Korea, South, 441; promotions, 150; Russia, 441

Philip Morris Magazine, 559
Philippines, 121, 427–28
Phillips, Michael M., 679
The Phoenecian, 575
Pierre, Robert E., 763
Pillsbury, 521
Pincus, Walter, 574
Pittman, Rhashad, 643
Planet cigarettes, 67; packaging, 5
Playboy, 193
Player's Navy Cut cigarettes, 141
Poetschke-Langer, Martina, 199
Poland, 143, 403, 433
political action committees (PACs), 599, 601
political contributions: AMA, 549; California, 500, 505, 507, 545
Pollack, Judann, 146, 149, 154, 159, 170, 172–74, 180
Polo cigarettes, slogans and themes, 85
Pool, Jessica Johns, 469
Pope Air Force Base, North Carolina, 411
Popper, Edward, 232
Porter, Eduardo, 498
Porter, John, 557, 560, 700
Power, Christopher, 112
Powerful Lion cigarettes, packaging, 17
Prager, Ronald S., 762

Prague, 256
preemption, 511, 514, 516–17, 545, 553, 562, 582–83
Preska, Loretta A., 486
Price, Charles, 500
Price v. Philip Morris, 641, 645, 768
price support programs, tobacco, 556, 569, 596, 622, 626, 628–29, 631
Price Waterhouse, 546, 554
Pringle, Peter, 701, 734
Prison Life magazine, 450
prisons and jails, 449; California, 519; federal, 450; Florida, 448; New York City, 447; Oregon, 447; Vermont, 450
Pristin, Terry, 486
Pritchard, Chris, 72, 181, 434
Pro Billiards Tour Association, 291
Procordia AB, 207
Progress and Freedom Foundation, 563
Prohibition News Update newsletter, 513
"Project Blue" campaign, 725
PROMA Technologies, 213
Promotional Marketing, Inc., 37
Proposition 99, California, 499, 500, 505–6, 509, 512, 514, 516
Proposition 188, California, 508, 511, 514, 517, 562
Pryce, Deborah, 590
psychology, depth, 152
Public Laws: PL 103-66, 523; PL 103-111, 525; PL 105-33, 671; PL 105-34, 671, 673, 680, 690; PL 105-78, 690; PL 105-119, 530, 531; PL 105-178, 595, 600, 603; PL 105-206, 600; PL 106-31, 740; PL 106-519, 612; PL 107-56, 389; PL 108-357, 631
Pyramid cigarettes, 447
Pytte, Alyson, 538

quota, tobacco, 596, 626, 629, 631
Quebec Health Department, 219
Quest cigarettes, 90

Racketeer Influenced and Corrupt Organizations (RICO), 648, 651, 655
Raffaelli, John D., 675
Ramhurst Corporation, 565
Ramirez, Anthony, 39, 247, 421
Rangel, Charles B., 561
Rashid, Ahmed, 275
Rayburn, Kelly, 655, 659
Raw, Martin, 352, 374

Real Edge magazine, 178–79, 190
Redhead, C. Stephen, 726
Red Kamel cigarettes, slogans and themes, 67
Reemtsma Cigarettenfabriken, 49, 85, 535; Formula One, 298; international markets, emerging, 420; packaging, 9, 19; promotions, 120, 199
Regal cigarettes, sports sponsorship, 293
Rembrandt Group, Ltd., 363
Rendezvous magazine, 151
Republican National Committee, 599, 680
Republican National Convention, 237, 542, 570, 611
Republican Party, 571
research sponsorships, 257–68
The Resistance newsletter, 513
retailers, 214, 461, 463–65, 480, 487; California, 515; cigarette displays and racks, 451, 452, 469, 473, 475, 481, 495–96; cigarettes, counterfeit, 393, 396; distribution system, 470, 484; Internet cigarette sales, 494; Kenya, 434; pharmacies, 456; promotions, 485; "store-within-a-store," 475; tobacco specialty stores, 459; youth smoking prevention programs, 462
Revenue Quebec, 410
Reynolds cigarettes, packaging, 28
Reynolds France, packaging, 46
Ribisi, K. M., 496, 515
Rice, Mary, 265
Richards, Anne, 545
Richards, John W., Jr., 139
Richardson, Sally K., 685
Rigby, Leslie, 364, 476
Riley, Richard W., 543
R. J. Reynolds International, 59; brand stretching, 162; Iraq, 390
R. J. Reynolds Tobacco Company, 35, 37, 38, 42, 43, 54, 60, 71, 83, 89, 92–93, 153–54, 213, 221, 459, 470, 550, 564, 573; advertising, empathy, 168; African Americans, marketing toward, 215; appeal-bond caps, 746, 747; arts sponsorship, 217, 243; brand stretching, 105, 142, 160; China, 432; cigarette displays and racks, 451, 495–96; cigarettes, duty-free, 315; cigarettes, smuggling, 370, 380, 384, 386, 387, 391–92, 395; cigarettes, supermarket, 472; *Choice* magazine, 559; *CML* magazine, 178–79; congressional testimony, 551; direct sales, 180; Everyday Low Pricing

program, 485; federal regulation, 629; Goldstone, Stephen F., 705; international markets, emerging, 420, 423–26, 428, 430–31; Internet cigarettes sales, 136; Kenya, 69, 434; legislation, federal, 524; litigation, tobacco, 639, 643–44, 647, 655, 779; lobbyists for, 548; marketing, database, 108, 112, 124, 127; marketing, research, 202; marketing, trend influence, 126, 200; Master Settlement Agreement (MSA) (1998), 729, 731, 737, 742, 750, 753, 759, 762, 774, 779, 783; military, 411–13, 415; "No Bull," 86, 155, 164, 168, 186, 302; packaging, 2, 12, 28; partnership programs, 453, 461; Partners program, 464; philanthropy, 248, 250; political contributions, 540–42, 563, 565, 568–70, 590, 592; price increases, 715, 731; promotions, 107, 112, 115, 117, 122, 127, 129, 134–35, 138–39, 143–44, 149, 155, 159, 161, 172–73, 176, 183, 185, 198, 214, 224; Retail Partners program, 488; retail stores, 485, 495–96; Russia, 429, 435, 444; Soviet Union, 421–22, 431; sports sponsorship, 106, 109, 147, 164, 270–73, 291, 296; testimonials, 555; Tobacco Settlement, Florida (1997), 676; Tobacco Settlement, Minnesota (1998), 714, 719; Tobacco Settlement, Mississippi (1997), 667; Tobacco Settlement, Proposed (1997), 661, 664, 666, 683, 733; Tobacco Settlement, Texas (1998), 696; trade-loading, 50; Vietnam, 436; Winston Cup, 66, 147, 271–72, 276–77, 281, 289, 295, 302, 728; World Brands International, 142; youth smoking prevention program, 605. *See also* Camel cigarettes; Doral cigarettes; Winston cigarettes; tobacco industry

RJR-Macdonald, Canada, 391

RJR Nabisco. *See* R. J. Reynolds Tobacco Company

Road & Track magazine, 135

Robb, Charles S., 571

Robbins, Carla Anne, 531

Robert, Diane, 61

Robinson, Robert G., 232

Rodriguez, Noelia, 611

Rogers, Danny, 283, 290

Rogers, Will, 102

Roig-Franzia, Manuel, 642

Rolling Stone magazine, 222, 750–51, 759, 762

Romania, 431

Rommel, Christian, 17, 29, 33

Ronderos, Maria Teresa, 381-82

Rose, Charlie, 524

Rosenberg, N. Jennifer, 296

Rosenberg, Stan, 766, 777

Rosenblatt, Stanley M., 752

Rosenfield, James R., 108, 169, 196

Ross, Chuck, 148

Rossel, Stefanie, 19, 298

Rossetti, Stephen, Jr., 419

Rostenkowski, Dan, 547

Rothfeder, Jeffrey, 733

Rothmans, Benson, & Hedges: arts sponsorship, 245; cigarettes, smuggling, 401; sports sponsorship, 288

Rothmans cigarettes, Lights, 114

Rothmans Foundation Education Division, 259

Rothmans International: brand stretching, 142; cigarettes, smuggling, 401; Formula One, 282, 303; *Icon* magazine, 133; packaging, 11, 46, 72; promotions, 158, 210, 212; *Rendezvous* magazine, 151; sports sponsorship, 278

Rowe, Stephen, 226

Royal Canadian Mounted Police, 337, 344

Royal cigarettes, promotions, 210

Royal Commonwealth Society Library, 264

Rubel, Chad, 56

Rubin, Alissa J., 635

Rubin, Robert E., 673

Rum Menthol cigarettes, 94

Rupert, James, 431

Russell Group, 264

Russia, 54, 62, 75, 143, 167, 392, 403, 429–30, 435, 441, 444–46, 522

Russian Orthodox Church, duty-free cigarettes, 318

Rutkowski, Liane, 27

Rutter, Terri, 260

Ryan, Kerwin, 311, 338

Ryan, Thomas M., 548

S&M Bailey's cigarettes, 756

S&M Brands, 756, 778

Sabanci, Sakip, 437

Sack, Kevin, 662

sacoleiros bag carriers, 407

Safer Smokes Corp., 70, 73

Saigon Cigarette Factory, 436

Sainsbury supermarket, 472

Salam newspaper, 43
Salem cigarettes: Black Label, 92; Green Label, 92; packaging, 12; Pianissimo, 71; promotions, 173; slogans and themes, 12, 71, 92
Samuels, Bruce, 501
Sandefur, Thomas E., 551
San Diego Museum of Art, 237
Sandomir, Richard, 132
Sanger, David E., 564
Sanson-Fisher, Rob W., 259
Santa Clara County, California, 515
Santa Cruz do Sul, 529
Sarajevo Tobacco Factory, 339
Sargent, James D., 191
Saudi Arabia, 411–12
Saueressig GmbH & Co., 13
Schapiro, Mark, 389
Schelzig, Erik J., 381–82
Schiffman, James R., 35
Schlueter, Stan, 545
Schmitt, Eric, 416
Schoenmarklin, Susan, 582
schools, 614
Schuler, Kate, 622
Schunk, Susanne, 199
Schwartz, John, 77, 376, 512, 685, 688, 691, 714, 729–30
Schwarzenegger, Arnold, 519
Scruggs, Ricky, 620, 733
Seaman, Debbie, 105
Sea Princess ship, 370
secondhand smoke, 527, 602, 634
Second Harvest National Food Bank Network, 231, 254
securitization, 744, 754, 763, 766, 770, 777
Sega Enterprises, 104
Segal, David, 380, 480
Seneca Nation, 498
Sepe, Edward, 200
Sesser, Stan, 427
Shag cigarettes, slogans and themes, 96
Shag Tobacco Company, 96
Shamasunder, Bhavna, 207
Shanghai Tobacco, 98
Shapiro, Eben, 550
Sharfstein, Joshua M., 549, 601
Sharfstein, Steven S., 549
Shatenstein, Stan, 267
Shearer, Brent, 257
Sheehy, Patrick, Sir, 264–65

Shen, Fern, 413
Shenon, Philip, 428
Shirouzu, Norihiko, 71
Shop Rite, 469
Shuit, Douglas P., 287
Shuqi, Wei, 353
Siegel, Michael, 295–96, 582, 743, 760
Silk Cut, United Kingdom, packaging, 46
Silk Cut cigarettes: promotions, 145, 150, 177; slogans and themes, 177
Simmons Research, 750–51
Simple Living magazine, 179
Simpson, Glenn R., 568
Singapura United Trading, Ltd., 382
Siragusa, Gail, 41
Skolnick, Andrew, 447
slogans and themes, 11, 435; Benson & Hedges, 26, 665; Benson & Hedges 100mm, 125; Camel, 109, 129, 149, 159, 176; Camel Turkish Royal, 89; Capri, 188; Capri Superslims, 188; Carlton, 170, 196; Dakota, 37; Davidoff, 199; Death, 44, 67; Doral, 135, 198; Eclipse, 185; 555 Equinox, 317; HB907, 63; Hollywood, 64, 171; Kool, 25, 111, 156, 187; L&M, 143; Lark, 424; Lucky Strike, 52, 184, 196; M (Philip Morris), 87; Marlboro, 39, 427; Marlboro Mediums, 48, 110; Marlboro Milds, 182; Merit, 189; Midnight Madness, 93; Mild Seven, 40, 94; New West, 49; Pall Mall, 192; Polo, 85; Red Kamels, 67; Salem, 12; Salem Black Label, 92; Salem Green Label, 92; Salem Pianissimo, 71; Shag, 96; Silk Cut, 177; Virginia Slims, 141, 174, 239, 428, 752; Winfield, 26; Winston, 2, 118, 155, 164, 168, 173, 186, 428; Winston S2, 83; Winston Select, 118; Yava Gold, 75
Slovak Republic, 238, 468
Slovakia International Tabak, arts sponsorship, 238
Slovakia Tabak, arts sponsorship, 238
Smith, Craig, 356
Smith, Elizabeth A., 216, 225, 621
Smith, Jan, 759
SmithKline Beecham, 287
Smith, K. M. Clegg, 773
Smith's Food & Drug Centers, 127
Smithsonian Institution, 102
Smoker Friendly International, 491
Smoker's Rights Alliance magazine, 559
Smokewear company, 30

smoking cessation, 84, 207, 287, 303, 585
Smoking Cessation Newsletter, 207
Snook, Dennis W., 603
Sobieski cigarettes, 433
Solomon, Alisa, 235
Sony Pictures Entertainment, 783
Sosnowski, Tom, 13
South Africa, 329, 371, 522
South Florida State Hospital, 448
Southern Lights cigarettes, 447
Souza Cruz, 59, 64, 171
Soviet Union, 331, 421–22, 431, 433, 444. *See also* Russia
Spain, 160, 326, 369–70, 385, 395
Special Events Report, 109
Specialist Publishing, 151
Specter, Arlen, 700
Specter, Michael, 37
Spethmann, Betsy, 127
Spin magazine, 222
Spitzer, Eliot, 774
Spolar, Christine, 269
Sponsors Report, 295, 299
Sporting Events Report, 109
Sports Illustrated magazine, 104, 185, 750–51, 759, 762
Sportsman cigarettes, 69
Sports Marketing Enterprises, 270
sports sponsorship, 66, 103, 106, 109, 143, 147, 164, 236, 244, 269–310, 423, 425–26, 434, 694, 728, 742
Sri Lanka, 275
Srivastava, Ambika, 439
Stacchini, Alexis, 441
Stamler, Bernard, 193
Stamler, Rod, 351
Star cigarettes, packaging, 15
Star Scientific, Inc., 82, 84, 756
Star Tobacco Company, 57
Star Tobacco and Pharmaceuticals, 782
State Affairs Company, 571, 576
State Express 555 cigarettes: China, 432, 438; promotions, 167
state pension funds, investments, tobacco, 608
Statesman cigarettes, 472
Stecklow, Steve, 390
Stone, Peter H., 543, 545, 547–48, 553, 565, 670, 675
Stout, David, 637
Stowecraft Brook Distributors, 57
St. Regis Mohawk Indian Reservation, 376

Sudetic, Chuck, 339
Sullivan, Barbara, 58
Sullivan, Louis W., 35
Sumatra Tobacco Group, 535
Sumer cigarettes, 623
Sumner, Walton, II, 138
Sunbelt Video, 104
Sunday Times newspaper, United Kingdom, 522
Superkings cigarettes, 228
Supreme Court of Florida, 650
Surinam, 359
Sutton, Charyn, 232
Sweanor, David, 350
Sweden, 62, 367
Switzerland, 362
Symphony of Fire, 245
Szymanczyk, Michael, 471, 752

Tabak, 468
Taiwan, 121, 333, 404, 424, 426–27
Tallon, Robin, 548
Tarr-Whelan, Keith, 232
taxes, tobacco: California, 499, 518; Canada, 336–38, 340, 342, 344, 349–50, 391, 400; China, 353, 356; excise, 91, 524, 544, 546–48, 678; federal, 346, 552, 554, 586, 736; international, 345, 354, 359, 365–66, 369–71, 373, 613; Korea, South, 440, 617; revenue losses, 454; state, 346–47, 357, 360, 378, 704, 708, 763; Sweden, 367
Taxpayer Relief Act of 1997 (Public Law 105-34), 671, 673, 680, 690
Taylor, Andrew, 586
Taylor, Cathy, 136
Taylor, Jeffrey, 669, 703, 707
Teach for America, 249
Tedeschi, Bob, 493
Teinowitz, Ira, 148, 153–54, 182, 488, 677, 727–28
Tekel, 437
Television Broadcasting (TVB), 103, 106
Tempo magazine, 437
Tenenbaum, Jeff, 521
Tesco supermarket, 472
Texas, 545, 699
Thailand, 426–27
Tharp, Twyla, 241
Thatcher, Margaret, 522
Themba, Makani, 232
Third World, 382
Thomas, Daniel, 223

Thompson, Francis, 400–1
Thompson, J. Walter, 105
Thompson, Les, 391
Thompson, Tommy G., 615
Thurgood Marshall Scholarship Fund, 249
Tickle, Jennifer J., 191
Time, Inc., 179
Time magazine, school edition, 774
Time 2002 cigarettes, 203
Tin, Annie, 556
Tisch, Andrew H., 551
Tobacco Advertising and Promotion Bill (2002), United Kingdom, 210–11, 223, 228
Tobacco Advertising and Promotion (Point-of-Sale) Regulations (2004), 229
Tobacco Advertising Prohibition Act (1992), Australia, 220
"Tobacco Belt," 538
Tobacco Exporters International, 401
Tobacco Free Sport, 299, 300
Tobacco Grower Settlement Trust, National (Phase II), 764
tobacco industry, 521, 572, 573, 618; African Americans, marketing toward, 232; antismoking legislation, 516; appeal-bond caps, 746, 747; arts sponsorship, 232, 236; ASSIST, 624; Bangladesh, 395, 439; brand coloring, 157; Brazil, 529; California, 499, 500–5, 507–8, 512, 515, 516–17; China, 438; cigarettes, counterfeit, 397; cigarettes, duty-free, 316, 329; cigarettes, fire-safe, 584, 627; cigarettes, smuggling, 352, 354, 362, 389, 395, 402; cobranding, 301; "dark market," Australia, 220, 497; distribution system, 470; economic dependence on, 613, 708; economics, 538, 546; entertainment industry, 201; farmers, 737; Formula One (F1), 279, 285, 305–6, 308, 310; Freedom of Information Act (FOIA), 566, 583; India, 439; international markets, 121, 531–32; international markets, emerging, 426, 433; limbic branding, 218; lobbyists, 561, 590; marketing, database, 193; marketing, relationship, 487; marketing, research, 202, 205; military, 413, 416–18; movies, 191; Nepal, 439; packaging, 24, 31; Pakistan, 439; paper, tipping, 227; philanthropy, 251; political contributions, 500, 507–8, 538, 565, 567–68, 570, 574–75, 589, 592, 594, 599, 606, 611, 663; preemption, 502–4, 511, 514, 516–17, 545, 562, 582–83; price increases, 678; prisons and jails, 450; promotions, 166, 200; public relations, 472, 662; research sponsorship, 258–60, 262–64, 266–68; retail stores, 487, 496–97, 515; Russia, 444; sports sponsorship, 236, 2743–74, 277–78, 295–96, 299, 301, 304; Tobacco Settlement, Proposed (1997), 702, 707, 709, 712, 717, 723, 727; trademarks, 535. *See also* individual brand names and individual company names
tobacco industry: advertising, bans and restrictions, 4, 13, 103, 136, 211, 223, 229, 236, 244, 526–27, 534; television, 273, 295; tipping paper, 227
Tobacco Institute, 512, 546, 578; lobbyists for, 547, 548; political contributions, 540, 565, 569, 575, 589, 602; public relations, 693
Tobacco Manufacturers' Association, United Kingdom, 365, 383
Tobacco Outlet Business magazine, 491
Tobacco Products Control Act, Canada, 236
Tobacco Research and Development Council, Australia, 259
Tobacco Settlement, Florida (1997), 676, 692, 772; antismoking campaign, funding of, 677; appeal-bond caps, 748; attorneys' fees, 682, 689, 722, 732; Bush, Jeb, 744, 748; General Accounting Office report, 710; securitization, 744; Wall Street, 630
Tobacco Settlement, Liggett Group (1997), 79, 660
Tobacco Settlement, Minnesota (1998), 701, 714, 719, 772; attorneys' fees, 722
Tobacco Settlement, Mississippi (1997), 667, 676, 734, 772; attorneys' fees, 722, 732; General Accounting Office report, 710
Tobacco Settlement, Proposed (1997), 474–75, 586, 661, 664–66, 668, 695, 703, 733–34; advertising, bans and restrictions, 693; asbestos manufacturers, 670; CBO report, 713; cigarettes, smuggling, 368; Clinton, Bill, 698, 700, 706; CRS report, 726; economic impact, 679; farmers, 669; FTC analysis, 681, 683, 687; General Accounting Office report, 708; Goldstein, Steven F., 705; HCFA, 685, 688, 691; "Little Tobacco," 702; lobbyists, 675, 702; McCain tobacco bill (S. 1415), 606, 707, 709, 711–12, 716–17, 720, 722, 723, 724, 725, 727, media coverage, 743; Native Americans, 704; "orphan tax credit," 671,

673, 680, 690; "payment protection," 701;
  price increases, 678; "Project Blue"
  campaign, 606, 725; sports sponsorship,
  694; U.S. Department of Defense, 684; U.S.
  Treasury Department study, 672; U.S.
  Veterans Administration, 686; Wall Street,
  630
Tobacco Settlement, Texas (1998), 696, 772;
  attorneys' fees, 697, 699, 722, 732; General
  Accounting Office report, 710
Tobacco Settlement, U.S. (1998). *See* Master
  Settlement Agreement (MSA) (1998)
tobacco specialty stores, 459–60, 466–67, 469,
  474, 476, 491
Tobar, Hector, 407
Torigan, Puzant C., 70, 73
Toronto-Dominion Centre, 194
Toronto Film Festival, 245
Toronto Jazz Festival, 244
Torry, Saundra, 175, 376, 605, 697–98, 718,
  720, 723–24, 729–30, 736, 739
Tourism cigarettes, 436
Townes, Edolphus, 561
trade loading, 50
Transportation Equity Act for the 21st Century
  (Public Law 105-178), 595, 600, 603
Traynor, Michael P., 503, 505, 508
Trueheart, Charles, 412
TSO Packaging, 13
Turcsik, Richard, 459
Turkey, 59, 387, 390, 437, 607
Tuthill, Don, 116
Twisted (film), 783
Tyebjee, Tyzoon, 515

Ukraine, 431, 444
Ultramar Diamond, 475
United Kingdom, 145, 160, 223, 229, 278, 349,
  383; Department of Health, 293;
  Department of Trade and Investment, 406
United Nations, 386, 390, 392
United States of America v. Philip Morris
  (DOJ), 648–49, 651, 653–55, 659
United Way of Cabarrus County, 250
University of Bristol, 264
University of California at San Diego, 539
University of California at San Francisco, 557,
  560
University of Missouri-Columbia, 257
University of Sydney, 262
University of Washington, 249

Unlimited magazine, 146, 178–79
Uptown cigarettes, 35, 37, 215; U.S. Bureau of
  Alcohol, Tobacco, Firearms, 408, 494
U.S. Centers for Disease Control and
  Prevention, 615, 757, 775
U.S. Chamber of Commerce, 720; McCain
  tobacco bill, 709
U.S. Congress, Congressional Task Force on
  Tobacco and Health, 681
U.S. Congressional Budget Office (CBO), 591,
  713
U.S. Court of Appeals: for the 2nd Circuit, 493;
  for the 4th Circuit, 638; for the 9th Circuit,
  64; for the 3rd District, 642; for the 4th
  District, 779
U.S. Customs and Border Protection, 408
U.S. Department of Agriculture (USDA), 543,
  596; Foreign Agricultural Service, 525, 536;
  Market Promotion Program, 521, 523
U.S. Department of Commerce, 528
U.S. Department of Defense, 411–13, 416–17,
  419, 635, 684; Office of the Inspector
  General, 418; Morale, Welfare, and
  Recreation, 414
U.S. Department of Health and Human
  Services, 35, 521, 543, 694
U.S. Department of Homeland Security, 620
U.S. Department of Housing and Urban
  Development, 609
U.S. Department of Justice, 132, 272, 730;
  litigation, tobacco, 635, 637, 648–49, 651,
  653–55, 659
U.S. Department of the Treasury, 672
U.S. Department of Veterans Affairs, 580, 586,
  591, 593, 595, 600, 603, 635
U.S. District Court of Columbia, 655
U.S. Environmental Protection Agency;
  Science Advisory Board, 539
U.S. General Accounting Office (GAO);
  cigarettes, smuggling, 368, 408; exports,
  536; international markets, 426; Internet
  cigarette sales, 494; Tobacco Settlement,
  Proposed (1997), 708; tobacco settlements,
  710, 758, 764, 767, 781
U.S. House of Representatives, 626, 628;
  Appropriations Committee, 557; Commerce
  Committee, 691; Energy and Commerce
  Committee, 551; Ethics Committee, 567;
  Government Reform and Oversight
  Committee, 599; National Security Panel on
  Morale, Welfare, and Recreation, 419;

Veterans' Committee, 686; Ways and Means Committee, 552, 612
U.S. Immigration and Customs Enforcement, 408
U.S. Junior Chamber of Commerce (Jaycees), 605
U.S. National Park Service, 269
U.S. News and World Report magazine, (school edition), 774
U.S. Office of the Trade Representative, 528, 536, 543
U.S. Senate, 629, 721, 724; Agriculture Committee, 521; Commerce Committee, 615, 703, 704, 705, 706, 721; Democratic Task Force on the Tobacco Settlement, 683; Judiciary Committee, 630
U.S. State Department, 530–31
U.S. Supreme Court, 638, 646
U.S. Surgeon General, 124, 539, 573
U.S. Tobacco Associates, 521
U.S. Treasury Department, 672
USA Patriot Act of 2001 (Public Law 107-56), 389
USA Today newspaper, 723
Urban Latino magazine, 208

Valero, Greg, 454, 553
Van Bang, Le, 564
VandeHei, Jim, 620
Vanity Fair magazine, 97
van Kolfschooten, Frank, 492
Van Natta, Jr., Don, Jr., 606
Vantage cigarettes, direct sales, 180
Vector Tobacco Company, 88, 90
Vega, Michael, 281
Venezuela, 381, 532
vending machines, 558; Germany, 199, 477, 489; Netherlands, 492
Verhovek, Sam Howe, 699
Vermont State Department of Corrections, 450
Verner, Liipfert, Bernhard, McPherson, and Hand, 675
veterans, smoking-related, 580, 586, 591, 593, 595, 600, 603
Viceroy cigarettes, prisons and jails, 450
Vietnam, 382, 436, 522, 564
Vinataba cigarettes, 436
Virgin Mary, 428
Virginia, 746
Virginia Slims cigarettes: international markets, emerging, 428; "One," 71; promotions, 174; slogans and themes, 141, 174, 239, 428, 752; tennis tour, 269, 742
"virile females," 38
Vogue magazine, 751
Voinovich, George V., 691

Waddell, Ray, 231
Wakefield, M. A., 24, 26, 773
Wales, Princess of, Diana, 242
Walker, Adrian, 588
Wallison, Ethan, 686
Wall Street, 630
Walsh, Molly, 256
Walsh, Raoul A., 259
Walt Klein & Associates, 547
Wander, Nathaniel, 632
Warner Brothers, 212, 783
Warner, Fara, 48, 117–18, 128–29, 142, 455
Warner, John W., 604
Warner Nu Metro, 212
Warren, Peter M., 738
Washington, 532, 704
Washington Group, 675
Washington Legal Foundation, 563
Washington Post newspaper, 38, 723
Washington State, 368
Washington State Department of Health, 368, 566
Watkins, Michael Lee, 649
Waxman, Henry, 569
Weber, Vin, 675
Weiss, Edward, 69
Weisz, Pam, 134–35, 460
Wendy I ship, 361
Wentz, Laurel, 150
West cigarettes: duty-free, 321; Formula One, 298; international markets, emerging, 420; packaging, 9, 19
West Virginia, 768
Whalen, Jeanne, 271, 465
White, David, 369
White, Jenny, 624
Whitley, Charles, 548
Whitman, Christine Todd, 565
wholesalers, 214, 458, 461, 463–64; distribution system, 470; partnership programs, 453
Wigand, Jeffrey, 572, 668
Williams, Bob, 360
Williams, Marjorie, 540–41
Williams, Merrill, 572, 733–34

Williams, Mike, 692
Williams, Nigel, 265
Williamson, Debra Aho, 137
Willis cigarettes, promotions, 275
Wilson, Pete, 512
Wilson-Smith, Anthony, 344
Winfield cigarettes, slogans and themes, 26
Winston cigarettes, 198, 760, 783;
  advertising, television 295; Bistoon, 43;
  cigarettes, smuggling, 361, 370; Evo
  Flask, 213; gray market, 377; international
  markets, emerging, 428; Iraq, 390; movies,
  191; packaging, 2, 28; promotions, 122,
  155, 186, 224; S2, 83, 86; Select, 118,
  122; slogans and themes, 2, 83, 118, 155,
  164, 168, 173, 186, 428; "smoking
  lounge," 230
Winston Cup, 66, 104, 147, 271–72, 276–77,
  281, 289, 295, 302, 728, 742
Winter, Greg, 762
Wisconsin, 763
Woman's Day magazine, 134
Woman Thing Music, 239
women smokers, 174, 232

Women's Campaign Fund, 541
Women's Leadership Forum, 590
women's liberation movement, 169
women's organizations, 251
Women's Research and Education Institute,
  540–41
Wong, Edward, 623
World Brands International, 142
World Cup soccer, 36, 203, 275, 300
World Health Organization (WHO), 299, 300,
  324, 327, 354, 387, 402, 534
World Trade Center, 542
W. R. Grace & Company, 670

X cigarettes, 57
X, Malcolm, 57

Yale University, 632
Yava Gold cigarettes, slogans and themes, 75
Yellin, Emily, 746
Younger, Sue, 232

Zegart, Dan, 640
Zinn, Laura, 123

About the Author

Tom Diamond is the head of Reference Services at Louisiana State University (LSU) in Baton Rouge. Formerly, he served as the Social Sciences Collection development coordinator and as the business librarian. He has been at LSU since September 1989. He earned his master's degree in library science at the University of Kentucky and his bachelor of science in business administration at the University of Nebraska at Omaha. He enjoys cinema, reading, jazz, and vocal jazz.